A Tale of Three Cities

"In a timely and masterfully executed work that is both humbly honest and shockingly truthful, Douglas Matthews deftly lays out the prospects of the three cities over the course of a truly grand, even cosmic, history befitting the saints. I give this engaging and eminently readable work my highest recommendation."

—KENNETH J. COLLINS,
professor of historical theology and Wesley studies, Asbury Theological Seminary

"In a culture with lots of competing voices, we are often better at identifying the problems than we are at proposing solutions and seeing God's will done on earth as it is in heaven. *A Tale of Three Cities* beautifully describes where we are living with a healthy dose of wisdom for how Christians can be 'salt and light' and live as ambassadors for reconciliation and redemption. This book is a gift to the church and a call for Christ followers!"

—KEITH NEWMAN,
president, Southern Nazarene University

"The church has often been divided over the best way to engage the world for the kingdom. As such, the church needs wise voices to shape our future work, and our approach must be both faithful and effective. Douglas Matthews's *A Tale of Three Cities* is a welcome contribution to that discussion and is a must-read for anyone concerned with this kind of work."

—JAMIE DEW,
president and professor of Christian philosophy, New Orleans Baptist Theological Seminary

"*A Tale of Three Cities* cuts through the cacophony of voices offering the church quick fixes to today's complicated issues by masterfully addressing what it means to live in the light of the New Creation. Matthews brilliantly demonstrates that we can be people of hope and citizens of the coming age even in the midst of a painful, broken world."

—CHRISTINE JOHNSON,
assistant professor of historical theology and Wesleyan studies, Asbury Theological Seminary

"D. K. Matthews' *Tale of Three Cities* provides *profound clarity* related to the role and work of the Christian in a world standing in opposition to the tenets of the gospel message. Grounded in the clear teachings of the Bible, a Christian, while faced with potential suffering, persecution, and false doctrines, should respond with humility, grace, and conviction. Imagine the body of Christ, acting like Christ in love, care, patience, endurance, suffering, and sacrifice as witness of Christ to the world. To this end, Matthews calls his readers."

—BRENT ELLIS,
president, Spring Arbor University

"Occasionally, I come across a book I wish I had written. *A Tale of Three Cities* by Doug Matthews is just such a book. Not only does it offer a sobering critique of inadequate hermeneutics characterizing different eschatological assumptions in and outside Christendom, it also provides a Judeo-Christian, future-vision alternative that withstands current pushbacks to Christendom we find in Western culture. I endorse it wholeheartedly."

—JOSEPH B. ONYANGO OKELLO,
professor of philosophy, Asbury Theological Seminary

"Between a pandemic, toxic politics, and the dizzying advance of technology, there couldn't be a more critical time to re-evaluate the focus and priorities of Christ's church in our age. D. K. Matthews' work has given an important new tool to local church leaders—whether laymen or clergy. His 'Third City' model gives us an eschatological lens for the Church's ministry that is both deeply grounded and broadly useful. It envisions a way forward that is full of biblical optimism and tactical clarity."

—GEOFFREY A. FULLER,
professor of biology, Mount Vernon Nazarene University

A Tale of Three Cities

Best or Worst of Times? Antichristism, Constructive Cultural Engagement, and the Resurrection of the Cosmos

D. K. MATTHEWS

CASCADE *Books* · Eugene, Oregon

A TALE OF THREE CITIES

Best or Worst of Times? Antichristism, Constructive Cultural Engagement, and the Resurrection of the Cosmos

Copyright © 2024 D. K. Matthews. All rights reserved. Except for brief quotations in critical publications or reviews, no part of this book may be reproduced in any manner without prior written permission from the publisher. Write: Permissions, Wipf and Stock Publishers, 199 W. 8th Ave., Suite 3, Eugene, OR 97401.

Cascade Books

An Imprint of Wipf and Stock Publishers

199 W. 8th Ave., Suite 3

Eugene, OR 97401

www.wipfandstock.com

PAPERBACK ISBN: 978-1-5326-3952-4

HARDCOVER ISBN: 978-1-5326-3953-1

EBOOK ISBN: 978-1-5326-3954-8

Cataloguing-in-Publication data:

Names: Matthews, D. K. [author]

Title: A tale of three cities : best or worst of times? Antichristism, constructive cultural engagement, and the resurrection of the cosmos / D. K. Matthews.

Description: Eugene, OR: Cascade Books, 2024 | Includes bibliographical references and index.

Identifiers: ISBN 978-1-5326-3952-4 (paperback) | ISBN 978-1-5326-3953-1 (hardcover) | ISBN 978-1-5326-3954-8 (ebook)

Subjects: LCSH: Christianity and culture. | Eschatology—Biblical teaching. | Popular culture—Religious aspects—Christianity. | Christianity—21st century. | Christianity and politics.

Classification: BR115.C8 M388 2024 (paperback) | BR115.C8 (ebook)

VERSION NUMBER 08/16/24

All direct Scripture quotations, unless otherwise noted, are from the New American Standard Bible copyright© 1960, 1962, 1963, 1968, 1971, 1972, 1973, 1975, 1977, 1995, 2020 by The Lockman Foundation. Used by permission.

Scriptures marked KJV are from the King James Version, public domain.

Scriptures marked NIV are from The Holy Bible, New International Version®. Copyright© 1973, 1978, 1984, 2011 by Biblica, Inc.™ Used by permission of Zondervan.

Scriptures marked NRSV are from the New Revised Standard Version Bible, copyright © 1989 National Council of the Churches of Christ in the United States of America. Used by permission. All rights reserved worldwide.

Scriptures marked ESV are from The ESV® Bible (The Holy Bible, English Standard Version®), copyright © 2001 by Crossway, a publishing ministry of Good News Publishers. Used by permission. All rights reserved.

IT WAS THE BEST of times, it was the worst of times, it was the age of wisdom, it was the age of foolishness, it was the epoch of belief, it was the epoch of incredulity, it was the season of Light, it was the season of Darkness, it was the spring of hope, it was the winter of despair, we had everything before us, we had nothing before us, we were all going direct to Heaven, we were all going direct the other way.

—Charles Dickens, *A Tale of Two Cities*

CONTENTS

PREFACE AND INTRODUCTION: FUTURE-VISION TECTONICS | 1

CHAPTER 1
THE QUESTION FOR THE AGES: AGE OF ANTICHRIST OR KINGDOM INFLUENCE AND APPROXIMATION? | 36

CHAPTER 2
THE EPIC VISION: AN APPROXIMATED BUT NOT YET FULLY RESURRECTED NEW CREATION | 55

CHAPTER 3
THE COSMIC CAST: ANTICHRISTS, APPROXIMATORS, AND ENABLERS | 74

CHAPTER 4
THE SYMPTOMS, ROOTS, AND FRUIT OF TOXIC VERSUS REGENERATING FUTURE-VISIONS | 98

CHAPTER 5
THE IRREFUTABLE EVIDENCE: FUTURE-VISIONS RULE IN SCRIPTURE— AND EVERYWHERE | 121

CHAPTER 6
THE EXTRAORDINARY HISTORICAL MOMENT: OUR NEW AGE OF POST-CHRISTENDOM ANTICHRISTISM | 154

CHAPTER 7
THE BIBLICAL MANDATE: TRUE KINGDOM CITIZENS ARE ALWAYS PREPARED FOR THE AGE OF ANTICHRIST | 186

CONCLUSION
ALWAYS BE PREPARED FOR THE THREE CITIES AND NEW CREATION | 222

APPENDICES

APPENDIX A
Future-Vision Distortions and Corrections | 249

APPENDIX B
Nietzsche and Truth | 259

APPENDIX C
The Incremental Advance of Nietzsche's City of Antichrist? Historical Snapshots from 1995 and 2016 | 261

APPENDIX D
How to Always Be Prepared for Antichristism | 273

Appendix E
A Kingdom Approximation Manifesto: Tentative and Foundational Elements of a Kingdom Approximation Manifesto and Strategy | 295

Appendix F
Seven Representative Objections and Misunderstandings Briefly Considered | 304

BIBLIOGRAPHY | 309

PREFACE AND INTRODUCTION
FUTURE-VISION TECTONICS

Future-visions rule, and the preeminent future-visions today sweeping across the globe are toxic for church, synagogue, and state. Such visions or eschatologies largely determine whether cultures and civilizations embrace an age of antichristism or allow for kingdom influence and human flourishing.

Shall faith communities mobilize behind something akin to King's biblically influenced "I have a dream" and focus on the content of one's character? Or should they follow the many "justice" and "compassion" rainbows of various Marxist influenced liberation theologies that emphasize widespread and irredeemable economic, gender, and racial oppressors, the victimized oppressed, and the elect and enlightened liberators? Is true "compassion" and "justice" best aided by preserving, reforming, or enhancing more perfect union experiments that emphasize political, economic, and religious "freedom"? Or is civilization collapsing, and should God's faithful focus on increasing the numbers of the faithful who will escape the dawning age of antichrist and "tribulation, such as has not occurred since the beginning of the world until now, nor ever will again" (Matt 24:21)? Or, as with Rod Dreher, are we simply moving into another temporary dark ages, and believers should learn from history and the Benedictine monks and plan today for how they can influence culture and civilizations in, say, the year AD 2500?[1] This central question for the ages, how dark or bright is the age we are living in and how shall we respond, will be addressed throughout this work and especially clarified in chapter 1.

Future-vision mega-tectonic shifts went largely unnoticed for decades and centuries, yet the earthquakes and aftershocks can no longer be ignored. At the epicenter of much of our civilizational fragmentation is

---

1. Dreher, *Benedict*.

the confusion, redefinition, corruption, or militant rejection of the future-visions of biblical faith communities who were called to salt, enlighten, and leaven the spirit of the times. Tragically, faith communities often spew self-fulfilling fatalistic prophecies or distorted visions that only enable the spirit of antichristism.

This work will argue that, at an even deeper theological level, those who believe that the cosmos will be annihilated tend to drift toward such fatalism and escapism or respond to the worst of times by engaging civilization with anger, bewilderment, fear, inconsistencies, or arrogance. It will be documented that these cosmic annihilationists are everywhere, global, and most influential in what is often referred to as evangelical Christianity. Those affirming that the creation will be or is being restored or renewed often accommodate to culture and political fads, or adopt naively optimistic views of the future, or both. These cosmic restorationists properly value the creation, culture, and the continuity between Eden and the Heavenly City, but underestimate the radical nature of human depravity, the powerful presence of the present spirit of antichrist, and the organic or systemic nature of cosmic brokenness. The biblical and theologically sound vision of the future, in contrast to these two other options, is the death and resurrection of all things, cosmic resurrection, centered and grounded in the bodily resurrection of Christ. Cosmic resurrection properly frames our cultural, political, and civilizational engagement and avoids many of the misguided responses of the faithful throughout history to culture and the best and worst of times.

In contrast to misguided and ineffective faith communities, the Gospels and Acts serve as textbook and narrative illustrations of how to be rightly guided by the power and future vision of cosmic resurrection, and always be prepared to respond to antichristism, including persecution. Jesus, Stephen, Paul, Apollos, Priscilla, and Aquila were Spirit-led (see Acts, known as the Acts of the Holy Spirit), Trinitarian, persistent, persuasive, creative, shrewd (Paul before the Council, Acts 23:6; Jesus and taxes, Matt 17 and 22; Jesus, his authority, and the baptism of John, Matt 21:23–27), well-prepared with "great learning" (e.g., Acts 26:24; Acts 17), aware of and sensitive to cultural and intellectual realities and details (the unknown god, quotations from obscure Greek poets and philosophers, Acts 17), biblically grounded and saturated, appropriately gentle or firm, respectful and bold, compassionate, passionate, long-suffering, forgiving, rejoicing, singing, strategic and tactical (being led to key cities to advance the kingdom), and they all biblically and "powerfully refuted" (Acts 18:28) antichristism in word and deed (the resurrection, lordship over the creation, healing, casting out demons and darkness, reasoning with Jews and Gentiles, and verbally defending the faith).

Their responses to antichristism and anti-Semitism were overflowing with advanced knowledge, wisdom, truth, and love, "full of faith and of the Holy Spirit" (Acts 6:5), and even robed with "the face of an angel" (Acts 6:15). Acts was certainly written for every generation and is especially relevant to our present pluralistic and multicultural generation as great cities and civilizations are crumbling across the globe under the crushing and cancerous burden of antichristism. This entire work, and especially the last two chapters, directly addresses how to always be prepared for both antichristism and kingdom influence in our chaotic and oppressive present moment (1 Pet 3:8–22).

The genesis for *A Tale of Three Cities* is the seeming inability and floundering of Judeo-Christian believers, especially globally influential American evangelicals. The faithful seem largely incapable of framing their cultural, intellectual, and civilizational engagement within a biblical, consistent, coherent, practical, and effective future-vision. My academic and PhD training and teaching focused on theology, philosophy, and ethics, with a minor in political science and specialized research on how future-visions (i.e., eschatology) impact faith communities and their cultural and political engagement. My professional experience has regularly involved strategic and tactical planning for successful outcomes. These areas of research, analysis, and application have only deepened and expanded over time.

It became clear after working with thousands of youth group, undergraduate, and graduate school leaders that their future-visions were defining, guiding, and typically hampering their self-understanding, holistic growth, ministry preparedness, and effectiveness. One brilliant individual, in particular, chose not to attend college in large measure because the rapture of true believers was going to take place, she was told, in a specific year and within a matter of years. Higher education seemed pointless since the age of the antichrist and the rapture had arrived.

This tragic anti-intellectual and anti-cultural decision reflects the ongoing future-vision confusion in Judeo-Christian faith communities concerning how or if one should rigorously prepare for influencing civilization today, tomorrow, and reigning on earth someday in the New Creation. Other future, and now current, leaders I engaged simultaneously insisted that we were already in the final years' countdown to the rapture, Great Tribulation, and Armageddon, while they also were trying to "save America" or "make America great again."[2]

---

2. In the United States, "Let's Make America Great Again" was the campaign slogan for the Ronald Reagan presidential campaign (1980). "Make America Great Again," known as MAGA, is of course associated with former president Donald Trump's campaigns. The focus here is not on assessing these political movements but on the

In addition, my background in administration as a senior vice president, provost, and other cabinet-level and administrative positions has confirmed not only that toxic future-visions often rule in faith communities, but that more biblical and constructive future-visions often falter due to poor strategic and tactical planning, implementation, and the effective assessment of outcomes in faith communities and beyond. Those who are getting much of the biblical future-vision right are often getting it entirely wrong on how to execute and assess the vision. Toxic future-visions and inadequate planning certainly have served as enablers of our accelerating civilizational fragmentation and decay in many parts of the globe (see especially chapter 3).

SYMPTOMS AND FUTURE-VISIONS

Believers who are fervently engaged with culture and civilization are typically focused on symptoms, symptoms, and more symptoms, and they confuse the plentiful and inexhaustible poisoned fruit with the root of the current civilizational crisis (see especially chapter 4). Others are seduced by naive or utopian dreams and programs. Anything remotely resembling a safe, free, rational, genuinely compassionate, truly civilized, physically and spiritually flourishing, and morally decent culture will continue to collapse if the faithful don't move beyond addressing symptoms or promoting naive pipe dreams—as important as symptoms and dreams truly are. Identifying the root of the problem and the solution will determine which visions of the future will actually triumph.

Eschatomania and Cognitive Dissonance (Mental Contradictions and Confusion)

Some believers are disengaged, obsessed or shaped by end-times mania, predicting or claiming we are in the last generation or decade (Last-Generationism), while waiting for escape just prior to the end of the world (Rapture-Escapism). Theologian Millard Erickson once referred to this future-vision orientation and psychological state and groupthink as "eschatomania"—excessive or inappropriate enthusiasm, or a mental health challenge, concerning the last (eschaton) things (eschatology), perhaps

---

prevalent mixture of last-days fatalism with politically conservative programs to save America.

providing a way of escape from tribulation and/or this world destined for annihilation.³

While working on my PhD at Baylor, research confirmed that a common contradiction was prevalent among Judeo-Christian believers who were trying to "save America." Amazingly, for at least over half a century, and earlier to some degree, a sizeable group of American evangelicals have simultaneously tried to save civilization while also charting its certain slide toward Armageddon. This mental contradiction or confusion, referred to as cognitive dissonance, has been rather evident more recently and for decades among some supporters of "Let's Make America Great Again" #1 (Reagan, 1980), and "Make America Great Again" #2 (Trump, 2016–present). This observation is not intended to be a positive or negative commentary on these "Great Again" movements or slogans; the point here is the future-vision cognitive dissonance.

A New Monasticism and Coming Dark Ages

Others, whether they properly interpreted Rod Dreher's *Benedict Option* or not,⁴ doubt if believers will escape the coming new and global dark ages and are particularly convinced that the curtain is now falling on Judeo-Christian–influenced Western civilization. The time has arrived for a new or neo-monastic Christianity that strategically retreats from culture and preserves a faithful testimony, digs in for the long haul, and transmits and creates beneficial Christian culture, beliefs, and values to future cultures and ages—with civilizational light emerging from the darkness only after multiple centuries of this new dark age.

ADDICTED TO DARKNESS

Interestingly, much of popular culture (e.g., humor, entertainment, dystopian movies), the new monastics, and the evangelical end-times' last-generationists all seem to be addicted to darkness. Darkness has triumphed, for now, and the correct game plan must simply acknowledge the temporary triumph of darkness. Indeed, the long shadows are seen everywhere as the sun—and the influence of the Logos—dips below the cultural horizon amid *This Present Darkness*.⁵

---

3. Erickson, *Christian Theology*, 1152.
4. Dreher, *Benedict*.
5. Peretti, *This Present Darkness*.

The Triune Logos is the Wisdom of God (Proverbs, especially chapters 2–11), and the personal and revealed Word of God (in Jesus of Nazareth, the Christ or anointed Messiah King). This very personal concept of the Logos and Word includes and births the written word of God (Spirit-inspired Scripture). The Logos is the true image of the Father, the Son of God, whose revelation in history, Scripture, and through the Spirit is the true light of the world. The Logos is the creator, sustainer, and consummator of all things—the Alpha and Omega and "I Am" of reality (Exod 3; John 8).

The light of the world will eventually and forever vanquish darkness, yet darkness often seductively appears as future-visions of angelic light and seeks to move families, communities, faith communities, and nations further and further into the darkness and out of the orbit and influence of the Logos and the only real future. The Logos rules and shall rule forever, yet the influence of the Logos, the light of the Son, is sometimes overcast on the cultural horizon by shadowy cultural and civilizational darkness—especially in formerly Logocentric kingdoms.

OTHERWORLDLY FUTURE-VISIONS

Throughout the history of the Judeo-Christian movement, many who have not been addicted to darkness and eschatomania have, nevertheless, often unconsciously adopted a key assumption of this Judeo-Christian fixation with darkness. This massively influential assumption is an otherworldly, non-Hebraic, and Greek-influenced vision—borrowing and perhaps distorting some of Plato's and Augustine's ideas. N. T. Wright credits Plato with this trajectory, but that may be somewhat unfair to Plato's actual teachings.[6]

Regardless, in this view physical life on earth in the present is devalued or diminished. Heaven is all that really matters, and heaven is an escape from this inferior and shadowy world. Such believers do not view the redemption and enhancement of this present physical world, culture, and civilization, and our physical bodies, including our thoughts, as central to understanding God's glorious plan for their individual salvation and the coming New Heaven and Earth. Salvation is individual escape.

Heaven is "somewhere out there," largely or entirely spiritual or non-physical, and the goal of the Christian is viewed as, "When His chosen ones shall gather to their home beyond the skies, And the roll is called up yonder, I'll be there."[7] And yonder is not a transformed cosmos and is certainly "be-

---

6. Rogers, "N. T. Wright"; and N. T. Wright, *Day the Revolution Began*, 28–37 (see especially p. 34), and much of Wright's entire book.

7. Black, "When the Roll."

yond the skies"—not a redeemed and resurrected cosmos. Our true destiny is fully beyond and totally distinct from the present cosmos, which will be entirely destroyed after Christ's return.

This belief in the total destruction or annihilation of the cosmos is based on a simplistic reading of a number of biblical passages, including 2 Pet 3:10 ("the elements will be destroyed or [melt] with intense [fervent] heat").[8] "When we all get to heaven" is largely portrayed as a non-bodily existence where we enter a "perpetual worship service."[9] As per Chris Tomlin, the "earth shall soon dissolve like snow," and we are viewed more as otherworldly "aliens" than influential sojourners like Daniel. We are nonresident aliens rather than the more biblical *Resident Aliens* (1 Pet 2:11):[10]

> This world is not my home
> I'm just passing through
> My treasures are laid up
> Somewhere beyond the blue.[11]

These lines could have been penned by some of Plato's otherworldly followers, or even some early Christian anti-Creation heresies that went so far as to view the physical creation as very inferior if not outright evil (e.g., Docetism, Marcionism, Gnosticism).

Such believers do not see the earthly reign of Messiah (or Christ) and the co-reigning (co-regency or vice-regency) of the saints as their north star, defining who they are and who they should become. Preparation for time and eternity is often reduced simply to saying the sinner's prayer. That prayer is very valuable and was my gateway to salvation, but biblical salvation and reconciliation, as rightly understood by the early church, John Wesley, and N. T. Wright, is large, "great" (Wesley), profound, rich, cosmic in scope (Irenaeus), and as broad as God's biblical covenants and the coming New Creation.

With the otherworldly and unbiblical view, the incarnation (the Word becoming flesh) and physical return of Christ are not viewed as a clarion call today to influence the world that God so loved that is being redeemed, restored, *and resurrected*. There is no need to understand or prepare for co-regency or vice-regency with the Messiah on earth.

The church and synagogue are not preparing the faithful to be priests, princesses, princes, kings, and queens; instead, the church is the convenient dispenser of tickets to heaven, ecstatic praise and worship, and spiritual

---

8. See the comprehensive argument in Juza, *New Testament*.
9. Middleton, "Singing Lies."
10. Hauerwas and Willimon, *Resident Aliens*.
11. Carter, "This World."

therapy. This otherworldly future-vision seems to have moved away from this exalted concept: "But you are a chosen people, a royal priesthood, a holy nation, a people for God's own possession, so that you may proclaim the excellencies of Him who has called you out of darkness into His marvelous light" (1 Pet 2:9).

Otherworldliness views intellectual, holistic, and cultural growth; leadership; and competencies as marginal at best to the real goal of getting out of here, going to heaven, and taking others with us. Or, to illustrate with a common sentiment expressed by many, "What does excelling at quantum physics, cosmology, political philosophy, architecture, sociology, engineering, nursing, leadership, psychology, athletic development, art, or music have to do with being a faithful and Christlike Christian in terms of preparing for Christ's reign on earth? Just tell me how to get to heaven. That is all that really matters for eternity." The goal and vision—eternity—are otherworldly rather than a resurrected and transformed world.

This otherworldly outlook contributes to viewing spirituality (or Christlikeness) as a private or individual rather than a cosmic, kingdom matter. Spirituality is primarily about avoiding a lifestyle of sin and being blessed and protected from all harm. Prayer and worship focus more on "me, me, me," rather than the kingdom and coming New Creation. The faith journey is about my blessings and merely getting to heaven.

LIVING IN THE LIGHT AND DAWNING OF THE NEW CREATION

The biblical mega-drama of the redemption of all things (Rom 8; Isa 11; Revelation), and the heavenly city descending to planet Earth, have been reduced to the individual Christian escaping our increasingly dark *Terminal Generation* and our *Late Great Planet Earth* as we *Countdown to Armageddon*.[12] The highest good is to escape our sinful world and physical body and cash in our eternally secure ticket to heaven. This assumption is truly Greek philosophy at its worst, and definitely more Greek than biblical or Hebraic or Christian.

In Scripture, the redemption of God's world is normative for all we believe and practice, and bodily resurrection lies at the nonnegotiable core of our faith and the very center of history and the cosmos. In some varieties of Greek thought, salvation is the escape of the soul from the body and from the shadowy physical world to true rational and spiritual reality in the heavenly stars above.

---

12. Lindsey and Carlson, *Late Great Planet*; Lindsey, *Terminal Generation*; and Lindsey, *1980s*.

For otherworldly believers, salvation is often framed as escape, not sacrificial engagement with the present and co-regency with Christ already initiated in the present and fulfilled in the future. The essence and central affirmation of Christianity, for this flawed view, is not the kingdom of God, central to Jesus, or the New Heaven and Earth, which sums up the whole of Scripture. For these sincere faithful, the theological centerpiece is the sinner's prayer,[13] not only for how to get to heaven but in terms of the oversimplistic purpose of life and the mission of the church. The Great Commission (Matt 28) has become the Great Omission, for it leaves out the discipling of all peoples and nations so pervasive in Jesus' kingdom teaching, ministry, and mission—namely, "teaching them to follow all that I commanded you [concerning *all* things pertaining to the kingdom]" (Matt 28:20).

The integrated redemption of all things and the kingdom of God, which includes and properly defines or contextualizes the true meaning of the salvation of individual sinners through the sinner's prayer, is marginalized rather than foundational to understanding salvation, discipleship, and the mission of the church. Being saved and Christlike have little to do with actually being fully like Christ (or Messiah), the Logos (Word), the very creator and sustainer of all things, including the creator of the relativity of the space-time continuum and the complex beauty of music, subatomic particles, and words (language and communication).

MERELY GETTING TO HEAVEN OR FIT FOR HEAVEN

Christians have, to redeploy a famous phrase of John Wesley,[14] often reduced salvation to merely getting to heaven rather than becoming fit for heaven and reigning with Christ (Messiah) over the very good and complex cosmos and civilizational tapestry that God set in motion. Such a vision is the "great" salvation for Wesley and must be central to the "General Spread of the [authentic] Gospel." It should be no surprise that late in Wesley's life and

---

13. One example: "*Dear God, I know that I am a sinner and there is nothing that I can do to save myself. I confess my complete helplessness to forgive my own sin or to work my way to heaven. At this moment I trust Christ alone as the One who bore my sin when He died on the cross. I believe that He did all that will ever be necessary for me to stand in your holy presence. I thank you that Christ was raised from the dead as a guarantee of my own resurrection. As best as I can, I now transfer my trust to Him. I am grateful that He has promised to receive me despite my many sins and failures. Father, I take you at your word. I thank you that I can face death now that you are my Savior. Thank you for the assurance that you will walk with me through the deep valley. Thank you for hearing this prayer. In Jesus' Name. Amen.*" Crosswalk Editorial Staff, "Sinner's Prayer."

14. Wesley, *Farther Appeal*.

ministry one of his summative sermons (1785), and a theme that increasingly pulsated through his writings, was "The New Creation" (Sermon 64).[15]

NEW CREATION CHILDREN OR OLD CREATION CHILDISHNESS?

In contrast, escapist Christianity implies that believers are not just to exhibit a totally trusting childlike faith but that it is largely acceptable to remain childish, underdeveloped, anti-cultural, anti-intellectual, dependent children in this age and the next—as long as one goes to heaven. This toxic future-vision has reduced the saints to children, perhaps even fools and morons (Proverbs) who negatively illustrate this biblical command: "Brothers and sisters, do not be children in your thinking; yet in evil be infants, but in your thinking be mature" (1 Cor 14:20). Higher education and personal, intellectual, psychological, physical growth—holistic growth—are merely options for those who enjoy or need such things for their careers, rather than a key implication of genuine salvation and being truly "fit for heaven"—co-regents with the Logos who made and redeemed all things in heaven and earth. In Scripture, authentic faith works and bears fruit. Dead faith (James 2:26) makes claims to gaining heaven without the claimant being increasingly heavenly—increasingly fit for dwelling in creative harmony with God and others for eternity. The believer who is restored to the image of God will co-steward, co-discover, and co-create the future of the cosmos and the never-ending flowering of the eternal city. We are not called to be dog-like dependent creatures, but citizens and rulers of a royal nation and holy priesthood.

The childish believer asks, "Why spend years being holistically educated, especially developing the mind, if the simple goal of life is to escape life on this earth and land on the shores of an otherworldly heaven as blissful and dependent children who never mature into priests and compassionate cosmic rulers?" "Why rigorously learn the details of music theory, history, marine biology, political philosophy, or physics—or even theology?" The childish vision for such believers is simply to sing praise hymns for all eternity rather than co-creating the future, or to dwell in a non-physical heaven, or to remain childishly dependent forever, or for death to instantaneously change everyone and everything in a magical moment apart from any growth, consent, culture building, or a relational and communal journey.

The childish approach is "just me and Jesus" getting to heaven. The biblical approach is "the Kingdom of the world has become the kingdom of our Lord and Savior Jesus Christ; and He will reign forever and ever" (Rev 11:15).

15. Wesley, "General Spread"; and Wesley, "New Creation."

To illustrate the application of the otherworldly childish vision, studying and learning piano or tennis with excellence for decades might have value for those who get into sports or music, or play such for a career, but it's not for everyone and is viewed as having no or a very narrow relevance to becoming like the Logos and preparing for vice-regency in the restored creation. Learning piano may assist a local church on Sunday morning, perhaps with escapist worship, but it is not viewed as contributing to the fulfillment and restoration of our creation in the image of God, or the actual realization of the cosmic New Creation symphony and our *essential* spiritual, personal, holistic, and communal growth. Playing piano or tennis well is not viewed as thinking God's thoughts, co-creating, or actually contributing to the coming but already New Creation.

We prepare ourselves for necessary jobs, making money, having a meaningful career, specific tasks, and to be providers, which of course all have value, but often see little connection to our preparation for time and eternity and our eternal future reigning in a redeemed and resurrected body and cosmos. That Achilles heel is due to an inadequate future-vision. We don't know why we are spending decades on planet Earth other than to witness, provide for our family, remain faithful, and get saved and go to heaven—this is small and immature thinking indeed in view of the glorious biblical future which no eye has fully seen and no ear has perfectly heard (1 Cor 2:9).

We are more concerned with our retirement plans than with our earthly and eternal co-regency with the Messiah. And what is the consequence of this theology? As with political and economic systems that create dependency, many believers only do what is absolutely necessary (pray the sinners' prayer, avoid gross immorality) to qualify for and secure the ticket to heaven. We, therefore, concern ourselves only with how to escape to heaven, rather than how to be fit for heaven.

Heaven will never be very heavenly if its inhabitants are not radically transformed in every way and at their very core, which is necessary for New Creation perfection and glory. Citizens of heaven certainly must be saved by grace, radically transformed, and overflowing with love for God and others, but also equipped to understand, lead, and reign over all of the complexities of heavenly civilization. "Blessed are the gentle, for they will inherit the earth" (Matt 5:5). We simply have not taken the death and resurrection of all things with utter seriousness in our thoughts, passions, discipleship, and actions.

EMBRACE LIFE?

Is it any wonder that harsh and often unfair critics of Judeo-Christian faith and practice, such as Friedrich Nietzsche, sense that the Judeo-Christian faithful really don't fully embrace life and the fullness of God's good creation? This deficiency is not new, for Nietzsche lived in the nineteenth century, and other scholars from Roman writers to modern authors (e.g., Deists), right or wrong, found Christianity to be devoid of life, honor, world-affirmation, intelligence, creativity, love for intellectual and scientific discovery, and courage.

From a biblical and Hebraic perspective, faith communities that devalue God's creation, the full restoration and fulfillment of the image of God, the bodily resurrection, and the New Creation consummation are corrupt and cancerous to the church's true mission. Such corruption impacts daily life, attitudes, values, human sexuality, preaching, teaching, worship, education (or anti-education and anti-intellectualism), the training of children, and cultural and intellectual engagement. Such corruption defines what we really love,[16] which norms how we actually live.[17] Otherworldliness loves personal salvation, comfort, peace, spiritual therapy, and prosperity more than risking all for God's New Creation kingdom.

OUT OF THE WORLD AND BACK INTO THE SALTSHAKER?

Others are less otherworldly and rather suspicious about cocksure claims that we are living in the "last days," or the last days of the last days, before the rapture and Great Tribulation. Yet this group of believers fatally accepts the absurd notion that Judeo-Christian core convictions, values, and assumptions have no relevance to the health and true *Desire of the Nations*.[18] Rather than answering the question and attempting to dialogue on what is or should be the true desire of nations, meaning what kind of civilization we should aspire to in the present age before Messiah's rule, some simply defer to others without a biblical orientation. Such believers who are best positioned to answer the question forfeit their biblical calling to contribute to the debate and quest for the common good prior to Messiah's return.

These separatist or isolationist saints affirm that such beliefs and practices cannot or should not try to bend the public marketplace of ideas, politics, and culture toward God's true future. One version of this toxic

---

16. Smith, *You Are What You Love*.
17. Schaeffer, *How Should?*
18. O'Donovan, *Desire of the Nations*.

future-vision for the era prior to Messiah's earthly reign proposes a likely unconstitutional and strict separation not just between church and state but between culture and the biblical, life-giving values and living waters of God's people. These are the living waters that can, in part, redefine, redeem, nourish, "salt," "light," and positively "leaven" our communal and civilizational life together.

UTOPIANISM—A NAIVE FUTURE-VISION[19]

In contrast to those who distance themselves from civilization for various reasons, other Judeo-Christian believers have naively affirmed that the kingdom can be ushered in prior to the return of the Messiah. Such believers should be commended for leading numerous movements and ministries to rescue lives, communities, and nations.

This untold story includes the fact that countless major social reform movements—in revivalistic colonial America, Wesley's England, revivalistic America on the eve of the Civil War, and during much of the nineteenth and early twentieth centuries in America and across the globe—were led by Judeo-Christian saints. Indeed, Timothy Smith has documented that every major social reform movement on the eve of the Civil War in America was led by Christian revival influenced reformers who typically believed that they could usher in God's rule on earth *before* the return of Christ.[20] How far we have fallen from being true kingdom Christians who incarnate life, love, and truth in the trenches and crucible of history and civilization.

Yet such naively optimistic and utopian (or postmillennial) future-dreams ultimately collapsed under the weight of history and the realities of fallen human nature. This naive optimism taught that the world could be largely transformed or Christianized, and/or democratized—that a *Christian Century* was near.[21] Many referred to this future golden era of at least one thousand years as the millennium. And the millennium would become a global reality *before* Christ literally returned—the actual Messiah would return after (post) the one thousand–year Spirit-led reign of Christ's

---

19. Utopianism is the belief that a perfect or nearly perfect world can be established on earth, even apart from a supernatural act of God such as the return of the Messiah.

20. Smith, *Revivalism and Social Reform*.

21. The *Christian Century* magazine of the 1800s (it had different names) viewed the coming twentieth century as becoming a great century of Christian influence on civilization. Some even believed that the thousand-year reign of Christ could be fulfilled before Christ returned by the advance of Christian influence and the work of the Spirit. *Christian Century*, "About Us."

kingdom influence on earth (the millennium); hence, *post*millennialism was undiscerningly embraced.

In contrast, Scripture affirms that culture can be positively and partially influenced but not redeemed or fully Christianized, prior to Messiah's actual earthly rule and reign. Postmillennialism is naive and dangerous. Church-state unions are naive and dangerous. Banning Judeo-Christian influence from nations and cultures is dangerous. Common sense suggests that Christ's return must come *before* his kingdom rule is largely or entirely realized on earth, in contrast to postmillennialism.

DISILLUSIONMENT AND FATALISM

Disillusionment with such grand, naive, utopian schemes and dreams fed the previously referenced monsters of fatalism, escapism, and eschatomania that devoured the will and wisdom of Judeo-Christian cultural engagement and influence. After the Civil War in America, this disillusionment sparked a future-vision shift that was more pessimistic, fatalistic, and tended to view the world as inevitably (or inexorably) sliding toward Armageddon. End-times prophecy conferences multiplied like rabbits in late nineteenth-century northern America, which had a global impact through the Great Century of Missions.

When Israel became a nation in 1948, many were convinced that "last days" prophecy was literally being fulfilled and that the rapture would take place within roughly forty years, and certainly no more than seventy years. Even Josh McDowell, one of the most popular college and university speakers in history, argued in the 1970s that in 1948 God had taken all of the puzzle pieces of history and thrown them out on the table so that we could piece together God's plan and timetable for the end times. This work will document the widespread conservative Judeo-Christian view that things are getting worse and worse, and that we can waste time better spent on saving souls if we naively try to bend the present toward God's true future and improve the world before Messiah's return.

Today's successors of the valiant faithful trying to bend the present toward the true future have remained in the cultural trenches seeking to make a real difference for time and eternity while often suffering abuse from unbelievers and suspicion from escapist or separatist believers. Such criticism of the valiant also has come from more politically and theologically liberal believers who tend to accept, accommodate to, or even approve of many cultural fads that counter traditional Christian beliefs and morality—such as redefining Christian doctrine, marriage, ordination, gender, freedom, and democracy. Yet, as noted, these valiant ones often have schizophrenic or inconsistent future-visions—they are going to "save America and the world" in these last days before everything collapses.[22] This contradiction, referred to previously as (eschatological) cognitive dissonance, will be more fully explored in this work.

PRE-RESTORATIONISM AS A KEY

It will be argued that the biblical future-vision not only acknowledges but clearly affirms the presence and persistence of some measure of civilizational darkness prior to Messiah's return. There is no utopian or globally golden era prior to the Messiah's earthly victory and reign. Yet the present has already been invaded and influenced by the future victorious kingdom. A utopia or something akin to one thousand years of peace and Christ-influenced wholeness is not possible in the present era.

Hence, it will be argued that the idea that the Christ returns after the millennium—postmillennialism—contradicts Scripture and mountains of historical, sociological, psychological and theological (e.g., human nature and sin) evidence. Likewise, the rejection of the earthly reign of Christ—no millennium or amillennialism—undermines core biblical affirmations concerning the restoration of the creation (Isaiah, Revelation). To be fair, some amillennialists today do affirm the restoration of the creation after Christ's return as we move toward the New Jerusalem and the New Heaven and Earth. The idea that Christ returns before the literal thousand-year earthly reign of Christ—premillennialism—has become so attached to claims like we are living in the last generation or decade or literal years prior to Christ's return, the antichrist may be alive today, and believers will be raptured out of the world before the worst part of the Great Tribulation (a literal seven years), that the term premillennialism fails to communicate important and helpful biblical truths.

Premillennialism is right on much. Sin and the spirit of antichrist are potent in every age and in the present age, and we should take into account many antichrists, radical human depravity, and the folly and arrogance of claiming to be able to usher in the Messiah's kingdom before the Messiah returns. The most popular forms of premillennialism, as noted, are also wrong on much, including the flaws already referenced (fatalism, pessimism, escapism), and the insistence that the thousand years must be a literal thousand years. The thousand years of the millennium, symbolic of the literal fullness

---

22. Schizophrenia is used here as a confused mental state, characterized by inconsistencies, contradictions, and cognitive (mental) dissonance (discord).

of God's blessings and presence, might point to a much deeper, richer, and longer transitional fulfillment of the Creator's purpose for the creation as we move toward the New Creation. A transitional period of at least one thousand years where evil is mostly but not entirely subdued until the fullness of the New Creation is sound theology.

One could try to create new terms for the position of this book, such as pre-transitionism, where Christ comes back before a lengthy transition to the New Creation. Pre-transitionism, however, only speaks to the transition and not the full glorious future-vision. Pre-resurrectionism could emphasize that Christ returns before the fullness of individual and cosmic New Creation resurrection, but that term does not highlight the need for a transitional period prior to the final New Creation resurrection of all things. The same omission (the important transitional period) would apply to something like a pre-New-Creationism new term (or neologism). Pre-utopianism avoids naively optimistic views of the future by placing the Messianic return before utopia, but utopia is not a biblically based term and is inferior to pre-New-Creationism.

Hence, barring a better suggestion, all of these new terms, as well as the traditional terms (premillennialism, amillennialism, postmillennialism) should be retired or greatly qualified, at least for a season, as summaries of the biblical future vision. Premillennialism can be salvaged but the term is sometimes less than helpful in an age of escapism and fatalism. Some are trying to salvage amillennialism by emphasizing the New Creation restoration, but this approach uses a term that literally denies ("a") the earthly reign of Christ, and more importantly does not acknowledge the practical and theological need for something like an actual transitional period of a thousand years or more prior to the fullness of the New Creation. Amillennial New Creation Restorationism is attractive but inadequate.

Hence, pre-restorationism seems to be the only available remaining alternative to capture the argument of this work. Restoration is a biblical term and concept. Restoration of the creation is biblical and theologically sound. Pre-restorationism properly places Christ's return prior to his reign on earth and rules out much naivete and flawed and dangerous messianic movements and dead ends that seek to usher in the kingdom, or total social justice, or the classless society, or the people's rule, or full inclusion and equity, or even claim to end war, which was popular before and after World War I. Pre-restorationism views the transitional period from the present to the New Creation as absolutely essential and lengthy, and points to the restoration of the Creator's intent. However, restoration is not final fulfillment and total, glorious, cosmic, New Creation consummation and the resurrection of all things. Pre-restorationism is a premillennialism purged, an amillennialism salvaged via the transitional period and reign of Messiah, and postmillennialism emptied of its dangerous Messiah complex yet affirming of postmillennialism's insistence on historic and cosmic fulfillment and that believers play a critical role in the restoration and fulfillment of cosmic history as vice-regents of the Logos.

Pre-restorationism not only properly frames the future and ultimate future (eschatology), but it properly guides the present. The present has already stepped into the future via the Christ-event, cross, resurrection, and sending of the Spirit. The present cannot be perfected, but because of Christ's victory already the present can be significantly influenced by the future. Present Spirit-filled impact and influence, however, will largely be determined by robust and sound theological strategy and tactics. Unfortunately, many faith communities today either disengage or try to change the world by playing the missional equivalent of Whac-A-Mole.

WHAC-A-MOLE ATTEMPTS TO "SAVE" CIVILIZATION

Courageous and profound theological strategists of past and present generations, such as Augustine, H. Richard Niebuhr, and James K. A. Smith, try to counter ideologies and toxic future-visions that are corroding and fragmenting families, communities, and nations by offering profound theological analyses (e.g., *The City of God*, *Christ and Culture*, or *Awaiting the King*) to which, the reader will see, this present work is indebted.[23] However, many of the proposed and less profound solutions offered today by politically and culturally involved believers amount to playing Whac-A-Mole, meaning, "a situation in which repeated efforts to resolve a problem are frustrated by the problem reappearing in a different form."[24]

Rather than overtly, clearly, and publicly announcing that biblical and Judeo-Christian influence and influencers must be silenced or removed from culture and civilization, the more shrewd leaders and soldiers of the City of Antichrist have shattered the pillars and cornerstones of the City of Kingdom Influence, drawn the faithful into endless and single Whac-A-Mole issues while missing the deeper tectonic shifts, and redefined and relabeled believers, Scripture, and Judeo-Christian values—not only as unhelpful or irrelevant (ABC)[25] to the common good but hateful, non-in-

---

23. See the bibliography concerning all three of these works.
24. *Free Dictionary*, s.v. "whack-a-mole."
25. ABC, anything but Christian, is a concept borrowed from Os Guinness. Decision Staff, "Hostility."

clusive, and unjust. Those strategically guiding the moles behind the curtain are often the victors, and to the victors go the civilizational spoils.

Politically engaged evangelicals are to be commended for many of these mole-whacking initiatives if the activities are expressions of overflowing love for God, others, and God's good creation, especially when other spiritual doves simply remain supposedly pure and stay on the sidelines while criticizing the players self-sacrificing in the trenches. These doves also and often parasite off of the valiant and Herculean efforts and sacrifices of those in the trenches.

Some criticism of cultural and politically engaged Christians comes from believers who already seem to be in the boost phase of flight, no longer earthbound.[26] However, the evangelicals with their feet firmly on the playing field often lack a clear, compelling, consistent future-vision, much less strategic and tactical envisioning and planning. Perhaps of equal or greater importance is that such efforts lack true and needed collaboration and winning teamwork with other workers amid the crisis of a dying civilization.

Recently, over a million copies were sold in just months with a battle plan for exposing and countering *American Marxism*, the alleged cause of the majority of the moral, economic, cultural, and political decline of America.[27] Numerous other works propose to understand and overcome "the postmodern, neo-Marxist faith" and "toxic new religion" that seeks to "destroy the Judeo-Christian culture of the West."[28] Senator Ted Cruz's 2023 Amazon bestseller offers a battle plan for "how to defeat cultural Marxism in America."[29]

Nearly all proposals that try to identify the key threat or enemy and the correct solution perpetuate the nearly daily and endless game of Whac-A-Mole.

Marxism could be eliminated today across the globe with some likely and potential benefits, yet many countries would still be in the advanced stages of decomposition or cultural rot.[30] Russia is illustrative. The attempts to establish democracy in nations without the prerequisite historical experience and shared values are also illustrative.

This work will contend and explain why the only enduring silver bullet relative to approaching the reality of the City of Kingdom Influence or

---

26. Mojtabai, *Blessed Assurance*, xii.

27. Levin, *American Marxism*.

28. One such recent illustrative work, with well-known author Stan Guthrie, is Scott D. Allen and Darrow Miller, *A Toxic New Religion: Understanding the Postmodern, Neo-Marxist Faith That Seeks to Destroy the Judeo-Christian Culture of the West*.

29. Cruz, *Unwoke*.

30. Oden, *After Modernity*.

Approximation in this age, meaning authentic kingdom influence on civilization, includes the many dimensions, layers, ripple effects, light, salt, spirit, Spirit, and healing cultural leaven of God's true future already. That true future is centered in the Messiah, Word, or Logos. The only hope for the healing presence of the true future already is thus Logocentric.

To be Logocentric is to be kingdom-centric—to be lovingly passionate and steadfastly and appropriately committed as a citizen to the kingdom rule of the Logos. Kingdom faithfulness before Messiah's return does not mean that adultery, divorce, and homosexuality should be punishable by death. Kingdom faithfulness does require shrewd and loving assessments of appropriate goals for the era prior to Messiah's return. Authentic citizenship means not ignoring the relationship between healthy families and the common good, and identifying how the faithful can influence families and communities even though not all will convert to the faith.

The terms city and citizen are related, for a citizen is one who inhabits and is subject to a nation, state, commonwealth, province, territory, or city. In our current age, a faithful or good citizen or citizenry contributes positively to the community, nation, and world—referred to collectively as the City of Kingdom Approximation. Judeo-Christian believers define that contribution biblically and in terms of flavoring and bending present kingdoms and history toward the true future. The faithful hold multiple citizenships in the present, the future kingdom that is already, and the ultimate future (see Heb 11). However, for the faithful to be effective, they should focus on their larger future-vision citizenship and move beyond important though not ultimate single hot topic issues.

Whac-A-Mole civilizational reform is an inch wide and an inch deep. Know your true disease, know your true cure.[31] And the only real cure for our radically diseased historical moment and culture is the influence and current reality of the City of Kingdom Approximation, which will be introduced, explained, and illustrated in this work. The singular answer and antidote to the City of Antichrist prior to Christ's return is this City of Kingdom Approximation.

Cultural changes, upheavals, and hemorrhaging cause some Christian and cultural conservatives to take flight, curse the darkness, and focus on a way of escape via the rapture or ecstatic religious experience. Other social and religious conservatives orient more toward fight than flight and directly engage one or a cluster of issues and perceived threats. Well-intended books,

---

31. "Know your disease! Know your cure! Ye were born in sin: Therefore, 'ye must be born again,' born of God. By nature ye are wholly corrupted. By grace ye shall be wholly renewed. In Adam ye all died: In the second Adam, in Christ, ye all are made alive." Wesley, "Original Sin."

videos, sermons, conferences, rallies, churches, families, organizations, and individuals seek to influence or save culture by whacking one mole after another, or flittering from one threat and proposed solution or cause to another. Some go to battle, some seek escape, and some proclaim that the last decade or years prior to the rapture have now arrived while also seeking to stem the floodwaters of perceived threats such as:

- Same-sex marriage;
- Nonbinary sexuality and gender fluidity;
- The new polygamy, "polyfidelity," polyamory, and "sologamy";
- Toxic or shallow theologies of the body;
- Advocacy for pederasty (advocacy to normalize homosexual relations with minors; pederasts are now being reclassified as "minor attracted persons");
- Oppressive vaccine and mask mandates;
- The Enlightenment or modernist intellectual movement (which enthrones reason over Scripture, the church, and traditional belief);
- Theological and/or Political Liberalism or Progressivism;
- Postmodernism and deconstruction, Existentialism and Nihilism;
- Utopianism, Secularism, Humanism, or Secular Humanism;
- The cultural revolution;
- Radical environmentalism;
- The sexual revolution;
- Abortion and the alleged growing acceptance of infanticide (killing of the born);
- Marxism, Woke-ism, and American Marxism;
- Neo-Marxism or seductive Marcusian Marxism;
- Liberation theology;
- Critical Race Theory (CRT);
- The new atheism;
- Socialism;
- Victimization;
- Educational indoctrination;
- Pornography;

- Moral relativism, including the rejection of absolute truth and morality;
- Corrupt, manipulative, state-sponsored corporate media, technology, and fake news;
- Anti-Western and Anti-Christian movies;
- The "Great Reset";[32]
- Lack of prayer by the faithful and taking God and prayer out of the public schools.

A thousand other causes and solutions for alleged contemporary cultural rot have been proposed, so this list is truly illustrative. As noted, an obsession with single issues engenders escapism and/or reckless cultural engagement rather than shrewd and loving kingdom approximation. This list also contains possible wedge issues, where the real goal may not simply be to win on a single issue, but to dislodge civilization from its increasingly drifting orbit from Judeo-Christian Scripture and the Logos.

The intentions of these religious, social, and political cultural warriors when addressing such single-issue concerns may at times be noble, but they never seem to identify or focus on the underlying root and spirit of antichristism that increasingly animates, guides, and norms these "moles'" legion movements, future-visions, and social issues. For issues and concerns that are legitimate, it is critical to remember that all of these are grounded in a rejection of the person, truth, values, wisdom, and cultural influence of the only true Messiah or Christ, the Logos or Word of God.

Avoiding Whac-A-Mole approaches to influencing culture and civilization requires at least three key elements. First, while some are called to constructively address single issues and should be honored, church and synagogue will fail to be salt and light apart from a strategy that connects the dots between the single issues. Profound strategy, wise planning, stellar teamwork, and constructive tactics are indispensable. Second, the epic drama of whether individuals, families, communities, cities, nations, and global culture will align more with and love the City of Antichrist or the City of Kingdom Approximation connects the dots of legion single issues. Third, prayerful, Spirit-led apologetics and evangelism (see the book of Acts) flowing forth from genuine, historic, world-influencing revival and renewal inside of faith communities must lie at the core of authentic and sustainable kingdom influence, but such prayerful revival is not the entirety of a biblical response to the current crisis of proliferating antichristism.

---

32. Beck and Trask Haskins, *Great Reset*.

Western and global antichristism has now reached an inflection point and a crisis moment. Antichristism is ancient and timeless but is also the new and progressively acceptable form of anti-Semitism now emerging in formerly Judeo-Christian-influenced nations.

Antichristism and anti-Semitism are anti-Logos, anti-Messiah, and anti-Scripture. Some forms of antichristism seek to marginalize biblical faith communities. Others seek to silence, cancel, or criminalize biblical faith and practice. Antichristism, in contrast to some distorted contemporary claims of oppressive intersectionality and victimization, is a legitimate manifestation of spiritual "intersectionality." Antichristism includes the interconnected (or intersectional) nature of increasingly militant opposition to Judeo-Christian civilizational influence and the Judeo-Christian faithful who dare to emerge from their privatized and over-spiritualized closets and exercise actual political freedom and impactful freedom of speech.

Many less religiously and socially conservative foot soldiers, even inside of faith communities, sincerely believe they are courageously advancing values and causes such as justice, compassion, inclusion, equity, and diversity. The ordination of practicing homosexuals, for example, is viewed as the caring, just, and progressive response to a changed world. Yet all of these allegedly noble causes and virtues—justice, inclusion, and compassion certainly can be virtuous if properly defined—are redefined in today's context and quickly drifting out of orbit of the Logos.

More discerning and militant social justice progressives and antichrists (e.g., Nietzsche), however, understand very well that, for them, the true or root problem is Judeo-Christian and scriptural influence on culture. They are correct, given their assumptions. The influence of the Logos has to go if legion symptomatic causes and values are to fully triumph. Logos-influenced culture must become an unfortunate memory of a supposedly and entirely oppressive past era.

For such cultural warriors, if Judeo-Christian influence is marginalized, vaporized, or criminalized, then countless so-called social justice causes can progress. Christianity is the root problem. Judaism is the root problem. For some today, accelerating anti-Semitism may be more about political power and core values than ethnicity alone. Judeo-Christian Scripture is viewed as the root problem. Yet simply eradicating what is arguably the world's largest religious orientation and belief system (Judeo-Christian) is not so simple. So while Judeo-Christian influence may not always be able to be eradicated or criminalized, it can at least be redefined, and such a redefinition can take place initially and willingly through undiscerning faith communities—from within.

Again, the fruit is not the root, and the symptoms are not the same as the disease. Falling out of orbit of the influence of the Logos (the person, relational love, and biblical truths) can take place inside and outside of faith communities and can be direct and oppressive or subtle and subversive. The individual cultural conflicts are important, but these hot button issues often run cover and blow smoke for the larger game plan of eclipsing the influence of the biblical Logos on church, synagogue, culture, and civilization. Hence, mole-chasing is a very dangerous and failed strategy and tactic for those defined and led by the Logos.

The spirit of antichrist and antichristism certainly includes bad ideas, especially toxic future-visions. Yet at the unifying and animating core is what John the apostle refers to as the spiritual force (1 John 4:3; 2:18–24) that opposes confessing the Messiah and opposes the work, influence, beliefs, practices, values, and affections of or love for the Logos who became flesh.[33]

The future-vision problem is much deeper, systemic, and profound than any one issue, ideology, or future-vision. The many cancerous future-visions reviewed in this work are the fruit of the core future-vision and spirit of antichristism. And the solution, the biblical future-vision, certainly includes sound ideas concerning the future, but it especially is a lionhearted human spirit and Spirit-led and Spirit-realized combination of right ideas, right affections or loves, and right action—the true and potent solution employs head, heart, and hand.

As noted, eliminating any political system, future-vision, or unethical practice tomorrow would still leave in place incalculable and toxic cancers that devour families, faith communities, and nations. Or, to use familiar biblical imagery and a contemporary issue, you can cast out the civilizational demon of partial-birth abortion, yet myriad fallen angels still remain intact and flourish. A small victory can easily morph into a large defeat. The demon will just possess another cause, such as human trafficking, and/or use the reaction to the defeat of a practice to justify an even more evil practice. Why? Unless the underlying spirit and future-vision of antichrist is truly addressed, the fruit of antichrist will continue to find ways to blossom, proliferate, and seed the future of the entire planet. Many theologians (e.g., Tillich) have noted that culture reflects the true soul or spiritual state of nations. Changing cultural or legal practices without addressing the soul is a short-lived strategy, almost certain to backfire.

To illustrate further, Mark Levin's million copy bestseller is a call to arms against the future-vision and American "counterrevolution" of

---

33. The loves or affections of the Messiah simply refer(s) to that which the Messiah loves and draws upon, the general concept found in Smith, *You Are What You Love*.

American Marxism, which is "everywhere" and single-handedly "threatens to destroy the greatest nation ever established, along with your freedom, family, and security," and "impose autocratic rule." Hence, Levin states that the purpose of his "book is to *awaken* millions of patriotic Americans" to the reality, threat, and proper response to American Marxism and to spark the creation of a "unified, patriotic front of previously docile, divergent, and/or disputatious societal, cultural, and political factions and forces, which have in common their belief that America is worth defending . . . [and] immediately galvanize around and rally to the cause." Otherwise, quoting Ronald Reagan, Levin warns that "one day we will spend our sunset years telling our children and children's children what it was once like in the United States where men were free."[34]

Let's assume for now that Levin has properly diagnosed and identified a real or even primary threat to church and state in the American context. The problem is that if you eliminate American Marxism today, you would still have moral relativism, a post-truth society, shameless spin, the redefinition of everything, and corrupt media and government to contend with tomorrow—just to name a few threats (see the previous list).

ANTICHRISTISM AND THE REJECTION OF THE INFLUENCE OF THE LOGOS

Indeed, not only do these toxic future-visions share assumptions, values, beliefs, and the spiritual force of antichristism, they also reinforce, nurture, fuel, and feed each other. They also have become a constant barrage on the City of Kingdom Approximation, and the city walls are nearly, if not already, breached around the globe, especially and ironically in formerly Logos-influenced nations.

For example, our post-truth moral relativism provides potent ammunition to those who argue that since there is no normative truth or ethics (Nietzsche), all that remains is saying and doing whatever is necessary to advance the individual or the individual's tribe (radical political tribalism). The intentional or unintentional relativistic and postmodern goal is to redefine every term, value, and even history itself. Not only is spin on steroids in, but constant lying is morally acceptable because morality is about who wins, not timeless truth, and it is time for Christians, especially white Christians, and Westerners, to lose. Thus ends the long quest in the West and across the globe for Justice with a capital J. The new king and future-vision that

---

34. Levin, *American Marxism*, 1, 12–13.

triumphed is "just us," with a small j but presented as a capital J in order to persuade or manipulate.

To illustrate this organic or systemic connection opposing Messiah or Logos, once the relativistic and post-Logos fuel is poured on the Marxist fire, you then have a potent recipe for anarchy or revolution at any cost—and by any means necessary. And the necessary means for dealing with anyone who gets in the way are consistent with the French Revolution's Reign of Terror: chop, chop, chop. As one Seattle revolutionary articulated to a crowd of protesters:

> Has anybody here ever heard of the French Revolution before? That is another revolution (that happened) because people started putting property over lives! They started putting money over people! Does anyone here know what happened to the people who did not get on board with the French Revolution? "Chopped!" the crowd replied. Again. And again. That is the message we need to send! We are serious! This is not a joke! As the demonstrators walked back toward Capitol Hill, they chanted, "No justice, no peace. No racist police."[35]

Failing individual police, police training, and police oversight systems need addressing and accountability, but the proposed solution above is less than helpful and enables evils far greater than those being "chopped." History has demonstrated time and again that liberators, as with the French Revolution, often exceed the tyranny of the tyrants they depose and release even more pathological forces on the masses and especially the vulnerable.

The spirit of antichrist and anti-Logocentrism is a collection of loves, passions, ideologies, and practices that come from the same poisoned fruit, interface, cross-pollinate, and coalesce in the spirit of legion future-visions. They are often seductive, mixing half-truths (e.g., the lack of social justice) with virulent and deadly lies and toxic solutions. They have done much to establish the superiority and reign of the City of Antichrist over the City of Kingdom Approximation. And ever so tragically, it is often the poor and powerless that suffer the most in the City of Antichrist.

---

35. *Seattle Times* Staff, "Seattle-Area Protests"; Perrotta, "CHOP"; and Urbanski, "Menacing Speaker."

ACCOMMODATION AS A POWERFUL ENABLER OF ANTICHRISTISM AND SEDUCTION

This work will demonstrate that unbiblical or anti-biblical future-visions not only share normative assumptions and beliefs but are also empowered by the spiritual forces of antichristism and the attempt to banish the Logos and Logocentric influenced language, words, culture, and civilizations. Unfortunately, many of those claiming to follow the Messiah are essential and strategic enablers of false future-visions and antichristism—often inside of churches and other faith communities and organizations.

This enabling frequently takes the form of escapism, cultural separatism, prideful or angry cultural engagement, all of which have been previously introduced, or accommodation to culture. A classic example of cultural accommodation or compromise inside of faith communities is when pro-abortion and pro-partial-birth abortion religious leaders sing, "This little light of mine, I'm gonna let it shine," at the dedication of abortion clinics. "We affirm the work of abortion care as sacred."[36]

Similarly, the seductive slogan "pro-faith, pro-family, pro-choice,"[37] used in countless states and nations, reflects such accommodation to culture and a redefinition of Judeo-Christian beliefs and practice. The historic faith of biblical Jews and Christians concerning the unborn is simply ignored, redefined, and shamed. The destruction of preborn children is the ultimate attack on the family. Family is also redefined by such pro-choice advocates while they pretend to affirm traditional Judeo-Christian values. Unfortunately, the choices of millions of preborn children and fathers are viewed as irrelevant to the dialogue. The truly consensual approval of abortions by the marginalized is also arguably overridden at times by incomplete information and manipulation by abortion crusaders. Mothers who have complete information and visuals concerning the developmental stages of the distinct person inside of them often conclude that the unborn are more than body parts or potential human beings. They are human beings with great potential, as many have noted.

Abortion is a blind faith religion and false god. Some who worship at the altar of this carnage are deceived, and others are militantly antichrist, which is the only possible explanation for how abortion, especially late-term abortion, and now infanticide, is presented as a just and compassionate cause that occupies the moral high ground.

---

36. Religious Coalition for Reproductive Choice, "Clinic Blessings."
37. Religious Coalition for Reproductive Choice, "Clinic Blessings."

In Scripture, the opposition to God's rule inside and outside of faith communities is the spirit of antichrist, the spirit of antichristism, the spirit of false prophets, and the spirit of seductive angels of light (1 John; 2 Pet 2; Matt 7:15; 24:24; 2 Cor 11:14). The opposition to God's current and future rule inside and outside of the church is increasingly militant and especially includes the unbiblical or anti-biblical, though sometimes seductive, redefinition of virtually every belief, term, and value—a process Nietzsche referred to as the reevaluation or transvaluation of all values.

Everything is redefined everywhere and always. The contemporary illustrations are in the news daily. Those advocating for consensual sexual relationships with children now redefine those seeking or engaging in this relatively widespread ancient desire and practice, pederasty, and the current practice of so-called consensual child molestation, as "minor attracted persons." The compassionate adoption of children by Judeo-Christian parents is now viewed by increasing numbers as psychologically damaging, unconstitutional, and anti-democratic. In contrast, polyamorous (multiple partners) and non-heterosexual adoptions are loving, inclusive, healthy, constitutional, and pro-democratic. The use of terms like boy and girl must be banned as oppressive. The massive centralization and expansion of governmental power or control is the only path to justice and compassion, and any opposition to such plans are hateful and, ironically, seductively redefined as anti-democratic.

Civilization has been flipped on its head. The Logos that once held many of the cultural and civilizational pillars in majestic and synchronized orbit in submission to the only true future is now being eclipsed or drowned out by countless clamoring and often conflicting voices from tribal messiahs of liberation. Transgender tribes and messiahs seek to devour the formerly powerful feminist tribes, or vice versa. Tribal truth and justice is self-devouring and short-lived. Many proclaim "follow me" but lack the divine and eternal status to truly lead. Messianic movements reject the true Messiah and futilely seek to hold the civilizational system together by attracting a few here or there for a season. This will not end well. The present influence of the Logos is the secret sauce for a better world prior to the return of the Logos.

CIVILIZATIONAL ECLIPSE OR POTENTIAL REEMERGENCE OF THE INFLUENCE OF LOGOS?

The removal of the Word, the Logos who created and upholds all things, the Messiah who redeems the present and future, as the invisible norm and center or glue of civilizational influence, communication, and language, results in language and communication chaos and anarchy. Human communication and civilization once, while often failing, sought unity out of a healthy diversity, while often unaware of the invisible norms and contributions of the Logos and the more secular quest for the common good and self-evident truths.

The attempted banishment of the Logos norm and the truth quest has resulted, as noted, in the "just us" tribalistic redefinition of virtually every term, concept, value, belief, and moral standard. Antichristism is the long term and inevitable consequence, though it often emerges subtly and slowly. It typically begins with word, phrase, and value redefinitions in centers of education, including both religious and non-religious schools. This has happened repeatedly with educational institutions in the American context. Schools founded by prayer, revival, and the sacrifices of Bible-believing faithful not only drift from the original mission and faith but often become militantly anti-biblical.

Over time the truth quest in such centers displaces the influence of the Logos and education increasingly moves toward indoctrination rather than discovery, and the new post-Logos definitions, values, and one thousand commandments eventually redefine culture and civilization. Though this is typically a long process, one day a nation wakes up, well aware of its weaknesses, but asks if the world had gone mad.

Formerly Logocentric civilization is now marginally Logocentric, if not anti-Logocentric—happily so for many. Justice has been replaced with "just us," and marriage, gender, and most every term and value has been craftily redefined in the name of "justice," "equity," "compassion," and "inclusion." The new definitions have fallen mostly if not fully out of orbit of the biblical Logos plumb line. Some still claim to be in orbit when in fact they have migrated to a new universe where all has been redefined, everywhere and always. And the subtle and eventually aggressive removal of Ten Commandment Logocentrism, originally sold as "freedom" and "tolerance," has resulted in a myriad of fleeting tribal commandments, gods, dark angels attempting to control everyone and everything, and a new almost infinite set of commandments, regulating actions, words (Logos means Word), and even thoughts.

The vision of the City of Kingdom Approximation that lives within and runs counter to the City of Antichrist in the present age rejects church-state union, while remaining fully and graciously Logocentric and New Creation centered. Influence is not indoctrination or manipulation. The City of Antichrist is ultimately anti-Logos and anti-freedom. And both cities have their cultures, languages, and lexicons (i.e., the underlying vocabulary, values, and verbal assumptions of a civilization even if there are distinct and multiple languages).

The anti-Logos agenda is for the key terms and values taken for granted in Judeo-Christian–birthed and influenced civilization to be subtly or militantly redefined, banned, replaced, or transcended (i.e., to move beyond them). For Nietzsche (d. AD 1900), Judeo-Christian values needed to be replaced (or transvalued) with what he absurdly viewed as more humanity and culture-affirming values from Greco-Roman or other cultures and civilizations superior to Logocentric influenced culture. These civilizations also had moral standards more in line with Nietzsche and the contemporary culture. Is it any wonder that we are rushing toward the moral standards of ancient Greece and Rome (polyfidelity, homosexual practices including advocacy for pederasty, late-term abortion, infanticide, antichristism, the king is the law rather than the God-given law rules over the king)?

Marriage, truth, gender, morality, justice and social justice, civilization, faith, freedom, freedom of speech, democracy, compassion, love, Christian, Jesus, tolerance, terrorism, inclusion, diversity, equality, and multiculturalism—to name only a short list—have all been radically distorted and redefined. Biblical and Judeo-Christian dissenters need to be marginalized, shamed, criminalized, or permanently silenced. The real agenda, however, is to silence the Word, the Logos, and place the spirit of antichrist on the throne.

We live in an age of verbal or semantic seduction, manipulation, and warfare, fueled by the spirit of antichristism and the love of the City of Antichrist. Judeo-Christian love for and the seeking of the influence of the only true and enduring eternal City is love for approximating the only true future in the present. This means seeking first the City of Kingdom Approximation—realistic kingdom influence—already in the current age before Messiah's return when our seeking of the kingdom is gloriously fulfilled.

Yet, as noted, the sirens of verbal seduction and truth manipulation also have enraptured many inside faith communities—individuals, organizations, denominations, and religious traditions. As already observed, in Scripture this subversion is the work of "false prophets," false "messiahs," and "many antichrists" (Matt 24:24; 1 John 2:18). The religiously seduced, while still naming and claiming the name of the God of Abraham and Christ, especially serve as enablers of antichrist and assist with empowering the City of Antichrist.

Many religious leaders of Jesus' day were anti-Messiah, or anti-Christ in a religious community, claiming to be the children of Abraham, children of the promise, and the special, favored children of God. They rejected the very Messiah for whom they were waiting. Jesus turned to others inside and outside the elect community to find the true children of the promise and children of genuine faith in the Logos. Jesus claimed that many who thought they were Abraham's children were not and that their true father was the devil (John 8:44–45).

Amazingly, the leaders in this graced and favored community were determined to be whitewashed tombs and hypocritical, false prophets. Jesus predicted that "false christs and false prophets will arise and will provide great signs and wonders, so as to mislead, if possible, even the elect" (Matt 24:24). The elect are the objects of seduction, and religious leaders are often the causes of seduction.

Those who oppose, subvert, or distort the faith, even inside of faith communities, are antichrist, and their deception targets everyone, including the elect. Such is the spirit of antichrist and antichristism. Such is the work of many antichrists.

And these seducers are enabled by the faithful who are deceived or who misunderstand their own faith (e.g., fatalistic escapism) or the implications of biblical faith for kingdom service and cultural engagement (such as cultural escapism or compromise and accommodationism). God's kingdom influence is hindered by antichrists, false christs or messiahs, false prophets, and especially by *enablers* inside and outside the community of faith.

This work will argue that antichristisms include toxic future-visions such as the many corrosive varieties of modernism and postmodernism (see chapters 9–10). These perspectives will be briefly introduced, simplified, integrated, and assessed as forms of antichristism—and then rapidly countered.

Enablers include many erroneous and toxic future-visions, with some addressed in this preface and introduction and others (e.g., Libertarianism) introduced or more fully defined later (e.g., see chapters 2, 4, and 7), As noted, these perspectives will be briefly introduced and refuted while focusing on the underlying root of these toxic or less than helpful future-visions.

While political and cultural engagement are essential and must be loving and shrewd, the epicenter or root of God's solution and program to redeem individuals, families, communities, and nations in the present age resides within transformative, transforming, and Spirit-led biblical faith communities. Relative to biblical communities, the church or synagogue is both the problem and solution for fragmenting and collapsing civilizations.

The City of Antichrist destroys, distorts, oppresses, kills, and flees from or opposes the coming City of God. Some cities of antichrist actually claim the name of Christ by misleading or deluding many. The City of Kingdom Approximation steps into the better and true future already. Unfortunately, faith communities, including churches, are often stellar enablers of antichrist ideologies and future-visions due to playing Whac-A-Mole, being seduced, or via the fatalistic and escapist future-visions referenced previously that will be further explored.

Hence, this book responds to the reality that the present moment is plagued by significant biblical distortions inside church and synagogue and accelerating opposition to Scripture, God's people, Judeo-Christian values, and God's Logos and rule outside faith communities. This reality can no longer be blissfully ignored by escapists. The impact is increasingly touching every community, family, church, synagogue, and future generations.

The present escalating civilizational crisis impacting the entire globe has, therefore, resulted from seduction and corruption from within, opposition from without, and valiant but fragmented and Whac-A-Mole responses by the Judeo-Christian faithful. This very same historic crisis is also fueled by the enabling of false prophets and the spirit of antichrist by God's own people with grave consequences inside and outside the circle of faith.

We have met the principal enemies or cast of characters, and, to modify a well-known phrase, some of them are us. Faith communities bear a profound and impactful responsibility and opportunity. This work seeks to focus on the root of the crisis, the spirit of antichrist, and the root of the solution, which is the biblical future-vision, theology, and Spirit-generated City of Kingdom Approximation. The perennial and epic challenge prior to the Messiah's return is to diminish and disempower the City of Antichrist and enable and advance the City of Kingdom Approximation.

As noted, my multi-decadal background in strategic and tactical planning in higher education, including institutional effectiveness, assessment, accreditation, and continuous improvement, also has contributed to the contours and goals that will frame this work and its conclusions and recommendations. To repeat and to be blunt, the current response of God's people to the present crisis is typically an exemplar of anemic, flawed, and fragmented strategic and tactical planning.

As we have seen, the toxicity of the enablers, sometimes well-intended, takes on many, many forms. If C. S. Lewis were still with us, he might note that Screwtape's strategy is brilliant and succeeding by luring the people of God down incalculable rabbit trails.

In addition to eschatomania, perhaps one of the more prominent enablers among the truly faithful is referred to in this work as the "Lone Ranger" response of many Judeo-Christian leaders. The Lone Ranger strategic planning vision simply accepts the fact that everyone is peddling or marketing some variety of an independent solution to civilizational collapse. Everyone is saving civilization, or America, which has some value, but not truly working together amid our historic crisis and major challenges will be fatal.

As Benjamin Franklin aptly said on the eve of the American Revolution, "We must all hang together, or, most assuredly, we shall all hang separately."[38] The time is long overdue for all people of faith to "hang together" with key elements of a broad, true, biblical future-vision and then engage in a teamwork approach to integrated strategic and tactical planning and continuous improvement relative to constructive Judeo-Christian influence.

This work hopes to make a modest contribution to this essential, communal, future-vision project throughout the book. Chapters 1 and 2 will address the central question of this work and provide a foretaste of options and answers. Chapter 3 will identify how three representative groups—antichrists, enablers, and approximators[39]—harm or heal civilization and frustrate or fulfill the true mission of God's people. Chapter 3, after laying a foundation for and expanding the thesis of this work, will clarify the limitations of the remainder of this work and further preview the remaining chapters and argument.

Chapter 4 addresses the symptoms, roots, and fruits of both toxic and regenerating future-visions. Chapter 5 reviews the irrefutable evidence that future-visions are central and dominant in Scripture, and everywhere. Chapter 6 describes and assesses the significance of our new age of post-Christendom antichristism. Chapter 7 and the conclusion seek to guide faith communities on how to always be prepared for the age or City of Antichrist, the age or City of Kingdom Approximation, and the New Creation—the three cities.

Appendix A will provide an instructive table that illustrates how future-vision distortions can be corrected or eliminated and then harnessed or replaced with future-vision alternatives that birth, nurture, and sustain effective kingdom influence in orbit of and guided and empowered by the true Logos. This material will "preach." Appendix B clarifies Nietzsche's influential teaching on truth that guides life in the City of Antichrist. Appendix C explains how Nietzsche's City of Antichrist incrementally vanquished countless civilizations and nation states. Appendices D and E provide very practical guidance or steps for how faith communities can always be fully prepared, as true kingdom citizens of time and eternity, for the City of Antichrist, the City of Kingdom Approximation, and the New Creation City.

---

38. Isaacson, "Benjamin Franklin."

39. An approximator is "one who, or that which, approximates." *Free Dictionary*, s.v. "Approximator."

Throughout this text, based on observations of the reading patterns of laity, students, and professors, some repetition between the chapters will be intentional. In addition, clarifying the argument for the reader will require some repetition in relationship to the different contexts of each chapter.

"I'm not a prophet, the son or daughter of a prophet or prophetess, and I work for a non-profit organization." The source of this quip and quote is uncertain, though it was often used by Dr. Walter Kaiser. The truth of this sentiment is especially evident and relevant today given the pace and complexity of cultural and civilizational change.

Two things seem certain regarding the current and next chapter of history. First, marginalizing and militant antichristism and even the persecution of present and future generations of Christians in formerly Judeo-Christian nations will likely spike within a generation—apart from grace and an appropriate response from the faithful. Antisemitism, which is one form or subset of antichristism, seems to be flourishing globally and in formerly Judeo-Christian–influenced nations. Or at a minimum, antisemitism and antichristism are increasingly and publicly acceptable in many circles once thought to be safe or sacrosanct. Such dark shadows are already lengthening. Subtle or sweeping redefinitions and the deconstruction and reconstruction of freedom and democracy, combined with new technological and media capabilities that enable technological tyranny, are pregnant with potential oppression and persecution. Open season is near or imminent. Second, this work will argue that the laying aside of flawed future-visions and the energetic and broad affirmation and advocacy for the grand and authentic biblical future-vision of kingdom approximation is the best hope for mobilizing the effective and influential faithful.

RECAP

Hence, sound biblical theology suggests that we currently live in both the best and worst of times, prior to the truly best of times that accompany Messiah's return. The mission that God has called us to requires understanding or navigating three if not four or five cities, though three are most immediately relevant and guide our epic journey to the New Creation.

The City of Eden is no more, though not forgotten and someday fulfilled in the New Jerusalem and New Creation. The City of Antichrist is a present reality that already can be countered by salt, light, and leaven, and this rebellious city was, in one sense, as a foretaste of the only true future, already defeated by the victorious Christ event and sending of the Spirit "upon all flesh [or people]" (Joel 2:28 ESV). In the present age this dark city will ebb and flow in power and influence, with a possible future intensification, yet the cornerstone and foundational walls are crumbling and it ultimately will be defeated forever.

The City of Kingdom Approximation is a present possibility, largely determined by the Spirit-dependence, faithfulness, cross-formed (cruciform) sacrifices, and the creative and constructive cultural and civilizational engagement of Judeo-Christian faith communities. The City of Kingdom Approximation partially restores the intent of the City of Eden, withstands and frustrates darkness, brings healing and wholeness, approximates, points to, and participates in the future flesh-and-blood Spirit-ruled Triune City of God. The fourth city, the transitional City of God, is established after Messiah's return, and prepares the way for the final state of the cosmos and the eternal City of God—the radiant and celestial fifth city.

Yet in this present age the faithful especially navigate the best and worst of times, fluid antichristism and antisemitism, discipling all nations (Matt 28:19–20), the spirit and City of Antichrist, the Spirit's outpouring, the City of Kingdom Approximation and constructive and creative cultural engagement, and the morning star and dawning of the City of God. The mission and journey of God's people today primarily engages and prepares for the three cities of Antichrist, Approximation, and the still future and transitional earthly City of God.

Those who affirm the complete annihilation of the present cosmos often try to navigate the three key cities by flight, fight, escapism, angry cultural engagement, or some combination thereof. The resurrection is viewed more as a past event and Christ's kingdom is viewed almost entirely as a future event. Discontinuity between the present and ultimate future is typically emphasized.

Those who affirm the complete renewal or restoration of the present cosmos are often tempted to baptize or accommodate to programs for renewal or revolution that seem promising but almost inevitably drift from biblical and historic Judeo-Christian core convictions. These New Creation restorationists also tend to flirt with flawed and utopian or nearly utopian programs for changing the world. The death and resurrection of the Messiah is viewed as the beginning of the great revolution that issues forth in a restored creation, without adequately emphasizing the need for the actual, real space-time nature and return of the Messiah. The role of the literal, historical, physical, bodily resurrected Messiah in this ultimate future restoration is often less than clear. Is the Messiah's return actual, literal, and necessary for global restoration? Continuity between the present and ultimate future is often emphasized at the expense of clear biblical teaching concerning the discontinuity between the present and future. Nineteenth-century

American evangelical postmillennialism, which explicitly taught that the millennial kingdom could be established before Christ's actual return, would be the classic, naive, and extreme example of overemphasizing continuity between current efforts at creation restoration and the glistening City of God.

The biblical bedrock for navigating the present and future is centered in the bodily resurrection of the Messiah and the sending of the Triune Spirit. Just as with the physical body, the cosmos will neither be annihilated nor merely restored. Humanity, the very crown of creation (Gen 1), very much connected to the cosmos, will follow Christ in bodily death and resurrection. If the very crown of creation is bodily resurrected, it follows that the physical cosmos will also be resurrected. The biblical vision is neither cosmic annihilation nor merely restoration, but cosmic resurrection—the resurrection of all things. Such a future vision (1 Cor 15; Revelation) affirms both radical continuity and discontinuity with the present. The posturing of God's faithful is neither anger and fight, nor escapist flight. The biblical emphasis is not on Christ's death sparking a political or cultural revolution that restores the creation, which too easily opens the door to accommodation, but on the death and resurrection of the entire cosmos initiated by Christ's bodily resurrection.

Faithful biblical witness prophetically and hopefully proclaims both death and resurrection to the present age and the entire cosmos. Utopianism, fatalistic escapism, and accommodation to culture (accommodationism) reflect unfaithfulness. The quest for the City of Kingdom Approximation affirms God's very good creation, condemns a creation still caught in the quagmire of rebellion, hopes for an approximate and potent presence of the true future already, and simultaneously emphasizes both continuity and discontinuity between the present and ultimate future. These themes will of course be explored and persuasively presented throughout this present work.

The health of church, synagogue, and state are at stake. Faithful believers, faith communities, and organizations can not only win individuals to Christ but also serve as salt, light, and healing leaven by influencing and at times even redirecting nations toward their ultimate center and future. The Logos is the only resurrected, redemptive, regenerative, and true *Desire of the Nations*.

CHAPTER 1

THE QUESTION FOR THE AGES

AGE OF ANTICHRIST OR KINGDOM INFLUENCE AND APPROXIMATION?

The jacket cover description of *The Return of the Gods* predicts the following:

> From the author that brought you 6 New York Times bestselling books including *The Harbinger*, *The Book of Mysteries*, *The Oracle* and *The Harbinger II* [Jonathan Cahn]. Is it possible that behind what is taking place in America and the world lies a mystery that goes back to the gods of the ancient world . . . and that they now have returned?[1] . . . The mystery involves the gods. Who are they? What are they? And is it possible that these beings, whose origins are from ancient times, are the unseen catalysts of modern culture? Is it possible that these gods lie behind the most pivotal events, forces, and movements taking place in our nation and around the world at this very moment? Are the gods at this very moment transforming our culture, our children, our lives, and America itself? . . .
>
> Is it possible that the gods lie behind everything from what appears on our computer monitors, our televisions and movie

---

1. The book description also includes the following: "*The Return of the Gods* is the most explosive book Jonathan Cahn has ever written. . . . Cahn takes the reader on a journey from an ancient parable, the ancient inscriptions in Sumer, Assyria, and Babylonia that become the puzzle pieces behind what is taking place in our world to this day, specifically in America. . . . Could this mystery have even determined the exact days on which Supreme Court decisions had to be handed down? . . . Could the gods have returned to New York City and an ancient mythology played out on the streets in real time? Cahn, *Return*, jacket cover.

screens; to the lessons given in our classrooms; to the breakdown of the family; to wokism; to the occult; to our addictions; to the Supreme Court; to cancel culture; to children's cartoons; to every force and factor that has transformed the parameters of gender; . . . to that which is, at this very moment, transforming America and much of the world?[2]

A CENTRAL QUESTION FOR EVERY GENERATION

One of the most important queries of the present generation, and every generation and age, is whether we are on the precipice of living in something like Cahn's age and City of Antichrist. Or is the present generation potentially the age and city of significant kingdom influence—the City of Kingdom Approximation? This is arguably the most consequential assessment for faith communities seeking an appropriate and biblical framework for how to interact with and serve as "salt and light" and good "leaven" for civilizations and cultures. Jonathan Cahn's answer is unequivocal and clear in his most recent, prior, and immensely popular works.

Those suffering persecution, past and present, might at least concur that they are certainly living in the City of Antichrist, regardless of how near we are to Christ's return. And yet in some regions and cities around the globe—sometimes referred to as the majority Christian world—kingdom influence seems nearly unbridled. Those living in formerly Judeo-Christian–influenced civilizations, like Jonathan Cahn, tend to equate the decline of their civilization with the end of the world. Others view the fate of nations, such as the United States, as irrelevant to whether we are in the last days. Some, very naive, almost seem giddy not just concerning the collapse of church-state unions but also about the decline of Judeo-Christian influence on the culture and desires of nations.

The answer to the central question of this book—What age are we living in?—needs to encompass far more than the perspective of one person, faith community, civic community, tribe, city, region, age, or nation. The question is and must be global in scope and biblical/theological in nature. The crumbling of Judeo-Christian–influenced civilizations does not necessarily mean that we have moved into the last generation or age of antichrist, but pretending that the global repercussions of such decline to kingdom work are not important is shallow, flawed, naive, misinformed, and precarious.

Everything is now largely connected everywhere and always. Rapid kingdom influence in one region and accelerating decay in another global

---

2. Cahn, *Return*, jacket cover.

city or nation must inform a sound answer to this central question of the ages. Even within single nations regions and cities vary relative to antichristism and kingdom influence. Cities vary greatly concerning the degree to which they are spellbound by the City of Antichrist. The game plan for kingdom influence must be biblical and shrewd.

A directly related question is whether Judeo-Christian believers have any constructive truths and values to offer all peoples, religious groups, communities, cultures, and civilizations of good faith concerning *How Should We Then Live* prior to the return of Messiah. Such a daunting and energizing task is known as public theology. Public theology addresses how our Judeo-Christian religious and biblical insights, values, and beliefs can contribute to the common or public good and the dialogue concerning authentic human social and spiritual flourishing for all who respond to God's grace. Other religions and philosophies also have public theologies.

Should we Judaize or Christianize the world and mandate beliefs and practices in a fashion more akin to the early Puritans? Is the world about to end and it is pointless to try and improve civilization through a very difficult and decades- or centuries-long project? Are we in the last generation and the last days of the last days? Is it truly possible that Christ's return may be hundreds or thousands of years in the future, and while we cannot and should not try to Christianize civilization (known as theocracy),[3] perhaps the faithful have contributed and can contribute to the multi-faith dialogue concerning a better future before Messiah returns? Have Jews or Christians ever bent the arrow of history toward a better future and God's true future?

RUDDERLESS, ESCAPIST, LIFEBOAT EVANGELISM

Or should we, more in line with Jonathan Cahn, simply expose, condemn, and assume the posture of a well-entertained spectator concerning the greatest show on earth amid *This Present Darkness*? Have we arrived at the age of the antichrist and militant antichristism at our historical *Tipping Point: The End Is Here*?[4]

Was D. L. Moody right that this old world is like a wrecked and sinking ocean liner, and God has given us a lifeboat and a Great Commission to save all we can?[5] Is our mission and ministry goal to point people to faith in Mes-

---

3. *Theos-kratia* (theocracy) refers to (*theos*) God-rule (*kratia*) and suggests that it is appropriate to essentially Christianize culture and civilization.

4. Evans, *Tipping Point*. The foreword for this 2020 Amazon-bestselling publication is by popular author Max Lucado.

5. Moody, "Return," 185.

siah so they will be miraculously raptured off of the sinking Titanic, a.k.a. *The Late Great Planet Earth*?[6] In this vision, Messiah returns before (pre) the kingdom (thousand-year reign of Christ; the millennium) is established on earth. Messiah's literal return establishes Messiah's global kingdom, but true believers are rescued and removed from the earth (raptured) before the ship slips below the turbulent waters (the Great Tribulation) prior to Messiah's return.

This rather gloomy and often escapist view of the present age or generation is one version of premillennialism—where the rapture and return of Messiah occur before Christ's literal reign on earth. Hence, premillennialism. There is often very limited premillennial guidance provided for *How Should We Then Live* in culture and civilization, other than to get saved, get others saved and ready for the rapture, perhaps engage in small-scale, compassionate social concern, and trust and obey before the tribulational age and earthly reign of the antichrist. However, as was discussed in the preface and introduction, some try temporarily to save civilization in spite of its certain demise in the present generation, resulting in a confused approach to impacting culture and cognitive dissonance.

NAIVE OPTIMISM

Or, in contrast, many have argued that truly faithful Judeo-Christian believers can establish God's kingdom rule on earth *before* Messiah returns through revival, and/or cultural, political, and economic influence. This belief, known as postmillennialism, was common in the West as recently as the seventeenth, eighteenth, and nineteenth centuries. Messiah returns after (post) Messiah's global kingdom rule and pervasive influence is established on earth—the earthly millennium. Hence, postmillennialism. Hence, much historical optimism.

This upbeat and transformational view of the future time period before Messiah's return powerfully guided Christian engagement with the world—indeed, this perspective informed their Christian public theology. For example, nineteenth-century conservative and liberal Christian leaders sensed that the twentieth century could well become the global Christian century—with social justice or social gospel liberals even founding a magazine in 1884 that would become known by 1900 as *The Christian Century*—a rather optimistic future-vision prediction and public theology title! "Founded in 1884 as the *Christian Oracle*, the magazine took its current name at the turn of the 20th century. Notable contributors in the early

---

6. Lindsey and Carlson, *Late Great Planet*.

decades included Jane Adams [advocate for world peace; co-founder of the ACLU] and Reinhold Niebuhr [former pacifist who guided many American churches through World War II]. In 1963, the *Century* was the first major periodical to publish the full text of Martin Luther King Jr.'s 'Letter from Birmingham Jail.'"[7] King is best known for his "I Have a Dream" future-vision.

REJECTION OF THE CHRISTIAN CENTURY

The *Christian Century* magazine, especially under the influence of Reinhold Niebuhr and C. C. Morrison, became more realistic concerning the future as the troubled twentieth century progressed—a century that had been predicted to be the bloodiest century in human history by Friedrich Nietzsche, the author of *The Antichrist*. Nietzsche was known for his proclamation that "God is dead" and "we have killed him." Nietzsche died in the year 1900, with his most influential and critical works being published in the same decade that the optimistic *Christian Oracle/Century* emerged—works including *The Antichrist, Genealogy of Morals, Beyond Good and Evil*, and *The Madman*.

Nietzsche's work from the 1880s not only proclaimed the death of Judeo-Christian influence on culture and the death of the Judeo-Christian God, but rebuked the inferior Judeo-Christian prejudices and slave morality which were based on glorifying weakness due to the resentment of the ruling class by weak Jews and Christians. He is still most relevant and influential today.

In the West, according to Nietzsche, corrupt and inferior Judeo-Christian morals and values tragically had been exalted, somehow triumphed, and replaced the superior individual and cultural virtues such as courage, strength, power, mastery, and the refined but unbridled passion, will, and creativity of what Nietzsche believed were superior ancient civilizations, such as Rome.[8] It was now time, according to Nietzsche, to move beyond (transvalue) the corrupt Judeo-Christian understanding of good and evil that plagued civilization. It was time for superior humans (*Übermenschen*) to rise to power and lead.

Nietzsche's *Antichrist* "is a condemnation of modernity [modern civilization] as a sickness brought about by Christianity. Nietzsche blames Christianity for 'the corruption of man,' especially that Christian tenets of virtue and godliness have contributed to a decadence that has caused man to lose his natural instinct [which was more prominent in ancient Roman

---

7. *Christian Century*, "About Us."
8. Anderson, "Friedrich Nietzsche."

culture]."⁹ Hence, Nietzsche's public theology relative to Judeo-Christian theology is truly a form of antichristism; an anti-theology or an atheological public theology. "Instead of time [and civilization] being defined by Christ's birth and death, Nietzsche felt that it should be calculated by the death of Christianity."¹⁰ Antichristism is used in this work to refer to far more than anti-Christianity or anti-Christian. Nietzsche clearly understood that, because for him, the problem was the foundational Judeo-Christian approach to reality—beliefs, practices, and passions. For those who truly understand this critique, this means that Nietzsche especially rejects Messianism, the belief that the biblical God redeems the cosmos and ultimately rules history and all civilizations through a Messiah figure or an anointed cosmic king. Many religions have messianic figures, but Nietzsche and those in his crazed orbit primarily view loving allegiance to the biblical Messiah figure in the Abrahamic religions (principally Judaism and Christianity) as absolutely toxic for the past, present, and future of civilization.

Hence, for Nietzsche, and his countless minions today, the City of Antichrist is a good thing, the snake in the garden of Eden is the hero,¹¹ and Judeo-Christian terms, values, and virtues must be replaced or redefined. As with many other ideological movements (e.g., Marxism or the French Revolution), the Christian calendar and all it represents must go—history and civilization must start over again with a born-again year zero or year one. Culture and history must be taken out of orbit of BC and AD, before Christ and the year of our Lord. The Logos center must go. Nietzsche offered the world a radically pessimistic optimism. With the civilizational death of God and Logos, the world was unravelling and headed toward unprecedented fragmentation and butchery, but superior humans and values would emerge from the carnage and chaos and restore the grandeur of BC or BCE civilization and morality. Nietzsche has increasingly ruled for two centuries.

LEGION MARXIST-INFLUENCED LIBERATION THEOLOGIES

The more economically and/or politically Marxist-influenced religious versions of a hopeful future period before Messiah's eternal reign is known as

---

9. Elkins, "Antichrist by Nietzsche." This source is not particularly impressive or scholarly, but in contrast to many other sources, it does encapsulate or quickly and briefly summarize key ideas of Nietzsche. Nietzsche's primary sources will be engaged directly throughout this work. This chapter only seeks to introduce key themes clearly relative to influencing civilization.

10. Elkins, "Antichrist by Nietzsche."

11. Alinsky, *Rules*, ix.

liberation theology. Some religious liberators affirm an actual return and earthly reign of the Messiah, while others simply believe that Christ will eventually bring a cosmic liberation and triumph—before and typically without belief in an actual earthly reign or millennium (amillennialism).

Liberation theology has many varieties and children such as gender liberation, sexual orientation liberation, gender fluidity liberation, non-monogamous liberation, racial or ethnic liberation, economic liberation, regional (e.g., South American) or hemispheric liberation (e.g., southern, eastern, majority world), social justice liberation, anti-capitalist liberation, anti-American liberation, victim and intersectionality liberation, and "woke" liberation movements.

A critical ingredient for liberation theology is the intentional inclusion of theology in the mix. God is the great liberator who liberates the have-nots from the oppression of some sort (e.g., economic, ethnic, geographical, gender) of the haves. For Marx, the working class or proletariat (economically in chains) will overthrow the bourgeoisie ruling class. In contrast to atheistic political ideologies (traditional Marxism), these liberation theologians connect or synthesize their religious beliefs and, especially, practices (praxis) with their understanding of God and proper engagement with culture and civilization. Liberation theology is very public theology. Their God is at the center of their unbreakable spirit and a glorious Exodus-like liberation from oppression.

Some liberation theologies are more optimistic than others concerning the present age before Messiah's ultimate triumph/victory. Many liberationists today are relatively optimistic though shrewd in the sense of a lucid recognition that global liberation may take centuries or millennia. God is patient, and God's people utilize prayer, social justice activism, culture-changing suffering, political power, and, for some, if needed, the justifiable use of force.

Other liberationists not only are suspicious of claims to improve the world dramatically (utopian views) and quickly, but find such views dangerous and manipulative. Promises of a better future easily can be used, they argue, to manipulate and oppress others, especially the poor and marginalized. Yet these liberationists often are not aware of how their own more peaceful liberation movements, which often patiently pursue strong centralized governments to establish and ensure justice, often, over time, become like the very oppressors or naive liberators they condemned. And some social justice warriors are very cautious about making any optimistic or utopian claims and press on in spite of affirming a nonutopian or dystopian (chaotic or desolate) future.

N. T. WRIGHT'S COSMIC REVOLUTION

Popular author and scholar N. T. Wright's view of the future directly connects the crucifixion, *The Day the Revolution Began*, to the larger biblical narrative and a cosmic future-vision (eschatology) where heaven comes down to earth (Rev 21:2) and restores all things. Heaven is the cosmos transformed, or, to quote a dated but famous and chart-topping rock song, "Heaven is a place on earth."[12] The traditional otherworldly heaven, Wright argues, is not our true home.

Wright attempts to avoid both naive optimism (utopianism) and escapist and fatalistic pessimism concerning the present age before Messiah's return. Unfortunately, in the present historical context, the language of "revolution" is easily interpreted as naive or Marxist or socialist, and he apparently never clearly articulates how much positive influence is possible before Messiah's return. For example, can all slavery and human trafficking be abolished even prior to Messiah's return? Can war become an anomaly or be eliminated altogether? These are essential questions for a public theology which will be addressed throughout this work and in appendix A.

This lack of precision in Wright's eschatology and strategic and tactical planning is ultimately terminal relative to guiding the church on how it interacts with communities and nations. Wright directly connects and grounds his understanding of how believers can positively influence the world (public theology) with his take on the biblical future-vision of cosmic redemption, but he ultimately leaves church and synagogue with insufficient strategic and tactical guidance. He also joints those, noted in the Preface and Introduction, who are less than precise on the nature of the return of Christ.

It is critical at this juncture to note that public theology is fundamentally or ultimately eschatology. Public theology is something of a misnomer, for theology applied to the question of *How Should We Then Live?* is primarily eschatology.

TWO CITIES OR KINGDOMS

As with Wright, both Augustine and Luther brilliantly construct a framework for guiding Judeo-Christian faith communities that want to contribute to the common good and true human flourishing for time and eternity. Both suggest a public theology duality of competing loves, loyalties, or spheres, namely the two cities (God and man) or the two kingdoms (God and the world). Yet, as with Wright, who critiques Luther's otherworldly dualism,

---

12. Carlisle, "Heaven Is a Place."

the genius of their visions is undermined by their lack of clarity and specificity concerning the how, what, when, and where of influencing earthly kingdoms or cities prior to Messiah's return.

In addition, while loyalties and loves lie at the core, public theology needs to directly address, if not primarily address, what is appropriate and possible relative to civilizational and cultural influence and outcomes. That is, after all, the real point of public theology. The loves and motives and loyalties need to be understood and harnessed by an appropriate future-vision for time and eternity. Being faithful and innocent as doves regardless of the consequences must be balanced with being shrewd and wise as serpents concerning strategy, tactics, and probable outcomes (Matt 10:16).

Again, the lack of strategic and tactical specificity in these brilliant future-visions is terminal. As with the old adages, if you aim at nothing you are bound to hit it, and if you aim too high or too low you will most certainly miss the mark (*hamartia*). In business terms, prior future-vision models for defining the church's precise role, goals, outcomes, tactics, and responsibility for influencing culture and civilization had beautiful visions (two cities or kingdoms) yet were typically lacking in the specific blocks and tackles of strategic goals, planning, tactics, outcomes, and measures. Faithfulness, purity, and outcomes are all appropriate performance metrics. Or stated differently, the faithful doves have had ambiguous and soaring visions that were utterly lacking anything remotely resembling the shrewdness of a well-honed business model. Doves are sometimes sacrificed, but flying into a wall may have more to do with a bad flight plan.

The point here is not to reduce the Judeo-Christian future-vision to a business model, so the analogy is admittedly weak or at least limited. Yet the analogy can help as many failed businesses launch without a clear understanding of their vision, mission, strategy, distinct contribution, specialization, tactics, and outcomes relative to the why, how, and what that they hope to accomplish. And some failed business ventures have so many outcomes and products or lofty goals that they inevitably fail.

As a prior senior vice president, this deficiency became striking to me when evaluating these Judeo-Christian future-visions throughout church history. While the majority might be inspiring and profound on some levels, vision clarity and practical planning and tactical guidance were either lacking, opposed, or hopelessly ambiguous.

The church is not a business, but the church clearly has been floundering on every level—vision, mission, strategy, goals, outcomes, tactics, assessment, and use of results. We desperately need to clarify and hone our future-vision for the era prior to Christ's return and assess its implementation and use of results relative to improving missional effectiveness. We desperately need to understand and assess the present culture and historical moment—analogous to market or mission field analysis. What do Scripture and historically orthodox (non-heretical) theology tell us concerning specifically what can and should be the influence and impact of faith communities prior to Messiah's return, in any given context?

Clarity on the role of the church and shrewd and sustainable cultural and civilizational impact and influence, for better or worse, has been rare. Possible and illustrative exceptions would be the more optimistic revivalism of the nineteenth century and their countless social reform movements or the Marxist-influenced liberation theologies of the twentieth and twenty-first centuries and their often specific economic and political goals and outcomes.

To be fair, those embracing escapist and fatalistic future-visions have often been very clear for decades on their opposition to influencing civilizations. "I think the whole thing [trying to improve culture] is wrong-headed. . . . I just can't buy . . . [the] basic presupposition that we can do anything significant to change the world. And you can waste an awful lot of time trying [time better spent on evangelism]."[13] This fatalistic and "wrong-headed" approach leaves the church and the mission of God either with nothing to say or offer to culture and civilization concerning the era before Christ's return—or only the message of how to escape the coming Armageddon, get off the sinking ship, and get to heaven. The hope is that this work can begin to synthesize the specificity of some of the optimistic but flawed future-visions just referenced with a robust future-vision that learns from but avoids some of the either/or pitfalls of the past.

TOXIC "PAN-MILLENNIAL" ESCAPISM

Somewhat humorously, concerning the age prior to Messiah's second advent, some try to avoid committing to utopian views (postmillennialism) or pessimistic and fatalistic views (escapist premillennialism), or perspectives that deny the actual reign of Messiah on earth (amillennialism). These tongue-in-cheek armchair theologians thus sarcastically advocate for "pan-millennialism"—it will all pan out in the end, so quit quibbling because such matters cannot be resolved.

Pan-millennialism is great humor but very bad theology and even worse future-envisioning, and a most destructive approach to the question of how faith communities can and should interact with culture, politics, communities, and nations. Eschatologies rule and guide church, synagogue,

13. Hoehner, "Is Christ," 42–44. Hoehner taught at Dallas Theological Seminary.

individuals, organizations, communities, nations, and multinational entities. The suggestion that millennial views don't matter is easily refuted by the facts and realities of church history. Christian cultural and civilizational engagement, optimism, pessimism, or escapism, has been guided for centuries by whether believers have affirmed premillennialism, amillennialism, or postmillennialism. This thesis will be explored and defended further in this chapter.

Future-visions rule and shape the future from Irenaeus's anti-gnostic New Adam redemptive history, to Augustine's *City of God*, to King's "I Have a Dream," to Hitler's thousand-year kingdom (Third Reich or Kingdom), to America's Manifest Destiny and Trail of Tears, to Puritanism's City Set on a Hill, to Marxism's communist utopia (classless society), to Japanese emperor worship and territorial expansion, to ancient Egyptian culture and architecture (with pyramids as resurrection chambers), to the utopian "war to end all wars" or "making the world safe for democracy," to Colonialism, to Anti-Colonialism, to Black Lives Matter, to social justice, to Wokism, or to Michael Novak's defense of virtuous and Trinitarian free enterprise (democratic capitalism). "Pan-millennialism" should be welcomed as light humor if not taken seriously, but it is ultimately a form of irresponsible escapism. Much, if not everything, is at stake relative to millennial views and future-visions.

AMBIGUOUS FUTURE-VISIONS AND FLOUNDERING CHURCH-STATE RELATIONS

Relative to eschatologies, Judeo-Christian scholars typically reject irresponsible pan-millennialism and strive to advocate for a particular view that is biblical and/or makes the most sense of Scripture and historical realities. Most future-visions today are tolerated and debated by scholars and non-scholars with the occasional exception of perspectives that go to excess, such as fatalistically predicting the last generation, naming the antichrist, or claiming that believers truly can usher in the kingdom before Christ returns. Yet this work will point out that millions in the present generation, including many pastors, seem to affirm unequivocally that we are or likely are living in the last generation—and especially the rapture generation.

This work argues that it is virtually impossible to guide the church on how to relate to the state, culture, and civilization apart from deciding which general future-vision is more biblical and theologically superior and which perspectives touch the very edges of heresy. Likewise, future-visions should be replaced or rebooted if they do not provide a general framework

THE QUESTION FOR THE AGES

for the specific questions of how much "world changing" is appropriate to attempt before Christ returns.

N. T. Wright properly and creatively calls for us to participate in the cosmic "revolution" that began the day Christ died but, as noted, is less than clear and specific on key elements in his future-vision that are needed to guide this revolution *before* Christ returns.[14] Yet to be fair, his scholarly output is immense and others may need to more carefully scrutinize his perspective.

Wright is likely and primarily referring to the cosmic theological revolution that began on the day Christ died, the crucifixion, and which culminates in the New Creation. Yet he connects this cosmic revolution to our daily, "cruciform" participation in cultural and civilizational change now and implies that vast positive change is possible already.[15] Wright clearly connects this theology, repeatedly, with the kinds of actions, applications, and causes that flow forth from the first day of the revolution with a capital R—The Revolution. He implies that our actions are part of or flow from The Revolution yet does so in our historical context today on the heels of many cultural revolutions, especially in an age obsessed with social justice revolutions, without ever providing clarity on precisely what the church can and should seek to accomplish prior to Messiah's return.

Yes, Wright's Christ-centered revolution, The Cosmic Revolution, will win and Messiah will reign forever and ever, but that is not the issue at hand with public theology in the present age. What can be expected or should be pursued before Christ returns? Will Christ literally return to earth—Wright could be more precise in key works like *The Day the Revolution Began*—and is that return the only real hope for anything remotely resembling a truly transformative revolution on a large or global scale? And is the only real hope for major and perhaps fleeting regional advances, or for seemingly intractable (irremovable) immoral practices? Is it possible that Wright's understanding of the ripple effects of our participation in Christ's revolution could result in planet Earth experiencing, say, one thousand years without war, slavery, and human trafficking in almost every nation? These are essential questions.

The term and call for revolution should be handled like an explosive device—with precision and extreme care. The same care should be applied to future-visions that might suggest escapism. At points Wright sounds naively utopian or postmillennial without defining the upper limit of change implied by the human and historical condition before the actual return of

---

14. See Matthews, *Theology*, ch. 11.
15. See Matthews, *Theology*, ch. 11.

Christ. At other points he sounds ambiguously hopeful on specifics and amillennial (his likely view), yet with an emphasis on a restored creation.

These are significant flaws, ambiguities, or imprecisions in Wright's brilliant articulation of the Judeo-Christian future-vision and in his pastoral guidance to believers on how to interact with culture and civilization (public theology). No one knows the future, but, theologically speaking, what can and should be improved in the present age—when, where, how, who leads, and to what degree? What civilizational reforms are naive or even counterproductive in the present age before Messiah returns? Should we ban slavery but not abortion or polygamy?

Wright and others, including Augustine, Smith, and Luther, have given us compelling but incomplete strategic future-visions that lack specificity, planning, tactics, goals, and measurable outcomes. Organizations with ambiguous future-visions inevitably flounder and fail. Judeo-Christian faith communities have had short-term wins but ultimately failed relative to long-term (longitudinal, measured in millennia) and constructive initiatives and interactions with civilization. This present work has and will present evidence for this failure and seek to alleviate at least a small portion of this theological and eschatological ambiguity and poor planning.

IRREFUTABLE EVIDENCE OF FUTURE-VISIONS INTERACTING WITH HISTORICAL CONTEXTS

The historical evidence is irrefutable. When believers opt for one future-vision over another, everything changes. Future-visions interpret reality and influence reality. For example, premillennialism dominated Christian churches for the first few centuries after Messiah amid much persecution and marginalization. Otherworldly amillennialism dominated Christianity for over a millennium once fourth-century Christians not only were no longer running for their lives but were walking with emperors and becoming emperors. Postmillennialism ascended the civilizational throne in the West as expansion, colonialism, the hope of a new promised land, medical progress, scientific progress, labor-saving devices, economic and social mobility of the lower classes, increased lifespans, and increased economic and political progress proliferated.

It would be overly simplistic to suggest that the eschatological view of a given era either was entirely caused by the historical context or created and/or only interpreted the spirit of an age or historical context. The evidence suggests two-way traffic. Postmillennialism may have emerged in part due to optimistic modernism, but the vision of establishing Christ's rule on earth before the return of Christ took optimism to a new level and fueled countless world-changing movements.¹⁶

As the dream for a Judeo-Christian or *Christian Century* began to unravel in the later nineteenth and twentieth centuries in the West, a more realistic or pessimistic kingdom future-vision, premillennial eschatology, began to rule many politically and theologically conservative faith communities. Clearly, or so it seemed at the time, civilization was more likely to devolve downward rather than evolve upward, and only the Messiah's literal return could stabilize and redeem the staggering planet.

Once again, eschatology ruled and rules, and this pessimistic, premillennial vision of the future prior to Messiah's return made for many of the bestselling books and movies of the last one hundred plus years. It truly seemed to many that the *Present Darkness* was getting darker and that we had entered the age of the antichrist and burgeoning antichristism.

Regardless of the relationship between future-visions and historical eras, the classic chicken and egg debate concerning causes and consequences and the pessimistic, escapist, and fatalistic versions of premillennialism have, as noted previously, often become self-fulfilling prophecies. Such eschatologies have guided the lives of millions and the very nature and mission of the church, including its political and cultural involvement—or lack thereof.

It seems safe to affirm that in all historical periods, eschatologies both reflected and fueled how faith communities interacted and interfaced with civilizations. Future-visions rule. Eschatology rules. Pan-millennialism is, to be blunt, humorously irresponsible, historically consequential, and nearly heretical. Pessimistic and fatalistic premillennialism, as noted, was and is a fatalistic self-fulfilling prophecy of escape.

Traditional otherworldly amillennialism is an abandonment of the clear biblical narrative and vision of a fully redeemed cosmos. The age of amillennialism was also the age of an otherworldly redefinition of Judeo-Christian faith more indebted to Greek than biblical or Hebraic thought. This vision influenced everything, from architecture, art, music, and religious practices to the very nature and means of salvation. Too often, salvation became an otherworldly and individualistic escape from divine judgment divorced from the biblical and redemptive narrative of the cosmic resurrection of all things.

Postmillennialism, as noted, certainly to be credited with many and sometimes successful movements for social betterment (e.g., abolition, education), was ultimately and hopelessly naive or utopian. Its collapse

---

16. Smith, *Revivalism*; Dayton, *Discovering*; Olaskey, *Tragedy*.

and subsequent disillusionment became the fertile soil for many faithful to become almost obsessed with pessimistic premillennialism's cultural disengagement, Last-Generationism, and spectator-sport escapism. It also encouraged pan-millennialism for those weary of failed dreams and eschatological debates.

MORE THAN CRATERS OF THE GOSPEL (O'DONOVAN AND SMITH)

O'Donovan and Smith have correctly pointed out that the gospel, or I would say the full-orbed biblical gospel, has verifiably and positively influenced civilizations. These impact points are referred to by both scholars as craters of the gospel.[17] This present work is indebted to Augustine, O'Donovan, and Smith but will argue that this verifiable impact of future-visions on history, such as the Puritan's City Set on a Hill or King's "I Have a Dream," if indeed such impact was primarily positive, are better classified as symphonic approximations of God's true future or artifacts of the full-orbed gospel (good news) influence.

Craters are impact points, and Smith and O'Donovan are simply using an analogy for significant impact or influence on civilization, but craters are often destructive events. Smith (drawing on O'Donovan) affirms that one of these craters of the gospel is the idea that kings and kingdoms are temporary stewards of civilization and not ultimate rulers. Hence, rulers of kingdoms should view themselves as subjects to a higher law, and checks and balances should exist on the power and authority of rulers. Rulers serve on bended knee toward the true future, true kingdom, and only true King.

Defining kings as humble stewards is certainly a crater or impact point of a gospel that proclaims there is only one true King of Kings and Lord of Lords, before whom every knee shall bow. However, this crater may be far more significant than an impact point in history.

Kingdom approximations actually step into the true future, to one degree or another, already. Approximations of the future, such as kings, presidents, and prime ministers, when defined as temporary, humble stewards of civilization, are more analogous to symphonic contributions to the never-ending masterpiece of the New Heaven and Earth. Nations and kingdoms that strive, however imperfectly, to remain "under God," the one, true, personal God, are provisionally stepping into the true future already.

Every genuinely treasured and beautiful musical, artistic, or architectural creation, every authentic act of compassion and justice, and every legitimate life, family, community, and political kingdom contribution

---

17. O'Donovan, *Desire*. Smith, *Awaiting the King*, builds upon O'Donovan.

endures, participates in, and contributes to God's enduring masterpiece and ultimate future. Such living artifacts serve as future-evidence or down payments already. Living artifacts are "something characteristic of or resulting from a particular human institution, period, trend, or individual [including God, one might add]."[18] There is continuity between the present and future, and fulfillment of present approximations in the future. The only true future is partially being written already as God's faithful people navigate the historical and redemptive journey between the three cities.

The abolition of slavery anywhere, for example, is a symphonic overture for, approximation of, and contribution to the compelling melody of cosmic liberation, including liberation from the slavery of sin. The Judeo-Christian and revival-influenced abolition of slavery is also a living and fertile artifact of the kingdom's intrusion into the present and the divine-human-civilizational interface through the church, the Quakers, the Enlightenment, and through individuals such as John Locke, John Wesley, William Wilberforce, Harriet Beecher Stowe, and Abraham Lincoln.

A PRELIMINARY ANSWER TO THE QUESTION FOR THE AGES

So, are we (1) in the age of antichrist or (2) in the age of potential and significant kingdom influence? Are we in an age when we can roughly approximate, in a very temporary and limited fashion, God's ultimate kingdom triumph already even beyond faith communities? This work will affirm a resounding and biblical yes to the second question, and a qualified yes or no to the first question. And relative to constructive influence and impact on civilizations, all is at stake regarding how these questions are framed, articulated, and answered. The reality is that while there are two ages and civilizational spirits or souls, there is also a continuum in any given historical moment or location between the two ages and the two cities of kingdom approximation and kingdom opposition. History and culture are fluid and multi-complex.

Fortunately, we are not plowing totally untouched, concretized, and infertile soil. In addition to luminaries from the past such as Augustine and Wesley, others such as Oscar Cullmann, G. E. Ladd, G. R. Beasley-Murray, C. F. H. Henry, N. T. Wright, Oliver O'Donovan, James K. A. Smith, and J. Richard Middleton have prepared the way for understanding and partially realizing the coming of the kingdom both already and forever.[19] Indeed, the forever is misunderstood apart from the already, just as the already easily

---

18. *Merriam-Webster*, s.v. "artifact."
19. Middleton, *New Heaven*.

becomes naive or fatalistic apart from acknowledging the *Presence of the Future*.[20] O'Donovan and Smith, for example, affirmed that in some cultures and civilizations there are craters of positive cultural influence that have radiated or are radiating still from the gospel, such as subordinating every nation to a higher law, or the principle of freedom of speech (see chapters 6 and 7). A healthy church can continue to leave craters of the gospel or approximations of the gospel future. An unhealthy church enables the City of Antichrist.

What has become apparent in light of over a century of biblical scholarship is that through the Christ event the kingdom rule of God already has broken into history in a decisive, provisional, approximate, anticipatory, or initiatory fashion. God has already provided the theological hors d'oeuvres through the Christ-event such that we can begin to live in some respects as if the future already exists, which is called proleptic theology and living. Oscar Cullmann uses the analogy of D-Day (turning point victory) and Victory Day (final, complete victory) to illustrate the already-but-not-yet nature of God's coming kingdom and kingdom service:

> The decisive battle has already been won. But the war continues until a certain, though not as yet definite, Victory Day when the weapons will at last be still. The decisive battle would be Christ's death and resurrection, and Victory Day, his parousia. Between the two lies a short but important span of time already indicating a fulfilment and an anticipation of peace, in which, however, the greatest watchfulness is demanded. Yet it is from the decisive battle now won and the Victory Day yet to be achieved that this span of time gets its meaning and its demands.[21]
>
> Just as the "Victory Day" does, in fact, present *something new* in contrast to the decisive battle already fought at some point or other of the war, just so the end which is still to come also brings something new. To be sure, this new thing that the "Victory Day" brings is based entirely upon that decisive battle, and would be absolutely impossible without it.[22]

Believers are to live in some respects as if God's true future kingdom exists now. Hence, the true and normative center of kingdom influence and positive civilizational influence is and should be in and through the church.

Because the church is salt, light, and healing leaven and the church is destined to reign with Christ in Messiah's New Creation, then even before

---

20. Ladd, *Presence*.
21. Cullmann, *Salvation in History*, 44.
22. Cullmann, *Christ and Time*, 141.

Christ returns the ripple effect of the kingdom can impact lives, families, communities, culture, and civilization. The influence and impact of the kingdom is not limited to being inside the walls of the church, for such a limitation would be a profound misunderstanding of the nature of the church, its mission, neighbor-love, and of God's grace. The church is the eschatological church, the called-out ones to image-bear God's true future in an age characterized by the Spirit being poured out "on all mankind" (Joel 2:28; also Acts chapter 2).

COGNITIVE DISSONANCE

Yet the kingdom approximation and kingdom influence of the American and global evangelical movement is confused, fragmented, and diluted due to double-think. As noted in the Preface and Introduction, some call this cognitive dissonance, meaning affirming things that are clearly contradictory. Especially since at least the mid-twentieth century and the founding or refounding of Israel (1948), and since the wildly popular speculations (e.g., Hal Lindsey) concerning whether the last or terminal generation (forty years) has arrived, American evangelicals have been truly and cognitively dissonant—mentally conflicted.

Many of the same evangelicals trying to "save America" or support Reagan's "Let's Make America Great Again" (1980) agenda for four-plus decades have also fully embraced a rather fatalistic, escapist, and pessimistic view that the last generation has arrived. Indeed, Lindsey also authored *The 1980s: Countdown to Armageddon*, another bestseller,[23] just as Jerry Falwell's Moral Majority movement was ascending in national cultural and political influence. Falwell, on the heels of the American bicentennial (1976), affirmed that if the moral majority sleeping giant could be awakened (as with America in World War II after Pearl Harbor), then Christian America could be "saved."

This work will demonstrate that this fatalistic future-vision was and is not anecdotal but widespread, even global, and impactful. Many were and are singing the mantra, "It's the end times, the last days, things are getting worse and worse, and there is not much of anything that can be done to stop, reverse, or delay the ultimate and predicted slide to Armageddon that started in 1948." For some, the very details of civilizational collapse and American future-history were divinely determined and unalterable.

This work will provide evidence that this widespread pessimism, fatalism, escapism, and cognitive dissonance have persisted until the present

---

23. Lindsey, *1980s*.

among last-generationist "Make America Great Again" evangelicals. This dissonant narrative persists at the same time that more politically liberal social justice evangelical sentiments skeptical of American greatness (past or present) seem to be gaining influence, at least among American evangelical leaders. The ideological and political civil war or polarization in the broader culture exists within American evangelicalism.

Hence, American evangelicalism tends to be dominated by those who are relatively certain we are living in the *Terminal Generation*,[24] those who are trying to return to the American experiment, and social justice or woke evangelicals who tend to view the American experiment as inherently flawed, oppressive, an "original sin,"[25] and in need of significant liberal or progressive reforms—if not a wholesale renovation or replacement. The title of one of evangelical Jim Wallis's more recent publications sums up this more politically liberal or woke perspective very well: *America's Original Sin: Racism, White Privilege, and the Bridge to a New America*.[26] Perhaps the stalemate and overt conflict between these American evangelical options can be somewhat mediated by a clarified and more biblical future-vision.

---

24. Lindsey, *Terminal*.
25. Wallis, *America's Original Sin*.
26. Wallis, *America's Original Sin*.

CHAPTER 2

THE EPIC VISION

AN APPROXIMATED BUT NOT YET FULLY RESURRECTED NEW CREATION

To be clear on the biblical future-vision, it is necessary to be somewhat controversial. Christian future-visions that are so utterly escapist, fatalistic, deterministic, and non-world affirming that they cut the nerve of constructive cultural and civilizational engagement, such as some forms of premillennialism, are touching the very edges of heresy.

PESSIMISTIC PREMILLENNIALISM

Premillennialism at its biblically defensible best and core simply affirms that Christ literally returns before the glorious and blessed reign of Christ on earth. Premillennialism does not require affirmation of excessive and speculative details regarding the millennium, Great Tribulation, the antichrist, the false prophet, or the rapture. Indeed, for some, the millennium may be symbolic of a lengthy reign of the Messiah on earth (perhaps far more than one thousand years), and the view of the rapture as escape before the seven-year Great Tribulation may be denied. For some, the catching up of the church in the air to meet Christ (1 Thess 4:17) takes place when Christ returns and when the saints return with Christ to reign on earth. The biblical focus is not on the literalistic and physical direction of the rapture ("up"), or the physical location of the cosmic meeting ("air"), but on our radical transformation and glorious reunion—"and so we will always be with the Lord." This essential, wise, and noble vision, however, has often been corrupted by otherworldly and escapist tendencies along with shallow biblical interpretation.

Nevertheless, this pessimistic future-vision often got it right concerning the pregnant, latent, and powerful presence of evil and "many antichrists" (1 John 2:18) in *every* present moment and *every* generation. This new kind of premillennialism thus affirms Any-Generationism rather than constantly predicting or implying Last-Generationism.

Premillennial sensitivity to the potential and spirit of antichrist and extreme darkness in every generation should characterize any future-vision claiming to be biblical and grounded in historical reality. Unfortunately, this often escapist view got it terribly wrong when endlessly naming the decade or generation of Christ's return while also birthing a toxic self-fulfilling prophecy of cultural impotence that muted the light, salt, and good leaven of Christ's church and mission.

NAIVELY OPTIMISTIC POSTMILLENNIALISM

On the other end of the continuum, some have argued that Christ's kingdom on earth (the millennium) can become a historical reality *prior* to the actual return of Christ on earth. Christ's return comes after Christ's glorious but indirect or mediated kingdom rule on earth—hence, *post*millennialism. Christ reigns through the Spirit and the church, even though Christ is not literally or physically on earth. This perspective often and commendably harnessed the explosive fuel of eschatologies—future-visions rule—and successfully launched thousands of world-changing movements, such as abolitionism (anti-slavery), prison reform, evangelical feminism, and urban relief efforts.

Unfortunately, this naive model of the future also touches the very edges of heresy by misunderstanding human nature, history, and Scripture concerning the era before Christ's actual return. This approach, over time, almost inevitably leads to world-changing arrogance (triumphalism), cultural accommodation, and/or, in the realities and crucible of history, extreme disillusionment. Indeed, disillusionment with this popular optimistic view in the late nineteenth-century America—due to war, economic panic, and seemingly irresolvable social problems (industrialization, urbanization, massive immigration)—led to extremely popular, toxic, proliferating, fatalistic, escapist future-visions from the latter 1800s to the present day. Revivalist Charles Finney ironically and historically birthed Hal Lindsey, Tim LaHaye, Frank Peretti, and Jonathan Cahn.

OTHERWORLDLY AMILLENNIALISM

While there probably is no true middle ground between pessimistic premillennialism and optimistic postmillennialism, the denial of an actual, literal, or historical reign of Christ on earth at least provided an alternative and widely held future-vision. Amillennialism, literally meaning a view that is against or opposed to belief in the literal reign of Christ on earth, arguably has dominated more centuries of church history than alternative eschatologies. The amillennial millennium meant many things, such as Christ's reign in heaven or through the church. Some versions of amillennialism did mediate between future-vision optimism and pessimism, by emphasizing that the "wheat and the tares" grow together until Christ returns—and takes us all away to heaven.

Some more recent amillennial views have self-corrected by becoming less otherworldly (Platonic or neo-Platonic) and emphasizing that the return of the Messiah—whether defined literally or not—will restore the entire cosmos and that "Heaven Is Not Our Home."[1] Heaven is earth transformed, which aligns greatly with a less speculative premillennialism. While there may be other challenges for Wright's thought, the return of Christ as cosmic creation restoration burns away many of the elements of escapist and Platonic amillennialism with intense, purifying, careful and biblical theological heat. In other words, amillennialism is itself restored or salvaged by returning to orbit around non-otherworldly Scripture and biblical theology.

The more traditional version of amillennialism, often reflected in the Middle Ages, was very influenced by some versions of Greek thought that were otherworldly. Wright refers to this as Platonic influence, which may do some injustice to Plato, but that debate exceeds the purpose of this work.[2] Salvation was viewed as getting out of this world or cosmos and going to a more nonphysical heaven. For some heaven was almost entirely nonphysical, which of course subverts the theology of the bodily resurrection of Christ. Viewing heaven or the eternal destination of individuals and the cosmos as nonphysical is arguably moving toward the same heretical camp as Gnosticism and Docetism.

Hence, the more Greek, Hellenistic, or otherworldly versions of the amillennial future-vision also touch the very edges of heresy, as they devalue the creation, the "in flesh" or incarnational and bodily resurrected life of Jesus the Christ, and subvert the central biblical narrative of a redeemed and fully resurrected creation. The creation affirmation biblical narrative is

---

1. Wright, "Heaven Is Not Our Home."
2. Rogers, "N. T. Wright's."

consistent, from paradise, to paradise lost, to paradise regained, through the incarnation, crucifixion, bodily resurrection, sending of the Spirit, and the actual return to earth of Messiah.

SCRIPTURAL AND FUTURE-VISION GLORIOUS ESSENTIALS

The perspective that it is necessary for Christ to return literally, restore, and/or resurrect the cosmos in order for Christ's kingdom truly and fully to reign on earth as it is in heaven is *the* central biblical, Jewish, and Christian hope and affirmation. He shall reign forever and ever in the very good cosmos he created. He redeemed all things by being incarnated, and history and the purpose of creation will be fully fulfilled and consummated by his final victory, cosmos purification or restoration, and resurrection. This core biblical narrative frames the entirety of Scripture.

The repentant—those who confess and mourn their spiritual poverty, the meek, the gentle, the pure in heart, the merciful, and especially the persecuted—will "inherit" the cosmos (Matt 5) and co-reign with him (2 Tim 2:12). And "with righteousness He will judge . . . and decide with fairness, . . . and He will strike the earth with the rod of His mouth, and with the breath of His lips He will slay the wicked" (Isa 11:4). "And the wolf will dwell with the lamb, and the leopard will lie down with the young goat, . . . and a little boy will lead them" (Isa 11:6).

> The nursing child will play by the hole of the cobra, and the weaned child will put his hand on the viper's den. They will not hurt or destroy in all My holy mountain, for the earth will be full of the knowledge of the Lord [YHWH] as the waters cover the sea. (Isa 11:8–9)

> And He [who is from Bethlehem and from long ago and from the days of eternity] will judge between many peoples, and render decisions for mighty, distant nations. Then they will beat their swords into plowshares, and their spears into pruning hooks; nation will not lift a sword against nation, and never again will they train for war. . . . For the mouth of the Lord of hosts has spoken. (Mic 4:3; 5:2)

> Then I saw a new heaven and a new earth; for the first heaven and the first earth passed away. . . . And I saw the holy city, new Jerusalem, coming *down* out of heaven from God, prepared as a bride adorned for her husband. [And the city has no need of the sun or the moon to shine on it, for the glory of God has illumined it, and its lamp is the Lamb. The nations will walk by

its light, *and the kings of earth will bring their glory into it*. (Rev 21:23–24)] And I heard a loud voice from the throne, saying, "Behold, the tabernacle of God is among the people, and He will dwell among them, and they shall be His people, and *God Himself will be among them*, and He will wipe away every tear from their eyes; and there will no longer be any death; there will *no longer be any mourning, or crying, or pain*; the first things have passed away." And He who sits on the throne said, "Behold, I am making all things new." And He said, "Write, for these words are faithful and true." Then He said to me, "It is done." . . . And he showed me a river of the water of life, clear as crystal, coming from the throne of God and of the Lamb, in the middle of the street. On either side of the river was the tree of life, bearing twelve kinds of fruit, yielding its fruit every month; and the leaves of the tree were for the *healing of the nations*. There will *no longer be any curse*; and the throne of God and of the Lamb will be in it, and his bond-servants will serve Him; they will see His face, and His name will be on their foreheads, . . . and they will *reign forever and ever*. (Rev 21:1–6; 22:1–5; emphasis added)[3]

QUARANTINING SEMI-HERESY

In view of the unified Hebraic and scriptural hope and witness, it will be argued that fatalistic and otherworldly premillennialism, otherworldly amillennialism, "pan-millennialism," and naive postmillennialism so thoroughly undermine or confuse core Judeo-Christian convictions and kingdom service as to touch on the very boundaries of heresy. Such views contradict or undermine Scripture and sound biblical theology, and should be marginalized, discounted, or at least quarantined. Yet this work already has and will continue to argue that some elements of truth in each of these views need to be heard, filtered, and appropriated.

As noted previously, pessimistic premillennialism is attentive to the reality and power of antichrists and prophetically critiques naive, elitist, and dangerous future-visions. Naive postmillennialism rightly understands that a Spirit-led harnessing of the power and energy of hopeful future-visions can energize the troops and radically impact culture and civilization, as with abolitionism. Shrewd postmillennialism, where the kingdom or millennium on earth can be realized before Christ returns after an immense period of time, is more defensible, perceptive, and realistic (Teilhard de

Chardin). Nevertheless, shrewd postmillennialism or utopianism can't save itself from its own fundamentally flawed view of human nature, frequent cultural accommodation, and the nature and necessity of Christ's return by adding thousands or millions of years to its utopian vision and game plan. The present age needs death and resurrection, not merely evolution, growth, enlightenment, and progress, prior to arriving at Christ's reign on earth. In Scripture, Messiah is the Omega point that lures the faithful and fulfills all things. Theologically speaking, to use a common expression, shrewd utopianism simply puts centuries of lipstick on the underlying pig of naivete.

Hence, it will be argued that the way forward is to reject "pan-millennialism" and postmillennialism and radically reform otherworldly amillennialism and fatalistic and escapist premillennialism. Fortunately, such reform is well underway, and common ground is now possible between a rebooted pro-creation amillennialism and a sanitized and trimmed down premillennialism.

RESURRECTED OR RESTORED CREATION APPROXIMATIONISM

When the biblical and all-encompassing and creation-affirming vision guides the church, the perfected and glorious future destiny of the cosmos is viewed as capable of limited and carefully defined approximation amid the present realities of church and civilization. The future victory frames, defines, lures, and bends the present toward God's ultimate victory.

This biblical orientation toward the future avoids naive views of present possibilities, as well as legion pessimistic, escapist, and fatalistic views. Claims that we are in, or know that we are in, the last generation are graciously interrogated and rejected. The City of Kingdom Approximation future-vision provides a foundation for robust, clear, and specific guidance on how the church can and should patiently engage culture and civilization—over the course of many centuries if not millennia, prior to Christ's return.

This work will argue that the future-vision of a reborn and/or resurrected creation—as opposed to a purified or restored creation—is truer to Scripture and a better guide to how the church should affirm and interact with culture and civilization today. The restored creation models of scholars such as N. T. Wright and J. Richard Middleton are most helpful, a nice corrective, and certainly in vogue, but are also fundamentally inadequate and less scriptural than a resurrection model for the New Heaven and Earth.

CREATION RESTORATION CONSENSUS AND APPROXIMATION

Whether the current cosmos is purified or resurrected is not the focus but will be explored in this book. The biblical certainty of a paradise restored and raised to a new level, however, is a nonnegotiable centerpiece for defining how the faithful interface with civilization now and forever—and to what degree civilization can be improved this side of Messiah's earthly reign. Conservative and liberal theological scholarship has largely rejected otherworldly conceptions of heaven not rooted in creation-affirmation. "They have plumbed the New Testament's Jewish roots to challenge the pervasive cultural belief in an otherworldly paradise."[4]

This work argues that the coming resurrected creation can be approximated already but is not fully a reality—fully manifest or consummated—until *after* Messiah returns. The City of Kingdom Approximation, the city of kingdom influence on civilization, eventually gives way to cosmic fulfillment in the heavenly city, the New Jerusalem. The debate about the literal details of the New Jerusalem that comes down to earth (Rev 21) often misses this essential and foundational biblical truth: "And he carried me away in the Spirit to a great and high mountain, and showed me the holy city, Jerusalem, coming down out of heaven from God, having the glory of God. Her brilliance was like a very valuable stone, like a stone of crystal-clear jasper" (Rev 21:10–11).

The City of Kingdom Approximation and the coming holy city of the New Jerusalem represent and illuminate far more than two literal cities. The cities represent two ages and the nature of two earthly civilizations that either approximate or ultimately consummate God's kingdom rule on earth.

Current civilizations can either approximate the true future or be ruled by the spirit of antichrist, to one degree or another. Both dynamics exist and persist on a continuum, yet one or the other ultimately dominates or rules. Civilizational and cultural relativism is unbiblical and sub-Christian theology, if not anti-Christian theology. We must discern the soul of any city, culture, kingdom, or civilization to be effective in kingdom work.

All civilizations before Messiah's return fall somewhere on the continuum between the City of Antichrist and the City of Kingdom Approximation, and all civilizations can and will be held accountable. In the present upside-down world, consistent with a theology of the cross,[5] accountability is often only articulated by scorned and persecuted prophets.

---

4. Murawski, "Our Idea."
5. Matthews, *Theology*.

The City of Kingdom Approximation anticipates and points toward the heavenly city, the New Jerusalem, that fulfills history and God's intent in creation. The first transitional phase of the Messiah's literal return and reign will be referred to as the millennium by some but is best viewed simply as the age of creation restoration. Creation restoration, as noted, occurs after Messiah's return and is phase one of creation restoration and resurrection. The proper goal (or true *telos*) of current civilizations is to approximate phase one of God's unfolding redemptive history (creation restoration), just as this restorative phase one approximates the eventual and final cosmic triumph, rebirth, or resurrection of all things.

It is unclear as to whether the holy city of Rev 21, the New Jerusalem, should be interpreted as phase one of cosmic restoration, or the final phase of cosmic resurrection, or both. It seems less than productive to obsess with this question and miss the central biblical theology of at least three cities (antichrist, approximation, and the New Jerusalem). Regardless, civilization is headed toward the heavenly city on earth, and that glorious future may be approximated at the individual, familial, ecclesial (church), communal, cultural, and civilizational levels already via the City of Kingdom Approximation.[6] The City of Kingdom Approximation exists where Judeo-Christian influence is evident, measurable, and significant.

This recommended future-vision is a true, biblical, real, incarnate, earthy, and heavenly hope indeed, for a unified future-vision of time and eternity. The unresolvable tension expressed in the *School of Athens* by Raphael (1511) of Plato pointing to true reality above and Aristotle pointing to true reality before us amid seemingly constant change and death is best resolved through the future-kingdom vision of an already-and-not-yet kingdom. Both real world marine biology (Aristotle) and lofty rational and ethical concepts (Plato) are essential aspects of the priesthood and co-regency of believers and authentic kingdom work. This is true hope in the restoration, healing, redemption, rebirth, and resurrection of all things in both present (the already) and future (the not yet) ages.

Pessimistic premillennialists often argue they are optimistic—Christ will return and rule, and, for some, they will *Escape the Coming Night* via the rapture.[7] Hence, they say, we are very optimistic; we are the ultimate optimists! This sleight of hand fails, however, as the question before us is how realistically optimistic the faithful can be for church and state *before* Christ

---

6. Or, as already noted, the Great Tribulation and antichrist's reign can be approximated in every generation, which is defined in this work as Conditional Tribulationism.

7. Jeremiah, *Escape the Coming Night*.

returns. The correct answer is neither pessimistic fatalism nor unrealistic or naive utopianism.

As I argued in *A Theology of Cross and Kingdom* and elsewhere,[8] and for decades, the present is the age when the faithful can assist with approximating the true future already. War, slavery, and tears are sometimes conquered, yet the total and global defeat of slavery, war, and suffering remains future tense. Slavery was abolished in many nations in recent centuries, which was often assisted by the true and revived church. Some rejoiced at the end of slavery. Such approximations of the future are glimpses of the New Creation and are truly glorious and worthy of celebration and adulation, yet human trafficking and slavery continue to surface and fester in the present. Such is the nature of life and the age between the current two rival cities.

The present always has the potential and all too frequent and common characteristics of the darkest City of Antichrist, yet the future of the true and only real and lasting earthly city—he shall reign forever and ever—is ever dawning already. Hence, Niebuhr's Serenity Prayer, illustrating Christian realism, should be reframed as a more precise, hopeful, and even indomitable creation-affirming optimism and fervent prayer. The prayer hopes and calls for the faithful to miraculously and aggressively approximate the kingdom already—in the light of the fullness of the dawning kingdom rule of God. Realistic and indomitable biblical hope in the present age and City—impossible to be defeated or subdued—may look something like this revision of Niebuhr:

> God, give me your Spirit and grace to accept with *discerning* serenity the things that cannot be changed,
>
> Courage to change the things which should *and can* be changed already in the Kairos kingdom moments of history,
>
> *Confidence, shrewd optimism, passion, and realism* concerning what can and cannot be changed prior to Messiah's return,
>
> and the *Wisdom* to distinguish the one from the other.[9]

---

8. Matthews, *Theology*.
9. Shapiro, "Who Wrote." As noted, this prayer has been eschatologically modified.

THE PERENNIAL CHALLENGE: THE CITY OF ANTICHRIST, ANTICHRISTISM, AND THE ANTI-JUDEO-CHRISTIAN MOVEMENT

This quest in the present age for the City of Kingdom Approximation is under siege from the City of Antichrist and proliferating antichristism, which can only be described as a global anti–Judeo-Christian (AJC) movement that is gaining momentum. This AJC movement is becoming entrenched especially in formerly Judeo-Christian–influenced civilizations and cultures.

Os Guinness's brilliant "ABC" observation of not many years ago—that we have moved into an "anything but Christianity" historical moment—is perhaps already dated. He argued in 2016 that we were moving into an ABC historical moment in the West, an "anything but Christian" norm for education, culture, and civilization.[10] However, the true mega-trend that seems to be emerging, especially in formerly Judeo-Christian–influenced regions of the globe, is that we are now moving from an ABC moment in history to an AJC moment. This macro-morphing is conterminously emerging from and influencing virtually every theological, political, ethical, and cultural term, phrase, concept, and issue within and outside faith communities.[11] In terms of the contemporary civilizational context, this AJC moment has emerged from antichristism and its many offspring or antichristisms.

It is somewhat ironic that the epicenter of much AJC activity is in regions where Judeo-Christian influence played a critical role in birthing nations and making constitutional provisions for freedom of speech, freedom of religion, freedom of the press, freedom of association with others, and inalienable God-given human rights. Indeed, Judeo-Christian–influenced values, culture, practices, founding documents, laws, entertainment, and education are often the primary targets of AJC proponents, militants, and political fascists.

Such educators, educational institutions, politicians, media spokespersons, entertainment spokespersons, sports figures, corporations, advocacy groups, political hacks, judges, and legislators increasingly seek to marginalize, oppress, ridicule, criminalize, and eradicate Judeo-Christian influence. Most striking is the additional irony that those attacking the Judeo-Christian and Enlightenment wellspring of political freedom, economic freedom and opportunity, religious freedom, and freedom of speech parasitize off of the very freedoms that allow them to assault the demonstrably Judeo-Christian– and Enlightenment-influenced roots or foundations of those very same freedoms. They use these freedoms, opportunities, and

---

10. Decision Staff, "Hostility."
11. See Matthews, "Seduced?"

economic successes to poison the very well of freedom and opportunity. The parasites rule.

The naive would suggest that AJC leaders are targeting only Judeo-Christian faithful who are trying to establish a dictatorial Christian government (theocracy), which is rare today. That outworn and straw person argument (i.e., "we're just opposing a Christian theocracy or Christian nationalism") rests upon a false choice or dichotomy—that either we have a complete church-state union or we have to banish Judeo-Christian influence from the marketplace of ideas, culture, and civilization—which means going AJC.

There are other civilizational options than theocracy or AJCism that will be explored in this work which align more with the City of Kingdom Approximation and nurture human physical and spiritual flourishing opportunities and increased freedom for all. The answer is not AJCism or radical secularism, communism, or Libertarianism, especially in light of contemporary historical developments and evidence.

It will be demonstrated, for example, that Libertarianism's limited government and "live and let live" model has not only proven to be an enabler of the City of Antichrist but is devouring itself due to lacking a stable foundation for civilization, virtue, and sustainable freedom. Libertarianism is also a leech on foundational Judeo-Christian values. The Wild Wild West does not promote liberty but tyranny and mob rule. Civilization needs a tolerant, pro-freedom civilizational glue and Logos norm to hold things together and avoid tyranny, tribalism, fragmentation, and anarchy.

"I SHALL BUILD MY CHURCH": THE CHURCH AS THE EPICENTER OF THE CITY OF KINGDOM APPROXIMATION OR THE ENABLER OF THE CITY OF ANTICHRIST

"I will build My church; and the gates of Hades will not overpower it" (Matt 16:18).

Nothing but kudos is appropriate for those laboring in the often risky trenches of political and cultural engagement while seeking a better world for all, the virtuous common good that is the True *Desire of the Nations*. I added "True" to O'Donovan's title (*Desire of the Nations*) because that is the real point—that the true desire of nations should cause kings and kingdoms, on bended knee, to know their proper role (temporary stewards of a healthy kingdom) while *Awaiting the* [Only True] *King*. "Only True" is added to Smith's title because that is also the main point relative to the appropriate role of nations, kings, kingdoms of this world age, presidents, and prime ministers. All are transitory or temporary kings and kingdoms that will be judged based on the plumb line of the Heavenly City.

Many spend their resources and risk their lives, reputations, and lifestyles in inner cities, or on mission fields, or in court cases, striving for a better world and opportunities for all in this present age. And they have made and do make a difference (e.g., Wilberforce in England; Mother Theresa in India; Pasteur in the lab).

Amazingly, I have had wonderful colleagues over the years, whom Reinhold Niebuhr would probably refer to as "doves," who unfortunately criticize those in the messy, dangerous, and exhausting trenches of culture wars who are preserving the very rights of the doves to fly freely and engage in free speech, freedom of association with others who disagree with the government, and the free exercise of religion. These heroes in the trenches are mocked as "too political." Such heroes should always speak the truth in love (Eph 4:15) inside and outside of communities of faith, but only those in denial would ignore that the culture wars are very real; hence, kudos and gratitude are inadequate expressions of appreciation to those overflowing with love for others. The good Samaritan helps individuals but also future generations and nations.

Yet the true scriptural epicenter of the City of Kingdom Approximation is, "I will build my church; and the gates of Hades will not overpower it" (Matt 16:18). The present only bows toward the true future of a resurrected creation when Judeo-Christian faith communities fully bow to the true King of kings and Lord of lords such that the faithful serve as authentic salt, light, and healing leaven in the present age. And this service usually requires a cross in an inverted world, which is what many have referred to as cruciformity. The kingdom Christian is the cruciform Christian following the Messiah and suffering for the world that God so loves on the way of the cross—the *Via Dolorosa*.

This work will document the fact that in the globally influential American evangelical church, many who hold to a very high view of scriptural inspiration and authority often have muted or sidetracked their divine calling to serve as light, salt, and healing leaven when discipling the kingdoms and the peoples of all nations (Matt 28:19–20). Why? Their future-vision has been corrupted by pipe dreams or unbiblical distortions and accretions (additions) that have cut the nerve of effective civilizational engagement and influence. The beacon light of the City of Kingdom Approximation pointing the way to the true future has been hijacked, eclipsed, or placed under a bushel.

Now that we have laid some foundations, and as a preview to or foretaste of many of the arguments that will be developed in this work, the list below briefly introduces and summarizes key future-vision distortions and possible corrections of such eschatological distortions. New terms or neologisms are utilized in order to clarify and abbreviate the material. The distortions and corrections are addressed throughout this work, and also summarized in a table in appendix A. The future-vision corrections strive to be grounded in enhanced biblical interpretation and careful theological and historical reflection.

The introduction of these contrasts in the following list should assist with clarifying the argument for and theology of the City of Kingdom Approximation:

- Last-Generationism (the claim to know that the last generation or decade or year has arrived) should be replaced with Any-Generationism (we should live as if the Messiah can return in any generation).

- Great Tribulationism (that we are on the verge of entering the literal, seven-year Great Tribulation) should be replaced with Conditional Tribulationism (many great tribulations come to the church and world throughout history; Jewish and Christian faith communities can play a critical role in influencing history; and the nature, timing, and duration of these horrendous tribulational periods are at least somewhat fluid rather than precisely predetermined.) Faith communities bear a significant though not total responsibility for the state of surrounding kingdoms. Yet the distortion of Great Tribulationism contains an important truth. Every generation and age is ripe for many antichrists, the seductive spirit of antichrist, and very harmful and powerful leaders and deceivers. Hence, the profound sense of human fallenness and the depravity of leaders, kingdoms, and systems at the core of Great Tribulationism—the gold in the dross—needs to be taken up into a robust and discerning theology of antichristism. Antichristism is crouching at the gates of every city and community, attempting to negatively leaven both church and state from within, and is very real, seductive, malevolent, dark, and pervasive in every generation and kingdom. And, in agreement with the New Testament, deceivers and antichrists may do their most damaging and globally influential work within faith communities and so-called faith-based education.

- The Historical and Theological Determinism of all things should be replaced with a recognition of Historical Fluidity and Providential Kingdom Approximation. By grace, through faith, service, and the way of the cross, kingdom influence can, under God's providential guidance, contribute to shaping history and edging it toward its true future.

- Premillennialism, not necessarily unbiblical at its essential core (see, for example, the works by Ladd, Henry, Beasley-Murray, Cullmann, and Matthews in the bibliography), in view of its tragic abuses, is best replaced for now with a theology of pre-restorationism. Messiah will return prior to the transitional and restorative phase that premillennialists refer to as the millennium, which they believe is a literal thousand-year reign of Christ on earth. Pre-restorationism views the thousand years as representing the fullness of God's redemptive and glorious restoration of his creative intent. The thousand years may last much longer (or be shorter) than a thousand years, and still retain providentially guided and grace-assisted historical fluidity and freedom that paves the way for the fullness of the resurrected New Creation.

- Contemporary Last-Daysism should be replaced with Biblical Last-Daysism. The last days, according to Scripture (e.g., Hebrews), clearly refer to the era from Christ's first coming to his second coming—the church has been living in the last days for two millennia. Yes, we are living in the last days.

- The Addiction to Darkness should be replaced with Kingdom Approximationism, which has already been introduced many times and which will be expanded upon throughout this work. The City of Antichrist has ultimately already been defeated by the death and resurrection of Christ, yet the fullness of the Heavenly City is still future and can only be approximated in these last days amid powerful and dark cities.

- Eschatomania (see the preface and introduction) needs to be replaced with Eschatopraxis, which means harnessing and utilizing the powerful future-vision impulse in valiant, courageous, and sacrificial practice or praxis, as with the postmillennialists, who significantly and positively impacted the world that God so loved. Similarly, the fear of eschatology due to its abuses, Eschatophobia, also needs to be replaced with Eschatopraxis. Eschatology is central to the ministry and teaching of Jesus, and the whole of the Christian faith and praxis, and therefore should neither be distorted as a spectator sport nor ignored as a toxin.

- Rapture-Escapism, Lifeboat Evangelism, Simplistic Evangelism and Discipleship, Experientialism (an overemphasis on religious experience and good feelings), and Entertainmentism (turning churches, worship, and preaching into entertainment centers) all need to be replaced with a theology and praxis of Kingdom Approximation and a sacrificial Theology of the Cross. Biblical kingdom influence is typically found on the road (or way or via) to the cross, as in the Gospels, the Garden of Gethsemane, and Calvary, and as documented in Heb 11 and 12.

- Pan-millennialism (it doesn't really matter what you believe about eschatology, it will all pan out in the end) should be replaced with Eschatopraxis. Eschatology matters. Views of the future and millennium matter and shape church, state, and history. Pan-millennialism is humorous but cancerous to the life, ministry, and impact of individuals and faith communities. Eschatology has been used and abused but lies at the core of biblical faith, teaching, and practice. We are all eschatological animals through and through, and the key is to purify eschatology then harness the powerful, world-changing eschatological impulse with robust theology and praxis, known as Eschatopraxis.

- While individuals figure prominently in Scripture and God's kingdom and New Creation where God dwells intimately with his people, the theology of Individual Eschatology should be replaced with the Theology of the City to better connect with God's larger and more integrated redemptive work. The ultra-complexity, demonic realities, and potential resurrection of civilizational and city life is better addressed by the theology of the City of Antichrist and the theology of the City of Kingdom Approximation than the typical theology of Individual Eschatology. The latter eschatology should be subsumed under the former cosmic two cities eschatology and the third and glorious City of the New Creation.

- Both Cosmic Annihilationism (the present universe will be entirely annihilated) and Restorationism (the cosmos will be purified and restored) miss the mark on the biblical teaching of Cosmic Resurrectionism. This has already been introduced multiple times and will be further explained and explored in detail in this work, but resurrection, which appropriately emphasizes continuity and discontinuity (1 Cor 15), is the proper theology and analogy for the fullness of the New Creation. Both humanity and the cosmos, which are tethered together in Scripture, must die and be physically resurrected.

LEARNING FROM THE DISTORTIONS AND POTENTIAL CORRECTIONS

The centrality of the church in God's redemptive work is why we can no longer entertain legion distortions and different eschatologies as merely different and inconsequential perspectives or options. The consequences of these different perspectives are grave and threaten core biblical beliefs and the very worship and mission of the church.

The resurrected creation of the next age, the City of Kingdom Consummation, and the City of Kingdom Approximation of the present age must guide not only the loves, loyalties, worship, and passions of God's people but also their strategic and tactical planning and engagement relative to culture and civilization. Too much hinges on the church's future-vision and planning to treat eschatology as a buffet of legitimate choices.

As a historical example, Judeo-Christian–led American Prohibition actually had some legitimate concerns (e.g., ending gambling, the abuse of women, the destruction of families, violence, lost employment, premature deaths, disease), but its future-vision and strategic and tactical plans were horribly flawed. Today it is increasingly difficult to suggest, even in the American evangelical church, that reducing alcohol consumption toward minimal thresholds or abstinence might be an expression of true neighbor-love. Even in the face of millions and millions if not over a billion alcohol-related deaths, including the sad truth that "1 million people died from alcohol-related causes between 1999 and 2017" in just the United States, recreational alcohol use is an untouchable sacred cow.[12]

The present age is characterized by abundance and excess, increased emotional challenges, addictions, increased social challenges, anger and outrage, broken families, legal and illegal drug abuse, poverty, the legalization of additional recreational drugs, needed technological and scientific precision that requires clear focus, and pervasive mobility in vehicles that can almost instantly morph into instruments of death and destruction. So why has the pendulum swung from the legal prohibition of alcohol in the United States (1920) to the sacred cow status of alcohol consumption today, even among the spiritual descendants of the prohibition warriors?

Prohibition was bad eschatology and strategic and tactical planning due to trying to legally enforce what any perceptive student of history and psychology would know is impossible in the early twentieth century, given alcohol's long cultural, religious, economic, and psychological history. However, the current and so-called responsible realism of increased recreational

---

12. National Institutes of Health, "Alcohol-Related Deaths."

drug and alcohol consumption is also bad eschatology in view of the magnitude of the daily carnage and trauma that far exceeds major wars and other tragedies that rightly consume our attention, compassion, or wrath. Shootings and natural disasters that take the lives and fortunes of hundreds or thousands are tragic, yet silent carnage is still carnage even if ignored by the media and so-called enlightened religious and cultural leaders. The last thing that faith communities and civilizations need in the present moment is an increase in recreational drug usage.

Similarly, "the war to end all wars" and "peace in our time" were naive, dangerous, and bad future-visions (eschatologies), yet so was and is hawkish international behavior that assumes that military force is the first or only means for solving economic and territorial disputes. Just War Theory, with all of its challenges today, at least served as a future-vision that tried to frame the possible need for the use of force within moral boundaries, including viewing war as a last resort—and only if there was a reasonable chance of a better outcome.

The church sheds light on the true spirit of the present and ultimate future that is also the true desire of individuals and nations. Those who have any sense whatsoever of authentic neighbor-love promote human and civilizational flourishing and strive to prepare properly all for time and eternity. This is because the church is the primary window into the true future, for via the Spirit of the future it directs our loves and gaze toward the City of Kingdom Approximation and the City of Kingdom Consummation.

The present and future kingdom rule of God was absolutely central to the entirety of Jesus' teaching, parables, mission, ministry, return, and reign. We are not seeking just any City of God or trying to avoid a corrupted City of Man. We are seeking the reality and specific characteristics, practices, and virtues of the already initiated and eventually consummated kingdom of God.

What are those kingdom teachings, virtues, attitudes, and practices? In Matthew, John the Baptist and Jesus both proclaim that all should repent, or radically change course, due to the in-breaking kingdom rule of God. A new City is on the horizon. Jesus then paints a picture of what that true future looks like with his kingdom teaching through the Sermon on the Mount and his kingdom parables, kingdom life, and sacrificial kingdom ministry. Blessed are the truly repentant, meek, humble, pure, and merciful, for they shall inherit and reign on the earth with the coming Messiah in the New Jerusalem.

The City of Kingdom Approximation shrewdly and lovingly discerns and identifies the when, what, where, who, how, and why of stepping into the true future already in the present age. The City of Kingdom Approximation purges and unifies otherworldly conceptions of a perfect heaven with the enfleshed and incarnational reality of the current and future cosmos.

Many sense that something in culture and civilization external to the church has truly gone off the rails. Fingers point at Marxism, or socialism, or capitalism, or Critical Race Theory, or a political party, or a politician, or moral relativism, or the media, or Black Lives Matter, or Trumpism, or secularism, or . . . . These issues matter and should be assessed, and, as noted, the labors of those in the cultural, social, and civilizational trenches are to be commended.

This work argues, however, that the primary problem and solution to the intensifying civilizational crisis is the church—the called-out ones—of the Messiah. The crisis in the church (the ecclesial crisis) lies at the heart of the crisis in civilization. Christ's church is often escapist or angry, or when engaged it is often corrupted by culture or contemporary movements and ideas concerning how to engage. And effective engagement with an upside-down world inevitably requires a gracious, cruciform life—a life patterned after the cross and overflowing with love and forgiveness. Believers are beckoned to take up their cross daily and follow the sacrificial Lamb who is also the coming Lion (Luke 9:23; Rev 5:5–6).

Hence, the church of Jesus Christ is the primary problem and solution to the present quagmire. The church often makes personal experience, feelings, health, entertainment, and economic success into idols. God is viewed, as Carl F. H. Henry once put it, as a cosmic bellhop, waiter, or waitress whose primary purpose is to meet our needs. Good feelings, enjoyable experiences, physical health and wealth, which are not inherently bad, exclusively signify God's blessings rather than biblical measures of success that often involve the way of the cross, the *Via Dolorosa*.

Christian leaders who "succeed" by worldly standards, which Luther referred to as the failed, false, and unbiblical theology of glory, self-congratulate and are congratulated by others, even if they politely trample on many behind closed doors. Terms such as advancing the kingdom, God, Jesus, the Spirit, and saving souls are often used to baptize very un-kingdom-like actions and attitudes. Inevitably, personal or organizational image management is confused with preserving and advancing Christian mission.

As was argued in *A Theology of Cross and Kingdom*, in an upside-down world the citizens of the City of Antichrist are often promoted and lauded, whereas the citizens of the City of Kingdom Approximation are crucified, literally or otherwise—often even within religious communities.

Some churches proclaim truth without lived faith, and others proclaim faith in faith or faith without truth—whatever feels good or works is the norm rather than the crucified Logos and his coming kingdom. From a biblical vantage point, faith without truth is dead, and truth without biblical faith and practice is dead. The church often emphasizes right beliefs or rules at the expense of having a Spirit-led influential community. Other churches sacrifice truth before the altar of experience or results. Some churches and families have rules without relationships, and others have relationships without rules and normative truth and ethics. Both approaches are toxic.

Entertainment, popularity, numbers, and finances are often the only real measures of church or Christian organizational success. "Successful" megachurches that can't possibly serve as models for the vast majority of small churches across the nation and globe sometimes have more in common with the personal comfort and good feelings of Starbucks, movie theaters, and rock concerts than the essentials of the church of the apostles and the New Testament (see Acts or the Epistles). And these illustrations are but a miniscule sampling of the fruits or symptoms of compromised or confused future-visions.

The self-proclaimed, Bible-believing churches need reformation. This work will argue that the primary obstacles to constructive kingdom influence on civilization lie primarily within the church, as the church has many enablers or even defenders of the City of Antichrist. It is instructive to remember that the primary opposition to the Messiah's first coming was by religious leaders and their distorted teaching, even though they shared the same general religious worldview or outlook (monotheistic Judaism) as the Messiah.

The church will continue to qualify as a problem, since bad eschatology rules apart from a future-vision reformation and appropriate and effective Spirit-led strategic and tactical planning. And an eschatological revolution could spark unprecedented opportunities for future kingdom influence. A true future-vision revolution will identify and disempower antichrists and enablers and prepare, equip, energize, and commission kingdom approximators, which is the subject of the next chapter.

CHAPTER 3

THE COSMIC CAST

ANTICHRISTS, APPROXIMATORS, AND ENABLERS

As the crisis of culture and civilization wanders in a thousand discordant directions toward the future, the self-proclaimed biblical, evangelical, and historically orthodox church in America and beyond is largely distracted, confused, and often theologically corrupt. Safe, economically and spiritually flourishing civilization is on life support and becoming increasingly if not militantly anti-Judeo-Christian.

Self-proclaimed biblical churches often are being seduced by toxic future-visions and are either accommodating or unbiblically reacting to and/or self-isolating from the present crisis. Church has often been reduced to something such as

- an ecstatic emotional experience,
- a Starbucks moment,
- a movie theater drama,
- a rock concert or theme park adrenaline rush,
- a social club,
- a spiritualized therapy or "posithink" gathering,
- an arena for the spectator sport of charting the riveting last days prior to the rapture,
- a woke community organization advocating for ill-defined social justice, or

- an escapist ghetto, providing tickets to heaven—or some combination thereof of some or all of the above.

Spurious and lethal future-visions rule the day in church, synagogue, and state. Some visions are overtly or covertly anti-Judeo-Christian. Inside faith communities those embracing eschatologies such as last-generation escapism perceive themselves as Christ-honoring while enabling legion toxic anti-Judeo-Christian future-visions.

When biblical leaven, salt, and light disengage or are hidden under a bushel, the consequences for families, communities, future generations, and civilizations are grave, as illustrated by a classic story and tragic reality. Edwin Lutzer shared recollections from a German man who had resided in Nazi Germany as the anti-Semitic fires of hate swept through the nation and kindled brutal and heartless torture and mass exterminations. The documentation of this story by Lutzer is less than desired, but the recollection vividly and accurately recounts how escapist spirituality ill prepared believers for authentic kingdom service and enabled antichristism during the age of the antichrist Hitler and the Christian martyr Bonhoeffer:

> I lived in Germany during the Nazi Holocaust. I considered myself a Christian. We heard stories of what was happening to the Jews, but we tried to distance ourselves from it, because, what could anyone do to stop it? A railroad track ran behind our small church and each Sunday morning we could hear the whistle in the distance and then the wheels coming over the tracks. We became disturbed when we heard the cries coming from the train as it passed by. We realized that it was carrying Jews like cattle in the cars! Week after week the whistle would blow. We dreaded to hear the sound of those wheels because we knew we would hear the cries of the Jews en route to a death camp. Their screams tormented us. We knew the time the train was coming and when we heard the whistle blow we began singing hymns. By the time the train came past our church we were singing at the top of our voices. If we heard the screams, we sang more loudly and soon we heard them no more. Years have passed and no one talks about it anymore. But I still hear that train whistle in my sleep. God forgive me; forgive all of us who called ourselves Christians yet did nothing to intervene.[1]

Dietrich Bonhoeffer's *Cost of Discipleship*, which applied Jesus' teaching on the kingdom from the Sermon on the Mount to this troubled historical context, concurs that countless Christians were more German or Nazi than

---

1. Lutzer, *Hitler's Cross*, 99–100.

Judeo-Christian during these dark days. These Christians did not respond to the call of the cross: "When Christ calls a man, . . . he bids him come and die."[2] The cross and the coming kingdom define true, real, incarnational and biblical piety, practice, and conformity to the likeness of the Messiah.[3]

Today, the time is long past for directly identifying and addressing the key life-destroying waters that are incrementally poisoning individuals, families, communities, church, synagogue, and state. Many are obsessed with looking for the signs of the times or an individual antichrist when, as previously noted, Scripture teaches that there are many antichrists and the spirit of antichrist present in every age. Perhaps Nietzsche and Saul Alinsky would celebrate this pervasive and pregnant antichristism if they were alive today.

This work will demonstrate that, according to Scripture, there are false prophets, false teachers, and antichrists inside and outside faith communities, seeking to seduce and subvert the mission of the people of God. Jesus warned of false prophets: "Beware of the false prophets, who come to you in sheep's clothing, but inwardly are ravenous wolves" (Matt 7:15). Scripture seems far more concerned with the in-house variety. If the people of God are led astray, then God's work in the world is muted or thwarted, and civilizational decay, rather than kingdom approximation, accelerates and advances.

The church is the primary civilizational problem and solution relative to bending the arrow of time toward its true future.

Jesus warned of false prophets, but it would have been odd for Jesus to warn of antichrists prior to the culmination of his ministry, since he was claiming to be the Christ. Paul, John, and other New Testament documents (e.g., Jude, Hebrews) warn of false teachers, false teaching, false prophets, and antichrists. Such antagonists to the faith operate inside and outside the church and synagogue. Unfortunately, many of God's people either follow their lead or enable their game plans by toxic future-visions that distort Scripture.

The church and synagogue are the centers and primary authors of future history. My PhD minor was in political science, and I taught philosophy, theology, and ethics for over two decades. Politics and intellectual and cultural engagement are essential tasks, but the state of church and synagogue is the key to the state of the culture and nations. In our own day, in

---

2. Bonhoeffer, *Cost of Discipleship*, 11.

3. This material that recounts and applies this story from Erwin Lutzer appeared previously in Matthews, *Theology*, 17–18.

contrast to many stellar moments from the past, the church of Jesus Christ is largely if not utterly failing to contribute significantly to directing the arrow of history. The craters of the gospel are vanishing. The future is being bent toward the City of Antichrist.

PUBLIC BELIEFS (PUBLIC THEOLOGY)

Many models have been proposed to understand the proper relationship between Christ and culture, such as two cities, two competing kingdoms, two domains, two loves, competing citizenships, various models of Christ and culture, and alternative loyalties and game plans. Leading thinkers have argued for approaches such as the strict separation of church/synagogue and state (separationism), or radical civilizational transformation, or Constantinianism (church-state union), or neo-Constantinianism (the significant influence of church on state), or life-boat escapist evangelism (save all you can before the kingdom ship sinks), or resident aliens (active and culturally influential separationism), or new monastic (neo-monastic preparation for a long, coming, new dark ages) future-visions.

All of these perspectives can contribute to the dialogue, yet all are incomplete, inadequate, flawed, or terribly flawed. A mortal problem with most of these approaches is that they are far too ambiguous, conceptual, or simplistic, and fall short of employing key biblical categories that define the major players who write the past, present, and future of church, synagogue, and state. They are often big on theory but small on clear strategy and tactics.

These models and other options also touch on how to relate our basic Judeo-Christian beliefs and loves to impacting our world positively, which some refer to as public theology. *I prefer to speak of public eschatology rather than public theology as the new academic discipline that navigates how our visions of the future contribute to our public and shared life together.* The fuel for change in synagogue, church, culture, and state are the basic beliefs (theology) as articulated and applied to the present moment via a potent, compelling, and persuasive Spirit-empowered eschatology.

Public theology is framed and guided by public eschatology. In most respects, good public theology is public eschatology. Theologically sound and biblical public eschatology allows the church to contribute to the enhancement of civilizations prior to Messiah's return.

Public theology is a bit of a misnomer if the argument of this work—that future-visions rule our public life—is correct. This is a work in public theology, refined and redefined almost entirely as public eschatology. Eschatology deals with present and future kingdoms and future-visions. The key and normative concept in Scripture for *How Should We Then Live*—public theology—is the present and future kingdom rule of God. This work will ceaselessly argue that in countless ways *eschatology rules and biblical eschatology should rule everything*.

AUGUSTINE'S CITY OF GOD FUTURE-VISION AS THE FIRST MAGISTERIAL PUBLIC THEOLOGY

Augustine's brilliant, massively influential future-vision and public theology are largely found in his classic, *The City of God*.[4] Rome was collapsing. Many blamed Christians—just like Nietzsche fifteen hundred years later—for the calamity and called for a return to pagan or anti-Christian values and gods. Augustine more than responded with a nearly eight-hundred-page *tour de force*. Augustine defended the faith (apologetics), preserved the faith inside of the church (polemics), and framed and merged this defense of the faith with his future-vision (eschatology). Hence, we have eschatological apologetics and polemics in the eschatological public theology of the *City of God*.

Rome, Augustine argued, was collapsing long before Judeo-Christian influence. Rome's future-vision was flawed and founded upon false gods, unsustainable and confused values and ethics, increasing barbarism, and civilizational-destroying moral decadence. The Judeo-Christian future-vision was the only true hope and remedy for this fifth-century AD crisis. *The City of God* was a multi-decade project that stretched into the later years of Bishop Augustine's life.

AUGUSTINE'S DUALISTIC FUTURE-VISION

Augustine's mature thought soundly rejects much otherworldly Greek thought, while also retaining key otherworldly (neo-Platonic) elements in his assumptions and the very structure of his perspective. He appreciates, appropriates both critically and uncritically, assesses, and redeploys Greek (Platonic-influenced) otherworldly assumptions.

At the heart of his future-vision is the surpassingly glorious City of God, which conflicts with the earthly city dominated by self, lust, pride, and abused power—to name but a few vices. Augustine and his father were non-Christians, in contrast to his Christian mother, Monica. Augustine was immersed in the lust and the pride of the many misdirected loves of the earthly city. He pridefully journeyed through multiple philosophical and

---

4. Augustine, *City of God*.

religious perspectives on his quest for something that truly endures before experiencing a humbling, heart-changing experience—just like Luther, Wesley, and countless others.

Converted Augustine's future-vision and view of history was that there are two cities, determined by two loves or passions, reflecting two peoples or groups, and ultimately resulting in two eternal destinies. The prideful earthly city loves self, seeks its own glory, and often opposes God (antichristism). The city of God or heavenly city overflows with humility, love for others, and love for God and seeks the surpassing glory of God and the heavenly city.[5] Augustine writes, "The glorious city of God is my theme in this work, . . . a city surpassingly glorious . . . [that] sojourns as a stranger in the midst of the ungodly . . . [toward] the fixed stability of its eternal seat, which it now with patience waits for . . . [and which it will] obtain, by virtue of its excellence, final victory and perfect peace."[6]

Augustine's glorious city "sojourns as a stranger," whereas the City of Kingdom Approximation, advocated for in this work and Scripture, while often treated as a stranger is also the true and rightful ruler of the present and the future. The City of Antichrist is the usurper and illegitimate kingdom. In truth, the City of Antichrist, while very real, is the true stranger, the true counterfeit, and the unreal future. The City of Kingdom Approximation is the rightful owner of the present and a foretaste of the Heavenly City on earth.

MISDIRECTED LOVE AND DUALISM

For Augustine, the present existence of the earthly city is characterized by false or misdirected and often demonic loves for things that do not endure but that destroy and are ultimately unreal. Sin is misdirected love and a distortion of the true love that lies at the core of the heavenly city; sin is a distortion of the good and, in one sense, lacks reality as a separate or positive thing. Misdirected love is a distortion of what God created rather than a separate or rival and ultimate reality.

For Augustine, God did not create sin and evil, and there is no force or power or reality outside of God. Augustine once held to a strong dualism known as Manicheanism, where God and evil are separate, powerful, and conflicting realities. Post-conversion Augustine's God created everything good; God and God's good creation constitute the only true reality. Sin and

5. Augustine, *City of God*, xi.
6. Augustine, *City of God*, 3.

evil are distortions of what God created, not separate or eternal forces opposing God. Augustine's God is in charge.

Humanity distorted love and God's creation. Fallen humanity now loves things that are false loves and false gods. This false love lies at the heart of the earthly city. And at the heart of this false love is the false kingdom "lust of rule," which opposes God's celestial city.[7]

OTHERWORLDLY DUALISM AS AN ENABLER OF THE CITY OF ANTICHRIST

Unfortunately, otherworldly dualism or Platonism remains in the structure of thought, assumptions, perspective, philosophy of history, and future-vision of Augustine. There are two cities, two peoples, two destinies, two loves, and the adversaries and those who love God. There is a changing world that is passing away and the unchanging eternal—the ultimately unreal and the ultimately real:

> Accordingly, two cities have been formed by two loves: the earthly by the love of self, even to the contempt of God; the heavenly by the love of God, even to the contempt of self. The former, in a world, glories in itself, the latter in the Lord. For the one seeks glory from men; but the greatest glory of the other is God, the witness of conscience. The one lifts up its head in its own glory; the other says to its God, "Thou art my glory, and the lifter up of mine head." In the one, the princes and the nations it subdues are ruled by the love of ruling; in the other the princes and the subjects serve one another in love, the latter obeying, while the former take thought for all. . . . And therefore the wise men of the one city, living according to man, have sought for profit to their own bodies or souls, or both. . . . But in the other city there is no human wisdom, but only godliness, which offers due worship to the true God, and looks for its reward in the society of the saints, of holy angels as well as holy men, "that God may be all in all."[8]

Augustine escaped his pagan dualism (Manicheanism) by demoting evil to the distortion of the good, but he retained elements in his Greek-influenced, oversimplistic, otherworldly two cities dualism and time and eternity dualism. This dualism has infected the church for centuries and up to the present moment, with more extreme distortions of Augustine being represented

---

7. Augustine, *City of God*, 3.
8. Augustine, *City of God*, 430.

by many varieties of contemporary escapism, including views that devalue created, physical existence.

The two destinies of the two peoples and cities led Augustine to conclude, in a very otherworldly fashion, that it is impossible to possess a "happiness in this unhappy life . . . [because] the end of our good is that for the sake of which other things are to be desired."[9] Yes, Augustine affirmed that true, enduring happiness can ultimately only be found in the eternal goal or *telos* of the heavenly city—yet much more is being affirmed by Augustine.

DUALISTIC AND OTHERWORLDLY, NOT APPROXIMATE, HAPPINESS

Augustine believed that the philosophers of his day vainly sought to identify a supreme good apart from Christ that could bring happiness in this life. Augustine was correct that Christ is the ultimate ground of happiness, but the implication that either there is no happiness or only real happiness in Christ treats every individual as if they have already arrived at their eternal destiny rather than being engaged in the fluid process of responding to grace over time and in history. Real happiness is partial but possible in this present life and fulfilled in the next.

In other words, for Augustine, who was theologically deterministic, either a person is eternally chosen to be in the heavenly city and, therefore, can experience real happiness, or a person is among those in the earthly city passed over by God's choice of the elect whose true end or destiny is unhappiness and whose present experience in this life is the unhappy and vain pursuit of happiness.[10] With Augustine, most everything is either/or.

For Augustine, there were no variations among the philosophers who sought the supreme good and happiness in life, though the more noble philosophers were (like Augustine before his conversion), perhaps, on a journey through different views that might lead, for some, to finding the supreme good. There is no partial or approximate happiness for those who are progressing in the journey and seeking higher and nobler values (e.g., Socrates and Plato). Either one is in the community of the heavenly city or not, and if not then "what flood of eloquence can suffice to detail the miseries of this life?"[11]

The challenge is not that Augustine believed there are two ultimate destinies for humanity—salvation or damnation. The problem is that for

9. Augustine, *City of God*, 605.
10. Augustine, *City of God*, 611.
11. Augustine, *City of God*, 611.

Augustine these two destinies are not dynamic or fluid and based on the grace-assisted free response to God's amazing love and grace.

DUALISTIC HAPPINESS, THE FLESH, AND THIS PRESENT LIFE

And what was Augustine's dualistic advice to those destined for the heavenly city while sojourning as aliens on earth? The answer is yet another black-and-white, flesh versus spirit, this life versus the next life dualism: "And as we cannot attain to this [state] in this present life however ardently we desire it . . . [where] the flesh should cease to lust against the spirit, . . . [therefore,] let us by God's help accomplish at least this, to preserve the soul from succumbing and yielding to the flesh that lusts against it, and to refuse our consent to the perpetration of sin."[12] We should not consent or succumb to the lusts of the flesh, but the very fact of existing in this life, in the flesh, means that sin is essentially inevitable and a necessary aspect of fleshly existence in this age. And this is why true kingdom approximation in the present age requires the belief that kingdom approximation includes the possibility, in this life, of having radically transformed believers who not only don't succumb to being dominated by sin and lust but who increasingly are dominated by the overflowing love for God and others in the Spirit.

Hence, dualistic Augustine added that we can't possibly experience "our final beatitude," virtue, blessedness, or happiness "already" in this life in any real or even approximate sense; hence, our focus must be on the virtues of perseverance and fortitude in the flesh versus spirit war so that we are sure to land on the beautiful and glorious shore of the eternal city.[13] We "ought to patiently endure, until we come to the ineffable enjoyment of unmixed good; for there shall be no longer anything to endure. Salvation, such as it shall be in the world to come, shall itself be our final happiness." Augustine concludes his defense of the faith as follows: "And this happiness these philosophers refuse to believe in, because they do not see it, and attempt to fabricate for themselves a happiness in this life based upon a virtue which is as deceitful as it is proud."[14]

The goal for Augustine was "the final blessedness, this is the ultimate consummation, the unending end. Here, indeed, we are said to be blessed when we have such peace as can be enjoyed in a good life; but such blessedness is mere misery compared to that final felicity."[15] While there is an ele-

---

12. Augustine, *City of God*, 612.
13. Augustine, *City of God*, 613.
14. Augustine, *City of God*, 615.
15. Augustine, *City of God*, 619.

ment of blessedness and peace possible in this life as mortals, for Augustine it did not approximate the future but was so provisional in nature that it only motivates us to endure to the "unending end." Indeed, even for members of the heavenly city, "the true blessings of the soul are not now enjoyed; for that is no true wisdom which does not direct all its prudent observations, manly actions, virtuous self-restraint, and just arrangements, to that end which God shall be all and all in a secure eternity and perfect peace."[16]

Augustine is to be credited for soundly rejecting Hellenistic views of non-bodily resurrection, for eternal "healing" is "also of the body renewed by the resurrection."[17] Yet his entire system radiates with an overstated and ultimately unbiblical, non-Hebraic, over-simplistic Hellenistic/Platonic dualism: two loves, misdirected or properly directed love, two cities, two peoples, two destinies, elect versus passed over or damned, temporal versus eternal, uncertainty versus total certainty,[18] heaven versus earth, and flesh versus spirit. While Augustine utilized biblical terms (e.g., sojourners or aliens), he distorted their meaning in Scripture by this extreme dualism.

DUALISTIC FAMILIES

In Augustine's vision there are also only two families: the family that does not "live by faith" and seeks "their peace in the earthly advantages of this life" and "the families which live by faith" who "look for those eternal blessings which are promised, and use as pilgrims such advantages of time and of earth as do not fascinate and divert them from God, but rather aid them to endure with greater ease, and to keep down the number of those burdens of the corruptible body which weigh upon the soul."[19] Those in the earthly city do not live by faith (everything is either/or for Augustine), and they seek only an earthly peace (again, either/or). The heavenly community in this life "lives like a captive and stranger in the earthly city"[20] rather than living as liberating agents of kingdom influence in the present.

---

16. Augustine, *City of God*, 631.
17. Augustine, *City of God*, 619.
18. Augustine, *City of God*, 629.
19. Augustine, *City of God*, 628.
20. Augustine, *City of God*, 628.

DETERMINISTIC SALVATION AS ESCAPE OR NEW CREATION SALVATION?

And while Augustine correctly affirmed the bodily resurrection and "social life" in the hereafter,[21] he also bordered on a negative and Greek/Platonic view of the body when discussing the final destination and state of members of the City of God: "When we shall have reached that peace, this mortal life shall give place to one that is eternal, and our body shall be no more this animal body which by its corruption weighs down the soul, but a spiritual body feeling no want, and in all its members subjected to the will."[22] And his affirmation of the importance of the social life is undermined by his obsession, which continues to dominate much of Western theology, concerning how the individual can avoid hell and achieve heaven rather than the mammoth biblical vision of how heaven can come to and transform earth, including individuals, families, communities, cities, and nations.

Augustine's Greek dualism leads to his dualistic and deterministic view of salvation—the present age consists of (1) the divinely predetermined saved and (2) the passed over ones who are the damned or non-elect. The present does not consist of multiple players on a fluid journey with authentic grace-assisted freedom and, at least to some degree, genuinely undetermined personal and historical futures.

Therefore, Augustine's future-vision is for true believers to persevere, as wheat existing among the tares in the church and beyond, until they reach their mostly otherworldly end. Good and evil, the two cities, will coexist until the final victory. Messiah will not reign on earth, but the Messiah and true believers (the true church) already reign symbolically or spiritually in heaven. Christ will not come back to transform the world but to judge the earth and take true believers to heaven. The present age is not an age when God's true future can be increasingly approximated, but, like the classic movie *Groundhog Day* (1993), each step up the stairway of history leads nowhere. Good and evil persist and the two cities remain until God's people are taken to heaven.

And herein lies the Achilles' heel of Augustine's entire system and the fuel for his unhealthy dualism: his otherworldly future-vision. He was initially a premillennialist, meaning Christ would return to and transform earth, and the heavenly city would, as N. T. Wright often points out and Scripture affirms, descend or come down to earth (Rev 21:2).

---

21. Augustine, *City of God*, 629.
22. Augustine, *City of God*, 629.

The biblical future-vision is a transformed new cosmos, heaven, and earth, not an escape from the very good world God created, like in some Greek thought. Augustine eventually rejected premillennialism as being too earthy, this-worldly, or carnal. Some premillennial versions were articulated as very carnal (gold, silver, grape clusters with thousands of grapes each), though some of the language may have been symbolic or hyperbolic for glorious abundance and provision. Ironically, many premillennial versions today—after Augustine's mammoth influence—are just the opposite (i.e., very escapist and otherworldly).

AUGUSTINE'S FUTURE-VISION RULES

Augustine became the champion of this relatively otherworldly amillennialism (no literal reign of Christ on earth).[23] This future-vision not only dominated over one thousand years of church history, but elements of his dualism that were part of his future-vision system continue to corrupt many who strive to hold to historic and biblical Judeo-Christian beliefs but who tilt toward unbiblical otherworldliness.

This amillennial future-vision affirmed that "even now His saints reign with Him, though otherwise . . . they shall reign hereafter; and yet, though the tares grow in the church along with the wheat, they [the tares] do not reign with Him [now or ever]."[24] Hence, the wheat who reign now (the millennium or thousand years is spiritual and already a reality) should lead the church and are central to dispensing, determining, and declaring grace and salvation. Augustine's amillennial future-vision sets the stage for Luther's reaction and the Protestant Reformation—Christ, grace, and faith, not primarily the church, must be central to biblical salvation for those seeking escape.

Augustine's true church, which reigns now with Christ, is the "kingdom militant, in which conflict with the enemy is still maintained, and war carried on with warring [good or evil] lusts, or government laid upon them as they yield, until we come to that most peaceful kingdom in which we shall reign without an enemy."[25] This escapism is also why Augustine applied the Abrahamic blessing—that all the nations of the earth shall be blessed through Abraham's seed—almost entirely to the age of the "new heaven and earth."[26] The mental picture many of us have of the medieval period,

---

23. Augustine, *City of God*, 654–55.
24. Augustine, *City of God*, 655.
25. Augustine, *City of God*, 655.
26. Augustine, *City of God*, 733.

sometimes referred to entirely as "dark ages" by those who overlook its contributions to learning and scientific progress, is not entirely inaccurate. The faithful were, as Augustine recommended, persevering through a dark earthly existence while gazing at and waiting for the reality of heaven in a kingdom living in the shadow of the towering and otherworldly church spires.

THREE CITIES, RATHER THAN ONLY TWO

As noted previously, there are three primary cities to navigate, not two, and a fluid continuum between the two current cities and ages (antichrist and approximation) as redemptive history progresses in various locations across the globe. Such a continuum exists even within individual nations, regions or cities—and even within individual communities and families.

Augustine's error, though he at times hinted at or implied the logical existence of this third city, was dualistically emphasizing the City of Man and the City of God and largely internalizing both. First, the City of Man (more internal motives for Augustine), as argued throughout this text, is better referred to as the broader reality (internal motives or loves *and* flesh-and-blood civilizations) of the City of Antichrist. In Scripture, psychology, and sociology, the internal and the external exist in a kind of chicken and egg relationship. Second, there certainly is a Heavenly City or City of God, God's cosmic restoration and resurrection future, but it need not be presented in such dualistic or internalized terms and ideas so as to be largely disconnected from the earthly, cultural, urban, municipal, flesh-and-blood realities of the present moment. Hence, and third, there are therefore the loves and complex earthly layers of the City of Kingdom Approximation which already participates to some degree in the only true future.

THREE MAJOR FUTURE-VISIONS AS ENABLERS

Augustine's (amillennial) future-vision was rather dualistic and otherworldly on a host of issues, even while attempting to counter some elements of otherworldly Greek thought. The view that the Messiah returns and then establishes the reign of Messiah on earth (premillennialism) was the dominant view in the early church, but in that age of extreme persecution the premillennial future-vision also tended to be pessimistic about the age before Christ's earthly reign. Augustine's formulation was still quite otherworldly—understandably so given the historical context.

It was not until the optimism of the age of Modernism, roughly seventeenth century, that the church broadly began to consider the possibility that the kingdom of God could decisively rewrite history even to the degree where the Messiah's reign on earth could be realized prior to the return of the Messiah to earth. This optimistic future-vision has been referred to previously as postmillennialism. The three cities framework preserves the best of the three Christian future-visions, both theologically and in practice (e.g., postmillennial abolitionism, premillennial awareness of the power and spirit of antichrist and the actual reign of Messiah on earth, and amillennial awareness and discernment that the wheat and tares will grow together in this present age).

Nevertheless, the three major future-visions in the church, while affirming some truths within flawed systems, basically got it all wrong relative to the biblical future-vision. We can't usher in the kingdom of God (postmillennialism) prior to Messiah's return as the last few centuries have heralded to every corner of the globe, which should have been observed in clear biblical teaching about human nature. Yet the Messiah did initiate the future kingdom, sending forth Spirit-empowered believers as salt, light, and healing leaven to approximate the true future already, which foreshadows that day when history will be fulfilled when the Messiah renews or resurrects, rather than destroys or leads us in escape from, the New Heaven and Earth.

Our salvation story, avoiding hell and going to heaven, is part of something epic, much larger and far more profound than mere individual salvation—as important as individual salvation might be. When we grasp this larger framework for salvation, then our salvation propels us into the darkest of days and generations as world-influencing salt, light, and leaven. We've done it a thousand times before throughout history, and we can do it again.

CRITICAL EXCURSUS: AUGUSTINE'S FUTURE-VISION, SIN, AND EVIL

It goes beyond the scope of this work to critique Augustine's understanding of evil and sin as the absence or distortion of the good things God created, including viewing sin as misdirected love. Perhaps Augustine is correct in wanting to avoid viewing sin and evil as something that God creates or that somehow exists apart from the God who created all things.

Regardless, even if sin and evil initially involve seduction and misdirected love, Augustine's oversimplistic dualism again rears its ugly head and, therefore, by his own logic, and rather absurdly, reduces torture, genocide, the satanic and demonic, barbaric dictators, discord, sin, and even the hell of war itself to the misdirected love of the citizens of the earthly city.

Even if Augustine's "evil as the absence of good" and "sin as misdirected love" are assumed to be true, his oversimplified dualism is less than helpful. Clearly misdirected love, with some, morphs into more than misdirected love. This concept of sin as love means that someone is misguidedly seeking an actual good and somehow wakes up and rapes, tortures, or engages in the genocide of millions. Misdirected love may more appropriately apply to the early or embryonic stages of sin and evil where some are either seduced by others or enabled to do wrong by others who may well be authentic believers.

In Scripture, even if misdirected love is in any sense the core of sin, it often rapidly progresses to stubborn, impure, unholy, and demonic evil and opposition to God, love, justice, and everything pure and right. Scripture affirms that there are those who have progressed in darkness to the point that they are now "antichrists," regardless of whether misdirected love ever was a gateway drug to unspeakable evil.

Augustine refers to adversaries, evil citizens of the earthly city, antichrists, and the antichrist.[27] He seems intuitively to know that misdirected love or the absence of good fails completely to take into the account the reality and hateful dynamic of sin and evil. Misdirected passions become demonic, heartless, and unrelenting desires to hurt others and oppose God. Evil is evil.

Loving a false god rather than the only true God or desiring a false kingdom as a mere distortion of the desire for God's glorious kingdom (see neo-Augustinian Oliver O'Donovan's *Desire of the Nations*) are inadequate explanations of the evil opposition to God's kingdom and the merciless destruction of the good and human life. Indeed, the argument is rather contradictory and convoluted that the underlying desire for God's true kingdom becomes a merely distorted or misdirected love that includes totalitarian barbarism and genocide.

The killing fields in southeast Asia or the German concentration camps emerged merely from a misdirected, distorted, and underlying desire for the true King of kings? The worship of and servitude toward Stalin, Hitler, Nero, and Romulus certainly was misdirected love and the worship by some who were deceived, but for many it was nothing other than demonic-inspired hate of God and others.

---

27. See Augustine, *City of God*, 601–75.

ANTICHRISTISM: MORE THAN MISDIRECTED LOVE

Yes, there is seduction, and there is misdirected love and the absence of good, but there are also

- positively evil antichrists,
- those with unbridled hate of God and others who despise grace,
- countless millions who are being seduced but who also can be redeemed, and
- many enablers of antichrists both inside and outside faith communities.

Augustine is right that there are ultimately only two destinies, but the timetable of his future-vision is confused because in the present age many are, like Pilgrim in *Pilgrim's Progress*,[28] still on the journey and can be assisted by Evangelist, Christiania, Mercy, Great-Heart, Faithful, Helpful, Hopeful, Shepherd-Boy, Shining Ones, Unnamed Saint, Valiant, and, of course, Messiah. And Bunyan's journey narrative does not require a deterministic framework for salvation.

Hence, a proper future-vision and discerning approach to the ebb and flow of history, culture, the possibility of positive kingdom influence in the present, and the fluid state of faith communities require a less simplistic dualism, less determinism, and more distinctions and careful nuance. Augustine's *City of God* is genius, academic, and often leans toward the poetic and artistic.[29] However, a more accurate reading of how our faith and culture interact utilizes key scriptural categories and theological concepts fashioned from Scripture, centuries of historical evidence, and persuasive argument.

INTERPRETING HISTORY AND CULTURE THROUGH THE LENS OF ANTICHRIST AND APPROXIMATION

The scriptural categories of antichrist and the already initiated kingdom provide a helpful and robust lens for interpreting history and culture.

> For many deceivers have gone out into the world, those who do not acknowledge Jesus Christ as coming in the flesh. This is the deceiver and the antichrist. Watch yourselves, that you do not lose what we have accomplished, but that you may receive a full reward. Anyone who goes too far and does not remain in the

---

28. Bunyan, *Pilgrim's Progress*.
29. Augustine, *City of God*.

teaching of Christ, does not have God; the one who remains in the teaching has both the Father and the Son. If anyone comes to you and does not bring this teaching, do not receive him into your house, and do not give him a greeting; for the one who gives him a greeting participates in his evil deeds. (2 John 1:7–11)

Augustine's future-vision and countless other future-visions chart how our faith in the Messiah should relate to culture and civilization. We must begin, but not necessarily end, with Augustine. All of these eschatologies add to the great conversation, yet this work proposes that the ebb and flow of culture and history, the state of church, synagogue, and state, the nature of the mission of the church, and the very contours of authentic discipleship are greatly assisted by identifying these three key and powerful streams and cosmic actors.

1. **Antichrists.** These individuals, groups, communities, organizations, and nations oppose both the Judeo-Christian God and Judeo-Christian influence and advocate for and mediate great tribulation on earth.

    a. *Internal Antichrists. Antichrists*, false teachers, and false prophets promoting future-visions mostly *inside* of Judeo-Christian faith communities distort or destroy the church and, thereby, drive the arrow of history toward multiple and destructive tribulations. As noted previously, this work affirms conditional tribulationism.

    b. *External Antichrists. Antichrists*, false teachers, and prophets mostly operating *outside* of authentic Judeo-Christian faith communities undermine biblically flourishing individuals, communities, families, and nations while also influencing and deceiving "even the elect" if that is possible (Matt 24:14). This antichristism or opposition to God's plan for and influence on the world "he so loved" is referenced in Scripture but in recent centuries culminated in the insanely and creatively religious genius of Friedrich Nietzsche—"The Madman" who assaulted and proclaimed the coming cultural death of the Judeo-Christian God.[30] Nietzsche, as noted, viewed Judeo-Christian–influenced culture as the problem not the solution, and therefore ultimately served as an apologist for *The Antichrist*.[31]

---

30. Nietzsche, "Madman."

31. Nietzsche, *Antichrist*. The idea, in view of Nietzsche's literary genius, that Nietzsche employed terms and phrases like madman or antichrist accidently, rather than

2. *Enablers*

    a. **Orthodox Enablers.** Deceived or seduced *enablers inside biblical faith communities* and Judeo-Christian educational institutions, often well-intended, serve as powerful enablers of the spirit of antichrist and many antichristisms destroying church, synagogue, and state.

    b. **Unorthodox (or Heterodox) and Toxic Enablers.** Deceived or seduced *enablers inside* of *nominal and orthodox Judeo-Christian faith communities* serve as powerful enablers of the spirit of antichrist. Today this especially includes faith communities and Judeo-Christian educational institutions that have allowed their faith, beliefs, and virtually every key term to be largely or entirely and unbiblically redefined in order to accommodate to and comport with contemporary trends and values. This would also include organizations that engage in mission drift and fail to "contend earnestly for the faith that was once for all time handed down to the saints" (Jude 1:3).

    c. **Centurion-Like Enablers** (Matt 8:5–13). These are grace-assisted individuals, groups, organizations, and nations not consciously aligned with Judeo-Christian values and belief in the Messiah who nonetheless assist with making a positive impact on or contribution to church, synagogue, culture, and state. These enablers provide essential assistance to kingdom approximators.

3. *Biblical, engaged, and historically orthodox* **Judeo-Christian Approximators.** *These individuals, faith communities, other communities, organizations, and nations* truly stand faithful and are to some degree in the orbit of the Logos and the biblical line of promise to Abraham and his faithful descendants, thus blessing all nations in a provisional sense. They mediate Abraham's present and future kingdom blessings to the nations and peoples already. Approximators serve as Spirit-empowered and life-giving leaven, salt, and light in the church and the world. They approximate God's pure future individually, in faith communities, and in their civilizational and global impact. They especially approximate, to some degree, the next phase of God's restoration of the creation, which is the blessed transitional phase of Messiah's reign on earth preparing peoples and nations for the fullness of the New

---

very deliberately, including redeploying the biblical warning on the antichrist, seems absurd. He clearly was redefining definitions and inverting or transvaluing values.

Creation. Yet such victories or approximations in the present era are often only temporary, regional, or local (e.g., the abolition of slavery, infanticide, pederasty, prostitution, and female circumcision are true victories but simply take on new manifestations and garb through the centuries). Such approximations are windows to and down payments of the eternal future. These faithful and sacrificial believers approximate God's true future already—they are agents of approximation for time and eternity.

ANTICHRISTS, ENABLERS, AND APPROXIMATORS

To sum, the matrix, drama, nature, and flow of history is primarily an interface between antichrists, enablers, and approximators. These classifications avoid a simplistic dualism and determinism, which devalues the creation and the present age, and recognize historical fluidity, illuminate history and Scripture, integrate core and helpful aspects of Augustine's two cities and competing loves, explain the ebbs and flow of history and civilization, discern the complex state of church, synagogue, and state, and guide our preaching, discipleship, and mission.

This approximation and three cities model implies, and this work will continue to affirm, that the Messiah has already won the decisive battle in history and secured ultimate redemption and the coming paradise regained known as the New Heaven and Earth. Yet prior to that earthly Messianic reign, a reign that is only possible via the Messiah's supernatural victory, history is to some degree fluid and plastic (as noted, slavery may be outlawed in parts of the globe, biblical human flourishing may increase, and all who respond to grace may be saved and all can respond).

In the age before Messiah's earthly reign, the influence of that already initiated future reign and rule may, to some degree based on localities, approximate God's true future. Approximation, however, is contingent upon the interplay or interfacing of antichrists, enablers, and the grace-assisted loves, passions, commitment, actions, and sacrificial self-giving agape of Abraham's true and faithful descendants.

This work hopes to take first steps by directly addressing the seeming inability and floundering of Judeo-Christian believers, especially American evangelicals, to frame their cultural, intellectual, and civilizational engagement within a consistent, coherent, and persuasive future-vision. Believers who are engaged are typically focused on symptoms, symptoms, symptoms, and they confuse the inexhaustible toxic fruit with the root of the current civilizational crisis, and they are utopian or fatalistic and escapist.

Enablers are everywhere. Many Judeo-Christian faithful are largely disengaged, obsessed with or shaped by end-times' Last-Generationism, eschatomania, and waiting for escape just prior to the end of the world. Others, whether they properly interpreted Rod Dreher's *Benedict Option* or not, doubt if believers will escape the coming centuries of a new dark ages and are convinced that the curtain is now falling on Judeo-Christian–influenced civilization. The church's mission is to preserve and create Judeo-Christian–influenced culture for future generations, like the monks of the dark ages.

As noted, much of popular culture (e.g., humor, entertainment, dystopian movies), the new monastics, and the evangelical end-times' last generationists all seem to be somewhat addicted to a future-vision of darkness. The long shadows are everywhere as the sun dips below the horizon in what is perceived as *This Present Darkness*.

Enablers are everywhere and in every age. Throughout the history of the Judeo-Christian movement, many who have not been fully addicted to darkness and eschatomania have, nevertheless, and often unconsciously, adopted a key assumption of this Judeo-Christian fixation with darkness. This massively influential assumption is the otherworldly, non-Hebraic, and Greek (or Platonic or neo-Platonic) future-vision. Physical life on earth in the present is devalued or diminished. Such believers do not view the redemption of this present physical world, and our physical bodies, including our thoughts, as central to understanding God's glorious plan for their individual salvation and the coming New Heaven and Earth.

The theology of the escapist ticket to heaven is a primary enabler of the spirit of antichrist.

Enabler beliefs are everywhere. Higher education and lifelong learning are viewed as optional, based on personal interests or fiscal or career goals, and often defined as a waste of time and energy if not a threat to the soul. Bad education is a threat to the soul when dominated by the City of Antichrist. The City of Kingdom Approximation, in contrast, gives the faithful minds to love God, eyes to envision, ears to hear, and hands to contribute to the glorious New Creation cosmic symphony and epic journey—already, not just in a "bye and bye" heaven. Unfortunately, despite countless works by authors such as Mark A. Noll, Os Guinness, Dallas Willard, Josh McDowell, Gene Edward Veith, J. P. Moreland, N. T. Wright, Nancy Pearcey, and Alister McGrath, the scandal of the Bible-believing Christian mind persists and enables the dark city.

Enablers are indeed everywhere. Being Christlike or holy remains largely disconnected from being like Christ, the Logos, the ultimate source of all truth and wisdom, the very agent of creation, and the King of kings and Lord of lords. Believers are often permanently dependent children, exalting childlike faith (Matt 18:3) while actually modeling a childish faith largely disengaged from the mind, culture, and civilization unless seduced by said culture to contribute to the enfeeblement of the City of Kingdom Approximation.

The cities and concepts of antichrist and approximation frame and counter poisonous dualism, undermine contagious enablers, chart the epic and cosmic kingdom journey, affirm the more comprehensive and biblical understanding of salvation, and ultimately illuminate and unify the reality of sin and evil, the very good creation, the gracious incarnation, bodily resurrection, and God's glorious heaven and earth, time, and eternity. And the City of Approximation lures the faithful to passionate, effective, and holistic growth, service, ministry, mission, and their true destiny.

We can do better. And the better hopefully presented here is the biblically, theologically, historically, psychologically, and philosophically grounded theology of Approximation.

OVERVIEW OF REMAINING CHAPTERS

Now that the foundational pillars are hopefully in place, an intentionally belated preview of the remaining chapters should be more understandable. Likewise, this is an appropriate juncture for better clarifying the limitations and cautions related to this work and argument.

The critical distinction between the root and fruit of the current crises in church, synagogue, and state are further explored in chapter 4. Chapter 5 further demonstrates the evidence and implications of the fact that future-visions rule in Scripture, individuals, families, influential and historic leaders, communities, history, culture, civilization, church, and state. This all underscores why the kingdom of God is the key and life-giving future-vision of Christ and the whole of Scripture. The historic, volatile, and watershed nature of the current historical moment is addressed in chapter 6.

Chapter 7 synthesizes much in this work and highlights the need and correct approach and tactics that prepare the faithful for always being prepared for the age of antichristism and the increasingly emboldened City of Antichrist. That essential preparation includes a clear grasp and love of the inspiring and world-changing biblical and kingdom future-vision, in contrast to the legion, distorted, and toxic future-visions of the present age of antichristism. Such cultural and individual persuasion (graciously defending the faith, or apologetics) and properly responding to contemporary marginalization, ridicule, harassment, and persecution are assisted by refining the definition and understanding of antichristism in Scripture and in contemporary thought. Antichristisms include or have become manifest as toxic future-visions such as the many varieties of modernism and postmodernism, which will be briefly assessed.

Many of these various attempts to be liberated from Judeo-Christian influence addressed in chapter 7 certainly have been intensifying recently and serve as striking illustrations of contemporary AJC liberalism, for which the faithful need to be especially prepared. Liberalism, *properly defined* in chapter 7, is the attempt to liberate church, synagogue, and state from being formed and/or influenced by authentic, revealed, Judeo-Christian and biblical convictions, practices, thoughts, virtues, and passions (things that we quest for, envision, love, value, and practice). Such liberalism, simply stated, seeks liberation from the Judeo-Christian future-vision for this age and the next and proposes deceptive, sometimes demonic, always destructive, and counterfeit alternatives. These destructive alternatives are more fully responded to in a forthcoming and longer academic publication.[32]

The conclusion, "Always Be Prepared for New Creation and the Three Cities," details how those within the orbit of the Judeo-Christian future-vision can best counter antichristism and toxic liberalism and contribute to approximating God's future-vision now, already—even prior to the earthly reign of Messiah. Such approximation in the present age contributes to and is lured, guided, and normed by the New Creation City. The appendices supplement the argument of this work, including the embryonic Approximation Manifesto in appendix E.

As noted, while political and cultural engagement are essential and must be loving and shrewd, the epicenter or root of God's solution and program to redeem individuals, families, communities, and nations in the present age resides within transformative, transforming, revived, and Spirit-led biblical faith communities. Unfortunately, faith communities are often stellar enablers of antichrist ideologies and future-visions due to responding to the legion assaults on God's future by playing Whac-A-Mole or via the utopian, fatalistic, and escapist future-visions referenced previously.

A key theme in the remainder of this book is a slight modification of a well-known phrase: "We have met the principal enemies, and one of them is us."[33] This work seeks to focus on the root of the crisis, the spirit of antichrist, and the root of the solution, which includes renouncing the role of being enablers and embracing the full-orbed and Spirit-empowered realization of

---

32. The title has not yet been finalized.
33. Kelly, "We Have Met."

the biblical future-vision and theology of Approximation, starting with the true heirs of Abraham's cosmic blessing.

As noted, my multi-decadal background in strategic and tactical planning in higher education, including institutional effectiveness, assessment, accreditation, and continuous improvement, also has contributed to the contours and goals of this work. To be blunt, the response of God's people to the present crisis is an exemplar of anemic, flawed, and fragmented strategic and tactical planning. The toxicity of the enablers is one illustration. The Lone Ranger response of many Judeo-Christian leaders, where everyone is peddling some variety of an independent solution to civilizational collapse, is another telling illustration.

LIMITATIONS CONCERNING THE REMAINDER OF THE ARGUMENT

As noted previously, this current and more popular and accessible academic work is premised upon the research of an already drafted and lengthier—four hundred page, nearly two hundred thousand words, and one thousand footnotes—specialized academic work that should be released in 2024 or 2025. While this present and more popular academic book includes substantial documentation and argumentation, many additional arguments and extensive documentation may be found in the forthcoming and more specialized academic publication.

The argument of this work clearly has global implications in our interconnected world. However, it should already be clear and the rest of the work will reinforce that the primary focus concerns how biblically grounded and historically orthodox faith communities can navigate the contemporary context of proliferating AJCism in formerly Judeo-Christian–influenced civilizational experiments.

CAUTIONS CONCERNING THE REMAINDER OF THE ARGUMENT

Even the semi-careful reader will readily observe the attempt to precisely define and nuance the usage of terms, such as enablers, antichrist, antichristism, liberalism, and postmodernism. Special attention to definitions is essential to track with the argument, even though such is not an exact and precise science. The goal is increased not perfect understanding and semantics.

According to Scripture there are many antichrists, false prophets, deceivers, and angels of light in the world, yet the point of discussing the age of antichrist and antichristism is not to curse the darkness or engage in name calling with everyone with whom we disagree. We don't always or easily know the motives of others, and some are hurt and/or deceived while others are deceivers.

And because all are fallen, and even the redeemed are in process of restoration to the image of God, this work notes that many inside communities of faith are unintentionally wreaking havoc on church, synagogue, and state with false future-visions (e.g., escapism) that enable toxic future-visions, antichristisms, liberalisms (properly defined), and the spirit of antichrist. Indeed, from a biblical perspective, it is often the failures of the people of God that play a major role in civilizational decay and collapse. The problem is not always "out there" or "them" but "us."

Hence, this discussion of antichrist and antichristism is an attempt to synthesize biblical teaching with our contemporary Nietzschean moment of increasingly overt and militant antichristism in order to explore the present crisis and propose workable solutions or responses.

A true watershed moment and a profound challenge for present and future generations has arrived. Many kingdoms and civilizations that once had ears to hear and eyes to see the church tower bells breathing life into church, synagogue, and state and ringing across communities, cities, and lands have entirely lost their footing and direction on the journey toward God's true future. In many respects, the cultural train has left the station in countless nations—some time ago. Formerly Judeo-Christian soil is often now toxic to the only authentic and enduring future. The life-giving waters of our Judeo-Christian–influenced civilizations and nations began to dry up more than a century prior. History plods along for some time before the supply lines run short such that we all feel the impact of the civilizational betrayal of the God of Abraham, Isaac, and Jacob. Many are now feeling it, seeing it, hearing it, and suffering under emerging counterfeit cities and kingdoms.

The future effectiveness of the church requires further exploration and analysis of the relationship between the fruit and the root of the present crisis. The church especially should proffer guidance on how to distinguish between symptoms and root causes and provide genuine, biblical, and long-term cures and solutions.

CHAPTER 4

THE SYMPTOMS, ROOTS, AND FRUIT OF TOXIC VERSUS REGENERATING FUTURE-VISIONS

UNBIBLICAL DETOURS

The grand biblical mega-drama of the redemption of all things (Rom 8; Isa 11; Revelation) and the heavenly city descending to planet Earth too often has been reduced to the individual Christian escaping our physical planet and their physical body and getting a ticket to a largely or entirely nonphysical, otherworldly, spiritualized heaven. This ethereal assumption is truly more Greek than biblical/Hebraic or Christian. Scripture looks forward to the redemption, restoration, enhancement, and resurrection of God's good world that he so loved. Bodily resurrection is biblically and theologically central, nonnegotiable, and redefines everything, including the very nature of our salvation and the future of the cosmos. Cosmic resurrection rules.

For many faith communities, salvation is escape and unrelated to sacrificial (i.e., cruciform) and influential engagement with the present and co-regency with Christ in both the present (Eph 2:4–6) and the future. For such escapists, the essence of Christianity is the sinner's prayer not the integrated redemption of all things, which includes but is not limited to the salvation of individual sinners through the sinner's prayer.

CHILDISHNESS FOREVER?

For many believers, being saved and Christlike is almost entirely spiritualized and has little to do with actually being like Christ in every way that is possible and appropriate in this life and the next. There is little urgency and attention paid to maturing in order to be like the Logos, the very creator and sustainer of all things in every area of our life and being and behavior—head, heart, and hand. Learning to love God with the entire mind or plumbing the depths and complexities of true neighbor love and exploring every detail of God's majestic creation are considered optional. To again paraphrase John Wesley, we want to get to heaven but are barely fit for heaven—reigning with Christ forever.

How often have you heard a sermon calling believers to be fully Christ-like and share in the knowledge, wisdom, understanding, and creativity of things like the Creator's space-time continuum relativity, quantum physics, human psychology, political philosophy, the nature and flow of history, the complex beauty of music, or the four or more key fundamental forces of physics and the ten or more dimensions of the universe? Has the next generation been challenged to take up the vision of thinking God's thoughts after him as did so many of the pioneering Judeo-Christian scientists? Have all believers been encouraged to begin, already, the never-ending eternal process of fully exploring, understanding, and co-creatively stewarding and vice-reigning over all things in heaven and earth? Do young believers rush into science and law to secure a career and get a degree or to share in the Logos's cosmic wisdom and glory eternally? Do they have any grasp of the eternal significance of the Logos for daily life throughout eternity?

Are we learning to think like and be Logos-like eternal kings, queens, princesses, and princes, or are we content to be childish forever? Believers should be encouraged to have a trusting childlike faith (Matt 18:1–3; Luke 18:17). Unfortunately, they are also intentionally or unintentionally encouraged to remain childish, dependent children in this age and the next. This toxic future-vision has reduced the saints to children, fools, and, in some cases, holy morons, which is an oxymoron just as is the phrase holy child-abusers. Scripture is clear: "Do not be childish in your thinking; yet in evil be infants, but in your thinking be mature" (1 Cor 14:20).

In corrupt, unbiblical, and un-Logos-centered faith communities, higher education and personal, psychological, and holistic growth are viewed as personal preferences for those who enjoy or need such things for their career rather than a key and required implication of genuine longitudinal (long-term) salvation and being truly "fit for heaven"—authentic incarnational citizens of time and eternity. Heaven will be rather unheavenly, shallow, and drab unless we are increasingly and radically conformed to the glory of the Logos, the Ruler and agent of creation. Apart from a total renovation, we won't even be able to dwell with each other in joyous and intimate unity, much less be enthralled with every eternal moment forever.

Why spend years being holistically educated and studying things such as the robust *trivium* and *quadrivium* (i.e., integrated learning, including things like logic, persuasive speaking, grammar, writing, arithmetic, astronomy, music and the arts)? If the goal of life is to escape life on this earth and get to an otherworldly and largely non-physical heaven, why bother?[34]

Most believers I have encountered in multiple states and other countries, and even thousands of students in Christian liberal arts educational institutions, have never even heard of the *trivium* and *quadrivium*. Those influenced by Wesley and/or Calvin are typically clueless concerning the import and positive impact of Wesley and Calvin's very rigorous education (e.g., Oxford, Paris, Orleans, Bourges, *trivium*, *quadrivium*, philosophy, theology, law, languages).

Those who have reduced the massive or colossal nature of biblical redemption and salvation from cosmic salvation to escapist salvation understandably ask, "Why rigorously learn the details of disciplines like music theory, sociology, marine biology, organizational management, or cosmology and cosmogony?" Escapist and spiritualized believers who are childish forever might view studying and learning piano or tennis for decades as having some value for those who get into sports or music or who play piano in church, but it's not for everyone. The biblical truth is that God created all things, which were created very good, and therefore to some degree all things are intended for everyone.

Instead of becoming vice-rulers or co-regents with Christ, many remain co-childish and entirely dependent childish children forever. Rigorous growth and training are viewed as having no or a very narrow relevance to becoming like the Logos and preparing for co-regency in the restored creation—reigning throughout the cosmos that God so loves. Moral and spiritual likeness is oddly divorced from wisdom and mental or intellectual likeness. Redemption and resurrection are narrowed, limited, and not holistic.

We prepare ourselves for necessary jobs, making money, having a meaningful career, completing specific tasks, and to be providers, which of course all have value, but we see little connection between such growth and our preparation for time and our eternal future. We are more concerned with our retirement plans or 401Ks than with planning for our earthly and eternal co-regency with and infinite inheritance from the Messiah.

And what is the consequence of this small salvation theology? As with political and economic systems that create dependency, many believers only do what is absolutely necessary (e.g., pray the sinners' prayer, avoid gross

---

34. Cleary, "Understanding."

immorality, tithe, evangelize occasionally, and try to raise a decent family). Yet even John Wesley's "great salvation" theology, as helpful as that has been to the church, has often been overly spiritualized and reduced only to being spiritually or morally pure or holy. Scripture teaches both holiness and co-regency, which are inseparable, and the great salvation of individuals while central also must be unified with a theology of cosmic redemption.

It's past time to elevate the commendable Great Salvation theology to an even Greater Salvation theology for time and eternity. The great salvation is actually Mega-Salvation. It is of the highest rank and importance and truly colossal and functionally infinite in potential and scope.

Is it any wonder that harsh critics of Judeo-Christian faith and practice, such as Deists (i.e., modernist thinkers) or the postmodernist Friedrich Nietzsche, sense that the Judeo-Christian faithful really don't fully embrace life and the creation? From a biblical and Hebraic perspective, faith communities that devalue God's creation, the full restoration of the image of God including mind and body, the bodily resurrection, and the New Creation Consummation are corrupt or at least feeble. Such corruption impacts daily life, attitudes, values, human sexuality, preaching, teaching, worship, education, and the training of children and adults—and undermines cultural and intellectual engagement and kingdom approximation in the present age. Such corruption defines what we really love (*You Are What You Love*), which norms how we really think, or don't think, and live (*How Should We Then Live*).

THE ROOT AND FRUIT OF AUGUSTINE'S UNBIBLICAL DETOUR

In the previous chapter, we all too briefly introduced the brilliant, magisterial, and immensely creative two cities/two loves/two desires of Augustine. Augustine's *City of God*, written as Rome crumbled, for which Christians were being blamed, is advocating for the relevance of authentic biblical and Judeo-Christian beliefs and values to the earthly, heavenly, and spiritually flourishing of humans and the earthly success of cities and civilizations. Augustine, as noted, was engaging in public theology—how Judeo-Christian beliefs can contribute to the common good for all—even those who are not believers.

Yet Augustine reduces the two cities almost entirely to the internal desires or loves of humans. Those desiring salvation, primarily, are authentic or *bona fide* members of Christ's church and citizens of the City of God and the heavenly kingdom. Those pridefully and lustfully desiring their own glory and earthly power are citizens of the City of Man.

Augustine masterfully scaled the theological mountaintops of understanding fundamental motivations and culture, but he went too far—or perhaps not far enough. He ultimately over-spiritualized or over-internalized the central biblical motifs or dominant themes of kingdoms, cities, the kingdom of God, the New Jerusalem, the heavenly city, and the New Heaven and Earth. Augustine shifted his early theology and tragically rejected the idea of an earthly reign of Christ: He was amillennial (without or against the idea of a millennium, though premillennialism was held by most church fathers before his time).[35]

Augustine had no choice but to over-spiritualize. Early in his theological journey, he abandoned the idea, affirmed by virtually all Judeo-Christian believers until roughly the Christianization of the Roman Empire in the fourth century AD, that the nonnegotiable core biblical teaching was that Messiah would literally return and actually reign on earth. Yes, there is a spiritual core, properly defined, that lies beneath the two cities of Augustine, but these cities should point to real, flesh and blood, incarnational realities of good and evil, which changes everything relative to salvation, our purpose, and *How Should We Then Live* today, already, and forever.

Hence, the era and cities prior to Christ's return include but are far more robust and earthy than loyalties, loves, or desires. The City of Kingdom Approximation actually includes such loves as well as real world civilizational forms, realities, and consequences. Reflect on all that exists within an earthly city, from culture and crime to architecture and music—all can be influenced by antichrist and all can be influenced by God's true future and can approximate that future. The false glory of cities will be judged and pass away. The true glory of cities will be taken up into God's future and cosmic resurrection. The city of the bodily resurrection is our future.

In the present age, cities and civilizations conform, to one degree or another, not merely to perfected heavenly, spiritual love, but to the coming and very physical New Creation kingdom, city(ies), and civilization. *All* things are redeemed, restored, reborn, and resurrected.

And while the City of Antichrist in the present age certainly includes internal and misdirected loves, pride, lust, and the futile quest for temporary earthly power, this dark City is actually a real, physical, flesh and blood, brick and mortar, fiber-optic, wireless, and agrarian civilization. The City of Antichrist includes flesh-and-blood structures and systemic or organic—social, political, economic, cultural—sin and fully incarnate evil.

Perhaps even more essential to understanding the present age and civilizations, evil includes but is far more comprehensive and real than

---

35. For a helpful summary, see Landes, "Views of Augustine."

misdirected love or prideful and lustful desires or power-mongering. The spirit of the City of Antichrist is evil. It is real. It is earthly. It is earthy. It includes intentional opposition to everything the infinitely loving God of Abraham, Isaac, Jacob, Joseph, Isaiah, Mary, John the Baptist, Jesus, Peter, Paul, and John the apostle desires for individuals, families, communities, nations, and civilizations. It is dark. It is demonic. It doesn't just improperly love, for it hates humanity and the only true God. It is genocidal. It tortures, maims, arrogantly decapitates, rapes, confines, despises, cancels, and rejoices in pain and suffering. It loves carnage. It cringes and trembles at the name of the Messiah and the thought that "He will wipe away every tear from their eyes; and there will no longer be any death; there will no longer be any mourning, or crying, or pain; the first things have passed away" (Rev 21:4). It hates the Messiah. It hates Jesus. It loves hate.

The spirit of antichrist is mediated through deceivers, false prophets, antichrists, and angels of light. Those seduced by the spirit of antichrist, inside and outside of Judeo-Christian faith communities, are enablers. The spirit of antichrist forever seeks to build the City of Antichrist creatively in the present age and futilely to thwart forever or at least oppose the New Jerusalem in the next age—a flesh-and-blood civilization, culture, and cosmos. The battle is ancient, present, real, spiritual, physical, physical-spiritual, and future. The City of Antichrist cringes before that Great Day when "at the name of Jesus every knee will bow, of those who are in heaven and on earth and under the earth, and that every tongue will confess that Jesus Christ is Lord, to the glory of God the Father" (Phil 2:10–11).

Augustine's theological detour was masterful, creative, constructive, biblical, somewhat unbiblical, overly dualistic, over-spiritualizing, enabling, and deadly to the church but also inevitable given his otherworldly amillennial future-vision presupposition. In contrast to amillennialism, the more biblical pre-restoration age task or agenda is lovingly but truthfully to overcome the City of Antichrist and advance the City of Kingdom Approximation now as we journey to the New Creation Victory Day "world without end" (Eph 3:21 KJV).[36]

The good news is that the turning point D-Day victory is already, for the City of Antichrist and its counterfeit ruler and imposter have been

---

36. Intriguingly, the KJV translation of "world without end" has properly been replaced by countless versions that affirm something such as "to all generations forever and ever," or "for all ages of the ages forever." However, in some respects, our otherworldly and over-spiritualizing assumptions concerning terms such as forever, ages of the ages, and all generations (seen as a time reference to eternity) almost make the dated KJV translation more theologically accurate. The world, the creation, is truly without end and forever—because of the certainty of resurrection.

judged and mortally wounded. The outcome is certain. These counterfeit christs may continue arrogantly to rampage like wounded animals, yet they also tremble at the sound of the name of the only true King. The ultimate death of the City of Antichrist is certain, and V-Day is coming and is gloriously nearer each moment.

OTHER ROOTS AND FRUIT

Others are less otherworldly and rather suspicious about cocksure claims that we are living in the last days, or the last days of the last days, before the literal seven-year Great Tribulation. Yet this group of believers fatally accepts the absurd notion that Judeo-Christian core convictions, values, and assumptions have no relevance to the health and true *Desire of the Nations*.

These saints affirm that such beliefs and practices cannot or should not be employed to try and bend the public marketplace of ideas and culture toward God's true future. Such toxic future-visions for the era prior to Messiah's earthly reign propose an unconstitutional (in the American context) and strict separation not just between church, synagogue, and state—but also between the state and the biblical, life-giving values and living waters of God's people and culture. The living waters that can, in part redirect, redeem, "salt," and "light" our communal and civilizational life together are hoarded, stagnated, or hidden in the present age by this impulse to isolate from the great issues of the day.

In contrast to those who distance themselves from civilization for various reasons, some Judeo-Christian believers, as previously discussed, have naively and absurdly affirmed that the kingdom can be ushered in *prior* to the return of the Messiah. Such believers should be commended for leading numerous movements and ministries to rescue lives, communities, and nations. Theirs is quite an epic story. This often-untold story is that virtually every major social reform movement in revivalistic colonial America, Wesley's England, revivalistic America on the eve of the Civil War, and during much of the nineteenth and early twentieth centuries in America and across the globe were inspired by Christian eschatology and revivalism and led by Judeo-Christian saints.

Most of today's spiritual successors of these valiant and socially concerned faithful rightly have abandoned naive optimism, postmillennialism, and utopianism for more pessimistic future-visions. Only the actual or literal return of Christ can usher in Messiah's earthly reign. However, many such saints remain in the cultural trenches trying to make a difference for time and eternity, often suffering abuse from unbelievers and suspicion from escapist and separatist believers.

Yet, as noted, these valiant ones sometimes have schizophrenic or inconsistent future-visions; they are going to "save America and the world" in these last days before everything collapses.[37] Or they have simply exchanged large-scale social concern either for *preservative* social engagement (i.e., preserve the good in civilization as long as possible) or *symptomatic* social concern (i.e., valiantly addressing the symptoms via soup kitchens, poverty relief, fighting substance addictions, rescuing the oppressed and abused).

Utopian (or postmillennial) future-dreams ultimately collapsed, especially after two world wars and nuclear terror, and under the weight of history and the reality of human nature. This work argues that culture can be positively and partially influenced, but not fully redeemed, prior to Messiah's actual earthly rule and reign.

Disillusionment with such grand, utopian schemes and dreams fed the previously referenced cancers of fatalism, pessimism, escapism, and eschatomania that largely devoured the will and wisdom of American and global evangelical cultural engagement. The ship is sinking, so grab the lifeboats and save as many as possible. As noted previously, in this model things are getting worse and worse, and we can waste time better spent on saving souls than on futilely trying to love and serve others and future generations by bending culture toward the New Creation.

The classic illustration of life-boat evangelism and eschatology is from D. L. Moody, who seemingly forever influenced American and global evangelicalism. He famously said: "I look on this world as a wrecked vessel. God has given me a life-boat, and said to me, 'Moody, save all you can.'"[38] The appropriate response to this future-vision, just like those going down with the Titanic, was to "save all you can." History is getting darker and darker. The darkness results from the fact that humanity is repeatedly a failure in every dispensation or historical age. Moody's pessimism is critical to the current conversation of root, fruit, and enabling, for he "did more than anyone else to shape the nature of evangelical revivalism during the second half of the nineteenth century."[39] This fatal vision became the foundation for much of twentieth-century American evangelical otherworldly, escapist, fatalistic, speculative, and pessimistic theology and eschatology, which spread globally through aggressive missions, often seeking to reach all people groups to

---

37. Schizophrenia is used here as a confused mental state characterized by inconsistencies, contradictions, and cognitive (mental) dissonance (discord).

38. Moody, "Return," 185.

39. Nash, *Evangelicals*, 52.

spark the return of Christ—or at least reach all groups before the return of Christ. This fatal vision remains influential in the present century.

Again, contemporary American and global evangelicalism, initially emerging out of the Protestant Reformation and John Wesley's heart-warming and heart-changing experience, emphasizes the evangel or good news, being born again through a personal relationship with Christ, biblical authority, and essential Christian and biblical beliefs. This movement has often been hijacked by Last-Generationism.

CERTIFIABLE COLLECTIVE INSANITY?

As an avid reader of historical works, novels, official communications, and even letters and diaries rising from the shadows, fires, and conflicts of World War II,[40] one common phrase used by many inside and outside of Germany was the query as to whether "the world had gone mad." Nearly a century later, many today of diverse perspectives, politically left and right, have concluded that, indeed, the entire globe, or at least significant regions such as North America and Europe, have become disconnected from reality and reached the point of certifiable collective insanity: "The World Has Gone Mad."[41]

This brave new world is no doubt emotionally jarring but from a biblical perspective should not be surprising, and I am not referring to the simplistic, reckless, and escapist analysis that claims to know that we are literally living in the last days or generation before "The" antichrist and Armageddon. Vast swaths of civilization, once influenced by the values and future-vision of the biblical Messiah or Logos, have vaporized the civilizational glue that grounded us and bound us together into a relatively joyous community, even while recognizing subcultures of injustice, oppression, and misery. Today many do actually revel in the glory of the loss of community, increasing fragmentation, anxiety, isolation, violence, and sadness. How sad.

The nearly omnipresent church towers that represented a culture influenced by the Messiah or Logos are now relics, or tombs and sepulchers (says Nietzsche) of the biblical God. We are increasingly, barely, and rarely Logocentric. This void from our loss of the Logocentric soul of civilization has been replaced with a so-called neutrality or pseudo-neutrality, which is

---

40. *Reader's Digest Illustrated Story of World War II.*

41. Veith, "World Has Gone"; Blumenthal, "In a World"; Lowry, "Australia"; Boteach, "Americans"; Black, "America's"; Livesay, "Have Americans."

often overtly or covertly engulfed by the spirit of antichristism or AJCism (see chapter 2).

The daily assault on Judeo-Christian–influenced faith communities and kingdoms is truly omnipresent, stunning, and toxic. This attack from the City of Antichrist is overt, covert, and frequent and frames our humor, politics, art, law, music, television shows, movies, communication, social media, and the very spirit of the age.

The definition or redefinition of virtually all words, concepts, values, and beliefs, both inside and outside of faith communities, is arguably one of the most critical roots producing the poisonous fruit of the City of Antichrist. As I have argued in numerous other venues dating back to writing and research in 2017, when we redefine the language, we redefine the future. Everything is being redefined everywhere and always.

In much of the world, language was to some degree in orbit around the Logos, the Word, the creator of humans in the image of God, and the very possibility and reality of communication, language, and words. Communication and civilization, with all its flaws, were largely Logocentric. On its best days, again with many admitted imperfections, civilization reflected the influence of the City of Kingdom Approximation.

Yet the City of Antichrist's endless seduction has been to compare better civilizations against perfection (utopianism) and then arrogantly declare that the best civilizations on the planet are irredeemably evil. Of course, AJC angels of light always have promises, solutions, and revolutions guaranteeing that if they are given endless power and resources, they can usher in antichrist's utopian kingdom.

The City of Antichrist's revolutionaries always deliver. They promise something approaching heaven on earth and actually deliver hell. They almost always replace flawed kings and kingdoms with even worse tyrants and genocidal maniacs claiming to liberate the people, the workers, and, finally, to implement social justice. Such is the consequence of the seductive City of Antichrist.

HEAD-IN-THE-SAND JUDEO-CHRISTIAN BELIEVERS AND ENABLERS

Amazingly, within this context, even believers who have not fully succumbed to escapism have often assumed cultural isolationism or pseudo-neutralism (false neutrality). One of the most seductive and toxic opiates of the present day is that as long as everyone remains neutral on controversial issues, there should be no reason why we "can't . . . all just get along." This seduction is central to many ideologies, including what is known as political Libertarianism.

Martin Neimöller's words, forged during the spreading fires of Nazism when the world was going mad, should be more than haunting and relevant today, and should serve as a sobering call to action:

> First they came for the socialists, and I did not speak out—because I was not a socialist.
> Then they came for the trade unionists, and I did not speak out—because I was not a trade unionist.
> Then they came for the Jews, and I did not speak out—because I was not a Jew.
> Then they came for me—and there was no one left to speak for me.[42]

The key is lovingly to speak out with true words (*logos/logoi*) before civilization disintegrates and offer the Logocentric solution of the City of Kingdom Approximation.

THE EXALTED ROOT: THE LOGOS AND YOU ARE WHAT YOU LOVE

The biblical Messiah or Logos, the very Word and eternal agent of creation, was never intended to be a superficial and simplistic means of escaping to heaven but the very spirit and truth of the ultimate future that changes everything and everyone now and forever—in this age and the glorious ages to come. Just as the Logos will someday establish the only authentic and enduring kingdom of justice and love, wise and humble cultures and civilizations sought, very fallibly because humans are fallen, to live in the shadow and dawning of that great day.

Can anyone seriously read and fully grasp John 1, Heb 1, and Rev 1 and not understand the absolute centrality of the Logos for literally everything in the present and future? The Logos brings approximation in the present and then final consummation and restoration in the New Heaven and Earth:

> God, after He spoke long ago to the fathers in the prophets in many portions and in many ways, in these last days has spoken to us in His Son, whom He appointed heir of all things, through whom He also made the world. And He is the radiance of His glory and the exact representation of His nature, and upholds all things by the word of His power. When He had made

---

42. Holocaust Encyclopedia, "Martin Niemöller."

purification of sins, He sat down at the right hand of the Majesty on high, having become so much better than the angels, to the extent that He has inherited a more excellent name than they. (Heb 1:1–4)

> In the beginning was the Word [Logos], and the Word was with God, and the Word was God. He was in the beginning with God. All things came into being through Him, and apart from Him not even one thing came into being that has come into being. In Him was life, and the life was the Light of mankind. And the Light shines in the darkness, and the darkness did not grasp it. (John 1:1–4)

> Then I saw a new heaven and a new earth; for the first heaven and the first earth passed away, and there is no longer any sea. And I saw the holy city, new Jerusalem, coming down out of heaven from God, prepared as a bride adorned for her husband. And I heard a loud voice from the throne, saying, "Behold, the tabernacle of God is among the people, and He will dwell among them, and they shall be His people, and God Himself will be among them, and He will wipe away every tear from their eyes; and there will no longer be any death; there will no longer be any mourning, or crying, or pain; the first things have passed away. . . . It is done. I am the Alpha and the Omega, the beginning and the end. I will give water to the one who thirsts from the spring of the water of life, without cost. . . . Behold I am coming quickly, and My reward is with Me, to reward each one as his [or her] work deserves. I am the Alpha and the Omega, the first and the last, the beginning and the end." (Rev 21:1–4, 6; 22:12–13)

Law, music, art, values, ethics, meaning, purpose, experiments in more perfect civilizations, and the entirety of cultures and civilizations have not and never can be perfected prior to Messiah's earthly reign. Yet on occasion and by grace the arrow or orbit of time and history sometimes has bent or been redirected toward Logos—the present has partially stepped into the future. By grace, in some respects the present approximated the coming kingdom—as when some nations outlawed slavery, established hospitals of mercy, launched Logos-centered education, properly defined their role as stewards and servants not lords, or elevated the rights of the weak and oppressed.

When Logocentrism was the exalted root and the fruit-bearing civilizational vine, kings, prime ministers, presidents, legislators, and justices sometimes understood they were merely *temporary* stewards,[43] humble subjects of a true and eternal King, and gracious servants of the King's children who sought fallibly to approximate the coming kingdom. This self-limitation of the powerful and the powers is right, proper, and *on bended knee*. The Logos, the wisdom, truth, future, and Messiah of God, became the life-saving oxygen of a better future already.

The values and ethics of ancient civilizations such as the Greeks, Romans, Egyptians, Assyrians, Babylonians, and Chinese have sometimes been moved toward the Logos. Civilizations like Rome were partially purified and redeemed, such as with the abolition of infanticide and pederasty. Yet many today, sometimes inspired by Nietzsche, the author of *The Antichrist*, want to return to the so-called glories, courage, "ethics," and drama of these civilizations.

"It has happened to them according to the true proverb, 'A dog returns to its own vomit,' and, 'A sow, after washing, returns to wallowing in the mire'" (2 Pet 2:22).

The crucified and coming Messiah or Logos was the undergirding Spirit and future-vision that touched and provisionally redefined and healed everything and everyone responsive to such sacrificial love and grace. Those willing to have their unresponsive hearts of stone replaced with living, responsive, and loving hearts of flesh finally capable of fully loving God and others (Ezek 36:26) truly stepped into God's future, provisionally fulfilled God's moral law, and became salt, light, and good leaven for the nations.

"Moreover, I will give you a new heart and put a new spirit within you; and I will remove the heart of stone from your flesh and give you a heart of flesh" (Ezek 36:26).

The promise that Abraham would bless all nations (Gen 22:18) has not been fully realized but was inaugurated and initiated wherever the Logos was received with genuine repentance, meaning a 180-degree turning away from sin and in sincere faith turning toward God.

"And in your seed all the nations of the earth shall be blessed, because you have obeyed My voice" (Gen 22:18).

Many sought to put the Messiah Logos at the center of all things, which overturned false thrones and persuasively rippled and shimmered across the waves of culture and civilization. Not only have truth, ethics, meaning, purpose, and the future been approximately or partially redefined by this Logocentric vision, but so have the very words that define reality.

Words lie at the center of cultures and civilizations and serve as the navigational chart for the spirit of the age. Today, our entire Logocentric

---

43. Smith, *Awaiting the King*.

vocabulary and values and the very definition of terms (i.e., our cultural lexicon) are being redefined or replaced, from marriage and gender to inclusion, justice, compassion, open borders, and love.

The Logocentric plumb line has vanished as we fall through the void into the arms of antichristism. Like a dog returning to its vomit, we passionately and sometimes militantly advocate for exchanging the City of Kingdom Approximation for the City of Antichrist. Indeed, we demonize the citizens of the only true city of the only enduring future.

"Hold on to the example of sound words which you have heard from me, in the faith and love which are in Christ Jesus" (2 Tim 1:13).

"The things which you have heard from me in the presence of many witnesses, entrust these to faithful people who will be able to teach others also" (2 Tim 2:2).

Everyday existence, even in less than perfect kingdoms once pulsating with the partial influence of the living waters of the Messiah, was often filled with meaning, purpose, a sense of undergirding truth and morality, shared community, and hope. The dark side can only celebrate the current denigration of the value of everything inherited from the City of Kingdom Approximation. Wild-eyed Nietzsche certainly is smiling concerning this redefinition or transvaluation of words, phrases, meaning, and values—Nietzsche's future-vision rules.

Hence, is it any wonder that when we flee the Logos we lose words, God, truth, meaning, purpose, freedom, and exchange less than perfect kingdoms for purgatory or hell on earth? Should we be surprised when every word and value is being systematically redefined, daily? Does it not naturally follow from the growth of the City of Antichrist that a majority no longer embraces any meaningful concept of normative truth and morality or even the meaning of meaning or the meaning of words?

If it seems we have lost touch with reality, does that not follow from the cultural eclipse of the rightful center of reality and agent of creation, the Logos? Why are we shocked at how quickly cultural sanity and what used to be viewed as common sense are on life support? Why do so many care less about common sense or deny its existence? Is it not inevitable that a variety of toxic future-visions, including dystopian visions, have captured the centers of creativity, imagination (or imaginaries), and power? The assault on the Logos and the words of the Logos inevitably birth cultural insanity and the refrain, "Has the world gone mad?"

WHAC-A-MOLE SOLUTIONS, ROOT, FRUIT, AND ENABLERS

As noted, the intentions of the valiant mole-whackers are noble, but they never seem to identify or focus on the underlying root and spirit of antichristism that animates, guides, and norms these legion movements and future-visions.[44] Whac-A-Mole refers to "a situation in which repeated efforts to resolve a problem are frustrated by the problem reappearing in a different form."[45] The spirit of antichrist is certainly full of bad ideas and especially toxic future-visions, but at the unifying and animating core is what John the apostle refers to as the spiritual force (1 John 4:3; 2:18–24) that opposes confessing Messiah, and the work, influence, beliefs, practices, and loves of the Messiah.[46] The problem is much deeper and more systemic and profound than one ideology or future-vision. Focusing on one future-vision is akin to chasing the unarmed robber in your garage while a platoon is taking over your house.

Biblically orthodox Jews and Christians try to use single issues, such as communism, moral relativism, and gender issues, as wedge strategies to influence and leverage their way back into the cultural conversation. While we may or may not have lost the cultural war or battle in any given kingdom, a reasonable gauge of civilization today confirms that this wedge or single-issue strategy clearly is failing.

This wedge strategy is also irrational. Those not sharing Judeo-Christian beliefs and assumptions are inhabiting different conceptual, worldview, literary, artistic, ethical, and verbal (i.e., semantic) universes.[47] Advocacy for single issues as a means to "save America" only exacerbates confusion, hinders effective communication, and inflames militant antichristism. This is especially and increasingly evident in social justice and gender conflicts. This is not to say that such legal and cultural issues should not be addressed, but we often have tactics without a strategy that touches on the root causes and solutions for civilizational decay.

As already argued, assuming that Marxist threats have been properly assessed, the elimination of Marxism (or *American Marxism*) tomorrow would still leave in place incalculable and toxic cancers that devour faith communities and nations. For example, not only would countless toxicities persist, but radical postmodern moral relativism, with its shameless

---

44. See the preface and introduction for a foundational background on the discussion in this chapter.

45. *Free Dictionary*, s.v. "Whack-a-mole."

46. The loves of the Messiah simply refers to that which the Messiah loves and draws upon the general concept in Smith, *You Are What You Love*.

47. Sire, *Universe*.

disregard for truth and meaning, its corruption of language, and its replacement of normative truth and ethics with deceptive tribal power games, would still remain. Indeed, many contemporary and new or neo-Marxisms have been rocket-fueled by such radical postmodern root assumptions.

Hence, to use familiar biblical imagery, you can cast out the civilizational demons of Marxism or partial-birth abortion yet myriad fallen angels still remain intact and flourish. Why? Unless the spirit of antichrist is addressed, the fruit of antichrist will continue to blossom, proliferate, seed the entire planet—and write the pages of future history.

Indeed, not only do these toxic future-visions share assumptions, values, beliefs, and the spiritual force of antichristism, they also reinforce, nurture, and fuel each other. For example, our post-truth moral relativism provides rocket fuel to those who argue that since there is no normative truth or ethics, all that remains is saying and doing whatever is necessary to advance the individual or the individual's tribe or cause. We are way beyond justifying spin today—all is spin, spin and lies are the same, lies are moral, and lies are powerful means of attaining social justice for oppressed tribes.

Such tribalism rules, but it is a symptom of something much deeper. The Logos creates the only true and enduring tribe, the children of Abraham, so the flight from the Logos into reality is a flight toward tribalism, fragmentation, and, ultimately, tyranny as someone or something seeks to bring order to the chaos or to exalt their very temporary tribe.

The spirit of antichrist is a collection of loves, passions, ideologies, and practices that coalesce in legion future-visions. And getting at the root recognizes that such future-visions not only share normative assumptions and beliefs, but they also are empowered by the spirit or spiritual force of antichrist. Unfortunately, many of those claiming to follow the Messiah are powerful enablers of false future-visions and antichristism (see chapter 3).

The spirit of antichrist runs far deeper than any single challenge, issue, or assault on the faith once delivered. It is a spirit. It is a spiritual force. It is ideology. It is the convergence and overlap of key affirmations by the opponents of Logos Messianism, from Voltaire, Feuerbach, Marx, and Nietzsche to Sartre, Russell, O'Hare, George Carlin, Foucault, Dawkins, and Oprah—to enumerate but a small list. It is most influentially, classically, and creatively articulated by Nietzsche as a stinging critique of Judeo-Christian culture, civilization, and its God. It especially is a spirit and future-vision where Judeo-Christian influence is marginalized, canceled, oppressed, criminalized, or eradicated.

POST-CHRISTIAN, POST-CHRISTENDOM, OR ANTICHRISTISM?

The tectonic level activity of the potent and pervasive spirit of antichristism today is often glossed over by terms such as post-Christian, post-Christendom, or postmodern. There never was and never will be a truly neutral age, especially after the age of Judeo-Christian–influenced civilizations, that can be referred to merely as post-Christian or post-Christendom. Present reality is more than "post."

It is preposterous to suggest that any civilization could traverse from foundational Judeo-Christian pillars and imbedded Judeo-Christian–influenced culture to another civilization or so-called neutrality without eventually and ultimately rejecting the biblical belief that Messiah is savior and King of kings—Messianism. As noted previously and throughout this work, religious neutrality, freedom of speech, and the strict separation of church, synagogue, and state—all concepts with some value if properly defined and contextualized—have proven to be used as tools for covert, incremental, wedge strategies and smoke screens that pave the way for an increasingly militant culture of AJCism.

Libertarianism, well-intended and properly concerned about governmental overreach, is naively and especially an enabler of antichristism. The banishment of the Logos and Ten Commandment morality from civilization does not yield toleration and "live and let live." It simply enables an intolerant tyrant to ascend the throne, redefine everything, and implement and despotically mandate thousands of new commandments at the end of a sword.

The allegedly biased Ten Commandments are never simply taken down in order to be neutral. The Ten Commandments are replaced with a hundred or a thousand new commandments. Humanity is innately communal and moral by nature. Even those rejecting morality create their own moral norms and commandments—which are often rather legalistic and oppressive even if sold as liberty or anarchy.

To illustrate, Germany in the late 1930s was far more than post-Semitic; it was becoming militantly anti-Semitic. The *Kristallnacht* (the Night of Broken Glass), not coincidentally the year prior to World War II, was not the neutralization of Jewish influence on culture but the first phase of breaking, crushing, and eradicating of Jews and Jewish influence. The vandalism and destruction of Jewish-owned businesses, synagogues, and homes that left broken glass everywhere was simply the first phase of the confiscation of all Jewish property, power, and freedoms—and eventually the theft of millions of Jewish lives.

The prefix *post*, in post-Christendom, post-Christian, and postmodern is less than helpful. Post does not define the new age or era or the conceptual and spiritual root of the age. Post-pregnant hardly captures the full-orbed and rich reality of being a new mother. Post-Semitic should be an insulting term for Jews as it glosses over the demonic. The myth of neutrality has resulted in our age being categorized in a nonspecific fashion, such as post-Christendom, or postmodern, which is also a strategy for subversion—this subversion illustrates Nietzsche's redefinition or revaluation of all values.

Post-Christendom is a particularly seductive term as it covertly implies that the underlying spirit of the age is simply the desire to move away from too-close association between church, synagogue, and state—perhaps a great thing according to many naive scholars and undereducated Judeo-Christian leaders. Hence, anyone who advocates for the value of significant Judeo-Christian influence on civilization is a theocrat or a dominionist, wanting to take over nations with Oliver Cromwell–like or Islamic-style conquests, caliphates, or Sharia law.

Many Judeo-Christian leaders and friends today almost seem welcoming or even giddy about the prospect of believers heading back to the monasteries or the catacombs—as if the only choice in a democracy is between church-state union or persecution. While such historic crucibles may well reveal and purify true believers, such a giddy approach or posture is the opposite of neighbor love, care for children, grandchildren, and posterity. It is the opposite of responsible citizenship relative to the biblical calling to serve as salt, light, and leaven and to disciple the peoples of all nations in this so-called postmodern age.

Syncretistic ultramodern or syncretistic late modernity are much better descriptors for the current age than postmodern for such terminology at least defines the present as the latter unravelling stages of modernity. Our age is like a vehicle running on fumes to some degree or like the rotting and decaying remains of the arrogant, so-called scientific rational and enlightened, modernist monster. The modernist experiment and modernist pride or *hubris* are fragmenting. Unfortunately, postmodernist pride and *hubris* are fomenting and now arguably overtaking modernist arrogance. Many modernists, who at least claimed to be in submission to the norms of science and reason, appear humble amid our late postmodern age of outrage, anger, suppression, and cancelation of people and free speech. Perhaps the modernist *hubris* of the French Revolution or communist liberators was equally arrogant, but many modernists (or classical liberals) defended free inquiry and speech guided by reason and science.

In rejecting any ultimate norm for truth and morality, such as Logos, all that is left for our age is tribalism and syncretism. Fight for your tribe, and since there is no ultimate standard for truth, mix beliefs and practices together even if they are contradictory as long as they work for you or your tribe (syncretism). Syncretism means merging beliefs and practices (syn, "together") that often are largely or entirely contradictory (Cretan, meaning "logically at war").

Indeed, our current age reflects the ultimate syncretism—the irrational mixing together of modernism and postmodernism or anti-modernism!

Many today are pro-reason and anti-reason and proudly contradictory. Buffet AJC spirituality is in. Some are antiscientific and anti-technological yet addicted to technology and parasitical on science. Many use words and technology to reject words and technology. The loudest critics of modernism often utilize and are dependent on the tools and benefits of modernism and thus self-devour the ground upon which they stand. Yet the fundamental root and passion at the core of much of this present age is the desire to move well out of orbit of the biblical Messiah and Logos. AJCism rules.

Today, Judeo-Christian ministers try to speak to the head when the head already has been either subtly or overtly indoctrinated by at least two generations of AJC education and culture. Or the head has been dismissed, in liberal churches and synagogues which have bowed to contemporary culture, as inferior to tribe, passion, self-expression, and revolution. Today evangelicals also often ignore the hurts, stories, loves, passions, and hearts of those who no longer or never have been servants of the Messiah, and whose hard, stony hearts have never undergone spiritual open-heart surgery and received a new responsive heart of flesh from Messiah. Unless root issues related to both head and heart are addressed respectfully, tactfully, tactically, and appropriately, antichristism will continue to advance and Judeo-Christian helping hands will be feeble.

To summarize and review, the opposition to the biblical God and God's rule inside and outside of faith communities is the spirit of antichrist. The opposition to God's current and future rule outside of the church is increasingly militant and especially includes the unbiblical or anti-biblical though sometimes seductive redefinition of virtually every belief, term, and value or what Nietzsche referred to as the reevaluation or transvaluation of all values. The emerging future-vision and spirit of the present age affirms that values taken for granted in Judeo-Christian–birthed and influenced civilization need to be replaced or transcended (move above and beyond such values). And with Nietzsche, Judeo-Christian values must be replaced with the values of superior Greco-Roman and/or other cultures and civilizations.

Marriage, truth, gender, morality, justice and social justice, civilization, faith, freedom, freedom of speech, compassion, love, Christian, Jesus, tolerance, democracy, terrorism, inclusion, and multiculturalism have all been radically redefined, and biblical dissenters need to be marginalized, diminished, demeaned, shamed, or permanently silenced. We live in an age of anti-Logos and verbal or semantic seduction, manipulation, and warfare.[48]

FALSE PROPHETS, FALSE WORDS, AND THE LOGOCENTRIC PLUMB LINE OF SCRIPTURE

Throughout history the biblical plumb line has sought to return individuals, cultures, and nations to increased alignment with God's standards and the coming New Creation—beginning with the people of God:

> Behold I am about to put a plumb line [righteous and holy standard]
> In the midst of My people Israel.
> I will not spare them any longer.
> The high places of Isaac will become deserted,
> And the sanctuaries of Israel will be in ruins.
> Then I will rise up against the house of Jeroboam with the sword. (Amos 7:8–9)

Deception inside and outside of Judeo-Christian faith communities, including verbal seduction, should come as no surprise to the biblical faithful. The Old Testament authors, Jesus, Paul, and other biblical writers such as Peter made repeated and passionate appeals to the saints:

> For we did not follow cleverly devised tales when we made known to you the power and coming of our Lord Jesus Christ, but we were eyewitnesses of His majesty. (2 Pet 1:16)

> But know this first of all, that no prophecy of Scripture becomes a matter of someone's own interpretation, for no prophecy was ever made by an act of human will, but men moved by the Holy Spirit spoke from God. (2 Pet 1:20–21)

> Therefore let's make every effort to enter that rest, so that no one will fall by following the same example of disobedience. For the word of God is living and active, and sharper than any two-edged sword, even penetrating as far as the division of soul and spirit, of both joints and marrow, and able to judge the thoughts and intentions of the heart. And there is no creature hidden from His sight, but all things are open and laid bare to the eyes of Him to whom we must answer. (Heb 4:11–13)

---

48. See Matthews, "Seduced?"

> But *false prophets* [*pseudoprophētai*] also appeared among the people, just as there will also be *false teachers* [*pseudodidaskaloi*] among you, who will secretly introduce destructive heresies, even denying the Master who bought them, bringing swift destruction upon themselves. Many will follow their indecent behavior, and because of them the way of the truth will be maligned; and in their greed they will exploit you with *false words* [*plastois logois*]; their judgment from long ago is not idle, and their destruction is not asleep. (2 Pet 2:1–3; emphasis added)

Peter, reaffirming the whole of Scripture, condemns false prophets, who are false teachers who use false and deceptive words and who contradict eyewitness testimony to the historical reality of God's mighty acts and revelation in history. False teachers also undermine the inspiration of Scripture and normative, revealed truth and morality and try to use false words to subvert, or transvalue, the truth. Enablers inside faith communities fail to discern the threat and presence of counterfeit words, teachings, beliefs, and practices.

The sirens of verbal seduction and manipulation have enraptured many inside faith communities—individuals, organizations, denominations, and religious traditions. In Scripture this subversion is the work of "false prophets," "false messiahs," and "many antichrists" (Matt 24:24; 1 John 2:18).

The Messiah, the Logos who created and who defines reality and meaning, and serves as the plumb line or north star for the proper use of words, stands in opposition to false words (*logois*), false prophets, false teachers, and false messiahs or christs. The restoration of Logos-centered loves, passions, beliefs, teachings, practices, and words is the antidote to the poisonous root of antichristism.

Many, but not all, religious leaders of Jesus' day were anti-Messiah or anti-Christ. They used and twisted words and Scripture to redefine the Messiah, Jesus, as a false Messiah. They rejected the very Messiah for whom they said they were waiting for centuries. They were, according to the Logos or Messiah, whitewashed, hypocritical, false prophets. Jesus predicted that "false christs and false prophets will arise and will provide great signs and wonders, so as to mislead, if possible, even the elect" (Matt 24:24).

Those who oppose, subvert, or distort the faith are antichrist, and their deception targets everyone inside and outside faith communities, including the faithful or elect. Indeed, history has demonstrated how the deception outside faith communities (e.g., Deism) becomes the deception and distorted beliefs within faith communities (Deistic or Latitudinarian "Christianity").

Such is the root spirit of antichrist and antichristism. Such is the work of many antichrists. And these seducers are enabled by the faithful who are deceived or who misunderstand their own faith (e.g., fatalistic escapism or liberal/redefined Christianity) and who fail to grasp the broad implications of biblical faith for kingdom service and cultural engagement. God's kingdom influence is detoured, delayed, hindered, redefined, and thwarted by antichrists, false christs or messiahs, false prophets, and enablers inside and outside the community of faith.

The way forward is going back to the biblical future-vision. What is needful is the Spirit-led and discerning return to and creative application to the present context and current crisis the individual's and the faith community's encounter with the Messiah/Christ and the plumb line of the inspired Word and the Logos. The Bible used to serve as a foundational and influential plumb line or measuring rod that influenced art, culture, law, humor, music, education ("The Old Deluder Satan Act," *McGuffey Readers*), the very definition of terms (e.g., justice, compassion, freedom, love), popular entertainment (*The Sound of Music*), literature and movies (*Ben Hur*), secret war codes, and future-visions of freedom ("I Have a Dream").

We have lost our plumb line. We have lost our center and cultural glue. The new glue and centers simply will not hold. We have lost the meaning of meaning and words and the very hope for hope. We have exchanged the pursuit of truth for shameless spin, lies, and militant and sometimes violent advocacy. We have made perpetrators victims and victims perpetrators. Civilization has been turned upside down or inverted. The world has increasingly gone mad. Nietzsche's future-vision rules.

We have lost the intangible spirit that binds us together, often joyfully, as a community. How tragic for new generations never to have experienced at least some sense of civilizational community, even in less than perfect kingdoms. We now arguably have lost most of our sense of community in the name of progress while birthing even worse kingdoms.

We have lost the safety and security that most need to improve their lives, families, and communities. We have lost love and forgiveness. We have taken incivility to a new low and tribalism to a new high. We no longer seek consensus and the consent of the governed on our journey toward a better future, but gravitate toward deception and raw power. Truth and morality have been entirely reduced to whoever wins; our meaning and purpose is less than artificial, self-created or tribally created, and fleeting. We have made the people servants and the public servants unaccountable gods who endlessly manipulate and disappoint.

We all know that something has gone terribly wrong as we careen out of orbit of the Logos.

We have lost ourselves and our one true God. Is it any wonder that, with Nietzsche, many are falling, falling, falling into the infinite colorless void, all the while unsuccessfully pretending that our new future-visions are leading us to a post-Judeo-Christian and much improved world?

CHAPTER 5

THE IRREFUTABLE EVIDENCE

FUTURE-VISIONS RULE IN SCRIPTURE—AND EVERYWHERE

Where there is no vision, the people are unrestrained,
But happy is one who keeps the law.
—PROVERBS 29:18

This is an age of the world when nations are trembling and convulsed. A mighty influence is abroad, surging and heaving the world, as with an earthquake. And is America safe? Every nation that carries in its bosom great and unredressed injustice has in it the elements of this last convulsion.... O, Church of Christ, read the signs of the times! Is not this power the spirit of Him whose kingdom is yet to come, and whose will to be done on earth as it is in heaven?... Christians! Every time that you pray that the kingdom of Christ may come, can you forget that prophecy associates, in dread fellowship, the *day of vengeance* with the year of his redeemed? A day of grace is yet held out to us.... Not by combining together, to protect injustice and cruelty, and making a common capital of sin, is this Union to be saved,—but by repentance, justice and mercy; for not surer is the eternal law by which the millstone sinks in the ocean, than that stronger law, by which injustice and cruelty shall bring on nations the wrath of Almighty God!

—HARRIET BEECHER STOWE, *UNCLE TOM'S CABIN* (1852)[1]

1. Stowe, *Uncle Tom's Cabin*, 267. In an irony of history, some today like to emphasize

The world will little note, nor long remember what we say here, but it can never forget what they did here. It is for us the living, rather, to be dedicated here to the unfinished work which they who fought here have thus far so nobly advanced. It is rather for us to be here dedicated to the great task remaining before us—that from these honored dead we take increased devotion to that cause for which they here gave the last full measure of devotion—that we here highly resolve that these dead shall not have died in vain—that this nation, under God, shall have a new birth of freedom, and that government of the people, by the people, for the people, shall not perish from the earth.

—Abraham Lincoln, "The Gettysburg Address" (1863)[2]

THE CENTRALITY OF KINGDOM FUTURE-VISIONS: ESCHATOLOGY RULES

Future-visions rule. This statement is repetitious but essential in order to redirect, recreate, and optimize faith communities. The way forward and only true hope for humanity, created to be in the image of the Logos, is the eschatology of the Logos. The Judeo-Christian future-vision is central to and pervasive throughout the entire biblical narrative, from Genesis and the Exodus to the Gospels and Revelation. This future-vision includes the incarnation, birth, teaching, prayers, parables, ethics, actions, attitudes, ministry, cross, resurrection, and ascension and sending of the Spirit that grounds and defines the return and final victory of Messiah, the Lamb and Lion, King of kings, Lord of lords, and Alpha and Omega.

The evidence is clear. Ancient, medieval, modern, late modern, postmodern, or ultramodern future-visions have ruled the masses, kings, and kingdoms:

---

the apocryphal nature of Lincoln's statement that Stowe was the "little woman that started" the "great war," and others claim that Stowe perpetuated and popularized negative stereotypes. In reality the apocryphal story contains some truth as the novel, one of the most popular in American history and during the decade prior to the Civil War, undoubtedly raised the consciousness of many, especially in the North. It is even more ironic and amazing that contemporary self-righteous ultramodern or postmodern scholars who regularly emphasize cultural context, historical context, and theological contextualization seem incapable of or unwilling to appreciate the historical context and contributions of others. Setting aside the perpetual debate about identity politics, the future-vision of Stowe's work was historic. Concerning debates on Stowe's legacy, see *Encyclopaedia Britannica* Editors, "Uncle Tom's Cabin."

2. Lincoln, "Gettysburg Address."

- from Greek, Roman, Asian, African, and Egyptian mythology to Augustine's *City of God*;
- from the Puritan influenced and American City Set on a Hill more perfect union to Harriet Beecher Stowe's abolitionist prophecy and eschatology that America must repent or perish;
- from Martin Luther King's "I Have a Dream," to myriad revolutionary ideologies (often rejecting King's future-vision and) advocating some form of manipulative socialism, to current dystopian denials of the possibility or even desirability of seeking paradise or utopia. Listen closely to King's kingdom eschatology:

> I say to you today, my friends, that in spite of the difficulties and frustrations of the moment, I still have a dream. It is a dream deeply rooted in the American dream. I have a dream that one day this nation will rise up and live out the true meaning of its creed: "We hold these truths to be self-evident: that all men are created equal." I have a dream that one day on the red hills of Georgia the sons of former slaves and the sons of former slave owners will be able to sit down together at a table of brotherhood. I have a dream that one day even the state of Mississippi, a desert state, sweltering with the heat of injustice and oppression, will be transformed into an oasis of freedom and justice. I have a dream that my four children will one day live in a nation where they will not be judged by the color of their skin but by the content of their character.
>
> I have a dream today. I have a dream that one day the state of Alabama, whose governor's lips are presently dripping with the words of interposition and nullification, will be transformed into a situation where little black boys and black girls will be able to join hands with little white boys and white girls and walk together as sisters and brothers.
>
> I have a dream today. I have a dream that one day every valley shall be exalted, every hill and mountain shall be made low, the rough places will be made plain, and the crooked places will be made straight, and the glory of the Lord shall be revealed, and all flesh shall see it together.
>
> This is our hope. This is the faith with which I return to the South. With this faith we will be able to hew out of the mountain of despair a stone of hope. With this faith we will be able to transform the jangling discords of our nation into a beautiful symphony of brotherhood. With this faith we will be able to work together, to pray together, to struggle together, to go to jail

together, to stand up for freedom together, knowing that we will be free one day.[3]

Humanity and civilization not only seek and desire God—which Augustine frequently emphasized. We are also thoroughgoing kingdom-seekers, desiring, loving, and seeking a flesh-and-blood kingdom city and community, whether it be Christ's kingdom, or Hitler's Third Kingdom (Reich), or Marx's classless society, or a City Set on a Hill, or Manifest Destiny, or the Great Society, or the War to End All Wars, or authentic existence (being real or true to ourselves), or economic flourishing, or spiritual flourishing, or Chinese social and familial solidarity, harmony, and balance. Kingdom-visions rule.

Some might say that technology not eschatology now rules. However, technology and even AI (artificial intelligence) exist within a cultural and political future-vision framework that guides its application. Unfortunately, some tech leaders today have mixed together technological utopianism, powerfully centralized technology and government (techno-socialism), and Stasi methods of power, control, and indoctrination. While they typically do not embrace the full ideology of Nazism, it is hard to resist labeling them as smiling Techno-Nazis. Physical violence or criminalization is a last resort and in most cases should not be needed if spin, smiling "compassionate/just" persuasion, and technologically assisted indoctrination are properly employed.

Most future-visions include the afterlife of the individual, if the individual persists, but, more critically today, they define the nature, character, culture, and desired outcomes of the present era in the dawning of the future of all things. And future-visions, once implemented in the present moment, approximate either heaven or hell, or some combination thereof. Public theology, as noted, is primarily or ultimately historical eschatology for the in-between times—between the first and second coming of Messiah. It is about *How Should We Then Live* now, before Messiah returns.

Nietzsche called for the mastery rather than the tyranny of the supermen (*Übermenschen*) over the inferior men (*untermenschen*). Hitler tried to implement the tyranny of the Nazi supermen with the extermination of the *untermenschen* (Jews) and by rolling out his millennium (thousand-year Reich or kingdom). Kingdom future-visions rule.

The very words, concepts, usage, and definitions of words in countless AD (*anno Domini*, the year of our Lord) civilizations, which is known as semantics, have been, to one degree or another, Logocentric or

---

3. King, "I Have a Dream." From 1963, one hundred years after the Gettysburg Address.

anti-Logocentric. The Word or Logos of God, the Messiah, and agent of creation of all things created words, language, communication, and the proper definition and usage of words and ideas (semantics) that sparked a new future—and changed the calendar. Change the meaning of words, change the future. Public theology without a careful analysis of the definition, meaning, usage, and impact of words (semantics) is akin to trying to surf without waves. This semantic truth also applies to evangelism, defending the faith (apologetics), and preserving the faith inside the church (polemics). This is why many toxic future-vision AJC revolutions have sought to replace the Judeo-Christian calendar and start history over again.

The Messiah sought to initiate and write a future of kingdom approximation until his return. His actual biblical vision was centered in normed love and true freedom. He initiated his own city for the in-between times—the City of Kingdom Approximation. The City of Antichrist opposed and opposes this City of Kingdom Approximation, which includes individual salvation and transformation but also influences everything private and public. He is Lord of all, or not Lord at all.

The semantics of the City of Kingdom Approximation are, by definition, Logocentric. The semantics of the City of Antichrist, by definition, reject and seductively or tyrannically replace or redefine Logocentric words in order to build and empower the counterfeit city. The dark city semantics are often and increasingly AJC-centric.

Words either serve as the solid pillars or the shifting sands of cultures and civilizations.

Everything is redefined everywhere and always: God is now whatever you believe in; justice is just us, just me and/or my tribe; the biblical Jesus is whoever you want him or her or "ze" to be; all faith is personal preference and biblical faith is blind faith; love is a designer emotional drug or manipulated equity outcomes; biblical compassion is centralized governmental redistribution and control; truth is whatever advances the individual or tribe; spin and deception are virtuous; male, female, and gender categories are oppressive; diversity, equity, and inclusion exclude biblical teachings, practices, and thoughts, increasingly with the force of law; censorship is relabeled as content moderation or disinformation canceling and hate canceling; educational neutrality is aggressively ABC or AJC; civilization is an oppressive Judeo-Christian concept; freedom and democracy no longer mean freedom from governmental tyranny but governmentally mandated and enforced "justice" outcomes; saving "democracy" means you agree with me or else; patriotism is either dangerous or redefined to cancel AJC cultural influence and AJC influenced political experiments in more perfect unions; tolerance requires intolerance; extremism, either by implication or directly stated, is Scripture and

Judeo-Christian influence; terrorism is the views or actions of anyone who disagrees; multiculturalism is not celebrating and learning from multiple cultures but canceling AJC culture; multiculturalism requires anti-Western and AJC multicultural moral relativism; multicultural moral relativism condemns biblically influenced culture; the biblical church is not a beacon of hope but oppressive and, perhaps, the sepulcher of the god of a dying and unjust Judeo-Christian civilization; heaven is a present feeling or experience or the reward for everyone; criminals and inmates are justice system involved persons; a secure border is an open border that assists with illegal immigration, returns land and citizenship to its rightful owners, and aids with "social justice" long-term voting demographics; illegal immigrants are undocumented citizens; reckless trillion dollar deficit spending is inflation-reducing and sustainable over the long-haul; and systemic racism is not intentional structural oppression or institutional and personal bigotry against different races but unequal outcomes. Amazingly, this list is a very small representation of the verbal seductions in the present age.

The entire lexicon of civilizations, including the shaming of the terms civilization and civilized, is being redefined in order to redefine the future. In the counterfeit city biblical terms and concepts like Jesus, gender, and marriage are redefined or countered with aggressive eschatologies of ABC, ABB (anything but biblical), or AJC.

While language and terms certainly can be improved and enhance community at times (such as rejecting the improper and unbiblical use of "boy"), today all terms and phrases, even things as seemingly harmless as brown bag lunches (that used to be literally brown), lowering the bar, and cakewalk must be banned or replaced, and are now viewed only as some kind of oppressive assault on or marginalizing of others. As noted, pederasts (those sexually attracted to children) are now minor-attracted persons. Student debt is now reclassified as policy violence. The pro-abortion Religious Coalition for Reproductive Choice (RCRC) redefines itself and key terms such as pro-faith, pro-family, and pro-choice. RCRC refers to abortion with the oxymoron "abortion care," and flies in the face of Scripture, Jewish tradition, the early church, and nearly two thousand years of Christian opposition to abortion and infanticide that links the two barbaric practices. RCRC seems unmoved or unaware that the two world religions framing their "justice" and "compassion" were birthed amid the unjust and tyrannical slaughtering of babies (Moses, Jesus), and that the Savior of one of these major religions came in a manger.

As noted, the RCRC gathers "Christian" and other "faith" leaders to blasphemously and demonically sing what has often become a children's song of biblical faith, "This Little Light of Mine," at the dedication of abortion clinics. How can this be? They simply redefine their activities as social justice and compassion for women.[4] Other "social justice" and "compassion" movements similarly redefine radical surgery on children as gender-affirming health care. The indoctrination of children on such reckless health care is gender-affirming education. Those defining the gender-affirming removal of breasts and genitalia as mutilation, or defining hormone therapy on children or young teens without parental consent as tyrannical governmental manipulation, are no longer viewed as caring and responsible families and parents but as hateful, sexist bigots who need to be ignored, censored, silenced, fined, or incarcerated.

A redefined Christianity that redefines historic and biblical faith and practice is no longer Christianity but another religion. And such a false religion and future-vision is arguably far more toxic for church, synagogue, and state than even Nietzsche's AJC rants.

Words and concepts evolve or devolve, mutate and morph. To repeat a message that faith communities simply are not fully absorbing: change the meaning of words, change the future-vision. Change the future-vision, change the church, synagogue, and world.

Changing word (or logos) definitions is far more profound and consequential than single terms, phrases, or issues. Words are the pillars of an organic, verbal, cultural, and civilizational system. This corruptive metamorphosis lies at the core of movements that seek to move the future completely out of orbit of the Logos, the true and eternal Word. This amounts to cosmic antichristism and anti-Logocentrism. Gender and justice issues are important and must be lovingly and tactfully addressed by faith communities with a positive vision for biblical justice and human sexuality, but many are seduced by these semantic or verbal gyrations inside and outside of church and synagogue. The architects and advocates of these verbal revolutions and so-called justice causes are also shrewdly using the individual issues and verbal seductions as comprehensive wedge strategies to eclipse the influence of the Logos on the present—one issue at a time.

Verbal warfare is a primary strategy, tactic, and means by which to write a new future and create an AJC and post-Logos civilization. It has often been incremental and often emanates from colleges and universities. Now it is increasingly militant, ironically and especially in formerly Logos-influenced nations. The goal is not simply to move beyond Christendom, advance so-called inclusion and fairness, and avoid church-state political unions. The goal is to ban Judeo-Christian influence forever from impacting the arrow of history, culture, and civilization. Faith communities are often

---

4. Religious Coalition for Reproductive Choice, https://rcrc.org/.

asleep at the wheel, separating from the messy trenches of civilizational change, or flailing away at single words, phrases, persons, political causes, or symptoms. Yet Scripture, the Old Testament, the Gospel of John, and the book of Revelation could not be more clear—the Logos was, is, and forever shall be the center or reality, the great I Am, even in the present in-between times.

Hence, public theology from a Judeo-Christian perspective must be eschatological and Logocentric. Such public theology must also engage in public and semantic apologetics. Apologetics refers to the gentle, respectful (1 Pet 3:15), "speak the truth in love" defense of Judeo-Christian faith and practice, including the Judeo-Christian meaning of words and the meaning of meaning. Once again, future-visions rule. Words rule. Word definitions rule. Word seductions rule. Words and concepts are inherently eschatological and future-creating.

Eschatologies, including the biblical kingdom eschatology, are more than spectator sports. Kingdom-visions are participatory and epic dramas that capture our heart, thinking, imagination, planning, allegiance, loves, and actions. They enslave, inspire, oppress, and liberate.

The purpose and function of future-visions is not merely to understand or analyze the present and future but to change both.[5] Future-visions build the City of Kingdom Approximation and the City of Antichrist.

When Jesus and John the Baptist (and Peter and Paul) proclaimed the future-vision kingdom of God, they used identical words to call for change: "Repent, for the Kingdom of heaven is at hand" (Matt 4:17; 3:2). Repentance includes a turning away from false gods, sin, false future-visions (e.g., polytheism), and then turning in true faith toward the God of Abraham, Isaac, and Jacob.

Repentance involves a 180-degree reorientation of thought, life, and desires, including both individual and communal life. A classic example is Abraham leaving polytheism to trust and follow the call of God, or Abraham forever renouncing both child sacrifice and the idolatry of claiming a miracle child and promise as his own.

Eschatology defines and frames our assumptions about everything now and forever: human nature, government, law, politics, art, music, family, truth, ethics, God's will, the church, the mission of the church, how we worship, the afterlife, and even our personal self-understanding. Eschatology rules.

---

5. This rough paraphrase of Marx is not intended to endorse Karl Marx's flawed view of human nature (anthropology), history, economics, politics, or the future. Marx did seem to understand the power and purpose of eschatology as future-creation.

Twentieth-century theology revived the importance of eschatology for Christian thought but simply did not fully develop the comprehensive nature and implications of future-visions for all areas of thought, life, and civilization before Messiah's return. Or these visions adulterated the biblical vision with unbiblical ideologies, such as nineteenth-century Manifest Destiny or the twentieth-century utopias of Marx and Hitler. Others distorted biblical eschatology either via escapism or by the naive and contradictory belief that paradise was possible apart from Christ's actual return (postmillennialism).

Kingdom future-visions rule, from the first gospel promise or Messianic *protoevangelium* (Gen 3:15) to the New Heaven and Earth when evil is finally and forever defeated (Rev 20 and 21). The *protoevangelium* announced that while the Messianic seed of the woman would be wounded by the serpent in this age, the serpent would ultimately be vanquished by the coming Messiah in the New Creation: "And there will no longer be *any* death; there will no longer be *any* mourning, or crying, or pain; the first things have passed away" (Rev 21:4).

Future-visions define critical realities such as how things can and should be, the nature and role of the church, and the purpose of education (in and outside of the church) and cultural engagement. From a Judeo-Christian perspective some are largely constructive, some are destructive, and some are mixed or more neutral. They prescribe *How Should We Then Live*, what we should love, and who we should become. Eschatology rules:

- From Jesus' and John the Baptist's word-for-word identical vision, "Repent for the kingdom of heaven is at hand" (Matt 3:2; 4:17; Mark 1:15), to Paul's "preaching the kingdom of God" and repentance throughout the Mediterranean, to Augustine's vision of two cities in the *City of God* while serving as bishop of the city Hippo in the Roman Empire.

- From Moses guiding the children through the waters of the Red Sea to Harriet Tubman, a second "Moses," risking everything and voluntarily returning to her land of captivity and leading her people through the secret watery underground railroad to the "Promised Land."

- From Plato's world of the forms to Gnosticism's secret knowledge concerning how to escape the taint of the material world—the latter of which has some parallels with contemporary Western New-Age future-visions (e.g., Dan Brown, *The Da Vinci Code*).

- From Romulus and Remus and the *Pax Romana* to *Pax Britannica*, *Pax Germanica*, *Pax Americana*, and *Pax Sinica*.[6]

---

6. *Pax Sinica*: Possible future Chinese or Asian world dominance or hegemony.

- From Augustine's *City of God* and heavenly city to John Bunyan's *Pilgrim's Progress* and the celestial city—"from this world to that which is to come."[7]

- From Luther's *Sola Scriptura* Reformation to Trent's Counter-Reformation.

- From Calvin's sovereignty of God to Arminius's sovereignly good God.

- From Wesley's "General Spread of the Gospel," to Edwards's "Sinners in the Hands of an Angry God," to Rob Bell's *Love Wins*.

- From colonial slavery to abolitionism—"Perhaps nowhere was this American Christian utopianism speaking the language of the Apocalypse more pronounced than in the antislavery movement," illustrated by "The Battle Hymn of the Republic" (1862).[8]

- From the shining "City Set on a Hill" of the Puritans and John Winthrop to the "City Set on a Hill" of John F. Kennedy, Ronald Reagan, and "Yes We Can" Barack Obama.

- From the pacifistic indomitable will of Gandhi to the nonviolent "I Have a Dream" of Martin Luther King Jr.

- From the workers' revolution (of the *proletariat* or working class) and the classless society of Marx and Engels to the Trinitarian democratic capitalism of former socialist Michael Novak.

- From year one of the AD and BC religious calendars to year one of the Common Era, to year one of the French Revolutionary calendar era of liberty, to the "Year Zero" of far Eastern communism.

- From colonialism and Manifest Destiny to anti-colonialism, pluralism, and anti-Western multiculturalism.

- From the divine right of kings to individualism to collectivism.

- From Charles Sheldon's *In His Steps*, to Civil Rights, to liberation theology to pluralism plus, to Black Lives Matter, to Antifa's anarchistic and anachronistic socialism.

- From the "Let's Make America Great Again" of Ronald Reagan to the "MAGA" of Donald Trump.

- From widespread belief in resurrection to increasing acceptance of reincarnation, even inside the walls of the church.

- From the pursuit of utopia to the popularity of postmodern dystopia.

---

7. Bunyan, *Pilgrim's Progress*.
8. Grenz, *Millennial Maze*, 58.

- From American fundamentalism to Billy Graham–style American evangelicalism, to worldly evangelicalism, to post-evangelicalism, to emergent evangelicalism, to fragmented evangelicalism.

- From Schaeffer's *How Should We Then Live?* to the Moral Majority, to *The Young Evangelicals*, to *The Worldly Evangelicals*, to *Resident Aliens*, to *The Younger Evangelicals*, to *The Benedict Option*, to *Awaiting the King*, to *Still Evangelicals?*[9]

- From "The kingdom of the world has become *the kingdom* of our Lord and of His Christ; and He will reign forever and ever" (Rev 11:15), to more Eastern eschatological concepts such as *samsara* (including the cycle of death and rebirth), *moksha* (liberation and enlightenment), and *nirvana* (ultimate state).

- From *Caesar Kurios* or *Kyros Kaiser* to *Christos/Iesous Kurios*. From Caesar is divine lord or king of the Roman Empire to Christ is Lord or King of heaven and earth, the Alpha and Omega, redeemer and restorer of all things.

When we attempt to identify or define the ultimate or supreme end and purpose of our existence, our true individual and civilizational *telos* (goal or end), we are asking what or who should rule the future. Who should we be? Who is the rightful or ideal king? Who qualifies as eternal citizens? We are also inquiring about and pursuing the ideal form and nature of our individual and common life together; our individual and flesh-and-blood civilizational existence.

What is the correct and desired kingdom? That is why Oliver O'Donovan confessed that "I set out to discover the kingship of Christ, and ended up, as I am told, with a 'defence of Christendom.'"[10] And for O'Donovan, a Christian-influenced civilization or kingdom in this age that is genuinely subordinate to the only true King is the present, common, and eternal good. In other words, his quest for authentic kingship led to him developing a full-orbed political theology—a theology that guides our life together, including our political life.

Hence, O'Donovan entitles his book on public theology as *The Desire of the Nations*, for what we as nations ultimately desire, or should desire, is the true King and kingdom. This desire and longing lie at the heart of the biblical future-vision.

---

9. Please see the bibliography concerning these works and others that have been documented numerous times in this work.

10. O'Donovan, *Desire*, ix.

BIBLICAL KINGDOM FUTURE-VISIONS

Last-generationists, needless to say, have emphasized that "the Bible dedicates more space to the subject of prophecy than almost any other. There are over eighteen hundred prophecies in God's Word concerning the first and second coming of Jesus Christ alone!"[11] Last-generationists have been emphasizing the centrality of such biblical prophecies for at least two centuries, dating back to John Nelson Darby and the Plymouth Brethren. Yet, as we have seen, last-generationists interpret and apply these many passages within the context of last-generation futurism and tend to neglect the mammoth implications of the in-breaking kingdom, *The Presence of the Future*, for the present generation—for today, already. The biblical *Presence of the Future* has been replaced with *This Present Darkness*.

Pannenberg ties together the centrality, meaning, and application of the biblical kingdom. He argues, "Jesus eschatology has often been misunderstood and viewed as a liability," or a false belief that he would return within a literal "generation of his death and resurrection."[12] In reality, Jesus taught that the kingdom was both imminent and future, relevant to every present moment yet also potentially historically distant. "The teaching of Jesus, including his ethical radicalism, was dependent on his message of the imminent Kingdom of God. He viewed every aspect of life in the light of the imminent end of the world."[13] Every goal, action, and attitude "was validated or rejected in terms of its conformity to God's [kingdom-redemptive] action. The coming Kingdom of God—this was the single, pulsating reality of Jesus' existence. All else could be lost, if only this were to be realized. And in the realization of the Kingdom all else would be saved."[14]

Thus, a Christ-centered or Christocentric approach to kingdom eschatology recognizes that

- Jesus and John the Baptist initiated and defined their mission and ministry with, "Repent [*metanoia*, meaning, as noted, to have a 180-degree reversal of heart and life], for the kingdom of heaven is at hand" (Matt 3:2 and 4:17). The entrance to the kingdom requires bended knees, repentance, faith, and the rebirth of new life transformation.

- The Sermon on the Mount should be recast or retitled as The Sermon on the Kingdom, for that is its true focus and character.

---

11. Jeremiah, *Book of Signs*, x.
12. Pannenberg, *Theology and the Kingdom*, 102.
13. Pannenberg, *Theology and the Kingdom*, 102.
14. Pannenberg, *Theology and the Kingdom*, 102.

- The parables of Jesus are the parables of the kingdom.
- The ethical teaching of Jesus, as noted previously, is fully eschatological—here we have future-vision ethics.
- The incarnation, life, teaching, cross, resurrection, ascension, sending of the Spirit and return or parousia are fundamentally a unitary eschatology or eschatological event—the Christ event.
- The Trinitarian nature of the Son is rooted in kingship and kingdom eschatology.
- The Great Commission (Matt 28) to evangelize *and disciple the nations* is eschatologically driven, kingdom driven, and more than simply distributing tickets to heaven or getting folks off of a sinking ship and onto an escapist lifeboat.
- As noted, the new birth or born from above piety so popular among evangelicals such as Billy Graham is and should be framed and reframed by the kingdom eschatology in John 3. To once again paraphrase and slightly modify Wesley's famous words, salvation is not merely getting to heaven but the great salvation that prepares us to be fit for sharing in the kingdom. Repetition is needed: *The eternal kingdom will fail; it is simply impossible apart from radically and completely transformed kingdom citizens of time and eternity. Heaven can only be heavenly if its citizens are heavenly inside and out*—totally and holistically Christlike and holy.
- The kingdom and New Creation reality initiated by Christ potentially changes everything before and after his return, and biblical believers live in the shadow of the cross and the dawning of this New Creation kingdom.
- The kingdom future-vision rules the Bible and should rule the church and influence any state seeking its proper public servant role and the true desire of humans and nations.

Yet sound theological, historical, and philosophical reflection reveals that the kingdom is about much more than nations with literal kings. We need not confuse a contemporary first-century illustration (kingdom) with a profoundly and universally relevant concept (nations, cultures, and civilizations).

When the revelator states, "The kingdom of the world has become the kingdom of our Lord and of His Christ; and He will reign forever and ever" (Rev 11:15), clearly this is not a statement that is limited only to nations with actual kings. Prime ministers, presidents, the *führer* or exalted leader, ruling elites, aristocracies, and ruling parties with "kingdoms" certainly are not excluded because, as Ladd pointed out, the biblical kingdom concerns God's rule over all things already and forever.

Hence, civilizations are kingdoms even if they include multiple nations with different political structures, leaders, or kings. Nations are kingdoms even if they include states with leaders or governors. States are kingdoms even if they include cities or mayors that function as kings. Indeed, communities, subcultures, and even and especially family units are kingdoms of sorts. Each kingdom has a ruler, or rulers, or ruling principles and a culture, ethos, spirit, and character that conform to or deform God's rule. The idea that the kingdom of God only has application to literal kings and kingdoms is irrational and unbiblical.

The theology of the City of Antichrist and/or City of Kingdom Approximation certainly applies to contemporary cities and nations. Such theology also applies to every family, street address, apartment, homeless encampment, and organization.

Hence, each family unit, community, culture, city, gang, school, church, workplace, corporation, state, nation, or civilization is in one sense a kingdom or mini-kingdom or subkingdom or kingdom pillar. And each manifests the City of Antichrist or the City of Kingdom Approximation. And some kingdoms or subkingdoms unfortunately approximate, "for then there will be a great tribulation, such as has not occurred since the beginning of the world until now, nor ever will again" (Matt 24:21).

Each mini-kingdom has rules, rulers, principles, taboos, mores, gods, subjects, culture, subcultures, ethics, a normative ten commandments of some sort—or a thousand commandments—and a foundational ethos and spirituality. This truth about cultural commandments applies whether the ethos is *a-theos* (contrary to or without belief in the biblical God) or superficially not religious or spiritual.

All kingdoms are subject to the influence of the kingdom of darkness and deceit or the kingdom of truth and light. The biblical kingdom rule of God and future-vision, whether embraced or resisted, are normative, central, and universally applicable and relevant.

Karl Barth, however, amid the smoldering ashes of the Great War, properly cautions us against a naive, proud, or arrogant kingdom triumphalism. Triumphalism is when we prematurely attempt to triumph and force or fully implement the kingdom, which is really our own very flawed kingdom, in these multiple kingdom venues before Christ's return.

Prior to Christ's return, liberators who promise to deliver a triumphal kingdom, or social justice, or the classless society inevitably fail because grace and transformation have not yet fully triumphed in human hearts, especially in the hearts of so many liberators. As noted, they promise some new version of heaven and deliver many varieties of hell on earth. Triumphalism and escapism, regardless of intentions, are coconspirators in approximating the hell of the City of Antichrist. Barth guides us:

> In our journey through time, we are still men who wait, as though we saw what we do not see, as though we were gazing on the unseen. Hope is the solution of the riddle of our "As though." We do see. Existentially we see what to us is invisible, and therefore we wait. Could we see nothing but the visible world, we should not wait; we should accept our present situation with joy or with grumbling. Our [eschatological] refusal to accept it and to regard our present existence as incapable of harmony, our certainty that there abides in us a secret waiting for what is not, is, however, intelligible in the unseen hope which is ours in God, in Christ, in the Spirit, in the hope by which we are existentially confronted with the things which are not. We can then, if we understand ourselves aright, be none other than they who wait. We are satisfied to know no more than the sorrow of the creation and our own sorrow. We ask nothing better or higher than the Cross, where God is manifested as God. We must, in fact, be servants who wait for the coming of their Lord.[15]

SUMMARY AND URGENT APPLICATIONS OF THE BIBLICAL FUTURE-VISION

Much, much, more can and should be added to this discussion, and much will be, as noted, in a forthcoming larger publication. However, at this juncture the discussion in this and prior chapters should be sufficient to reinforce, highlight, and understand key applications.

1. *Future-visions rule.* Eschatology rules. Kingdom-visions rule. The kingdom-vision rules in Scripture.
2. The constructive attempt of Judeo-Christian believers to contribute to the global discussion concerning *How Should We Then Live* (public theology) is *primarily public eschatology*—dialogue and discernment concerning future-visions.
3. Writing a better future involves how we define and use words (semantics), thus *semantic apologetics* is essential to *How Should We Then*

---

15. Barth, *Epistle to the Romans*, 314–15.

Live. Control the words, control the future. Civilizations falling out of orbit of the Creator Logos succumb to the darkness and demonic.

4. The otherworldly and unbiblical version of the Judeo-Christian vision has assumed that a *magic moment* will change believers and all things into heavenly perfection. This flawed vision affirms that we should certainly get saved and be as obedient as possible to Christ, but as long as we are really and securely saved, it is argued, when we either die or are raptured we will become totally like Christ in a magical instant.

    a. And while learning a trade or becoming a master of some skill or competency is necessary to contribute today to the world, pay the bills, and provide for a family, when we all get to heaven all that becomes largely irrelevant. Hence, we sing "I'll fly away."

    b. The magical instant of death or rapture solves everything. There is no need to prepare for heaven truly and comprehensively—to develop our mind, to think God's thoughts, to explore the mysteries of God's cosmos, or to become radically transformed in this life.

    c. However, this otherworldly argument is less than compelling. Yes, we will be like him in some sense (1 John 3:2), especially our core motivations, but "it has not appeared as yet [exactly] what we will be" (1 John 3:2). We shall see him and all things face to face (1 John 3:2; 1 Cor 13:12), but we currently "see in a mirror dimly" and partially.

    d. Scripture nowhere promises that we magically will become experts in piano, art, music theory, the general theory of relativity, singing, leadership, farming, or co-regency as princes and princesses in an instant or moment (1 Cor 15:52). That magical conception is more otherworldly and flawed, pagan Greek philosophy than scriptural. In some respects, it is heretically gnostic or docetic by implying that getting out of the physical world is the key to the kingdom and Christlikeness.

    e. The Bible only promises that in a "twinkling of an eye, at the last trumpet; . . . the trumpet will sound, and the dead will be raised imperishable, and we will be changed" (1 Cor 15:51–52). The emphasis is that the dead are changed to a new order of existence, bodily resurrection with new glorious bodies ruled by spirit (1 Cor 15) and not subject to sin, disease, tears, suffering, and death (1 Cor 15; Rev 21 and 22).

f. It is utterly counterintuitive and naively magical to suggest that everyone raised to new life will be transformed into identical clones with the same competencies and understanding and experience and memories needed to reign with Christ "over the nations" (Rev 2:26).

g. It is utterly counterintuitive, pagan, otherworldly, and frankly disappointing to suggest that at the moment of our bodily resurrection (or rapture of some sort) we possess all knowledge, learning, and virtues without any need for endless growth in love for God, others, and the virtuous wisdom to rule the cosmos. Love and wisdom are infinite.

h. This otherworldly conception of the magic moment of death makes death the great savior and transformer of all things rather than the Triune Christ in a real and reciprocal (two-way) relationship with his people. It is as if we step into a supernatural transporter that makes us completely like the Messiah, in every respect, in an instant, and then we are injected with an infinite happy drug such that we joyously float around singing praise songs for all eternity.

i. Infinitely deepening love, Christ-likeness, relationships, growth, learning, exploration, creativity, novel creations (e.g., music), competencies, problem-solving, co-creativity, and co-regency sound far more Hebraic, scriptural, holistic, human, incarnational, *imago Dei* grounded, *theosis* (becoming like God) oriented, and truly heavenly than the magical instant.

5. Co-regency or vice-regency and the biblical future-vision of rewards are strongly suggestive that *true faith works, bears fruit, prepares us for and has a bearing on our co-regent status, rewards, and roles in the New Creation.* Again, it seems counterintuitive that some will be allowed to remain in spiritual infancy or be magically and instantly transformed in all respects into the maturity level of the apostle Paul, Joseph, Daniel, or John the apostle, much less the divine Logos. Scripture does not seem to affirm spiritual or holy socialism or manipulated and equitable outcomes.

   a. First Corinthians 3:11–14 (the value and quality of each person's work will be tested by fire; some works are as wood, hay, and straw and will not stand the test ; also see point "k" in this list)

b. Second Corinthians 3:18 ("But we all, with unveiled faces, looking as in a mirror at the glory of the Lord, are being transformed into the same image from glory to glory, just as from the Lord, the Spirit.")

c. Matthew 5:12 (there is a great reward in heaven for faithfulness in persecution)

d. Revelation 22:12 (God will render to each according to what they have done)

e. Philippians 3:14 (faithfulness means pressing on to the prize)

f. Hebrews 11:26 (there are heavenly riches distributed justly)

g. Daniel 12:3 (those who lead others to righteousness will shine like the stars)

h. Matthew 25:20–23 ("You were faithful with a few things, I will put you in charge of many things; enter the joy of your master.")

i. Luke 19:15–19 ("And he said to him, 'Well done, good slave; since you have been faithful in a very little thing, you are to have authority over ten cities.'")

j. First Corinthians 3:8 ("Now the one who plants and the one who waters are one; but each will receive his own reward according to his own labor.")

k. First Corinthians 3:12–14 ("Now if anyone builds on the foundation with gold, silver, precious stones, wood, hay, *or* straw, each one's work will become evident; for the day will show it because it is *to be* revealed with fire, and the fire itself will test the quality of each one's work. If anyone's work which he [or she] has built on it remains, he [or she] will receive a reward.")

l. Luke 6:22–23 ("Rejoice on that day and jump for joy, for behold, your reward is great in heaven. For their fathers used to treat the prophets the same way.")

6. The biblical future-vision seems clear: *Learn now or learn later. Mature now or mature later. Christlikeness and holiness now is greatly rewarded and not optional in the afterlife. Investing in the present is very well-advised.* This learning includes the way of salvation, but the scriptural way of the great salvation includes radical Christlikeness and holistic Logos-likeness in this life and the next. There is no magic machine at the pearly gates that will bypass freely chosen grace and growth toward

authentic co-regency. Learn it now or learn it later—so why postpone our true purpose and delay rewards and co-regency?

7. Likewise, it is absurd to choose *false glory* now (Augustine, Luther) and shallow and passing praise over *true eternal glory*. The *Via Dolorosa*—the way of the cross—is the pathway to true and enduring glory and co-regency, and authentic kingdom influence, just as the Messiah despised the shame in view of the lost sheep and the heavenly city (Heb 12:1–2). The theology of the cross is the theology of true glory.

8. True citizens of time and eternity can choose true glory now, with temporary embarrassment or persecution, or they can choose false glory now, with no eternal benefit, often covering up one's actual state of spiritual and holistic growth, which amounts to deceptive image management. These genuine citizens are ultimately forgiven but will face loving but *profoundly embarrassing accountability and transparency later*: "For nothing is hidden, except to be revealed; nor has *anything* been secret, but that it would come to light" (Mark 4:22). "So do not fear them [religious antichrists or the City of Antichrist], for there is nothing concealed that will not be revealed, or hidden that will not be known" (Matt 10:26). "Accordingly, whatever you have said in the dark will be heard in the light, and what you have whispered in the inner rooms will be proclaimed on the housetops" (Luke 12:3). Truly glory in this life is the pathway to glorious co-regency in the next.

Hence, the history of God redeeming and transforming all things is not only an epic journey involving loyalties, loves, and passions. This epic journey winds its way through and between actual flesh-and-blood earthly and heavenly cities.

Radical, personal, transformational, incarnational, eschatological, saving, kingdom faith, according to the whole of Scripture, especially as illustrated in Heb 11 and 12, involves real history, relationships, cities, culture, temptations, suffering, kingdom influence, and civilizations. God's redemption moves in and through history and creation toward the New Creation heavenly city.

Jesus the Messiah was kingdom approximation incarnate. He changed everything—not just the spiritual state and salvation status of his followers but literally everything on heaven and earth. In addition to the gospel or good news securing personal redemption, Smith and O'Donovan refer to the craters of the Messiah's gospel, such as freedom of speech. A better way to frame the impact of Christ's first coming than craters is to suggest that little remained the same after the year of our Lord. Smith and O'Donovan provide numerous examples of such craters, or kingdom breakthroughs, such as

- The modern notion of the state as not divinely sanctioned or eternal.
- The very conception of liberty or freedom.
- The legal principle of mercy and the related concept of cruel and unusual punishment.
- The affirmation of human rights as eternally grounded.
- The divinely sanctioned protection of freedom of speech.[16]

Or, as noted previously, the influence already of the incarnation of the Lamb who will return as the Lion, even before final victory, has been palpable relative to the value of human life; rolling back pederasty, abortion, infanticide, prostitution; the abolition of slavery; enhancing prison reform; inspiring medical breakthroughs in healing and the relief of suffering; genuine scientific advances; prison reform; poverty relief; and novel and glorious creations of art and music. This is only a short list reflecting the tip of the tip of the tip of the kingdom iceberg that has uprooted and removed many cities of Antichrist in the dawning forward progress of the New Creation.

The leaven of the City of Kingdom Approximation often spread slowly and imperceptibly, but the promise to Abraham—that he stood in the line of promise that would bless all nations—has been literally approximated, already, in this present age before Messiah's final triumph. Even Abraham's physical children have not only inherited a large portion of suffering, but out of their historical crucible, arguably, have emerged countless global blessings—anti-Semitic critics notwithstanding.[17] And if one accepts the New Testament teaching that non-Jewish believers have been grafted into the faith of Abraham, and that Christianity has made beneficial civilizational contributions, the list only grows longer.

It goes beyond the scope of this work to demonstrate irrefutably this positive influence. Certainly distortions of the biblical kingdom have had

---

16. Smith, *Awaiting the King*, 100–105. See ch. 7 for an expansion on this material and how it relates to being prepared for and responding to the City of Antichrist and advancing the City of Kingdom Approximation.

17. Even if one disagrees with the thesis of Norman Lebrecht and others or has alternative explanations (e.g., Jewish privilege), the list of world-influencing Jews and their impact from a small demographic is stunning. Chemotherapy, relativity theory, Einstein, modern political theory, postmodern philosophy and Kafka, Google, and Freud are but a short representation of what can be found in Lebrecht, *Genius*. The Jewish Life Television network—regardless of whether one concurs with the thesis of positive influence in view of disproportionate numbers—regularly features the names and contributions of those born Jewish, such as the film director and genius Spielberg.

negative impacts, but other works have addressed this question and a larger expansion of this present work, as noted, is forthcoming.[18]

The Messiah, Jesus, was indeed the incarnation and mediator of the City of Approximation. Messiah changed all things while pointing to an even greater day of full kingdom consummation in the New Creation.

It seems rather peculiar, and underscores the very otherworldly nature of our view of Jesus and the kingdom, that we often affirm that followers of Jesus are potentially being transformed already, by the Counselor he sent, yet without significant impact on civilization today. Genuine believers are inevitably part of the warp and woof of present realities. The church and the faithful that embody and model the future create the future already, even in relation to culture and civilization, and most often through suffering and persecution.

The followers of the Christ are human beings, the very crown of creation, so if the crown of creation can approximate the heavenly city already, why not the rest of God's very good creation even in the presence of sin and the City of Antichrist? The most important and concentrated kingdom approximation in this age should be God's own people—the true church and true synagogue.

Given the inseparable nature of and connection between humans, the church, culture, and civilization, it would be peculiar and should be unexpected and lamented if Messiah's incarnation does not radiate throughout the world God so loves. Preach the good news (gospel) to all nations. Disciple all nations or peoples. Share Abraham's cosmic blessing already. Hence, the City of Kingdom Approximation and the City of Antichrist are more than spiritual principles or loyalties or loves—they are real, existing, cultural and civilizational realities. The death and resurrection of Christ truly has changed everything already. It is finished. The Messiah, Jesus, is already, in one sense, the ruler of the kings of the earth (Rev 1:5):

> [He is] the firstborn of the dead, and the ruler of the kings of the earth. To Him who loves us and released us from our sins by His blood—and He made us into a kingdom, priests to His God and Father—to Him be the glory and the dominion forever and ever. Amen. Behold, He is coming with the clouds, and every eye will see Him, even those who pierced Him; and all the tribes of the earth will mourn over Him. So it is to be. Amen. (Rev 1:5-7)

---

18. Again, see the works by Augustine, Smith, and O'Donovan for an introduction to this discussion. Or, for an example of more popular attempts to make this case, see works such as Kennedy and Newcombe, *What If Jesus?*

He has made us into and to be a kingdom and priests. Or, more simply stated (ἐποίησεν ἡμᾶς βασιλείαν), "He has made us into a kingdom, priests to His God and Father—to Him be the glory and the [kingdom] dominion forever and ever. Amen" (Rev 1:6). Yet, according to Rev 1–3, the City of Kingdom Approximation wars against and exists in the present age amid places where "Satan dwells" (Rev 2:13), where Satan's kingdom "throne" rules, where the false "teaching of Balaam" rules, where synagogues of God have become "synagogues" of Satan, where there are false "prophetesses," "apostles," and "Jews," and where the angel with the key of King David rules already but not yet inside and outside of the church.

Justice will eventually rule and overthrow the City of Antichrist, the persecutors from the City of Antichrist will be held accountable, the unjust will "bow down" before the justified, and true believers will reign forever: "The one who overcomes, I will grant to him to sit with Me on My throne, as I also overcame and sat with My Father on His throne" (Rev 3:21). In the shadow of these two competing cities, the faithful already have been given "authority" over "the nations" (Rev 2:26, 27), and someday God "will write" on the overcomers "the name of the city of My God, the new Jerusalem, which comes down out of heaven" (Rev 3:12).

John the revelator suggests that only the faithful truly have ears to hear or fully grasp the message of this inspired future-vision: "The one who has an ear, let him hear what the Spirit says to the churches. To the one who overcomes, I will give some of the hidden manna, and I will give him a white stone, and a new name written on the stone which no one knows except the one who receives it" (Rev 2:17).

As noted, the conflicting cities, representing influence or domination in the present age by either Christ or antichrist, certainly include the loves, loyalties, and journeys of all players. John the revelator, however, consistent with Scripture from Genesis to Revelation, views flesh-and-blood rulers, teachings, practices, idolatries, culture, kings, kingdoms, art, architecture, and civilizations as concrete manifestations, to one degree or another, of the kingdom rule of one of these two cities in the present age.

The City of Kingdom Approximation lovingly, truthfully, and sacrificially influences the present age. The City of Antichrist seduces and tyrannically rules by any means necessary. The City of Kingdom Approximation creates new realities by creatively defining words, concepts, and values in relationship to the Logos; hence, this radiant city is Logocentric.

The City of Antichrist is anti-Logocentric and temporarily and futilely attempts to redefine everything and rewrite history and reality. "Hath God said?" "You certainly will not die." All is redefined: apostles, Jesus, prophetesses, synagogues, Jews, Christ, gospel, the means of salvation, faith, works, biblical love, biblical justice, wisdom, circumcision, angels, marriage, divorce, the resurrection of believers, and even the resurrection of Christ. All becomes anti-Logos. Hence, scriptural evidence suggests that relegating spiritual things to the personal closet or Christian ghetto is fundamentally unbiblical and unchristian.

We typically affirm that Jesus will change everything someday, and Scripture agrees. We also must affirm that he has changed everything already, including our status, identity, and calling in the present age. Abraham's melody of a cosmic blessing (Gen 12) grows ever louder in each generation, even amid the fierce opposition of the City of Antichrist to the ultimately victorious City of Kingdom Approximation that eventually becomes the celestial city.

This proposed, realistic, optimistic, and beautiful conception of the biblical future-vision paints a picture of redemptive history ever moving forward in overlapping and integrated phases or stages. These are not stages, or dispensations, with different means of salvation, for salvation is by incarnational grace through incarnational faith that works in every generation, including Abel, Noah, Joseph, Moses, Debra, the prophets, and the early followers of Christ (Heb 11). Christ is the ultimate norm and model (Heb 12). Faith upholds the law, and we are created in Christ Jesus for good works (Eph 2)—works that approximate the true incarnational future already.

THE FLOWERING AND ADVANCE OF CITIES AND FUTURE-VISIONS THROUGHOUT HISTORY

These unified stages or phases of cosmic redemption and civilizational influence in and through history ever move forward toward the New Jerusalem and New Creation, beginning with the garden of Eden:

1. *The Edenic Birth or Genesis of the Kingdom of Approximation.* Eden was not the destination but the beginning of God's plan for all things, even in its unfallen state. The Eden story includes history but is fundamentally not looking backward but forward. Eden is primarily eschatology. Eden was the fountainhead or birthplace of the three cosmic cities: the pre-fallen Edenic City of Kingdom Approximation, the City of Antichrist, and the New Creation Eternal City.

2. *The Birth of the City of Antichrist.* The temptation and fall of humanity in Eden births legion and indescribable seductions, verbal and other deceptions, misdirected loves, sufferings, and evils that not only impact the first humans but all of history, culture, creation, and

all civilizations. The poisoning of humanity, the crown of creation, is inseparable from creation, culture, and civilization. Sin is cosmic in nature, scope, and consequences, just as with the grace-assisted antidote to sin—Abrahamic, biblical, kingdom faith in the anointed New Creation King of kings (Messiah). Abraham's grace-based faith mediates the cosmic blessing to all families, peoples, and nations (Gen 12:3). In sharp contrast, the narrative of this virulent plague of cosmic sin is quickly reinforced and illustrated by the biblical account of fratricide[19] and the flood, including the divine diagnosis of humanity and culture that "every intent of the thoughts of their hearts was only evil continually" (Gen 6:5).

3. *The Abrahamic Rebirth of the City of Kingdom Approximation.* The originally intended eschatology of Eden was never fulfilled due to the fall. The emerging paradise was lost but reborn through Abraham's cosmic faith. Land and descendants as vast as the stars are certainly a blessing, but the true blessing of the line of promise through genuine faith (*notitia, assensus,* and *fiducia*) is individual, familial, and universal in scope.[20] "And in you all the families of the earth will be blessed" (Gen 12:3). The City of Antichrist is on the losing side of history and His-story. In contrast, the City of Kingdom Approximation is already but not yet victorious.

4. *The Decisive-Day Invasion and Incarnation of the City of Kingdom Approximation.* The Christ-event, as noted, involving multiple *Kairos* moments, truly is a singular event, theologically speaking. The prophetic Messianic predictions, the incarnation, birth, life, good and miraculous kingdom works, kingdom teaching, kingdom-oriented victorious death, kingdom resurrection, kingdom ascension, and kingdom sending of the Spirit/Comforter "on all flesh [or mankind]" (Joel 2 ESV; see Acts 2) means that Christ's death and resurrection for human sin and a cosmos falling out of kingdom orbit proclaims, completes, and initiates the reality that "it is finished!" (*telestai,* John 19:30, Jesus' last word or *logos*) The D-Day or decisive final and cosmic sacrifice, invasion, and re-enveloping of all that which Logos created is redeemed by the Lamb, Lion, Logos, Alpha, Omega, and coming

---

19. Fratricide is the killing of a brother.

20. The dimensions of true, biblical, and saving faith from the Reformers and Melanchthon (*notitia, assensus, fiducia*) are understanding, agreement, and trust. Or as I have referenced previously in this work, radical, personal, transformational, eschatological kingdom faith. The demons "believe" or have a "faith" from the City of Antichrist but tremble before the Christ and his coming kingdom City (Jas 2:19).

King of kings and Lord of lords. Some may object to Oscar Cullmann's non-pacifist D-Day war analogy or hymns such as "Onward Christian Soldiers," but these are just analogies. Still, warfare is a biblical analogy and reality, and love is an influencer and victorious weapon in the spiritual war between the cities. And it is also undeniable that at certain *Kairos* moments Christ's kingdom does advance with force and power, including the shock and awe use of force—as in the Old Testament. The sacrificial Lamb is *also* the conquering Lion of the Second Coming.

5. *The Victory-Day Global Establishment of the City of Kingdom Approximation and Restoration.* This coming transitional age of restoration and enhanced approximation commencing right after Messiah's return is of course debated. However, this phase can be defended from the larger themes of Scripture and argued theologically in terms of a realism of human nature, an optimism of grace, and the persuasive logic of a needed, lengthy, and non-magical transitional historical phase prior to the final, final and unlimited victory—especially in view of the nature of God's love, grace, and the reality of cosmic sin, authentic human love, and free will. Hence, the next phase of redemptive history is the return of Messiah on earth and the establishment and nearly complete realization of God's rule on earth that largely restores God's original intent for the creation. This restoration phase provides continuity to the progress of civilization and truly universal redemption. This phase confirms and reveals the continuity of history and culture, and completes and fulfills all of the noble efforts throughout time toward creating a better world. All things are fulfilled through and on the very plane of history, and the New Creation work of God eventually transforms and glorifies history forever. The historical staircase leads somewhere rather than nowhere—it leads to a next phase of redeemed history. Prior history matters. Future history fulfills all of history and redeems not only every tear but every moment of historical time. A return of Christ that immediately and magically catapults all of reality into the perfection of the New Creation seems, as suggested previously, unbiblical, otherworldly, and unrealistic.

6. *The Final Death of the City of Antichrist.* This proposed transitional historical era (see number 5) also better coheres with the next step of redemptive history—the final death of the City of Antichrist. The last vestiges or stubborn roots of the City of Antichrist will not simply dissipate or walk away or be won over by love, but will require the final, forceful, and decisive defeat. This defeat will be much greater

than the use of force but certainly involves the use of force to conquer evil finally and forever and bring true justice to bear on the City of Antichrist and its destructive rulers, seducers, and minions—and set the stage for the eternal New Creation. The martyrs who spent themselves on the *Via Dolorosa* will, according to Revelation, finally be properly avenged. A neglected theme relative to Victory Day 1 and Victory Day 2 is Scripture's concern not for crude revenge but for true justice and accountability for the grace-resisting unrepentant. The perennial justice question of the martyrs, who had been told "to rest [or wait] for a little while longer" (Rev 6:11), will finally and forever be addressed and resolved via the impact of both Victory Days. "How long, O Lord, holy and true, will You refrain from judging and avenging our blood on those who live on the earth?" (Rev 6:10). This is not a question of hate-filled vengeance but a question of real individuals who sacrificed everything and they and their loved ones were scorned, shamed, robbed, tortured, and martyred. Justice will come to the tear-filled faithful, who for the cause of Christ suffered beyond imagination, and who left everything behind, including beloved grandchildren, children, spouses, and friends. The long wait for true justice and final victory over unrepentant darkness and hate will be over as all things are taken up into the transforming eternal light of the cosmos.

7. *The Final Victory Day and New Creation Consummation of the Eternal City.* Death, evil, suffering, and pain will be forever overcome and replaced with a New Creation that has continuity with Eden (light, fruit, rivers, fellowship with God and each other), but which is so much more—no human eye or ear has yet seen or heard what God has in store (1 Cor 2:9). The Day of the Lord will become the ultimate resurrection day of all things. Cosmic Easter is imminent.

COSMOS ANNIHILATION, COSMOS PURIFICATION AND RESTORATION, OR COSMOS RESURRECTION?

The theological framework for the New Creation certainly includes the concepts of purification and restoration of the Creation, but such emphases are woefully inadequate. The theology that affirms the annihilation of the universe in the name of heavenly, otherworldly perfection rightly pointed to the need for cosmic redemption but became escapist and thus a biblical and theological dead end. The theology that argues for the restoration or purification of the cosmos is a needed correction and theologically popular today, but perhaps there is a better and more biblical way to envision the ultimate future than either annihilation or restoration/purification. Cosmic annihilationism and restorationism are both inadequate.

Concerning the famous passage from 2 Peter (3:10) where some see annihilationism, others argue that the fire is merely a symbol of purification. Annihilationists argue that this passage clearly and repeatedly teaches the complete annihilation or destruction of the current universe, which is then replaced entirely by a newly formed cosmos, or a largely spiritual and perhaps less than physical cosmos. Perhaps the language of this less than crystal clear passage is too strong for mere restoration or purification, but too biblical and Hebraic for total cosmic annihilation. "But the day of the Lord will come like a thief, in which the heavens will pass away with a roar and the elements will be destroyed with intense heat, and the earth and its works will be discovered" (2 Pet 3:10).

If we affirm that Scripture should interpret Scripture, and John the revelator is consistent with Peter, then perhaps the correct theological category for the nature of the New Creation is cosmic resurrection. Resurrection includes purification and restoring the created intent and so much more. Resurrection also affirms that in some sense the universe dies, but rather than being annihilated it is gloriously resurrected.

Cosmos-annihilation runs counter to the biblical and redemptive-history narrative and valuing of the creation. Cosmos-annihilation rests on weak theological and exegetical evidence.[21] Though, to be fair, cosmos-

---

21. Middleton, *New Heaven and a New Earth*. See multiple works by or about N. T. Wright, such as Wright, *Day*; Murawski, "Our Idea"; Rogers, "N. T. Wright's"; Wright, *On Earth*; Wright, *Surprised by Hope*; Juza, *New Testament*. Exegesis refers to the proper and critical interpretation of a biblical text, including usage of the original languages. The term literally means to lead or guide the meaning out of the text. Juza provides a tremendously helpful and detailed exegesis of key passages related to the debate concerning the annihilation of the cosmos and the contrasting views on the future of the cosmos. Such detailed work exceeds the scope and purpose of this present work. The most relevant part of Juza's work is where he touches the very edges of beginning to develop a theology of the resurrection of the cosmos (especially see pp. 282, 290, 299–306). Juza repeatedly emphasizes the "*material transformation*" of the cosmos (p. 301, italics original), and notes that "perhaps" it is the case that "the most helpful analogy to describe this tension between [the] continuity and discontinuity [between the present and future cosmos] is the resurrection body" of Christ (p. 304). Indeed (see pp. 305–6), "The results of this study suggest that the [biblical] writers' contemplation of the future of the cosmos can not be separated from their reflections on the ongoing significance of the death and resurrection of Jesus Christ and on the final coming of God for the purposes of judgment and salvation. These events have cosmic implications for the writers of the NT." Nevertheless, I was unable to locate in Juza's work the kind of clarion, multi-layered, and broadly applicable cosmic resurrection theology explored and affirmed in this present work.

annihilation has served as a useful reminder to the faithful that the present age is not and cannot become the fullness of God's kingdom (Heb 11). Utopianism, especially postmillennial utopianism, as we have seen, has been a constant and problematic temptation, especially in recent centuries.

The New Creation as cosmos-resurrection may be a theologically and biblically superior future-vision with very redemptive and real-world implications. This present work can only introduce the biblical, infinite, glorious, and majestic cosmos-resurrection argument:

1. As argued previously, humans are truly the *crown of creation*. Humans are the most important part of creation. As glorious as the rings of Saturn, super nebulae, Webb space telescope images, and hummingbirds are, they don't hold a candle to the brilliance of humans created in, and restored and resurrected to, the very image of God. This means that the most important dimension or aspect of God's good creation, humanity, will with very rare exceptions be bodily resurrected from death. And any exceptions are ultimately forms of resurrection. These rare exceptions (Enoch and Elijah?) would still be radical and bodily transformations akin to bodily resurrection. The cosmic resurrection argument affirms that the core and crown of God's cosmos will be bodily or physically resurrected.

2. The *cosmos is more than a platform or stage* for an otherworldly drama. It is organically connected to human life, the very crown of creation—and to each human's nature and destiny, just as with families and history. For God to resurrect humanity but only restore or renew the creation obscures the unity and interconnectedness of all things, all peoples, human experience, and our common history. Such a resurrection is not centered in the cosmic biblical kingdom. The thesis that the cosmos (apart from human life) is like an eternal rock or chunk of matter that does not in some sense perish is scientifically and theologically false. Animals die. Civilizations perish. Stars burn out or explode. Galaxies collapse. Humans are inseparably connected to their cultural, historical, civilizational, and cosmic context and experience. Some civilizations, cities, structures, peoples, and people groups literally have ceased to exist and have been physically broken down into molecules and/or atoms that have become absorbed by other existing things. Creation purification (of sin) and restoration (to its intended purpose) is true but simply inadequate. Which time period will be restored or privileged, the one that exists when Messiah returns? Why? Which human creations and structures will be restored and purified? Suggesting none seems very otherworldly, non-Hebraic,

and unbiblical. Why would God restore all things to the state of the garden of Eden and wipe out the whole of human global and cosmic history, including genuine cultural advances? As noted, while Eden was without sin, it also was the genesis or beginning of all that God desired for the creation ("be fruitful and multiply"), and not the end or consummation. Eden is Genesis (beginnings). Eden is eschatology. There is no easy answer to all of these issues and questions, yet some things seem certain. The cosmos will be restored to its created intent rather than its original state—it ultimately will be better than Eden. The creation will be purified of sin. The only real way to resolve all the multiple layers, history, and complexities of the New Creation is more analogous to bodily resurrection. Those who have perished and whose bodies no longer exist in any physical sense are bodily resurrected. The resurrection is the fulcrum, foundation, and focus of universal biblical history and redemption.

3. The resurrection of the cosmos, like bodily resurrection, affirms both *continuity and discontinuity with the present cosmos*. The risen Christ was truly Jesus of Nazareth, in contrast to the heresy of Docetism that denied the Messiah took on human flesh—that denied the incarnation. The risen Christ walked, fellowshipped, ate, had crucifixion scars, and walked through walls and ascended into heaven. The biblical future-vision of physical resurrection affirms restoration, purification, continuity, and discontinuity. Reality is raised to a new level, for which physics might supply a crude analogy by referring to multiple dimensional existence, beyond our current dimensions. Regardless of how it is done, God will masterfully resurrect the whole of cosmic and human history and establish the New Heaven and Earth such that we dwell in the same cosmos, and complete and fulfill history, yet all will be gloriously resurrected. Perhaps there will be something like five hundred dimensions to resurrected New Creation space-time reality, but we will still be dwelling in some sense in the same very good but fallen cosmos and creation in which the Logos became incarnate, just as someone who perished thousands of years ago will be bodily resurrected into a continuous and discontinuous physical existence (1 Cor 15). Jesus truly died, but the scriptural narrative (crucifixion scars, eating fish) and teaching is that "this same Jesus" (Acts 2:23–24) arose. Likewise, we will be resurrected to our own though glorified bodies. This cosmos will not only be purified but will die, yet this same cosmos and world that God so loved will be resurrected. Scripture does not affirm either discontinuity or continuity, but affirms both with passion

4. Why death? Why not simple restoration for us and the cosmos? Because all is radically fallen and irreducibly interconnected, organic, and systemic in nature. This is not to suggest a horribly flawed and unbiblical pantheism or panentheism, but simply to affirm the beautiful, complex, interrelated, and finely tuned nature of God's glorious creation. Death judges all things in a fallen world. Cosmic Restoration is inadequate on both ends of the equation. It overlooks the profundity of the cosmic fall, and the glory of cosmic resurrection. We can't get to the glory of cosmic resurrection apart from cosmic death. We can't get to the full glory of the New Creation apart from cosmic resurrection. All of creation must die and be resurrected in order to realize the totality of what no eye can see, no ear can hear (1 Cor 2:9), and no tongue can express at the present moment. Cosmic restoration falls almost infinitely short on so many levels and too easily feeds into cultural accommodation in the present age. Cosmic annihilation also falls terribly short of the biblical future-vision and too easily feeds into escapism and confused, arrogant, or even angry cultural engagement. Cosmic bodily and physical resurrection properly preserves both continuity and discontinuity, just as with Paul in 1 Cor 15 and with John in the latter chapters of Revelation. The endless debates about annihilation versus restoration, and the proper interpretation of 2 Pet 3 and the book of Revelation, will never be settled apart from a broader theological argument that unites the major affirmations of Scripture. Debated passages (e.g., "the heavens will pass away with a roar and the elements will be destroyed with intense heat and the earth and its work will be discovered"; "Since all these things are to be destroyed . . . what sort of people ought you to be in holy conduct"; does Revelation imply something like a transitional millennium, and when John's heavenly city descends to earth is that the final or ultimate state or the transitional and penultimate state?) must be interpreted by major biblical themes and sound and comprehensive theological reflection.

5. While much remains unknown, *the bodily resurrection of Christ is the critical foundation and proper framework for understanding the direction or trajectory of universal resurrection.* Hence, the fundamentals of cosmic restoration certainly involve purification from sin and restoration of God's creation and eschatological intent. Yet the bodily resurrection of Christ is also the firstfruits of the resurrection of the crown of creation, humanity, and the entire cosmos which is humanity's natural and only true habitat. Jesus the Christ—the Logos, Alpha and Omega—redeems the past and charts the true future. He died

and was buried, raised, appeared, and ascended (1 Cor 15:3–7; Luke 2:50–51; Acts 1:10–11; John 14:2; John 20:17). Messiah's resurrection is a foretaste of our future and the New Creation where the perishable is resurrected to the imperishable, the natural is resurrected to a natural realm ruled by the spiritual—the Triune Spirit—the weak is resurrected to the powerful, and the dishonorable is resurrected to the glorious (1 Cor 15:42–45).

> And the wolf will dwell with the lamb,
> And the leopard will lie down with the young goat,
> And the calf and the young lion and the fattened steer will be together;
> And a little boy will lead them.
> Also the cow and the bear will graze,
> Their young will lie down together,
> And the lion will eat straw like the ox.
> The nursing child will play by the hole of the cobra,
> And the weaned child will put his hand on the viper's den.
> They will not hurt or destroy in all My holy mountain,
> For the earth will be full of the knowledge of the Lord
> As the waters cover the sea. (Isa 11:6–9)

And the theological capstone of this glorious future-vision that should define our present existence and kingdom service is the crystalline civilization and City of God with overflowing love for God, others, and God's creation, and co-regency and co-creativity and vice-regency with Christ. We are not fully and finally human, ourselves, or holy apart from history fulfilled, kingdoms redeemed, and a resurrected cosmos. The curse and sin will pass away, and the repentant, the pure, the meek, the merciful, and the peacemakers will inherit all things and reign with Christ. "And He will wipe away every tear from their eyes; and there will no longer be any death; there will no longer be any mourning, or crying, or pain; the first things have passed away" (Rev 21:4).

THE FUTURE ALREADY

This profound and majestic vision pours meaning, purpose, and living water into every macro and micro reality and moment of the present. To repeat, as it has been so often distorted, the resurrected cosmos underscores discontinuity with sin and present limitations but continuity with God's created intent and ultimate future.

Bringing others to Christ includes but is far more than escape from judgment. Lives are reoriented around the New Creation. True believers believe and step into God's future. Musical, artistic, and architectural creations, if truly beautiful and of God, contribute to forever culture and civilization. History and the lives of previous generations matter, contributed to the epic story, and will not only be remembered but will color and enhance our shared, resurrected, cosmic future.

Leadership, purity, and maturity learned today prepare believers for co-regency tomorrow. Curiosity, exploration, and discovery, which reflect and fulfill the image of God, don't end but begin again and intensify in the New Creation. Those standing for authentic justice now will reign with Christ and mediate divine justice forever. Our destiny is writ large in Scripture.

Education is not merely for lifelong learning but also for forever learning. Mastery of the *trivium, quadrivium,* liberal arts, philosophy, theology, history, and quantum physics not only enriches the present and preps for final exams. Such mastery is a prerequisite for *the* co-regency final exam and a foundation for everlasting, holistic, abundant, flourishing life everlasting.

Redeemed humanity, human experience, relationships, families, cities, kingdoms, joys, sorrows, history, culture, civilization, and the cosmos are all interconnected, born again, and raised from death to life. Every moment truly counts for time and eternity, and not one historical moment, tear, or smile are wasted as the groaning creation moves inexorably to its true end:

> For I consider that the sufferings of this present time are not worthy *to be* compared with the glory that is to be revealed to us. For the eagerly awaiting creation waits for the revealing of the sons *and daughters* of God. For the creation was subjected to futility, not willingly, but because of Him who subjected *it*, in hope that the creation itself also will be set free from its slavery to corruption into the freedom of the glory of the children of God. For we know that the whole creation groans and suffers the pains of childbirth together until now. And not only *that*, but also we ourselves, having the first fruits of the Spirit, even we ourselves groan within ourselves, waiting eagerly for *our* adoption as sons *and daughters*, the redemption of our body. For in hope we have been saved, but hope that is seen is not hope; for who hopes for what he *already* sees? But if we hope for what we do not see, through perseverance we wait eagerly *for it*. (Rom 8:18–25)

Hence, this is our defining future-vision that changes all things and already contributes to and becomes the future. "Things which eye has not seen and ear has not heard, And *which* have not entered the human heart, All that God has prepared for those who love Him" (1 Cor 2:9). Future-visions rule, and the biblical future-vision rules over all.

CHAPTER 6

THE EXTRAORDINARY HISTORICAL MOMENT

OUR NEW AGE OF POST-CHRISTENDOM ANTICHRISTISM

[In] many influential cultural, political, and intellectual precincts, C for *Christian* has become the new scarlet letter.... [Not to mention] the antireligious [missiles and shots fired or] fusillade [and "the ongoing vilification of Christians"] now riddling popular culture via movies, books, videos, cartoons, and related popular fare that denigrates people of faith.... [There is a] toxic new force [and future-vision] hurtling across the United States and other ... societies.... [And] the domestic campaign against belief looks increasingly like one front in a larger global campaign against Christians, period.... [Many are asking,] "What is a believer to do these days? ... Where will we go?" ... Today's historic explosion of intolerance toward [biblical Judeo-Christian] religious believers did not erupt out of nowhere. It has a long prehistory....[1]

—MARY EBERSTADT, IT'S DANGEROUS TO BELIEVE

Have you not heard of that madman who lit a lantern in the bright morning hours, ran to the market place, and cried incessantly: "I seek God! I seek God!" As many of those who did not believe in [the Judeo-Christian] God were standing around just then, he provoked much laughter. Has he got lost? asked one. Did he lose his way like a child? asked another.... Thus they yelled

---

1. Eberstadt, *It's Dangerous*, x, xi, xv, xvi, 1.

and laughed. The madman jumped into their midst and pierced them with his eyes. "Whither is God?" he cried; "I will tell you. We have killed him—you and I. All of us are his murderers. But—how did we do this? How could we drink up the sea? Who gave us the sponge to wipe away the entire horizon? What were we doing when we unchained this earth from its sun? Whither is it moving now? Whither are we moving? Away from all suns? Are we not plunging continually? Backward, sideward, forward, in all directions? Is there still any up or down? Are we not straying as through an infinite nothing? . . . Do we not need to light lanterns in the morning? Do we hear nothing as yet of the noise of the grave diggers who are burying God? . . . God is dead. God remains dead. And we have killed him." . . . Here the madman fell silent and looked again at his listeners; and they, too, were silent and stared at him in astonishment. At last he threw his lantern on the ground, and it broke into pieces and went out. "I have come too early," he said then; "my time is not yet. This tremendous event is still on its way, still, wandering; it has not yet reached the ears of men. Lightning and thunder require time; the light of the stars requires time; deeds, though done, still require time to be seen and heard. This deed is still more distant from them than the most distant stars—and yet they have done it themselves." It has been related further that on the same day the madman forced his way into several churches and there struck up his requiem *aeternam deo* [eternal rest to God]. Led out and called to account he is said always to have replied nothing but: "What after all are these churches now if they are not the tombs and sepulchers of God?"

—FRIEDRICH NIETZSCHE, THE PARABLE OF THE MADMAN, 1882[2]

It has happened to them according to the true proverb, "A DOG RETURNS TO IT OWN VOMIT," and, "A sow, after washing, *returns* to wallowing in the mire."

—2 PETER 2:22[3]

---

2. Nietzsche, "Madman," 181–82.

3. While this verse primarily applies to those who have fallen away from biblical faith, it certainly has a relevant application to entire civilizations, once immeasurably and often unknowingly blessed by being somewhat in orbit around the light and influence of the Logos, now rejecting Abraham's cosmic blessing, self-destructing, careening out of orbit, and ever plunging into darkness.

WHERE DID THAT COME FROM?

Have you ever wondered "Where did that come from?" Things seemingly have moved at warp speed toward cultural antichristism, even, and especially, in civilizations and faith communities that once openly sought to align with biblical Judeo-Christian values and Logocentrism. The majority of power centers, players, and younger generations now say that the Judeo-Christian faith may be "true for you but not for me."[4] Many view Christism as dangerous. Some essentially affirm that parents teaching biblical values are terrorists in a country that once placed the Ten Commandments in public buildings in the nation's capital. Others harass and persecute such parents.

What did we expect? The Great or Greatest Generation won two world wars, and is to be commended, but lost the cosmic spiritual conflict between the two cities. Everything has been redefined. Lies, deception, and tyranny are viewed as moral and defined as saving "democracy." The idea that postmodern relativism is a passing fad or fancy is absurd in view of the daily news and present cultural quagmire. In the Western context, God, truth, meaning, words, freedom, and America or the American experiment have all, to some degree, died culturally or been redefined or fundamentally transformed. We are seeing before our very eyes exactly what AJC relativistic *and* tyrannical postmodernism looks like and what was predicted.[5] Only gaslighting would suggest otherwise.

In any event, the real enemy of antichristism is not traditionally religious parents or any groups or individuals, but the Judeo-Christian Bible. The religion of the Bible (and its basic morality), once viewed as the principal support of free societies, has implicitly or explicitly been redefined as an intolerant hateful or terroristic manual. Some are still hesitant to attack directly the world's best seller and largest religion. However, increasingly, even in formerly Logos-influenced political experiments, such hesitancy is vanishing.

Other politicians, pastors, and priests maintain that they are genuine Christians or Roman Catholics by simply redefining "Christian" and/or rewriting, redefining, and revising many or most scriptural and historic Christian teachings, beliefs, ethical positions (e.g., marriage, unborn children, justice), beliefs, and terms. The Bible eventually has to be interred along with the Judeo-Christian God that the author of "The Madman" proclaimed is

---

4. Copan, *True for You*.

5. See Copan, *True for You*; Henry, *God*; Henry, *Twilight*; Schaeffer, *How Should*; and countless other works, many of which are included in the bibliography. Writers like Henry and Schaeffer are out of vogue and can be ignored, but on many levels they predicted much of what we are seeing.

dead.[6] Can you hear the echoes of the madman? The Bible is hate speech. Judeo-Christian faithful are potential or actual violent haters and must be dealt with.

While the growth and influence of Judeo-Christian faith communities are increasing in many regions of the world, in other areas of our increasingly connected globe, the West, and especially in America of late, we have reached a historic watershed moment relative to the future. My wife, Carol, and I lived near the Great Smoky Mountains National Park some years ago and loved to walk, hike, and explore these mountainous paths and pathways. I well remember one beautiful day, at a high elevation, when we came upon a sign designating that we were standing on a watershed. The sign also informed us that all the rain and water that shed or separated or drained on one side of the watershed went to the Atlantic Ocean, and all the water that shed on the other side of the watershed went to the Gulf of Mexico. A watershed moment has arrived for many nations, global culture, and civilization, and especially for faith communities.

Judeo-Christian influence and memory have been fading for some time in many regions with Europe often leading the way. Europe's watershed moment with Judeo-Christianity, barring a miracle, is past tense and did not end well for biblical faith. Significant documentation will be presented that hostility, including open hostility, toward Judeo-Christian practice, beliefs, and values is on the increase globally. Some regions have always been opposed, but the increase is especially noticeable and fruitful on formerly Judeo-Christian–influenced soil. In America, however, while the future still seems moldable, the cultural concrete will likely settle within fifty years or less.

Hence, we live in an age characterized by countless future-visions and ideologies that often directly oppose or radically redefine Judeo-Christian influence on the future. For these visions, opposition to or radical reconstruction of the Judeo-Christian or Messianic future-vision of God's kingdom rule on earth is viewed as essential to creating a better life on earth. Hence, these alternative future-visions are accurately, and not pejoratively, referred to as antichristisms: "To be antichrist is to choose to stand against or be hostile to Christ [Messiah], to purposely hinder what Christ stands for."[7] Christism, once seen as advancing human flourishing, is now viewed as regressive, dangerous, unjust, and non-inclusive.

If these antichristisms fully triumph, then the next age will be far more than post-Christian or post-Christendom. We are entering the age of antichrist or the City of Antichrist, where the dominant spirit influencing the

---

6. Nietzsche, "Madman."
7. Mains, *Rise*, 25.

city—representing civilizational, cultural, and community life together—is antichrist. Or the next age can witness incredible kingdom influence and approximation—with our civilizational city influenced by and bending toward the true future. The only possible and long-term means to counter the age of antichrist, given the spirit of antichristism and the brokenness of human nature and culture, is supernatural—a truly miraculous, Messianic kingdom approximation. This certainly includes revival but is far more rich and profound that what many faithful view as revival.

THE ROOT, FRUIT, AND DARK SPIRIT OF LEGION ANTICHRISTISMS

The number of future-vision antichristisms today are incalculable, increasingly militant, and it is difficult for anyone to track them all or serve as a specialist or expert on their key assumptions, beliefs, practices, and historical consequences. This means that even fewer still can "always be prepared" for effectively writing present and future history persuasively and directly. Hence, it is prudent to focus on the core or essence of antichristism, thus illuminating the cultural forest, in order to have a better grasp of how to navigate the limitless future-vision trees.

The spirit of antichrist emerged in Eden, as per the last chapter, and has coursed through the ever-flowing rivers and tributaries of history, yet it has taken a more specific and loosely federated form in recent centuries. That form is to one degree or another indebted to the general approach of Nietzsche, the philosopher and theologian of *The Antichrist*. However, *The Antichrist* in our day is simply the latest form, version, iteration, or incarnation of the biblical spirit of antichrist and false prophets operating inside and outside faith communities, from Genesis to Revelation:

> For false christs and false prophets will arise, and will provide signs and wonders, in order to mislead, if possible, the elect. (Mark 13:22)

> Beloved, do not believe every spirit, but test the spirits to see whether they are from God, because *many false prophets have gone out into the world*. By this you know the Spirit of God: every spirit that confesses that Jesus Christ has come in the flesh is from God; and every spirit that does not confess Jesus is not from God; *this is the spirit of the antichrist*, which you have heard is coming, and now it is already in the world. You are from God, little children, and have overcome them; because

> greater is He who is in you than he who is in the world. (1 John 4:1–4; emphasis added)

> I am amazed that you are so quickly deserting Him who called you by the grace of Christ, for a different gospel[the good news of how to be saved and transformed];[8] which is really not another; only there are some who are disturbing you and want to *distort the gospel of Christ*. But even if we, or an angel from heaven, should preach to you a gospel contrary to what we have preached to you, he is to be accursed! As we have said before, so I say again now, if any man is preaching to you a gospel contrary to what you received, he is to be accursed! (Gal 1:6–9 NASB 1995)[9]

> Children, it is the last hour; and just as you heard that antichrist is coming, even now many antichrists have appeared; from this we know that it is the last hour.... Who is the liar except the one who denies that Jesus is the Christ? This is the antichrist, the one who denies the Father and the Son. (1 John 2:18, 22)

> As a result, we are no longer to be children, tossed here and there by waves and carried about by every wind of doctrine, by the trickery of people, by craftiness in deceitful scheming; but speaking the truth in love, we are to grow up in all aspects into Him who is the head, that is, Christ. (Eph 4:14–15)

> For our struggle is not against flesh and blood, but against the rulers, against the powers, against the world forces of this darkness, against the spiritual forces of wickedness in the heavenly [or high and powerful, not otherworldly] places. (Eph 6:12)

Hence, this work strives to emphasize the underlying root of the antichristism fruit, as well as the foundational root of kingdom approximation fruit. The root of the solution is a robust, culturally and intellectually engaged theology, pathos, spirit, and praxis known or framed in this work as the theology of Approximation. Such a constructive theology needs to look beyond the endless and toxic future-visions and antichristisms to the source or root of these widespread pathologies.

---

8. Gospel is the message of salvation and good news; 1 Cor 15; Rom 1:16; Rom 10:9–13; Mark 16:15; Acts 2:38. The Greek uses *euangelion* and *euangelizo* with over one hundred biblical references to the noun and verb forms of the term.

9. As a reminder, all Scripture references are from the NASB 2020 unless otherwise noted.

NIETZSCHE RULES, FROM THE GRAVE

Tragically, though dark days often serve as a catalyst for kingdom influence, some of the more militant future-visions today have imbibed deeply of many elements articulated in *The Antichrist* of Friedrich Nietzsche—often referred to as the patron saint or most influential philosopher of our relativistic, antichristism, and postmodern age.[10]

These polluted nineteenth-century reservoirs of Nietzsche's antichristism build upon prior ancient, medieval, and modern antichristisms and now constitute the very air we breathe. For example, Nietzsche and the present generation increasingly want to return to the spirit and immorality of ancient Memphis, Rome, and Athens. Today, we often hear the call to embrace the bold and unbridled spirit of ancient conquerors and cultures and the virtues and morality of polyamory, homosexuality, abortion, and possibly even infanticide—to name a few.

These many future-visions are superficially and frequently treated as discreet or separate assaults on biblical faith when, in fact, they share the same root and are one in spirit. Such influential and toxic ideologies include occult Nazism, atheistic Marxism, neo-Marxism, AJC cancel culture, a victimization culture, individual and cultural moral relativism, anarchism, and some forms of what today is often referred to as radical postmodernism. This observation concerning antichristism visions does not overlook the reality that some toxic future-visions, like Manifest Destiny, claim to be Christian even while undermining authentic biblical Christianity. As noted, civilization's cast of characters consists of the seducers, the seduced, the enablers, and the true line of promise bringing Abraham's Logos-centered blessing to the whole world.

The spirit of antichrist is wafting through every moment of our civilizational life and air. Listen closely to post-Christian "saint" Nietzsche, who died in his fifties (1900) as an insane man—from brain cancer, or psychiatric illness, or his own nihilistic philosophy, or perhaps some combination thereof or some other disputed cause, such as syphilis:

> What is good?—Whatever augments the feeling of power, the will to power [or the proper and appropriate aspiration of superior and refined humans to rule and redeem feeble Judeo-Christian civilization], [thus true] power itself, in man.
>
> What is evil?—Whatever springs from weakness.

---

10. See Blackburn, *Truth*, 75.

> What is happiness?—The feeling that power increases—that resistance is overcome.
>
> Not contentment, but more power; not peace at any price, but war; not virtue, but efficiency (virtue in the Renaissance sense, *virtu*, virtue free of [the evil of] moral acid [Judeo-Christian morality]).
>
> The weak and the botched shall perish [rather than inherit the earth or cosmos]: first principle of our charity. And one should help them to it.
>
> What is more harmful than any vice?—Practical sympathy for the botched and the weak—[meaning] Christianity.[11]

Nietzsche assesses Christ and Christianity with much vitriol and immense historical consequences. Nietzsche predates and sways popular culture as illustrated by elements of very popular and well-known works such as John Lennon's "Imagine," Bertrand Russell's *Why I Am Not a Christian*, Christopher Hitchens's *God Is Not Great*, and Richard Dawkins's *The God Delusion*. Nietzsche's future-vision rules:

> We should not [try to salvage or] deck out and embellish Christianity: it has waged a war to the death against this higher type of man [superior man or humanity, *Übermensch*], it [Christianity] has put all the deepest instincts of this type under its ban, it has developed its concept of evil, of the Evil One himself, out of these [inferior] instincts—the strong man as the typical reprobate, the "outcast among men."[12] Christianity has taken the part of all the weak, the low, the botched; it has made an ideal out of antagonism to all the self-preservative instincts of sound life; it has corrupted even the faculties of those natures that are intellectually most vigorous, by representing the highest intellectual values as sinful, as misleading, as full of temptation. The most lamentable example: the corruption of Pascal, who believed that his intellect had been destroyed by original sin, whereas it was destroyed by Christianity!
>
> Christianity is called the religion of pity.—Pity stands in opposition to all the tonic [invigorating] passions that augment the energy of the feeling of aliveness [or well-being]: it [Christianity] is a depressant. A man loses power when he pities.

---

11. Nietzsche, *Antichrist*, sect. 2.

12. Note Saul Alinsky's dedication of his influential *Rules for Radicals* to Satan, referenced earlier.

Let us not underestimate this fact: that we ourselves, we free spirits, are already a "transvaluation of all values," a visualized declaration of war and victory against all the old concepts of "true" and "not true."

The fact that the strong races of northern Europe did not repudiate this Christian god does little credit to their gift for religion—and not much more to their taste. They ought to have been able to make an end of such a moribund and worn-out product of the *décadence*. A curse lies upon them because they were not equal to it . . . [and failed to repudiate] this pitiful god of Christian mono-theism!

Buddhism is a hundred times as realistic as Christianity, . . . [and] it puts the self-deception that lies in [Christian] moral concepts behind it; it is, in my phrase, *beyond good and evil*.

Buddhism promises nothing, but actually fulfills; Christianity promises everything, but *fulfills nothing*—Hard upon the heels of the "glad tidings" [the Christian gospel] came the worst imaginable: those of Paul. In Paul is incarnated . . . the genius for hatred, the vision of hatred, the relentless logic of hatred [of the true spirit of life; biblical Christians are thus haters]. *What*, indeed, has not this dysangelist [the anti-good-news preacher] sacrificed to hatred! Above all, the Saviour: he nailed him [Christ] to *his own cross.*

Christianity is to be understood only by examining the soil from which it sprung—it is *not* a reaction against Jewish instincts; it is their inevitable product; it is simply one more step in the awe-inspiring logic of the Jews.

The Jews are the most remarkable people in the history of the world, for when they were confronted with the question, to be or not to be, they chose, with perfectly unearthly deliberation, to be at any price: this price involved a radical falsification of all nature, of all naturalness, of all reality, of the whole inner world, as well as of the outer.

Our age *knows better*. . . . What was formerly merely sickly now becomes indecent—it is indecent to be a Christian today.

Christianity destroyed for us the whole harvest of ancient civilization.[13]

And just in case anyone is unclear concerning the radical nature of Nietzsche's future-vision, he offers and clarifies his own summary of his work *The Antichrist*:

---

13. Nietzsche, *Antichrist*, sects. 5, 7, 13, 19, 24, 38, 42, 60.

With this I come to a conclusion and pronounce my judgment. I condemn Christianity; I bring against the Christian church the most terrible of all the accusations that an accuser has ever had in his mouth. It is, to me, the greatest of all imaginable corruptions; it seeks to work the ultimate corruption, the worst possible corruption. The Christian church has left nothing untouched by its depravity; it has turned every value into worthlessness, and every truth into a lie, and every integrity into baseness of soul. Let any one dare to speak to me of its "humanitarian" blessings! Its deepest necessities range it against any effort to abolish distress; it lives by distress; it *creates* distress to make *itself* immortal.... For example, the worm of sin: it was the church that first enriched mankind with this misery!—The "equality of souls before God"—this fraud, this *pretext* for the *rancunes* [uncountable resentment] of [or by] all the base-minded—this explosive concept, ending in revolution, the modern idea, and the notion of overthrowing the whole social order—this is *Christian* dynamite.... The "humanitarian" blessings of Christianity forsooth! [Forsooth used here likely means surprised indignation.] To breed out of *humanitas* a self-contradiction, an art of self-pollution, a will to lie at any price, an aversion and contempt for all good and honest instincts! All this, to me, is the "humanitarianism" of Christianity!—Parasitism as the only practice of the church; with its anaemic and "holy" ideals, sucking all the blood, all the love, all the hope out of life; the beyond as the will to deny all reality; the cross as the distinguishing mark of the most subterranean conspiracy ever heard of,—*against health, beauty, well-being, intellect, kindness of soul—against life itself.*

This eternal accusation against Christianity I shall write upon all walls, wherever walls are to be found—I have letters that even the blind will be able to see.... *I call Christianity the one great curse, the one great intrinsic depravity, the one great instinct of revenge, for which no means are venomous enough, or secret, subterranean and small enough,—I call it the one immortal blemish upon the human race....*

And mankind reckons *time* from the *dies nefastus* [the death of secularity] when this fatality befell—from the *first day of Christianity!—Why not* rather from its [Christianity's] last day]?—*From today?*—The transvaluation of all values [reevaluation, repudiation, and transformation of all values]![14]

---

14. Nietzsche, *Antichrist*, sect. 61. Emphasis added.

The point of reviewing these many affirmations in detail is not to join the endless debates about questions concerning Nietzsche's spiritual journey, whether he was gay (in the contemporary sense), when or if he became an atheist or nihilist, or if he acknowledged any value whatsoever for religion. What is clear is that his "death of God" prophecy referred to the hoped for death of allegiance to the Judeo-Christian God and Judeo-Christian–influenced beliefs, practices, ethics, and culture. Nietzsche increasingly rules.

Believers today are unprepared for antichristism, the City of Antichrist, and bewildered by the seeming hate or animus toward Christianity and the redefinition of everything. While certainly and emotionally jarring at times, especially the pace of change, the Judeo-Christian citizens of Nietzsche's emerging City of Antichrist should have seen this coming. Many colleges and universities, for multiple decades, have increasingly become the training, reeducation, indoctrination, or boot camps and churches of the fanatical blind-faith religion of this dark city.

Nietzsche utterly rejected the idea that Christianity could be reformed or embellished; he found more to value in Buddhism. The point here is that Nietzsche, perhaps one of the most famous and influential philosophers in recent centuries, uprooted the City of Kingdom Approximation and articulated a massively impactful antichristism future-vision that shares key emphases with many other powerful and toxic beliefs, values, and future-visions:

- Christianity is the problem, not the solution (see also Russell, *Why I Am Not a Christian*).
- The Christian future-vision needs to be replaced; it is harmful to individuals and civilization (see also Marx and Engels, *The Communist Manifesto*); Christianity creates rather than abolishes distress.
- Belief in the Christian God and afterlife is illusory and escapist (Marx and Engels; Freud, *The Future of an Illusion*; Feuerbach, *The Essence of Christianity*; Dawkins, *Outgrowing God*); Christianity is the happy drug (or opiate) that props up unhealthy and toxic Judeo-Christian influence and economic, gender, and racial oppression.
- Christianity is hostile to life and honest instincts like non-heterosexual and non-monogamous sex, appropriate usage and pursuit of power by the deserving elite, health, beauty, well-being, and intellect.
- Christianity elevates the weak, is vengeful to the strong, and destroyed the harvest of pre-Christian civilization (long live Greece, this-worldly Greek culture, and some aspects of Roman civilization). The birth of Christ marks the death of glorious secularity; calendars should be

changed from orbiting the Logos and birth of Christ to orbiting the new post-Christian and anti-Christian values and the revaluation of all values (note that many modernist movements, the French Revolution, or Communism, actually created new calendars).

- Christianity cannot be fixed or reformed, and Christian values need to be repudiated entirely; we need to repudiate Christian influence on civilization and replace Christian values with the new values more aligned with the best of the strong and courageous who ruled ancient empires.

- Equality before God was a pretext for revenge by the mob against the strong in the name of a revolution for freedom and democracy—for a mob rule that removed the superior rulers from the throne of the civilizational city. Democracy is decadent, inferior, and anti-human and inspired by the weakness of Christianity.

- Judaism and Christianity are flawed and harmful, with Christianity taking the anti-life and anti-civilization glorification of weakness to the next level, and then Paul even further corrupting the world with the most cancerous form of Christianity; hence, anti-Semitism and antichristism are both appropriate.

- The enlightened strong should lead culture and civilization, rather than those appointed by life-denying churches or elected by the Judeo-Christian-influenced democratic mob; elitism is proper if the strong and smart rule; the masses are incapable of leading; democracy was birthed in part by Christianity and is indeed a toxic ideology and future-vision.

- Agnosticism, skepticism, meaninglessness, and atheism are the courageous and honest approaches to reality. Systems of belief and truth are not only impossible but irrational power plays where the weak try to subvert the rightful strong and true civilizational leaders in the name of God and religion. The true enemies of liberated humanity are systems of truth and beliefs, and the pervasive belief in absolute moral and ethical norms.

- Nationalism is merely an outgrowth of such beliefs being used as power and is the enemy. Nations and peoples must bow to true global leaders and abandon the illusion of truth that grounds us and all things. "There is no truth."[15] There is power—Christianity—masquerading

---

15. The context of the full quote is important for understanding Nietzsche (see appendix B).

as truth, beliefs, and religion. In an evolutionary world with eternally recurring cycles headed nowhere, what is proper or fit for the true elite is to possess the most power and rule.

- The human mind and heart are not radically sinful as the Christian Pascal concluded; the fit and strong use their intellect to adapt to the evolutionary world, whereas the masses, who need to be led, immerse themselves in illusions.

- Christianity gloried in and created weakness and distress around the globe, and the superior leaders of the coming glorious antichristism future should, somewhat ironically, view the masses as sheep-like and inferior, while also having a hypersensitivity toward suffering, oppression, and true victims—just as did Nietzsche, even for abused horses.

- Those who are strong and honest today will acknowledge that the quest for reason and cross-cultural normative truth has destroyed any rational belief in God; therefore, churches are now the tombs or sepulchers of the Judeo-Christian God. The funeral is past tense for much of the globe. It is time to accept this post-mortem civilizational reality and move on.

Nietzsche's rants are much more than a philosophy. Here we have an immensely influential, toxic, antichristism future-vision and global movement that has written history and polluted other future-visions. World War II and the Jewish genocide were at least in part not only the distorted consequence and application of Nietzsche's vision but also the direct application of some of his specific teachings.

As per Nietzsche's famous parable of "The Madman," quoted previously in this chapter, the age of antichrist has and will approximate hell on earth as civilization experiences the cultural—not the actual—death and absence of the Judeo-Christian God. While some in the nineteenth century were predicting that the next century would be the golden *Christian Century*, Nietzsche prophesied that unparalleled chaos and bloodshed would be poured out upon those who murdered, culturally destroyed and eradicated, the Judeo-Christian God—the central pillar of any meaningful expression of flourishing civilization for Judeo-Christian believers. *The Antichrist's* spirit fragments the pillar of belief in the Judeo-Christian God. God is buried in his own churches, which are now cosmic tombs or sepulchers.

Nietzsche is right in part. This work argues that the many antichrists, but also the less than faithful antichrist-enablers who have failed to incarnate authentic biblical faith communities, are his [the Christian God's cultural] murderers. But how did we do this? How could we drink up the sea? Who gave us the sponge to wipe away the entire horizon? What were we doing when we unchained this earth from its sun? Whither is it moving now? Whither are we moving? Away from all suns? Are we not plunging continually? Backward, sideward, forward, in all directions? Is there still any up or down? Are we not straying as through an infinite nothing? Do we not feel the breath of empty space? Has it not become colder? Is not night continually closing in on us?[16]

The attentive reader and cultural analyst increasingly will hear the reverberation and frequent resonance and amplification of this spirit in manifold areas of our contemporary world, especially "higher" education and contemporary "entertainment" and the media. For example, there exists a nearly constant assault by Hollywood on Judeo-Christian beliefs and practice, sometimes direct and sometimes indirect, and often delivered in high definition, very creatively and seductively, with world class choreography. The most effective attacks are often indirect, seductive, incremental (gradual and paced), superficially humorous, and subversive (not direct but overt or hidden).

Some attack Judeo-Christian beliefs and influence directly, like Nietzsche, but more common is the incremental dismemberment of Judeo-Christian cultural assumptions and influence—often one belief, one practice, one ideology, one future-vision, and one thought at a time. A short list of illustrations includes the repudiation or redefinition of these beliefs and practices: marriage, gender, monogamy, freedom and religious freedom, God-given rights, human sinfulness (the sinfulness of the liberators is especially denied), sinful and flawed human reasoning, the glorious image of God in humanity, absolute and cross-cultural norms for morality, the possibility of cross-cultural and normative truth, belief in the Judeo-Christian God, the centrality of the biblical God for all things, and the true hope for civilization or the proper role of the state prior to the rule of the Messiah and the New Creation.

Nietzsche was spot on concerning another prediction. He wrote that "[Judeo-]Christianity is a system, a view of things that is conceived as a connected whole. If you break off a major concept from it, [such as] faith in God, you break up the whole as well: there are no necessities left to hold onto anymore."[17] That day of cultural fragmentation arrived as early as 1750

16. Nietzsche, "Madman."

17. Nietzsche, *Twilight*, 53; Nietzsche, *Twilight of the Idols and the Anti-Christ*, 80–81.

in much of Europe and 1970 in much of the United States. Nietzsche also reveals how some, in attacking one piece of Judeo-Christian influence (e.g., traditional marriage), may have a much larger agenda than a single issue like so-called justice for nontraditional marriage partners.

Even a semi-attentive assessment of the movies, music, entertainment, humor, law, education, politics, and the media of the last fifty years in America, or longer in other formerly Christian-influenced regions, reveals a near constant assault on Judeo-Christian civilizational influence. Nietzsche's toxic future-vision and antichristism seem to be getting the last laugh while most of the religious faithful remain clueless as to the root and enormity of the problem and threat. Judeo-Christian believers are still trying to win over and be winsome with antichristism soldiers with boots on their necks. Love and forgiveness are biblical under persecution, but naivete is a losing game plan in the present moment relative to navigating and influencing the City of Antichrist.

The Judeo-Christian–influenced and constructed Titanic truly is about to sink. And covert incrementalism and the piecemeal dismemberment of Judeo-Christian influence are increasingly being replaced with manipulative and oppressive antichristism.

The creatively insane and poetic words of our postmodern patron saint Nietzsche, certainly apt for our times, do not have to be the final word for our generation or future generations. A persuasive and biblical answer to "plunging continually," no "up or down," and the "infinite nothing" is a resurrection and New Creation theology of Approximation, not an enabling theology of fatalistic escapism.

Everything is at stake, and the collaborative and approximating work together of Judeo-Christian faith communities and all people of good will, or lack thereof, will truly write the script for future generations. And this script will foster famine or flourishing, peace or war, economic stagnation or fecundity, a joyful sense of community or balkanization, true educational institutions or reeducation camps, God-given inalienable rights or governmental-given and fleeting rights, and religious and political freedom or oppression and persecution.

SNAPSHOTS, PREDICTIONS, AND EVIDENCE OF AN ACCELERATING NIETZSCHEAN WORLD

Most of us can read, see, hear, and simply and deeply feel the reality, significance, gravity, and import of the current watershed moment. Many feel the spirit of Nietzsche and antichristism everywhere, even in some of our churches and synagogues, and some are beginning to grasp the real world consequences of the deeper crisis of words, worldviews, beliefs, assumptions, loyalties, and loves.

Even an assessment of cultural and civilizational evolution or devolution in the short time frame of twenty years is telling. While I'm no particular fan of the American political family known as the Cheneys, Lynne Cheney's prophetic work (1995) concerning the alarming decay and powerful influence of the academy on culture is masterful and a must-read more than a quarter-century after its publication.

We were warned. Sometimes the truthfulness of the diagnosis is more compelling based on its predictive value—and Cheney was largely spot on, and certainly can say "I told you so."

It was all there in Cheney's *Telling the Truth*: discussions of critical race theory and systemic racism; Nietzsche; personal but not normative truth and ethics; the alleged morality of false accusations and bearing false witness; the accelerating and systemic attack on Judeo-Christian–influenced civilization; the relativistic abuse of the once noble concept of multiculturalism; the cleansing or purging of Messianism from the ivory tower; historical and Constitutional revisionism and demonization; the total rejection of even the possibility of objective history, truth, and morality; selective and hypocritical moral outrage; and the shameless call to replace the quest for truthful, balanced, fact-driven, objective journalism with the "New News," which is nothing more than seductive and manipulative propaganda and advocacy. Nietzsche's future-vision rules, and Cheney was the prophetic canary in the mine shaft.

Appendix C provides many additional illustrations, well-documented evidence and classic quotes—direct quotations that will preach and teach—of Cheney's prescient (foretelling) predictions. She surgically exposed the core of exactly how higher education was being taken over by AJC and APF (anti-political-freedom) assumptions and teaching in the decades prior to her publication, and how that academic revolution largely overthrew every controlling sector of culture and civilization. AJCism and APFism privilege rule in the haunting shadow of Nietzsche.

It is most instructive, and even eye-opening, to review Cheney's time-capsule snapshot of our watershed moment. Cheney's dated but ever relevant conclusion includes the following central affirmation: "I have tried to show, it is from colleges and universities that messages radiate—or fail to radiate—to schools, to legal institutions, to popular culture, and to politics about the importance of reason, of trying to overcome bias, of seeking truth through evidence and verification. Colleges and universities are the wellspring of the ideas around which we organize ourselves."[18]

Yet increasing numbers of educators have abandoned the noble task of free inquiry and created the poisoned and tribalistic well that chokes the very life out of civilizational community, regional communities, cities, faith communities, families, and individuals. The academy and culture in the mid-1990s, as was almost over-abundantly and prophetically documented by Cheney (see appendix C),[19] had drunk very deeply of this spirit of AJCism and APFism. This cancerous metamorphosis occurred decades earlier—I personally experienced an aggressive version of this at a state university even prior to the 1990s. This aggressive posture especially became very manifest in political, legal, and media leadership well prior to the twenty-first century, and has only accelerated thereafter.

Cheney ended her argument with the tragic Mr. Softee group murder story, a cultural omen, and observations that seems ever relevant, though perhaps this story is now mild by comparison to today's realities, more than one quarter of a century later:

> In the late spring of 1994 an incident in Philadelphia provided a chilling vision of life without . . . [any objective, externally real, and normatively and morally true] qualities. Forty-nine-year-old Mohammed Jaberipour was working a route in South Philadelphia in a Mister Softee ice cream truck when a sixteen-year-old tried to extort money from him. Jaberipour refused to give the sixteen-year-old what he demanded, and the youth shot Jaberipour. As the father of three lay dying, neighborhood teenagers laughed at him and mocked his agony with a song they composed on the spot—"They killed Mr. Softee." Another ice cream truck driver and friend of Jaberipour, who came on the scene shortly after the shooting, described what he saw. "It wasn't human," he said. "When I got there people were laughing and asking me for ice cream. I was crying. My best friend was killed. They were acting as though a cat had died, not a human being."[20]

Much more than Mr. Jaberipour dying is represented by this dark day in the so-called city of brotherly love, the city of the Declaration of Independence and the Constitution, and the city now increasingly known for its violence. Philadelphia has been redefined.

18. Cheney, *Telling the Truth*, 198.
19. Cheney, *Telling the Truth*.
20. Cheney, *Telling the Truth*, 204–5.

When God is dead in the City of Antichrist, a God who cannot be actually or objectively murdered but only culturally dethroned, it truly is we who have killed him, as Nietzsche put it. But more fundamentally, when AJCism kills God, it is not God who dies, but genuinely flourishing culture, freedom, and civilization that dies. And the *imago Dei* dies. We die.

We reduce ourselves to being sub-human, no longer the crown of creation and the image of God, and we approximate hell rather than New Creation heaven. When God dies, truth, meaning, words, humanity, freedom, love, and noble experiments in more perfect civilizational unions also die. And so do individuals like Mr. Jaberipour who are just trying to serve the community and provide for their families. The powerless are often the primary victims of elitist ideologies and programs that claim to protect or liberate the powerless and marginalized.

Cheney's snapshot of the mid-1990s argues that we have become a nation of spectators, reducing everything to a show or entertainment: "Without the idea that we live in reality with other people who are as real as we are, [genuine] compassion is impossible and so is any other virtue one could name. Nothing beyond the gratification of the moment [or the tribe] matters in such a world, not [authentic] fairness, not [true] justice, not responsibility, not honor. None of them matters because in such a world none of them exists."[21] The other—of another tribe—is the enemy. The other is by definition and in advance of any evidence, and without any assessment of the content of one's character inferior humanity—*untermensch* (sub-human). The *untermensch* (a term defined and used in various ways by Nietzsche and the Nazis), at a bare minimum, should not possess political power or voice—perhaps not even political freedom or life. The City of Antichrist must not be ruled (*kratia*) by the people (*demos*)—democracy. Democracy, which is mob rule and un-aspiring mediocrity or worse, must be banished from the city. The enlightened elite and self-deluded superior humans or*ubermenschen* must rule.

Though most instructive and rather prophetic in 1995, what Cheney did not foresee was how within two decades virtually every significant term and concept would be redefined out of orbit of the Logos—and essentially out of existence. Genuine, biblical, Judeo-Christian–influenced terms and conceptions such as compassion, virtue, fairness, justice, responsibility, and honor would be, with Nietzsche's antichristism, "revaluated" or "re-normed" to create a new reality and a new normal. Biblical and eternal justice, or even early American justice for those who even see any ongoing relevance/value

---

21. Cheney, *Telling the Truth*, 205.

of the American experiment, would be emptied of divine influence and reduced to personal and tribal advocacy and power games.

As many have said, probably going back to ancient Greece, justice has become "just us."

Nietzsche, the academy, and AJCism truly rule. Cheney observed in 1995, "Outside the protective environment of the campus, these ideas have real and devastating effects." She finally concludes, "The virtues that we have increasingly come to believe we must nurture if we are to be successful as a culture simply make no sense if we turn away from reason and reality; . . . [hence,] whether we as a society find the will to live in truth is more than a matter for idle speculation. The answer may well determine whether we survive."[22] And a civilization or city that banishes Logos is a civilization or city that has banished normative and life-giving truth (*veritas*) that sets us free (John 8:32).

Nearly a quarter century later, Mary Eberstadt documented how the emerging trends and concerning events of the 1990s have blossomed into a full-fledged and progressively militant opposition to Judeo-Christian believers and Judeo-Christian influence on culture—AJCism. In her more recent (2016) civilizational snapshot, *It's Dangerous to Believe: Religious Freedom and Its Enemies*, the spirit of Nietzsche and antichristism is demonstrated to be increasingly pervasive.

Eberstadt's documentation is extensive, and examples of her evidence—which also can preach and teach—are included in appendix C. *It's Dangerous* tracks the acceleration, expansion, and increasing militancy of AJC culture over three recent decades and thus updates key and foundational aspects of Cheney's argument. The spirit of the times (*zeitgeist*) that we breathe today now views historic and biblical Christianity as the primary problem or obstacle to social justice, DEI (diversity, equity, and inclusion), and civilizational progress. As noted repeatedly, good terms like social justice, diversity, multiculturalism, and inclusion have been hijacked, redefined, and corrupted. I would add that a redefined Christianity may be compatible with some or many aspects of AJC culture, but not biblical and historic Christianity or Judaism.

Doctrinally faithful Christians, according to Eberstadt, are the one remaining minority that can be "mocked—broadly, unilaterally, and with impunity. Not to mention fined, fired, or otherwise punished . . . ."[23] Surely Nietzsche's followers are smiling that millions are slandered as hateful "phobes" and theocrats (religious and fanatic militants demanding

---

22. Cheney, *Telling the Truth*, 206.
23. Eberstadt, *Dangerous*, 204. Also see appendix C.

church-state union). Hence, a new form of witch-hunting is now acceptable in many quarters of formerly Logos-influenced nations, nations influenced by the written and personal Word, and the witches now on trial are traditional/biblical Jews and Christians. And today, mere allegations of "isms" are treated as compelling evidence of guilt. For many believers today the choice is either "my faith" or my job/social standing and future.[24]

Unfortunately, after this brilliant presentation and documentation by Eberstadt, she proffers a solution that only enables the age of antichristism—a future-vision that will be addressed again and rejected later in this work. She assumes and promotes the myth of neutralism—that if we all protect each other's rights and liberty, then perhaps we can all get along. This is also the fatal flaw of what is known as the increasingly popular political perspective of Libertarianism—a sirenic and deceptive, shallow, and simplistic silver bullet in an age of pluralism, tribalism, and outrage.

Thus Eberstadt's solution is that "believers . . . can opt for what Thomas Jefferson and other Founders developed as an antidote to Puritan destructiveness, namely the shared understanding that one's own liberty isn't safe until everyone else is protected." This principle truly has value in terms of creating a legal and ethical principle (Jesus, Kant, Confucius) or world where one is willing to live by the rules prescribed for others. And it is true, as she puts it, that "people must [in many cases] agree to disagree. This is the *sine qua non* of a more civil tomorrow."[25]

Additional concerns with Eberstadt's shallow solution will be addressed later, but she essentially undermines the logic of her own position when suggesting that, during the famous Salem witch trials from which we can learn, "momentum for change had to come from the other side [the persecutors]."[26] Similarly, she again invokes this so-called Jeffersonian and neutralist solution: "The political model that points a way out for progressives and traditionalists alike has been there all along: Thomas Jefferson."[27] But then she hints that her neutralist civil solution is ultimately built on sand by rightly quoting Jacques Maritain: "These [founding experiment] documents [by Mason, Jefferson, Madison] owe their derivation to a Jewish and Christian worldview, and do not spring from any other."[28] Authentic freedom requires Logocentrism.

---

24. Eberstadt, *Dangerous*, 102.
25. Eberstadt, *Dangerous*, 103.
26. Eberstadt, *Dangerous*, 105.
27. Eberstadt, *Dangerous*, 122.
28. Eberstadt, *Dangerous*, 122.

The general principle of being willing to live by the laws or ethics that we want to impose on others is one helpful secondary test but certainly not a sufficient foundation for *How Should We Then Live?* When no norms exist for truth and ethics, and advancing "just us" for one's tribe or self is all that matters as it so often is today, civilization loses the Logocentric glue that binds us together, referees inevitable and non-resolvable conflicts, provides some real freedoms today, and moves us toward and anchors us in the only true future.

However, unless unending tribal conflicts and chaos are acceptable to those rejecting Logos, which they never are, a new civilizational glue or set of commandments (far more than ten) will inevitably emerge, rule, and be mandated due to the unsustainability of cultural fragmentation and chaos. Those mandating diversity today are often belligerent about what practices, beliefs, or even ethnicities should not be included in the enlightened diversity game plan. The thousand commandments of AJC culture are nearly in place in the centers of power in American culture and have been for some time in other regions of the globe—often backed by the force of law, imprisonment, and violence.

Again, there are sincere social justice warriors focusing on sometimes legitimate injustices. Yet for some key warriors the stated battles (a handful of so-called justice issues) are not the real war—the real war for some, with Nietzsche, is against the remaining civilizational influence of the Logos, the personal and written Word. For enlightened social justice ideological blue bloods, winning individual issues (redefining marriage) in the name of justice and inclusion is merely a stepping stone or wedge strategy to dismantle Logocentrism's influence piece by piece, pillar by pillar, and cornerstone by cornerstone.

If the primary Judeo-Christian influence or cultural glue is removed, the ultimate end result will not be Jeffersonian tolerance and the golden rule. Instead, another functional religion or "ism" of some sort—communism, secularism, wokism, liberationist syncretism, or an alternative much less gracious than tolerant Judeo-Christian civilization—will reign.

Two points should be obvious and telling. If, and clearly it is the case that, Judeo-Christian values and assumptions are built into the very warp and woof of civilizations pursuing a more perfect union in law, culture, freedom, and how we treat each other, then the solution in an increasingly antichristism age can hardly be that we all just agree to disagree. The Libertarian silver bullet of limiting government, or the popular neutralist sentiment and myth of "Can't we all just get along?" in the present moment, amounts to nothing less than extreme naivete and dated and flawed thinking.

THE EXTRAORDINARY HISTORICAL MOMENT 175

Eberstadt's prescription, that the momentum for cultural detoxification must come from the persecutors in an age of AJCism, is patently absurd. Those standing in front of tanks are simply flattened in non-Logos influenced cultures. The myth of neutrality and the myth that Judeo-Christian values are not central to some civilizational experiments simply enable the antichristism of the age.

Ironically, Eberstadt again senses her own contradiction and acknowledges, "Yet it is exactly this labyrinthine [Enlightenment-Judeo-Christian framed] religious liberty legacy that makes Jefferson our best guide out of the troubles of our times—at least for unbelievers of good faith."[29] One senses that she is well aware that the problem and the solution run much deeper, that good faith doesn't quite cut it, and that a resurrection of Judeo-Christian values and influence at the heart of church, synagogue, and state is the only cure for antichristism.

Perhaps this is why Eberstadt also acknowledges the trending toward a return to Nietzsche's glory days of Greece and Rome: "Within academia, infanticide [and to some degree pedophilia] has been considered a respectable subject of discussion for many years now."[30] Antichristism is not addressed or countered but instead is enabled by the myth of neutrality or the strict separation of Judeo-Christian values from countries that were birthed in large measure by Judeo-Christian values. Such observations are not rocket science.

Enduring religious freedom flows from the aforementioned wellsprings of the best days of Athens, Jerusalem, Hippo, Wittenberg, Leiden, Oxford, London, and Philadelphia. Antichristism runs much deeper and cannot be healed by the Jeffersonian solution—but much of that argument will be left for my longer and forthcoming book (already referenced) on public theology and eschatology.

In any event, it is obvious that "the beat goes on" as antichristism expands its grip on directing the present watershed moment toward darkness. As this book is being finalized, the nearly daily headlines continue to confirm the theses of Cheney and Eberstadt concerning anti–Judeo-Christian marginalization and oppression.

Additional updates since 2016 are peppered throughout this work, but one headline will suffice for now: "JK Rowling Not Invited to Harry Potter Reunion because She Said Men and Women Are Different."[31] As most are aware, "British author J. K. Rowling is the brains behind the [multimillion selling] Harry Potter book series and even worked closely with the

29. Eberstadt, *Dangerous*, 123.
30. Eberstadt, *Dangerous*, 111.
31. Amico, "JK Rowling."

producers for the movies based on the books. But she was nowhere to be found . . . when the movie's stars reunited for a 'magical' Harry Potter 20th anniversary special."[32] Rowling, as a progressive feminist, infuriates her critics by maintaining the scientific, biological, and creation order distinction between males and females.[33]

This work is arguing that discussions of Rowling, Harry Potter, and gender are important but not at the core. An inadequate ethic or theology of human sexuality is critical but not central. Logocentrism and antichristism, the City of Kingdom Approximation and the City of Antichristism, underlie the conflict, and the conflict is epic and cosmic in scope and consequences. A toxic or anemic theology of human sexuality or theology of the body is ultimately a toxic or anemic theology of the kingdom of God. That already but not yet kingdom is the biblical focus and solution.

All of the evidence of antichristism so far presented, however, probably fails to do justice to the magnitude of the assault on Messianism, Jews, and Christians, especially in recent decades and generations in formerly Messianic-influenced nations. For example, in the American (US) context, the assault on Judeo-Christian influence and biblical values, which has been covertly and overtly mushrooming for centuries, has literally morphed into a toxic, nearly daily, radioactive bombardment. Education, law, politics, entertainment, art, music, media, social media, and peer influence have indirectly and now more directly pilloried every aspect of Judeo-Christian belief, values, practice, thoughts, attitudes, and loves.

In the 1950s and 1960s in America, the covert then eventually overt assault on heterosexual monogamous marriage emerged in literature, education, and, perhaps even more powerfully, in movies and television. Monogamous marriage used to be the norm, and now it is the exception and too often only after significant premarital infidelity and serial fornication and adultery.

The same subversive pattern has and is replicating itself relative to gender issues. In the name of religious neutrality, which is actually pseudo-neutrality (i.e., a false neutrality), strict church-state separation, and freedom of speech, the one nonnegotiable commandment is that most any morality is acceptable except for Judeo-Christian morality. When the influence of the Ten Commandments on culture is removed from civilization, the end result, as noted, is not freedom and neutrality, but over time the Ten Commandments are replaced by thousands of other commandments and

---

32. Migdon, "Harry Potter"; Amico, "JK Rowling."
33. Taylor, "JK Rowling."

the eventual eradication of religious freedom and free speech. We are living in such days.

This antichristism assault is powerful, defining of our generation, and has every appearance of being orchestrated. Certainly, higher education, as evidenced previously, plays a key role in such coordination and integration, as well as certain political ideologies and parties typically birthed by such educational indoctrination. The convergence, however, seems far better orchestrated than what is possible through education.

There seems to be a growing spiritual force or spirit pulsating through the whole of culture and civilization, and much of that pervasive spirit was captured, integrated, and creatively articulated by "The Madman," Nietzsche. The good news is that the spirit of antichrist is no match for the Spirit of Messiah over the long haul—or even the short haul when the City of Kingdom Approximation rules the church and synagogue.

The solution, however, is not the way of adding fuel to the cultural fires, or the different trails blazed by the likes of Oliver Cromwell, Thomas Jefferson, or James Madison. The solution is to align approximation and New Creation theology with compatible beliefs of Logos-influenced more perfect union experiments. This means looking backward, forward, and upward toward our ultimate orbit around the Alpha and Omega of reality. Cultural reform must be cautious but never-ending. The true Rosetta stone for the present moment is the biblical teaching on the Messiah's kingdom that has already enveloped the present moment, and the present advance of the good leaven of kingdom light, salt, and approximation.

LEGION ANTICHRISTISMS VERSUS NEW CREATION APPROXIMATION

Within this framework, Paul's call to discernment is timely: "As a result, we are no longer to be children, tossed here and there by waves and carried about by every wind of doctrine, by the trickery of people, by craftiness in deceitful scheming; but speaking the truth in love, we are to grow up in all aspects into Him who is the head, that is, Christ" (Eph 4:14–15).

The mature must be childlike not childish, innocent as doves and wise as serpents (Matt 10:16) in the current context. The American context has morphed through three major stages, from viewing Christianity largely as a social positive to a social negative:

> Positive World (Pre-1994): Society at large retains a mostly positive view of Christianity. To be known as a good, churchgoing man remains part of being an upstanding citizen. Publicly being

a Christian is a status-enhancer. Christian moral norms are the basic moral norms of society and violating them can bring negative consequences.

Neutral World (1994–2014): Society takes a neutral stance toward Christianity. Christianity no longer has privileged status but is not disfavored. Being publicly known as a Christian has neither a positive nor a negative impact on one's social status. Christianity is a valid option within a pluralistic public square. Christian moral norms retain some residual effect.

Negative World (2014–Present): Society has come to have a negative view of Christianity. Being known as a Christian is a social negative, particularly in the elite domains of society. Christian morality is expressly repudiated and seen as a threat to the public good and the new public moral order. Subscribing to Christian moral views or violating the secular moral order brings negative consequences.[34]

Christian morality is now immoral. Christian beliefs are unbelievable, credulous, and malignant to culture and civilization—including children (e.g., transgender and non-binary children). While we may or may not be living in the age of *the* Antichrist, the last generation before Christ's return, we certainly are living in the age of an increasingly militant antichristism, and plentiful, toxic, and proliferating liberal and conservative future-visions.

Hard antichristism is a conscious, willful attempt to subvert or eradicate Judeo-Christian influence. Nietzsche, as has been documented, represents this perspective. Soft antichristism refers to those individuals, groups, and cultural players that have been seduced into undermining or opposing authentic, biblical, Judeo-Christian influence on church and state. Christian escapism—which creates faith communities and millions across the globe that serve as enablers of antichristism—reflects yet another version of soft antichristism. In some contexts, soft antichristism is actually more destructive than hard antichristism because hard antichristism can sometimes be more easily discerned and quickly countered by the biblically faithful. Enablers, just as in families, often go unnoticed when they are faith communities or are the faithful inside of faith communities.

Non-enabling individual believers and faith communities desirous of making a positive contribution to the public or civilizational good must factor the reality of antichristism into their recommendations and observations. Some have rightly emphasized the need, when possible, to find common ground with those outside of the circle of faith. Others have properly

34. Renn, "Three Worlds."

encouraged the faithful to be loving and winsome.[35] Recommendations have been made by many simply to "be the church" and model a better way or the true future to the world and not emphasize directly influencing or transforming culture—because transformational efforts are increasingly resented by the City of Antichrist. In addition, identifying, influencing, and redirecting the misdirected loves of others (Smith, Augustine), inside and outside of the church, is essential. All of these approaches are partial truths and can have value and reflect how theology attempts to contribute to the public good—they represent public theology, defined previously.

However, any enduring and lasting contribution to the public or common good—public theology or, better yet, public eschatology—must include counsel on navigating or surfing the ceaseless waves of darkness, evil, and surd evil—especially surd or irrational evil, which is often immovable or unaffected by winsome or charming Christianity. Such evil is often enabled by a winsome Christianity, which can devolve into a peace at any price accommodation that uproots the prophetic element from Scripture.

Being the best possible church, modeling life-changing social justice and reform, finding common ground, loving others graciously, and redirecting misdirected loves are inadequate if not tethered to or by a profound appreciation of the spirit of antichrist and the "many antichrists" (1 John 2:18) ever present in every generation. We try to lovingly persuade and influence but ridicule, suffering, and persecution cannot always be avoided, even when we are at our best. Jesus did everything right and was crucified. Jesus was compassionate, prophetic, and confrontational when appropriate.

Those obsessed with things getting worse, the end times, the last days, naming the antichrist, identifying the revived Roman Empire, or predicting the last generation or decade, certainly enable antichrist and create a self-fulfilling prophecy. Yet beneath the surface of this enabling eschatomania, this dross, this husk, is the kernel of theological gold.

The spirit, power, and City of Antichrist must be acknowledged and directly addressed, and sometimes lovingly, forcefully, or creatively countered, for those seeking real kingdom influence. A proper response to marginalization, oppression, and persecution must be in the City of Kingdom Approximation's playbook, strategical and tactical planning. Eschatology and biblical apocalyptic passages focusing on the momentous future, the catastrophic, and the end, properly stated and interpreted, should neither be ignored (eschatophobia) nor distorted and sensationalized (eschatomania).

Awareness of antichrist avoids naivete. Awareness of antichrist should guard against those, even believers, with dangerous Messiah complexes.

---

35. Muehlhoff and Langer, *Winsome Persuasion*.

Sensitivity to *This Present Darkness*, when divorced from eschatomania, becomes absolutely essential for properly understanding how to engage culture and civilization.

Scripture soberly and pervasively emphasizes the spirit and City of Antichrist as a present reality. Second Thessalonians 1 and 2, for example, highlight the certain coming of Christ and the day of the Lord; the apocalyptic nature of the momentous future; keeping one's composure; the expectation of apostasy (the falling away of believers); the self-exalting Man of Lawlessness; the mystery of lawlessness already at work in the world; the divine restraint of evil in the public domain; the very public activity, signs, wonders and power of Satan; the deception of those who perish; the widespread belief in what is false; the justice of retribution for those who have afflicted God's people; God's righteous judgment and the slaying of evil; and eternal destruction. Regardless of one's approach to interpreting Scripture—meaning there are different views on whether some of these passages refer to the past, present, or future—these truths certainly apply to attempts to influence culture in every age.

Second Thessalonians 3 provides exhortation and encouragement even when living in the City of Antichrist. Be prepared to navigate the dark city just as in Paul's day. The true word has spread rapidly. Believers can be rescued from those who are perverse and evil. God can strengthen and protect us from the evil one amid great temptation. Believers are not to regard a fallen fellow believer as an enemy. The Lord can direct his followers deeper into the love of God and the steadfastness of Christ. The Lord is always faithful. Follow the example of discipline, labor and endure hardship for the City of Kingdom Approximation. God can grant continual "peace in every circumstance" (2 Thess 3:16) and will be with his people.

Countless biblical texts frame, guide, and prepare the faithful for life in the dark city. Daniel speaks of past and future kingdoms and the coming Messiah who will be cut off. Isaiah exalts the suffering servant and Peter calls us to follow in his cruciform steps (1 Pet 2:21). Matthew alerts us to false christs, false prophets, wars between kingdoms, persecution, apostasy, lawlessness, betrayal, heartlessness, global gospel proclamation, great tribulation, great deception, and readiness for Christ's return. Paul's epistles are loaded with relevant counsel on many realities, from one who has influenced and suffered in the City of Antichrist: apostasy is coming; deceiving spirits are at work; pervasive spiritual blindness exists in the city; we struggle with spiritual forces and powers; the present age is evil and there will be difficult times for the faithful; Satan soon will be crushed; the resurrection is certain, proving that God will judge the world with justice; and expect scoffers, angels of light, false servants of righteousness, terrible times, lovers of self, and a form of godliness without true power or reality. Revelation, essentially the entire book, is framing kingdom service between the city of darkness and the city of light. We should expect tepid churches, cosmic conflict, judgment, and the hope of the New Creation. Being effective salt, light, and healing leaven cannot ignore the City of Antichrist. And the true and bright future is already emerging amid the dark realities of the ever-fluid present.

Believers need to understand and prepare for the reality of persecution: "Indeed, all who want to live in a godly way in Christ Jesus will be persecuted. But evil people and impostors will proceed from bad to worse, deceiving and being deceived" (2 Tim 3:12–13). Faithful endurance amid suffering advances the kingdom but is only one piece of the puzzle concerning how the church and Christian theology can contribute to the public good—public theology or eschatology—prior to Christ's return. As in ancient Rome, the most powerful nation for centuries, persecution waxed and waned, and eventually the Roman Empire itself, while never becoming the true kingdom of God, certainly experienced significant kingdom influence.

It is a dangerous false dichotomy to suggest that either Judeo-Christian believers are persecuted or they establish and enforce a fully Judeo-Christian kingdom before Christ returns.

There are other options. There have been other options in history. Judeo-Christian faith communities have and can influence culture and civilization and contribute to the true common good. Salt, light, leaven, and taking up one's cross can bend the arrow of history and civilization toward its true future. Kingdoms can accept their biblical role as temporary stewards of God's good world until Messiah returns. The City of Kingdom Approximation can, at times and in some limited respects, leave a larger footprint on history and culture than the Kingdom of Antichrist. Such kingdom influence may be the ultimate, though not simplistic, form of neighbor-love.

Nevertheless, last-generation Christians are on to something ever so true and important concerning the present reality and potency of antichrist, but their eschatomania results in getting their theology and cultural engagement game plan utterly and entirely wrong. Unfortunately, last-generation believers are enabling the age of antichristism and the bystander effect via their own fatalistic and self-fulfilling prophecies that the age of the Antichrist is upon us. Glenn Beck well captured this sentiment: "I'm not saying we're living in the time of the Antichrist but this is what it will look like just before. . . . Just sayin.'"[36]

---

36. Beck, *Glenn Beck Show*.

HAS THE AGE OF THE ANTICHRIST ARRIVED?

Many religious conservatives continue to view contemporary crises as evidence that we are living in the last days, last generation, or the age of the coming antichrist, which sensitizes us to the power of evil but also is a perfect recipe for disengagement and escapism. A solid majority of American evangelical pastors, especially conservative Baptists and Pentecostals, still believe and teach that the antichrist will be revealed and Christ will return in their current lifetimes. Younger pastors seem less certain and less fatalistic.[37] Yet many still affirm that we are living in the last generation—the age in which *the* antichrist has arrived. This work repeatedly affirms that the only verifiable certainty today is that we are living in the age of antichristism and myriad antichristisms and that the City of Antichrist and the City of Kingdom Approximation are both present realities and possibilities.

Last-generation end-times popularity, including massive book sales (e.g., Lindsey, Peretti, LaHaye, Jeremiah, Rosenberg, and Cahn), arguably have shaped evangelical thought, culture, sentiments, passions, anti-intellectualism, eschatomania, plus the very nature of political and cultural involvement—which is sometimes very confused and inconsistent. And this defining and formative influence on American evangelicalism and beyond, which has continued largely unabated for multiple centuries and especially the last half-century, is only rebounding in response to contemporary crises.[38]

The theological gold of the theology of antichristism has been replaced with the frenzied dross of eschatomania with nearly apocalyptic consequences for church and state. Distorted apocalypticism produces

---

37. LifeWay Research, *Pastor Views*.

38. See Amazon.com, "Best Sellers in Christian Prophecy"; Cahn, *Harbinger*, back cover, where Cahn argues that just as with Israel's destruction, nine—not seven or ten—dark omens or harbingers "are now manifesting in America with profound ramifications for American's future and end-time prophecy"; Cahn, *Oracle*, 278, which seems to suggest a very otherworldly or escapist view of heaven, uninformed by decades of biblical scholarship that has been oft articulated by N. T. Wright; Jeremiah, *Book of Signs*; Jeremiah, *Escape*, 205; Kestenbaum and White, "#MAGA Church"; Pew Research Center, *Life in 2050*; Matthews, "Approximating," 205, for additional context related to Jeremiah's 1990 publication; Matthews, *Theology*, 181; Rosenberg, *Kremlin*, see the cover concerning the popularity of this work; Sine, *Mustard Seed*, 69–72. Sales figures by themselves do not entirely prove but do suggest significant influence, especially when some works reach twenty to forty million sales. It is most doubtful that twenty million book purchasers of these works, for example, disagreed entirely with the eschatology of such works. It is very likely that evangelicals, especially American evangelicals, are the primary audience and consumers.

apocalyptic realities already, even if the actual return of Christ is a thousand years or more in the distant future.

To be fair, it certainly feels as though the age of the antichrist has arrived for many American evangelicals who have not experienced persecution like so many believers throughout history and around the world. American evangelicals often assume that the fall of America necessarily is the end of the world. Such a fall would be globally significant for the church, but that is no guarantee that the last generation is upon us.

Yet the emerging and shocking opposition to orthodox evangelical and Roman Catholic Christianity some two decades prior to the present—illustrated by Mother Teresa and Billy Graham being referred to by such terms as "Hell's Angel," "fanatic, fundamentalist, and fraud," "power-worshipping bigot," and "disgustingly evil"—is now a nearly constant occurrence in North and South America.[39] Such representative daily news items and headlines from conservative and mainstream media sources are pervasive, recurrent, and must be factored in to being prepared to live in the City of Antichrist today. Appendix D provides further documentation of contemporary AJCism.

In a timely and still relevant *Time* magazine article from less than a decade ago, Mary Eberstadt describes and assesses this contemporary cultural and ministry context. This quote is somewhat lengthy, and at times both dated and predictive, but immensely perceptive:

> Traditional American Christians have long been on the losing end of culture-war contests—on school prayer, same-sex marriage and other issues. But recent events, including the Supreme Court decision overruling Texas' restrictions on abortion clinics and the mandate that employers provide access to contraception, have added to the sense that religious expression is under attack.
>
> According to recent Pew Research reports, the percentage of Americans who describe themselves as religiously affiliated has shrunk while the percentage describing themselves as unaffiliated has grown from 2007 to 2014. The percentage who say they are "absolutely certain" God exists fell to 63% from 71% during the same time period.
>
> This new vigorous secularism has catapulted mockery of Christianity and other forms of religious traditionalism into the mainstream and set a new low for what counts as civil criticism

---

39. Hitchens, "Mommie Dearest"; Crawley, "Disgustingly Evil Man"; Gibbs and Duffy, "Why Christopher Hitchens"; *Time* magazine covers, April 8, 1966, and April 2017. See Matthews, "Seduced," 118–21.

of people's most-cherished beliefs. In some precincts, the "faith of our fathers" is controversial as never before.

Some of the faithful have paid unexpected prices for their beliefs lately: the teacher in New Jersey suspended for giving a student a Bible; the football coach in Washington placed on leave for saying a prayer on the field at the end of a game; the fire chief in Atlanta fired for self-publishing a book defending Christian moral teaching; the Marine court-martialed for posting a Bible verse above her desk; and other examples of the new intolerance. Anti-Christian activists hurl smears like "bigot" and "hater" at Americans who hold traditional beliefs about marriage and accuse anti-abortion Christians of waging a supposed "war on women."

Some Christian institutions face pressure to conform to secularist ideology—or else. Flagship evangelical schools like Gordon College in Massachusetts and Kings College in New York have had their accreditation questioned. Some secularists argue that Christian schools don't deserve accreditation, period. Activists have targeted home-schooling for being a Christian thing; atheist Richard Dawkins and others have even called it tantamount to child abuse. Student groups like InterVarsity have been kicked off campuses. Christian charities, including adoption agencies, Catholic hospitals and crisis pregnancy centers have become objects of attack.

What's a tolerant American to do? First we must understand that red-hot rhetoric about a "war" on Christianity is misbegotten: there is zero equivalence between the horrors of ISIS-led genocide against Christians in the Middle East and what Pope Francis calls the "polite persecution" of believers in the West. (According to Pew, 77% of Americans described themselves as religiously affiliated in 2014, down from 83% in 2007.)

Yet we must also acknowledge that when some American citizens are fearful of expressing their religious views, something new has snaked its way into the village square: an insidious intolerance for religion [especially Judeo-Christian religion] that has no place in a country founded on religious freedom.[40]

Again, this is not to say that the West holds a visible candle to the blinding level of antichristism and persecution in other global locations. And it seems pointless to get in the weeds concerning the complete accuracy of every headline. Yet the endless AJC actions confirm why many Western evangelicals at least perceive that the age of the antichrist is emerging if

---

40. Eberstadt, "Regular Christians."

not here already, and that, at a minimum, bigotry toward Judeo-Christian practice, beliefs, and even thoughts is increasingly mainstream.

As noted, antichristism should not simply be defined as or identified with anti-Christian. Antichristism refers to the external and toxic opposition to, or the internal (inside the faith-community) corruption of, essential and shared Jewish and Christian beliefs, values, loves and affections, commitments, practices, thoughts, and attitudes. Antichristism rejects or opposes biblical and Judeo-Christian influence on church and state.

The term antichristism literally means anti-Messiah or the rejection or distortion of lived allegiance to the biblical teachings on the Messiah. Judaism and Christianity are centered around the mega-conviction and historical drama that the Messiah will redeem paradise lost, move the cosmos toward paradise regained, and ultimately usher in the New Creation. That glorious day includes the reality that every tongue will ultimately confess that the Messiah will rule as Lord in this coming kingdom, to the glory of God. Hence, antichristism includes both anti-Christian and anti-Semitic discrimination and oppression.

It is important once again to note that our extraordinary AJC moment and acronym is anti-Judeo-Christian, and broader than simply anti-Jesus-Christ or anti-Christian. Hence, the present AJC hour reflects antichristism and many antichristisms. This is also why Roman Catholics, the Orthodox, evangelicals, biblical Jews and Christians, and all biblical faith communities and Roman centurion people of good will need to heed Franklin's counsel quoted previously: "Yes, we must, indeed, all hang together, or most assuredly we shall all hang separately."[41] Such focus, unity, and constructive collaboration is fundamental to always being prepared as effective and influential citizens for time and eternity who can navigate the City of Antichrist.

---

41. Isaacson, "Benjamin Franklin."

CHAPTER 7

THE BIBLICAL MANDATE

TRUE KINGDOM CITIZENS ARE ALWAYS PREPARED FOR THE AGE OF ANTICHRIST

Every demon in hell has been turned loose.
—Franklin Graham (2023)[1]

Hold on to the example of *sound words* [*logōn*] which you have heard from me, in the faith and love which are in Christ Jesus.
—2 Timothy 1:13; emphasis added

The things which you have heard from me in the presence of many witnesses, entrust these to faithful people who will be able to teach others also.
—2 Timothy 2:2

To sum up, all of you be harmonious, sympathetic, loving, compassionate, and humble; not returning evil for evil or insult for insult, but giving a blessing instead; for you were called for the very purpose that you would inherit a blessing.

---

1. These epigraphs, as with Karl Marx in a future chapter, do not constitute an endorsement of the entirety of the views of any person or organization. What became clear from the response to Franklin Graham's 2023 speech at the National Religious Broadcasters' meeting (e.g., Glen Beck and numerous Christian organizations) is that Graham's words captured the perceptions of many conservatives and evangelicals: The world has gone mad and every demon in hell has been loosed on the church and state. Stand firm. Preach the word and stand up for Jesus.

But even if you should suffer for the sake of righteousness, you are blessed. And do not fear their intimidation, and do not be in dread, but sanctify Christ as Lord in your hearts, *always being ready to make a defense* [*apologian,* ἀπολογίαν; related to apologetics or persuasively and graciously defending the faith] to everyone who asks you to give an account [*logon,* λόγον, a word, or reasoned word or account, or verbal defense] for the hope that is in you, but with gentleness and respect [or reverence, reverential fear, *phoboo,* φόβου]; and keep a good conscience so that in the thing in which you are slandered, those who disparage your good behavior in Christ will be put to shame. For it is better, if God should will it so, that you suffer for doing what is right rather than for doing what is wrong. For Christ also suffered for sins once for all time, the just for the unjust, so that He might bring us to God, having been put to death in the flesh, but made alive in the spirit.

—1 Peter 3:8–9, 14–18; emphasis added

Scripture should norm our response to the age and City of Antichrist, including our tone, attitude, and speaking the truth out of overflowing love.[2] Scripture does not bless accommodation and appeasement to AJC culture, perhaps best illustrated by Chick-fil-A in recent years, or defensiveness, anger, hate, belligerence, and tactlessness. The coming death and resurrection of the cosmos, as noted, rules out an overemphasis on either continuity or discontinuity between the present and the ultimate future. As we have seen, overemphasizing continuity between the present era prior to Messiah's return and the resurrection of all things tends to result in naive plans for ushering in the kingdom (postmillennialism).

The popular sentiment today that the cosmos is not annihilated but merely restored also overemphasizes continuity, which tends to lead to cultural accommodation by suggesting that more kingdom impact can be accomplished prior to Christ's return than is biblically defensible. Even those who have moved away from naive utopianism or postmillennialism

---

2. This statement is an intentional reference to Eph 4:15. The likely context for speaking the truth in love is internal issues in the church or body of Christ, though the broader context of the passage could have reference to false teachers. Regardless, Scripture is clear that the norm is to speak the truth in love in all situations, yet based on the examples of Jesus, Paul, and Peter, that does not rule out appropriate and firm rebukes of those inside and outside of faith communities as a last resort, and especially when dealing with toxic religious leaders. The cleansing of the temple by Jesus does not fit shallow, sentimental, and simplistic conceptions of speaking the truth in love.

still suggest grandiose social movements or revolutions that promise that which only Messiah can deliver. Perhaps even more sadly, an overemphasis on continuity, or mere restoration of the image or the cosmos, partially obscures the true glory of the biblical future and things which "eye has not seen and ear has not heard, and which have not entered the human heart, all that God has prepared for those who love Him" (1 Cor 2:9).

I understand the allure of Cosmic Restorationism. I used to affirm this future-vision. Unfortunately, this view engages in what can only be called "present-centrism." We all love the idea that our present civilizations, culture, history, buildings, favorite memories, will be purified and restored and not die or be destroyed. Yet we forget that endless civilizations, cities, homes, buildings, favorite spots and memories have become nothing but dust. Indeed, in some cases layers and layers of dust are all that is left of past, multiple, civilizations. What exactly will God restore? Just the present or present culture and civilization? Instead, all will die, but all will also, just like every human being and every physical body, be gloriously resurrected. Present-centrism must die, for it also too easily leads to cultural accommodation.

Likewise, the image of God is certainly being renewed or restored in humanity (Col 3:9–10). But image resurrection is so much more glorious and complete than image restoration (Rom 8:29; 1 Cor 15:49). In one sense Eden is being restored, yet paradise restored, while including elements of Eden, is almost ineffably so much more (Rev 21–22). Likewise, we are "being transformed into the same image from one degree to another" by the Spirit (2 Cor 3:18) already and forever, but that new reality, more glorious than the glory of Mt. Sinai (2 Cor 3), culminates in a reality that we can not yet fully comprehend (1 Cor 2:9) in the present. It is not fully clear exactly what image resurrection entails, but we "will be like Him" and "see Him just as He is" (1 John 3:2).

In God's redemptive future, the cosmos, including the crown of creation, humanity, will die. Why not just restore humanity rather than require the dreadful "wages of sin," which "is death" (Rom 6:23)? The divinely required horror of death can not be glossed over. The sting of death trumpets that only the return of Messiah and the resurrection of all things will bring the final victory day.

Wouldn't restoration be kinder and gentler than death? Humanity is gloriously created in the image of God, but also profoundly fallen, and that brokenness is inseparably connected to others, to past, present, and future history, and to the entire cosmos (Rom 8:22). Sin is systemic and cosmic on steroids; sin is cosmos-systemic.

We must die and be resurrected. The cosmos must die and be resurrected. The Messiah must bodily return. The discontinuity between the present and true future can only be bridged by bodily resurrection, sending of the Spirit, and the actual return of Christ.

Yet that very bodily resurrection of Christ past and humanity future, plus the physical resurrection of all things, also underscores a profound continuity. The future has already touched humanity and the cosmos. The decisive battle has been won. The Spirit is mediating the future already, from deeply transforming the faithful to influencing everyone and everything via being poured out on all flesh or all humanity (Joel 2:28; Acts 2:17). The Spirit proclaims humanity's sinfulness, God's righteousness, and the judgment of the first and second deaths to the whole world (John 16:8; Rev 21:8).

A biblical theology of death and resurrection rules out engaging God's world with naivete, accommodation, angry cultural battles, escapism, hate, tactlessness, seductive and overreaching reform movements, and unrealistic revolutions. A biblical theology of death and resurrection serves as the genesis or re-genesis for appropriately bending the arrow of history toward its true desire and only ultimate and certain outcome. It is within this broad and rich future-vision context (2 Pet 3:10) that Peter's famous admonition to defend the faith amid persecution and interrogation (apologetics), finds its true spirit (1 Pet 3:13–16). Peter's "always be prepared" is properly connected to the gracious and persuasive defense of the Judeo-Christian faith. The biblical context for this defense is clearly the strong opposition or persecution of believers in the Messiah—antichristism. Hence, at the very core of gently and respectfully defending the faith (biblical apologetics) is the command always to be prepared for a widespread, systemic, and structural AJCism and its many varieties, forms, and children.

THE CITY AS A MAMMOTH THEOLOGICAL ERUPTION AND MISSIONAL CHALLENGE

However, our individualistic culture—and thousands of my students, current and future pastors and Christian leaders—immediately reduce this apologetics charge to one person encountering one unbeliever and commendably trying to win this individual to a personal relationship with Jesus Christ. And the individual is typically a friend or family member. That ministry to the individual is critical, but the passage in question is addressing Christians being interrogated while likely being persecuted. The primary context is not individual apologetics or evangelism but cosmic kingdom influence—in the city.

Paul's repeated "defenses" of the faith (Acts), "according to Paul's custom," were in the context of cities, such as Jerusalem (religious center), Philippi in Macedonia ("a Roman colony," Acts 16:12), Athens (intellectual center), Corinth (a carnal and compromised church), Ephesus, and Rome (political power center). Paul longed to strengthen the Roman church, in part because their faith was radiating globally. These confrontations, as with Moses and Pharaoh in the power center and great city of Egypt, also included trials before Felix, Festus, and Caesar. These were historic conflicts between Messiah's kingdom and cities largely dominated by antichristism.

These are epic stories. The City of Antichrist is challenged and undermined by the City of Kingdom Approximation. The present is exposed by the true future, and the eternal future is despised by the fleeting and feeble present. The City of Kingdom Approximation is always under siege, to one degree or another, by the malevolent city, and vice versa.

The biblical imagery and references to cities and nations are pervasive, from Eden as the embryo of civilizations and cities, to Egypt, Canaan, Jerusalem, Tyre, Sidon, Nineveh, literal Babylon, Syria, Rome, symbolic Babylon, and the New Jerusalem. Many cities represent opposition to Abraham's God or exemplify antichristism, and many earthly cities in the present age reflect a mixture of hate toward—or an approximation of—the enduring city of God.

In the American evangelical context, many have appropriately called for the faithful to be persuasive, well-educated, influential, or winsome (attractive, appealing) in order to give a winning defense, effectively evangelize, and creatively impact culture and civilization. There have been cultural wins, such as the influence of C. S. Lewis on countless scientific and political leaders.

While a creative, winsome, and positive approach had and has value, it is increasingly becoming clear that our theology of how to interact with and influence civilization, the city, *must take into account the reality of opposition, antichristism, ridicule, and persecution.* This is apologetics and evangelism 101 already in many parts of the world. What's new is the intensity of Nietzschean AJCism in formerly Judeo-Christian–influenced cities. Judeo-Christian thought can only contribute to the public good if it properly discerns the times and context and identifies appropriate strategy and tactics.

Neither seeking refuge in hidden monasteries nor being gracious and endearing reflects a robust, complete, and shrewd response to accelerating and militant antichristism. We are ill-prepared today, at least in the West, for the City of Antichrist.

The city, not just individuals trying to get to heaven, matters. Indeed, heaven includes and is largely defined by the reality of the city that comes down from heaven. As we have already seen, the heavenly city was not designed by Plato or some otherworldly architect but by the Alpha, Omega, and the very agent and moment-by-moment sustainer of creation—the incarnate, resurrected, and glorified Messiah. He is the King of all kingdoms and cities, Lord and King of all temporary lords and kings, and the only King of the eternal community and city of God.

The city matters—profoundly so—as do all communities. The city includes loyalties, loves, political realities, power conflicts, culture, architecture, communal life, music, justice and/or injustice, rulers, the powerful, the plumbing and wiring (literal and symbolic), the political and spiritual powers and systems, the popular, the unpopular, the ruled, the oppressed, the persecuted, the marginalized, faith communities, religions, the moral and spiritual climate, the laborers, the families, the children, the education and/or indoctrination, the tyranny and/or the public servanthood, the celebrations, the tears, the flourishing, the suffering, and life and death decisions—and such illustrations only scratch the surface of the breadth and depth of city life.

The city is the very physical and spiritual air of which we partake, including the future reality of the New Jerusalem. And in Scripture, the city is ultimately redeemed, restored to its original intent, a place for the intimate dwelling with God that is inseparable from city/community life and authentic spiritual life. The final and victorious biblical city is resurrected to a glorious new reality and New Creation.

A true grasp and appreciation for the role of the city in God's biblical and redemptive history sparks nothing less than a mammoth theological eruption for the mission of the church, and even the very definition of what it means to be holy, loving, and Christlike. To reference and paraphrase John Wesley yet again and expand his theology, our highest good must not only include getting to heaven. It must include becoming fit for heaven—which is not Plato's heaven and is far, far, more multilayered and complex than Augustine's City of God.

In a lengthy but priceless quote Tim Keller challenges future Christian leaders and taps this deep theological reservoir and eruption. The city is God's invention, original intention, and ultimate destination or consummation of and for human history and culture:

> God designed the city with the power to draw out the resources of creation (of the natural order and the human soul) and thus to build civilisation. . . .
>
> God's future redeemed world and universe is depicted as a "city." Abraham sought the city "whose builder and maker is God" (Hebrews 11:10). Revelation 21 describes and depicts the

apex of God's redemption, as a city! His redemption is building us a city—the new Jerusalem.

In fact, when we look at the New Jerusalem, we discover something strange. In the midst of the city is a crystal river, and on each side of the river is the Tree of Life, bearing fruit and leaves which heal the nations of all their wounds and the effects of the divine covenant curse [and human depravity]. *This city is the garden of Eden, remade [and, as argued in this work, resurrected].* The city is the fulfilment of the purposes of the Eden of God. We began in a garden but will end in a city; God's purpose for humanity is urban! Why? . . .

The city is God's invention and design, not just a sociological phenomenon or [mere] invention of humankind. . . .

It is widely understood that when God tells Adam and Eve to "have dominion" and "fill the earth" he is directing them to build a God-honouring civilisation. They are to bring forth the riches that God put into creation by developing science, art, architecture, human society. Kline reveals, however, that since Revelation reveals that the "end" of creation (the climax of the work of the "Second Adam" Jesus Christ) is a city—that therefore God was calling Adam and Eve to be city builders. City building is [arguably] an ordinance of God just like work and marriage. And indeed, cities draw together human talent and resources and tap the human potential for cultural development [and the fulfillment of the image of God] as nothing else does.

There is no absolute way to define a "city." A human settlement becomes more "urban" as it becomes more a) dense and b) diverse in its population. God made the city to be a developmental tool, a form of cultural "gardening," designed to draw out the riches he put into the earth, nature and the human soul at creation. Even after the fall, cities are places of "common grace" though each factor also now can be used (and is!) for evil purposes.[3]

---

3. Keller, "Theology of Cities." Emphasis added. The literature on the theology of the city varies greatly in value and relevance to the argument of this work. The focus of this work is on understanding the broad biblical meaning of the city and the nature of the interaction between the City of Antichrist and the City of Kingdom Approximation. The following works in this footnote are relatively easy to skim so as to grasp the larger debate concerning the theology of the city better. In addition to Augustine's theology, already introduced, this list includes classic and contemporary works easily accessible online: Smith, "How a Theology"; Stockwell, "Enchanting City"; Biggar, "Theology in the City"; "David Leong"; Bakke, *Theology*; Cox, *Religion*; Van Engen and Tiersma, *God So Loves*; Johnson, *City of Man*; Ellul, *Meaning of the City*.

While this quote at times reflects a Reformed or Calvinistic viewpoint,[4] the key and correct point here is that the biblical faithful must always be prepared before Christ's return to encounter and advance the kingdom within the context of cities that are, to one degree or another, dominated by the City of Antichrist or the City of Kingdom Approximation. Cities are either enhancing or eradicating/muting the intent of Eden, or both. The present and the true future, after the decisive Christ event, coexist and intermingle, like wheat and tares, until Christ returns for the great individual and civilizational resurrection harvest.

God's saints, the people of the true future, can partially mediate the future to the present and contribute to the common good. That mediation, or kingdom influence, however, in light of the multiple layers of the city, includes and is far more profound and comprehensive than simply "saving souls." Indeed, apologetic and evangelistic endeavors that do not take into account the city—as well as the non-city or rural—are shallow, often inept, and incomplete.

The saints, who will reign with Christ in his coming kingdom and glorious and crystalline city, are already in the business of being used of God lovingly to save whole persons and influence all of the dynamics and realities of cities, cultures, and civilizations. Persons and cities are inseparable, and, if separated, both lose their true reality, meaning, and purpose. The restoration of the image of God is within the context of the city. Cities, communities, and individuals are increasingly inseparable and will be resurrected.

Which brings us back to the apostles, such as Paul. By God's grace Paul was always prepared for the City of Antichrist and turned the ancient world and cities upside down. Individuals, families, communities, cities, and mighty empires were nudged toward the biblical future. The spirit of antichrist, already defeated by cross and resurrection, lost its unrestrained grip on the city and the future. Athens, Rome, Jerusalem, London, Alexandria, Egypt, Mylapore, and colonial Philadelphia and Newport were or never could be the same.

Effective mission today requires always being prepared for the reality of the city, city building and redemption in the present age, and the biblical promise and mandate to reign ultimately with Christ. This truth, that our true destiny is not escape but to live as both city and country dwellers, changes everything. Even rural agrarians are, in one sense, called to be "city

---

4. The debate concerning the various kinds of grace (e.g., common grace and prevenient grace), based on Wesleyan-Arminian versus Reformed, Calvinistic, or Roman Catholic perspectives, and the cultural mandate, exceeds the scope of this present work. The point is that God's grace influences civilization and culture—the city.

slickers," and city slickers should have holy, rural, agrarian hearts, wisdom, and sentiments.

We should prepare for city ministry just like Paul under Gamaliel and with sensitivity to our dual or multiple citizenships. We understand and can navigate Jerusalem, Athens, Rome, Babylon, and Nazareth. We learn how to influence cultures and prepare to serve as a cultural creator and leader for time and eternity. We are lifelong learners and citizens of time and eternal life.

We are always prepared for all of the challenges from the City of Antichrist and always prepared for all of the present opportunities of the City of Kingdom Approximation. We move from a posture of just getting by or escape to a posture of faithful, often cruciform (sacrificial), kingdom influence. We overflow with love for God, others, God's good world, and God's invention and creation and destination—the very city of God.

ALWAYS BE PREPARED FOR THE SPOILED FRUIT AND ESPECIALLY THE POISONOUS ROOT

We prepare ourselves for the challenges of ministering—and we are all ministers—amid the ever-changing dynamics and tactics of the City of Antichrist. The sheer number of toxic future-visions and "isms" in our information explosion age requires us to "cut to the chase" with all of these perspectives and emphasize and highlight the core of the toxicity—or toxic-city—the antichristism orientation, and clear attempt to be liberated from the Logos.

No one can be an expert on all of these traitorous future-visions, many of which have been already referenced in this work. Yet every believer should be so well grounded in basic Judeo-Christian values and the core Judeo-Christian and biblical vision, and the application of that vision to culture and civilization, that counterfeit visions, false christs and kingdoms are readily recognized as such—as counterfeits. And the toxic-cities of antichristism are appropriately and lovingly challenged and influenced.

We should, as noted, avoid the simplistic, escapist, anti-intellectual, and shallow spiritualizing of these contemporary crises and assaults on the faith, such as

- it is the last days and things will most certainly get worse and worse,
- the devil is taking over,
- no worries, we will be raptured out of this mess,

- there is nothing we can do other than pray for revival,
- we need another Billy Graham, or
- all we can do is pray and preach the gospel.

We need to emphasize the spiritual core or root that is producing the toxic fruit without simplistically spiritualizing everything.

In Scripture, "spiritual" is not an otherworldly Greek concept but very much connected to the spirit and powers and systems that are guided or animated by the spirit of antichrist in contrast to being led by the Spirit of God. This helpful translation of Ephesians is illustrative: "For our struggle is not against flesh and blood, but against the rulers, against the powers, against the world forces of this darkness, against the spiritual forces of wickedness in the heavenly [ruling] places" (Eph 6:12). This verse is not otherworldly (or Platonic) but very much connected to the Hebraic doctrine of creation—and is not an isolated thought or departure for Paul.

In Colossians Paul argues, "For by Him all things were created, both in the heavens and on earth, visible and invisible, whether thrones or dominions or rulers or authorities—all things have been created through Him and for Him" (Col 1:16). And likewise, in Ephesians he reaffirms that such spiritual warfare is very much connected to this-worldly created realities and culminates in a New Creation victory on earth: "He raised Him [bodily] from the dead and seated Him at His right hand in the heavenly places, far above all rule and authority and power and dominion, and every name that is named, not only in this age but also in the one to come. And He put all [created] things in subjection under His feet, and made Him head over all things to the church, which is His body, the fullness of Him who fills all in all" (Eph 1:20–23).

In Philippians Paul summarizes how this ultimate spiritual victory includes this-worldly implications: "For this reason also God highly exalted Him, and bestowed on Him the name which is above every name, so that at the name of Jesus every knee will bow, of those who are in heaven and on earth and under the earth, and that every tongue will confess that Jesus Christ is Lord, to the glory of God the Father" (Phil 2:9–11).

Hence, Paul's unfleshly or spiritual response to antichristism in his own day is not escapist, otherworldly, and is clear:

> For though we walk in the flesh, we do not war according to the flesh, for the weapons of our warfare are not of the flesh, but divinely powerful for the destruction of fortresses. We are destroying speculations [or arguments] and every lofty thing raised up against the knowledge of God, *and we are taking every*

thought captive to the obedience of Christ, and we are ready to punish all disobedience, whenever your obedience is complete. (2 Cor 10:3–6 NASB 1995; emphasis added)

Fleshly does not mean that something is inherently wrong with the body or the flesh, but, consistent with biblical and Hebraic thought, it refers to the entire self or being in opposition to God—rather than filled or led by the Holy Spirit. Many of the "sins of the flesh" in the famous Pauline list of such sins are not physical or sensual but very spiritual in nature:

> Now the deeds of the flesh are evident, which are: sexual immorality, impurity, indecent behavior, idolatry, *witchcraft, hostilities, strife, jealousy,* outbursts of anger, *selfish ambition,* dissensions, factions, envy, drunkenness, carousing, and things like these, of which I forewarn you, just as I have forewarned you, that those who practice such things will not inherit the kingdom of God. But the fruit of the Spirit is love, joy, peace, patience, kindness, goodness, faithfulness, gentleness, self-control; against such things there is no law. (Gal 5:19–23; emphasis added)

> For since there is jealousy and strife among you, are you not fleshly, and are you not walking like ordinary people? (1 Cor 3:3)

And this is why Paul travelled throughout the Mediterranean targeting influential cities, yearning for Rome, reasoning and persuading Jews and gentiles daily (Acts), working day and night with his body, and toiling and striving mightily to take "every thought captive to the obedience of Christ" (2 Cor 10). This is why Paul was symbolically and emotionally "in the pains of childbirth," working toward that day when believers would be blameless at the coming of Christ, and thus he charged the faithful to make real Christ "formed in you" (Gal 4:19).

This future-vision is also why Paul went to Jerusalem and Athens (the Harvard or Oxford of his day) and longed to go to the capital city of Rome, his final providential and ministry destination in this life. Perhaps Paul will serve as the prince of Rome or Jerusalem in the next life or age, as a co-ruler or vice-regent of Christ. He certainly was and is being well prepared.

Therefore, in the present age where we especially navigate two cities, believers should at least have a basic understanding of the many future-visions that will impact the lives and future of our children, our children's children, the world God loved, the nature and mission of church and synagogue, and the very nature and future of freedom, true human flourishing, and civilization. The Judeo-Christian future-vision is increasingly under siege, and the pillars, reservoirs, and life-giving waters of Christian influence are beginning to crumble and evaporate. The proper informed and loving response to opposition and persecution, which is typically far more than the actions of one and reflects the spirit of the true city, is "always being prepared to make a defense to anyone who asks you for a reason for the hope that is in you; yet do it with gentleness and respect" (1 Pet 3:15 ESV).

These numberless antichristism future-visions, as with Nietzsche and many others, affirm that a post-biblical and post–Judeo-Christian world is an improved world. John Lennon's "Imagine" captures many key aspects of this spirit.

"Imagine," globally beloved and as familiar as national anthems to many, is annually featured almost as a New Year's Eve worship hymn. The lyrics, the usage of which has been the focus of legal battles, are readily available online but cannot be reproduced here. Lennon's affirmations and allusions are easy to discern. Heaven, hell, normative truth and ethics, divine judgment by a personal God after death, countries, private property, free enterprise, and Judeo-Christian just war theory ("nothing to kill or die for"), have to go. All exclusive religious claims are false (e.g., "I am the way, and the truth, and the life; no one comes to the Father except through me" John 14:6), and all religious beliefs and practices should be kept personal and private ("no religion, too").

Lennon's somewhat utopian future affirms or assumes materialism (only sky above); some sort of benevolent, Marxist-influenced, one world civilization; centralized global, political, and economic power; the "brotherhood of man"; living in the moment; and the ending of poverty and hunger. A beautiful world and peace on earth are within our grasp if we only imagine, re-envision, reboot, and unite.

Such hopes are understandable and resonate with the masses and the elite, but they are also replete with errors, half-truths, and many gross distortions of authentic biblical and Judeo-Christian hope. As with Marxism, "Imagine" is eschatological heresy. And "Imagine" ultimately rallies the troops around the cause of the City of Antichrist and the enforced cancellation of a biblically influenced and flourishing culture.

Antichristism is opposed to far more than just Christendom—the often clumsy fusion or near merger of church, synagogue, and state. Christendom defined as a church-state union is easily refuted, like Lennon's vision, as a naive (and utopian) pipe dream that truly misunderstands human nature and the true pathway to a better civilization in the present age. Judeo-Christian influence on the public good, not Judeo-Christian premature and total rule, is the proper goal in the present age. We seek the City of Kingdom Approximation, not the full realization of the New Jerusalem, prior to Christ's return. Such dreams require Messiah's return.

The liberal or liberated antichristism future-visions oppose any significant biblical and Judeo-Christian influence on life and civilization. And a growing and militant antichristism or liberalism increasingly seeks to quarantine, silence, oppress, criminalize, or even persecute the Judeo-Christian faithful and those who advocate and work for a Judeo-Christian–influenced church, synagogue, city, and state. Such a variety of liberalism is liberated from Logos.

Unfortunately, and this is critical and worth repeating, many Judeo-Christian people of faith are confusing the fruit of this growing marginalization/oppression—such as our contemporary toxicity, fragmentation, polarization, moral relativism, cultural decadence, and worship of the state—with the *root* of the crisis. The faithful are rightly concerned with such recent trends as the redefinition of marriage, ethical drifting (and ethical solipsism),[5] the attacks of modernism and postmodernism on traditional beliefs, our "feet firmly planted in mid-air" post-truth and post-morality "beyond good and evil" world,[6] or various forms of Marxism, socialism, and contemporary post-Logos political liberalism.

However, as noted in the introduction, those attempting to stall or reverse ecclesial corruption (corruption of the church) and civilizational collapse clearly are chasing after one flash-in-the-pan toxic future-vision, and one proposed solution after another, thereby trying to bring relief to one symptom after another while the patient is inevitably dying apart from a real, lasting, and miraculous cure. Hence, it has been argued that Judeo-Christian cultural engagement too often reflects the tactic of Whac-A-Mole.

ADDITIONAL SCRIPTURAL CONSIDERATIONS FOR FURTHER UNDERSTANDING, DEFINING, AND ENGAGING ANTICHRISTISM

Antichristism, the opposition to authentic biblical influence on individuals, communities, and especially church, synagogue, and state, has many manifestations and incarnations or reincarnations, hence antichristisms. Historical and biblical evidence demonstrates that antichristism exists both

---

5. Ethical solipsism refers to the belief that the only ethical reality is that which is perceived or created by a single individual or tribe.

6. As Pannenberg writes, "Nietzsche proclaimed the revaluation of all values, 'everything that was nailed down is coming loose.' . . . Nietzsche contended that values are created by the evaluating will [or will to have appropriate power over others]." Pannenberg, *Theology and the Kingdom*, 103. See Nietzsche's prelude in *Beyond Good and Evil*; and Nietzsche, *Antichrist*.

inside and outside of communities of faith. Antichristism future-visions may be found among what is today referred to as both politically liberal and conservative ideologies, though flawed conservative Judeo-Christian future-visions are typically more enablers of antichristism than militantly and essentially anti-Judeo-Christian.

Those trying to ground and connect the biblical material on antichrist with the present generation and contemporary political and cultural realities often use antichrist in the diverse ways as seen in the following list. Different organizations, perspectives, theological confessions, groups, and individuals emphasize one or more of these options relative to antichrist and antichristism:

- The end-times or last generation antichrists or, more specifically, a singular individual (past, present, or future) who can be correctly identified as *the prophesied antichrist* or the beast, who truly is the personified, singular pinnacle and consummation of opposition to God, God's nature, God's law, and God's people.
- *Past, present, or future religious or political leaders or antichrists* who exemplify, incarnate, and culminate the opposition to God and God's law throughout the entirety of redemptive history (e.g., the man of lawlessness, the beasts of Daniel and Revelation). These antichrists are multiple and recurrent over the centuries.
- Old Testament *false prophets* operating *inside* the Jewish faith community, yet opposing (anti) God's law.
- Old Testament *false prophets not necessarily or directly connected* to the Jewish faith community (e.g., priests, prophets, and magicians of non–Judeo-Christian religions). The Egyptian priests or magicians would be illustrative.
- Old Testament *nations* opposed to God's people, law, and emerging kingdom rule (through Israel). Such nations constitute much of the Old Testament narrative.
- *Religious leaders* with official status *in the midst of God's people* who deceive and mislead God's people ("blind guides," Matt 23:16) and who are lawless, hypocrites, snakes/vipers, persecutors of God's true people, whitewashed tombs, oppressors of the weak and poor, evil, and have hard and heavy (impure) hearts. They oppose the true Christ and God's true law.
- Numerous *false teachers, antichrists, and false teachings inside and outside of the New Testament era churches* or synagogues that seduce and

deceive believers (via legalism or works-righteousness, or Docetism and related views which call Christ Savior but deny that he had a body, or deny his full humanity and thus demean God's good creation).

- *False teachers and antichrists of all generations* who deny or redefine and distort essential biblical beliefs (e.g., those who "preach" a "different gospel" or different Jesus, 2 Cor 11:4).

Antichristism, then, as used in this work, utilizes, unifies, and integrates all of these biblical definitions yet does so without assuming that we can know or predict with certainty that we are near or in the very last generation of human history—the age of the antichrist—prior to Christ's return. Hence, to oversimplify, the term antichristism incorporates and refers to any or all of the following:

- A *singular Antichrist* who incarnated or who will incarnate opposition to God;
- *Multiple antichrists*, false prophets, and religious leaders distorting the faith within the faith community;
- *AJC nations and leaders and prophets and priests* outside of the community of faith especially opposed to God.

LESSONS FROM CHURCH HISTORY CONCERNING THE AGE OF ANTICHRIST

The lessons from church history are invaluable and stark. Every generation since the first generation of Christians has had proponents affirming that their generation was the last generation. This utter failure—and the cultural consequences—should be cautionary.

Such false predictions do not prove that someone living today is wrong if proclaiming that the present generation is the last generation (say, forty to eighty years) before Christ returns. Such false last-generation date setting should, however, suggest extreme caution and humility. Last-Generationism's endless failings also suggest that the attempt to connect the last generation or the biblical antichrist simplistically to one's own generation requires very careful biblical and historical interpretation (known as biblical hermeneutics).

A few examples of interpretive errors shall suffice. False claims of the antichrist include Nero and other Roman emperors, the popes, Napoleon, Mussolini, Hitler, Gorbachev, Hussein, and countless presidents and world leaders, including virtually every American president since John F.

Kennedy. Even Elvis Presley and Billy Graham made the list for being the false prophet. American last-generationist evangelicals are not known for leading the way on woke politics, but perhaps this movement is overdue for predicting a major non-male antichrist.

False claims that Scripture has been fulfilled in a specific generation (the ten nations of the revived Roman Empire or Cobra helicopters predicted in Revelation) have wrought understandable disdain from critics and embarrassment when latter day prophets attempted to prove the veracity of Scripture by such predictions. Political unions (e.g., Europe) shift over time, yet I still remember as a child when some predicted that the absolute proof that the last generation (defined as forty years and likely commencing in 1948 with the founding of Israel) had arrived was clear because the European Union would soon receive its tenth member. Things could change, but the European Union currently has nearly thirty members.

Similarly, numerous new versions of the Cobra helicopter and new state-of-the art attack helicopters (e.g., the Viper) have emerged since the early 1970s prediction of Hal Lindsey that Cobra helicopters fulfilled Scripture. What if Christ does not return for five hundred years? Treating the Bible like tea leaves (tasseography) relative to contemporary realities is reckless and discredits the cause of Christ.

Such predictions often reflect circular reasoning. Since it must be the last generation, contemporary realities must be fulfilling Scripture and thus prove that Scripture predicted the future. In many respects, American and global evangelicals of recent centuries have been using such simplistic, flawed, emotional, escapist, circular, and anti-intellectual reasoning to prove the Bible because they simply did not know how to defend the faith (apologetics) appropriately and lacked a theology capable of facilitating constructive civilizational engagement over multiple centuries. One might call this fast-food eschatology or desperate eschatological apologetics.

The last two examples illustrate how what seemed to be so obvious, connecting the Bible to contemporary events, turned out to be a total distortion of the biblical text. Many last-generation believers, again indoctrinated into and enraptured by circular reasoning, shallow theology, and flawed biblical interpretation, frequently referred to being in the "last days" or "last hour" of history before Christ returns.

A seemingly infinite number of evangelical conversations occurred in recent generations where challenging world events were quickly and simply processed and resolved by someone quoting a preacher or televangelist who supposedly was quoting the Bible. The false prophets' refrain went something like this: "Well, things look bad, but we are in the 'last days' or 'last hour.' We should not be surprised by any of this because it is the last days. We will soon be raptured and taken like a *Thief in the Night*."

Interestingly, the "days" and "hours" were never taken literally but were interpreted as a means of referring to the last generation or decade. And those not taking the days and hours literally tended to view anyone who did not take the days of Genesis literally as theologically backslidden.

When Scripture was actually consulted, it turned out that these last generationists were in one sense correct. We are living in the last days—and have been since the first coming of Christ, according to Scripture! The author of Hebrews writes that "in these last days [God] has spoken to us in His Son" (1:2). Similarly, John, in a verse quoted previously, writes, "Children, it is the last hour; and just as you heard that antichrist is coming, even now many antichrists have appeared; from this we know that it is the last hour" (1 John 2:18).

Yet it should be evident that, first, John's "hour" is clearly not a literal hour. Second, like "last days," John is referring to the age or time period initiated by Christ's first coming. We are living in that same "last hour" today. And, most importantly, John was saying that in his day, the first century, not only were they living in the "last hour" but they also were witnessing the fact that "even now many antichrists have appeared." Such is our lot between God's cosmic ages.

Perhaps Billy Graham was wise when he allegedly said that we should live in hope each day as if Christ will come today or tomorrow but also live each day as if we were preparing for the next one thousand years of history. Regardless of the source, such discernment begins to point to the value of the theology of Approximation, where some elements of the New Creation can be approximated before Christ returns, but only Christ can usher in the fullness of the kingdom of God. And the final events just prior to Christ's return are not easy to chart.

A BROADER, RELEVANT, AND NIMBLE DEFINITION OF ANTICHRISTISM, CRATERS OF THE GOSPEL, AND APPROXIMATION THEOLOGY

The term antichrist is in Scripture but not antichristism or antichristisms, though John does refer to "many antichrists" and the spirit of the antichrist (1 John 4:3). The concept of antichristism has been connected to and built upon key scriptural passages referencing opposition to God, God's nature, God's kingdom influence, God's revealed truth, and God's will. Antichristism is a helpful term today in order to connect to the biblical term antichrist, contemporary cultural realities, and numerous discussions and obsessions with the antichrist (Nietzsche) and the last generation (Peretti, Jonathan Cahn)—as well as the emerging antichristism that increasingly imbibes deeply of the spirit and tactics of anti-Semitism. Antichristism is also an umbrella concept that includes anti-Semitism.

Yet, much more importantly, antichristism refers to toxic opposition to Judeo-Christian influence on culture. Opposing authentic Judeo-Christian influence on culture (e.g., the sacredness of human life) is similar or analogous to nations that opposed God's people in the Old Testament (e.g., Egypt, Babylon, Assyria). This antichristism is especially conspicuous today amid a society that used to cherish freedom, and which was birthed in part by core Judeo-Christian values, or what James K. A. Smith and Oliver O'Donovan have well documented and referred to as the "craters of the gospel": "Like the surface of a planet pocked with craters by the bombardment it receives from space, the governments of the passing age [sometimes] show the impact of Christ's dawning glory."[7]

Smith, building upon O'Donovan, provides examples of the craters of the gospel, already introduced earlier in this work, which underscore the thesis of this book. Some aspects of God's ultimate future and glorious New Creation can be *approximated* and are appropriate types of goals for the era before Christ's return. A cautious and discerning theology of Approximation, rather than fatalistic escapism, or the naive belief that we can usher in the kingdom before Christ's return (utopianism), is reflected by these craters of the gospel.

Examples of these craters of the gospel include

a. The *modern notion of the state*.[8] The state is not divine or divinely sanctioned, temporal not eternal in nature and authority, and "accountable to an order and law and King who is eternal."[9] Government is limited to the secular or "confined to the *saeculum* [present extended age between Messiah's first and second coming], circumscribed by [restricted within the limits of] the eternal and ultimately passing away."[10] Why Smith apparently fails to reference directly Samuel Rutherford's distinction between *Rex Lex* (the King is the determiner of law and justice) and *Lex Rex* (the eternal law of God is the ultimate basis for law and justice) at this juncture is perplexing, especially given Smith's Kuyperian and Reformed tradition, for he goes on to affirm, "Rather

---

7. O'Donovan, *Desire*, 212; Smith, *Awaiting the King*.
8. Smith, *Awaiting the King*, 100–105.
9. Smith, *Awaiting the King*, 100.
10. Smith, *Awaiting the King*, 100.

than look for the expression of Christ's universal reign in a world ruler in the *saeculum*, the political thought of Christendom located this universality in *law*.... All rulers—Christian or not—were to be held accountable to a law that was higher than them, not dependent on their fiats, and to which they were accountable."[11] Perhaps Smith was attempting to avoid identification with Rutherford's less tolerant and less Lockean views of religious toleration, yet Rutherford deserves recognition for this pre-Lockean emphasis in O'Donovan summarized by Smith: "The announcement of the kingdom of God and the resurrection of the King of the Jews are signs that earthly kingdoms are passing away. The emperor is not God. Caesar is not Lord. The empire is not the kingdom."[12] Kings and states serve a temporary role on bended knee and are always subject to prophetic reform.

b. *The liberal democratic conception of liberty.* Since the state is not ultimate, God's law (*lex*) is king (*rex*), and since the gospel emphasizes freedom from all earthly idols and powers, a more generalized conception of freedom came to dominate Western ethical and political thought.[13] "Thus, despite all the ways that freedom has morphed into [a sometimes unhealthy] autonomy in late modernity [or postmodernism], we shouldn't demonize freedom or liberty as such."[14]

c. *The mercy principle of modern jurisprudence.* "Judgment is reoriented in light of the cross, renewed by the resurrection, but also tempered by the eschaton [New Creation]: we judge [well, lest we be judged based on how we as sinners and hypocrites often judge,] as we await an ultimate judgment."[15] Smith, again following O'Donovan, is less than crystal clear at this point. Perhaps Smith's focus on mercy in judgment is due to our sinful and hypocritical nature, our limited or subordinate (under God) role in judging others, the injustice of Christ's crucifixion, the judgment of the cross on those playing the role of God while judging the Son of God, the Christian emphasis on and high calling to unjust suffering at the hands of those who abuse power, and the Christian gospel message to all of forgiveness and transformation. This message especially applies to those in shackles and in prison.

---

11. Smith, *Awaiting the King*, 101.
12. Smith, *Awaiting the King*, 100.
13. Smith, *Awaiting the King*, 102–3.
14. Smith, *Awaiting the King*, 103.
15. Smith, *Awaiting the King*, 103.

d. *The principle of human rights grounded in the coming New Creation.* "In other words, the 'creational' theology that underwrites a Christian political imagination [or vision] is not a merely nostalgic return to 'creation order' or an ahistorical appeal to 'natural law [something we learn simply from reason].' . . . So the affirmation of *natural right* that emerges in modernity is not a rationalist, 'natural' phenomenon but instead reflects a Christological renewal of the face of the earth and the plane of the human."[16] In other words, to perhaps give Smith and O'Donovan a partial assist, emerging modern democratic political theory's emphasis on human rights was birthed amid a near total obsession with Christ's coming kingdom, which was viewed as increasingly being realized in Western, Judeo-Christian–influenced history. History was not just returning to an unpolluted beginning and fresh start; it was fulfilling that beginning by a glorious end—the New Creation—already initiated by Christ's resurrection. Human rights come from God and are grounded in God's original and coming New Creation for we are citizens and royal priests of that future kingdom.

e. *The principle of freedom of speech.* The fearless gospel proclamation, which includes speaking truth to power (e.g., "We must obey God rather than human beings!" [Acts 5:29 NIV]), based on the eternal law of God and the coming kingdom, "unleashed habits of mutual address, prophetic challenge, and public confidence that began to seep into the expectations of citizens as well as those noncitizens—the underclass, the plebs [ordinary persons of the lower class], the disenfranchised—who had found citizenship in the [already/not yet] city of God [and coming New Creation]."[17]

The theology of Approximation seeks to discern what is an appropriate presence of the future already in this age, based on the decisive nature and victory of Christ's finished work and resurrection victory. We live in the in-between times when hell on earth is not necessary and the fullness of heaven on earth is not possible—before Christ's return.

Hence, our response to antichristism recognizes that AJC is present but so also is the in-breaking of Christ's glorious kingdom—already. Victory is certain, and antichristism is temporary and passing. Craters of the gospel are not only possible given the theology of Approximation—they are everywhere, global, and present in all generations and nations.

---

16. Smith, *Awaiting the King*, 104.
17. Smith, *Awaiting the King*, 105.

Being prepared as citizens for the City of Antichrist inevitably includes being prepared as citizens for effective kingdom influence via the City of Kingdom Approximation. Responding to antichristism is a positive, proactive future-vision and ministry, rather than a negative, reactionary, angry, and tactless engagement.

Yet we must also acknowledge, as per Scripture and historical experience, that antichristism, antichristisms, antichrists, false prophets, and deceivers are found within our Judeo-Christian faith communities, distorting and weakening Judeo-Christian influence and impact inside and outside church and synagogue. Scripture is clear on this internal threat.

One extremely valuable insight from contemporary thought, sometimes referred to as postmodernism or ultramodernism, is that people often use words as a means of power, control, manipulation, and distortion—even inside faith communities. To be clear, there are many varieties of postmodernism or ultramodernism, and many cancerous affirmations, especially with the more extreme representations. However, the old adage aptly applies here that even a stopped postmodern clock is right twice a day.

We all have witnessed manipulation and the abuse of power, and religious language, inside of faith communities, faith-based organizations, and even believing families. And this darkness is often glossed over, or hidden, or justified, or baptized, so to speak, by religious words and affirmations or appeals to God, Jesus, the leading of the Spirit, or even Scripture. How tragic. And so many have been seduced. A key manipulation tactic is convincing believers that questioning these leaders is questioning Scripture or God.

My wife and I once had a friend who, for years, was prayed with by an abusive church elder after being sexually assaulted by that same church leader. We all have heard religious leaders try to present themselves or their movement or organization as blessed by God, especially due to programs or alleged numerical or fiscal success, even though their actions, lives, lack of integrity, treatment of others, and example before believers is far from godlike or Christlike. In working with thousands of students, I have seen this kind of self-baptized "Christian" hypocrisy enable many to question their faith commitment, if not their faith altogether.

There also exists a level or type of distortion concerning Judeo-Christian values and biblical teachings that can only be labeled as direct opposition to God, which is the essence of antichristism. Hence, for the purpose of this work, true or hard antichristism and antichristisms exist inside and outside the church and synagogue, and they directly assault the faith once delivered.

Such hard or militant antichristism is often enabled by unintentional biblical distortions or soft antichristism. For example, respect for religious leaders is a biblical command, yet undiscerning respect for and submission to pastoral or rabbinic or organizational authority can enable or advance true or hard antichristism.

We should never forget that the staunchest opponents of Christ in the first century were exalted religious leaders with powerful status inside of the religious community. They were certainly against or anti-Christ, and primarily responsible for the persecution of Jesus.

Postmodern sensitivity to how words are used as unjust power over others is a helpful reminder. Yet some postmodernists suggest that all language and "truth" are about power, which not only contradicts the biblical teaching that the Word and some words about the Word are liberating. This claim about words and power also suggests that the postmodernists themselves are not speaking any truth about reality or words; they are just babbling to gain their own power and privilege! In contrast, "If you continue in My word, then you are truly My disciples; and you will know the truth, and the truth will set you free" (John 8:31–32).

REVIEW OF THE ESSENCE OF ANTICHRISTISM

Antichristism is the accelerating and increasingly contemporary and systemic/structural/widespread opposition to the Judeo-Christian and biblical way of salvation which is part of the cosmic restoration and resurrection through the Christ or Messiah. This includes opposition to biblically oriented Jews and Christians, opposition to the Judeo-Christian vision of a renewed and restored culture and creation, and thus opposition to—and the attempt to obliterate or eradicate entirely—authentic biblical influence on culture and civilization.

Antichristism affirms that Christians and Jews belong in the privacy of their closets, in jail, in reeducation camps, or in the grave. This antichristism has often been covert, slow-paced, and incremental in public domains such as art, media, entertainment, education, law, and politics,[18] but in recent decades has blossomed into overt if not militant antichristism.

The level of militancy during the bloodbath of the French Revolution has not yet been reached in the West, but there are parallels emerging today with some militants even utilizing the rhetoric of the French Revolution:

---

18. One key usage and meaning of *public*, *publics*, or *public domains* includes those areas of culture that impact or influence or affect most or all the people of a region, nation, culture, and/or civilization or that even impact worldwide or global realities and, therefore, people across the entire world. This global influence is increasingly a reality in our digital age.

"Menacing Speaker Asks Far-Left Seattle Protesters What Happened to Those Who Didn't Support French Revolution. 'Chopped!' They Reply."[19] We are not there yet, but history certainly has taught us how quickly a French Revolution or Nazi culture can emerge. Hitler came to power in 1933, the *Kristallnacht* took place in 1938, and the world was plunged into war on September 1, 1939.

Antichristism includes anti-Semitism (racial and religious), for the Messiah lies at the center of both Jewish and Christian hope. What better core definition could exist for the essence of anti-Semitism than opposition to the biblical Messiah—captured by the term antichristism? Antichristism opposes God's people, Jews and Christians, Jewish ethnicity, and their Judeo-Christian God, their worldview, their beliefs, (and increasingly) their thoughts and attitudes, their biblically influenced actions and behaviors, their message of salvation, their presence in and influence on culture, and especially their future-vision for the present and the future, for time and eternity.

After reviewing key Scriptures, this chapter will further explore representative faces and toxic future-visions of antichristism that are responsible for the lion's share of the following in recent decades and centuries: the endless and growing human carnage; cultural, community, and family breakdowns; and the increasing fragmentation and decay or rotting (or "mod-rot"[20]) of Logos-influenced civilization.

The attempt to be liberated from Judeo-Christian influence—the definition of liberalism in this work—promised heaven on earth and generously served up hell. Or as Lance Morrow put it best, liberalism's AJC "Utopia, this century has learned the hard way, usually bears a [remarkable] resemblance to hell. An evil chemistry turns the dream of salvation into damnation."[21] Contemporary liberalism typically is, at the core, ideological antichristism.

OLD TESTAMENT SPIRIT OF ANTICHRISTISM

The concept of antichristism is rooted in the anti-kingdom spirit and actions of the enemies of God, including nations and rulers (e.g., biblical beasts) who oppose God, God's law, God's influence on the nations, and ultimately oppose God's way of salvation (Messiah) and the Abrahamic blessing to all the nations. Hence, at the heart of opposition to God, and God's already present and future Messianic kingdom, is the spirit of anti-Messiah

---

19. Urbanski, "Menacing Speaker."
20. Concerning mod-rot, see Oden, *After Modernity*.
21. Morrow, "Evil," 51.

or antichrist. God's rule is through the Triune Messiah, and those opposing that true future are of the spirit of antichrist.

Anti-Messianism or antichristism opposes the Abrahamic blessing: "And in you all the families of the earth will be blessed" (Gen 12:3). "The Scripture, foreseeing that God would justify the Gentiles by faith, preached the gospel beforehand to Abraham, saying, 'All the nations will be blessed in you'" (Gal 3:8). "It is you who are the sons of the prophets and of the covenant which God ordained with your fathers, saying to Abraham, 'And in your seed all the families of the earth shall be blessed'" (Acts 3:25).

As demonstrated previously, the blessing of Abraham encompasses far more than merely getting out of the world and arriving on heaven's spiritualized or ethereal shores—it encompasses the entirety of God's program for a renewed creation. It encompasses real and glorious seashores and oceanfronts now and forever. Hence, antichristism opposes God's redemptive work in and on the world, including past, present, and future kingdom influence.

This anti-Messianism, which resurfaces in the book of Revelation, is vividly portrayed by Daniel via the epic conflict of kingdoms and the beast:

> This is what he said: "The fourth beast will be a fourth kingdom on the earth which will be different from all the other kingdoms, and will devour the whole earth and trample it down and crush it. As for the ten horns, out of this kingdom ten kings will arise; and another will arise after them, and he will be different from the previous ones and will humble three kings. And he will speak against the Most High and wear down the saints of the Highest One, and he will intend to make alterations in times and in law; and they will be handed over to him for a time, times, and half a time. But the court will convene for judgment, and his dominion [kingdom] will be taken away, annihilated and destroyed forever. Then the sovereignty, the dominion, and the greatness of all the kingdoms under the whole heaven will be given to the people of the saints of the Highest One; His kingdom will be an everlasting kingdom, and all the empires will serve and obey Him."
>
> At this point the revelation ended. As for me, Daniel, my thoughts were greatly alarming me and my face became pale, but I kept the matter to myself. (Dan 7:23–28)

Unfortunately, these potent passages have often been relegated to the sport of predicting the timing of the last generation rather than understanding that, even if there is reference to a last generation before Messiah's rule, there is evident applicability here to every generation. A scriptural approach affirms Any-Generationism rather than Last-Generationism. Any generation may experience the blessings of the Spirit of Christ or the fruit of the City of Antichrist. Preparation is key.

The spirit of antichrist includes nations and cities opposed to God's coming kingdom, false prophets claiming to speak for the biblical God opposed to God's coming kingdom, religious leaders within biblical communities opposed to God's coming kingdom, and God's own people, who were not truly God's people and inwardly opposed to God's coming kingdom (Rom 2:28; John 8:39). This spirt emanates from false children and people of God opposed to God's coming kingdom, even while claiming the opposite, and the physically but not spiritually circumcised opposed to God's coming kingdom.

The strongest opposition to the New Testament Messiah was not Rome but the whitewashed tombs, vipers, and hypocrites ruling over God's people. While there certainly were commendable religious leaders in Israel (e.g., Nicodemus), these false religious leaders and "priests" of the first century sent the Messiah to the cross—antichristism ruled.

Antichrist cannot be reduced to a single satanic leader "out there" and/or at the end of history as we know it. Antichrist and antichristism can exist in God's house. Antichristism certainly exists outside of God's house—outside of the Judeo-Christian communities of faith.

NEW TESTAMENT SPIRIT OF ANTICHRISTISM

The New Testament reinforces the truth that, while there may be a singular and historical antichrist, the concept of antichrist has many additional if not more central meanings and applications:

> [According to John,] we should probably understand the force of *anti* as indicating opposition, rather than a false claim, i.e., the antichrist is one who [primarily] opposes [the work and influence of] Christ rather than one who claims to be the Christ. ... The concept is introduced in John as already well known; ... there is a temper, an attitude, characteristic of antichrist, and that already exists. Indeed, he can speak of "many antichrists" as already in the world (1 John 2:18).[22]

Opposition to the kingdom of God, the Messiah, and kingdom influence is the core and ultimate motivation for antichristism:

---

22. Morris, "Antichrist," 69–70.

> If the world hates you, you know that it has hated Me before it hated you. If you were of the world, the world would love you as its own; but because you are not of the world, but I chose you out of the world, because of this the world hates you. Remember the word that I said to you, "A slave is not greater than his master." If they persecuted Me, they will persecute you as well; if they followed My word, they will follow yours also. But all these things they will do to you on account of My name, because they do not know the One who sent Me. If I had not come and spoken to them, they would not have sin; but now they have no excuse for their sin. The one who hates Me hates My Father also. If I had not done among them the works which no one else did, they would not have sin; but now they have both seen and hated Me and My Father as well. But this has happened so that the word that is written in their Law will be fulfilled: "They hated Me for no reason." (John 15:18–25)

D. A. Hubbard explains the relationship between the personal antichrist, the many antichrists, and the pervasive and underlying spirit of antichrist: "Opposition to God's kingdom [and God's kingdom influence and people] is [viewed as] opposition to him. . . . The disciples are warned that false Christs will attempt to deceive even the elect (Matt. 24:24; Mark 13:22). . . . [The] Antichrist is [therefore] the personal culmination of a [deceptive] principle [of rejecting God's law and will that is] already working [pervasively and] secretly."[23]

The New Testament affirms the reality of cosmic conflict, personified evil, and historic antichrists, as well as the pervasive timeless spirit of antichrist, many antichrists, and many false prophets and deceivers. Paul references a singular and blasphemous "man of lawlessness": "No one is to deceive you in any way! For it [the day of the Lord] will not come unless the apostasy comes first, and the man of lawlessness is revealed, the son of destruction, who opposes and exalts himself above every so-called god or object of worship, so that he takes his seat in the temple of God, displaying himself as being God" (2 Thess 2:3–4).

Revelation has been interpreted in a variety of ways, such as affirming that the narrative applies only or primarily to past events, or recurring events throughout history, and/or future events, or some combination thereof. In any event, the language certainly connects to the beast concept of the Old Testament and portrays a personified, evil, antichrist figure possessing enormous power:

---

23. Hubbard, "Antichrist," 55–56.

It was also given to him to make war with the saints and to overcome them, and authority was given to him over every tribe, people, language, and nation. All who live on the earth will worship him, everyone whose name has not been written since the foundation of the world in the book of life of the Lamb who has been slaughtered. If anyone has an ear, let him hear. If anyone is destined for captivity, to captivity he goes; if anyone kills with the sword, with the sword he must be killed. Here is the perseverance and the faith of the saints.

Then I saw another beast coming up out of the earth; and he had two horns like a lamb, and he spoke as a dragon. He exercises all the authority of the first beast in his presence. And he makes the earth and those who live on it worship the first beast, whose fatal wound was healed. He performs great signs, so that he even makes fire come down out of the sky to the earth in the presence of people. And he deceives those who live on the earth because of the signs which it was given him to perform in the presence of the beast, telling those who live on the earth to make an image to the beast who had the wound of the sword and has come to life. And it was given to him to give breath to the image of the beast, so that the image of the beast would even speak and cause all who do not worship the image of the beast to be killed. And he causes all, the small and the great, the rich and the poor, and the free and the slaves, to be given a mark on their right hands or on their foreheads, and he decrees that no one will be able to buy or to sell, except the one who has the mark, either the name of the beast or the number of his name. Here is wisdom. Let him who has understanding calculate the number of the beast, for the number is that of a man; and his number is six hundred and sixty-six. (Rev 13:7–18)

Then another angel, a third one, followed them, saying with a loud voice, "If anyone worships the beast and his image, and receives a mark on his forehead or on his hand, he also will drink of the wine of the wrath of God, which is mixed in full strength in the cup of His anger; and he will be tormented with fire and brimstone in the presence of the holy angels and in the presence of the Lamb. And the smoke of their torment ascends forever and ever; they have no rest day and night, those who worship the beast and his image, and whoever receives the mark of his name." Here is the perseverance of the saints who keep the commandments of God and their faith in Jesus. (Rev 14:9–12)

Regardless of how futuristically one interprets these passages, it is less than helpful to the mission of the church not to recognize how discerningly relevant these passages are to *every* generation and abuser of power and oppressor of others.

Perhaps even more stunning and relevant for every present moment and every generation, however, is the magnitude of opposition to the Messiah that exists inside so-called biblical faith communities. Those who only obsess over the end-times, last-generation antichrist are forgetting that the antichrist is often in the house. That should be most instructive today:

> Woe to you, scribes and Pharisees, hypocrites! For you are like whitewashed tombs which on the outside appear beautiful, but inside they are full of dead men's bones and all uncleanness. So you too, outwardly appear righteous to people, but inwardly you are full of hypocrisy and lawlessness [ἀνομίας, *anomias*, the same root term for Paul's "man of lawlessness" in 2 Thess 2]. Woe to you, scribes and Pharisees, hypocrites! For you build the tombs for the prophets and decorate the monuments of the righteous, and you say, "If we had been living in the days of our fathers, we would not have been partners with them in shedding the blood of the prophets." So you testify against yourselves, that you are sons of those who murdered the prophets. Fill up, then, the measure of the guilt of your fathers. You snakes, you offspring of vipers, how will you escape the sentence of hell? Therefore, behold, I am sending you prophets and wise men and scribes; some of them you will kill and crucify, and some of them you will flog in your synagogues, and persecute from city to city, so that upon you will fall the guilt of all the righteous blood shed on earth, from the blood of righteous Abel to the blood of Zechariah, the son of Berechiah, whom you murdered between the temple and the altar. Truly I say to you, all these things will come upon this generation. Jerusalem, Jerusalem, who kills the prophets and stones those who have been sent to her! How often I wanted to gather your children together, the way a hen gathers her chicks under her wings, and you were unwilling. Behold, your house is being left to you desolate! For I say to you, from now on you will not see Me until you say, "Blessed is the One who comes in the name of the Lord!" (Matt 23:27–39)

Scripture clearly views the spirit of opposition to the biblical God, God's kingdom, and kingdom influence as manifesting itself in manifold ways: Cain, Pharaoh, Pharaoh's magicians and false prophets, religious leaders residing within Judeo-Christian communities, false prophets, nations and kingdoms, deceivers attempting to seduce the faithful, many antichrists, multiple beasts, and, for those who believe in a single future antichrist, the antichrist who, in epic fashion, incarnates and exemplifies and consummates the spirit of antichrist throughout history.

This timeless, widespread, and systemic opposition is appropriately captured by the biblical references to many antichrists and the spirit of antichrist. Indeed, John properly equates or conflates false prophets and antichrists: "Beloved, do not believe every spirit, but test the spirits to see whether they are from God, for many false prophets have gone out into the world. By this you know the Spirit of God: every spirit that confesses that Jesus Christ has come in the flesh is from God, and every spirit that does not confess Jesus is not from God. This is the spirit of the antichrist, which you heard was coming and now is in the world already" (1 John 4:1–3 ESV).

Paul is far more concerned about those operating inside rather than outside faith communities—about those who deceive, distort, and redefine basic beliefs and terms:

> I am amazed that you are so quickly deserting Him who called you by the grace of Christ [Anointed One, Messiah], for a different gospel, which is not just another account; but there are some who are disturbing you and want to distort the gospel of Christ. But even if we, or an angel from heaven, should preach to you a gospel contrary to what we have preached to you, he is to be accursed! As we have said before, even now I say again: if anyone is preaching to you a gospel contrary to what you received, he is to be accursed! (Gal 1:6–9)

Why is Paul so animated? From a biblical perspective, the root and fruit of the global problem and the solution are one. Paul warns the faithful concerning the distortion and corruption of their beliefs: "A little leaven leavens the whole lump of dough" (Gal 5:9).

God's people must remain faithful to the revealed and biblical terms, definitions, beliefs, and practices found in Scripture. Those who redefine God, Jesus, Spirit, gospel, salvation, faith, marriage, gender, freedom, apostle, servants, love, compassion, justice, and kingdom inside communities of faith are the greatest threat to kingdom influence in the world. They are anti-Logos (opposing the Messiah, Christ, Alpha, and Omega). They are anti-Logocentric. They reject defining words and reality and the future based on the plumb line of the Logos who created all things, including the communication, language, meaning, and the meaning of meaning:

> For I am jealous for you with a godly jealousy; for I betrothed you to one husband, to present you as a pure virgin to Christ.

THE BIBLICAL MANDATE

> But I am afraid that, as the serpent deceived Eve by his trickery, your minds will be led astray from sincere and pure devotion to Christ. For if one comes and preaches another Jesus whom we have not preached, or you receive a different spirit which you have not received, or a different gospel which you have not accepted, this you tolerate very well! (2 Cor 11:2–4)

> For such men are false apostles, deceitful workers, disguising themselves as apostles of Christ. No wonder, for even Satan disguises himself as an angel of light. Therefore it is not surprising if his servants also disguise themselves as servants of righteousness, whose end will be according to their deeds. (2 Cor 11:13–15)

> I say this so that no one will deceive you with persuasive arguments [or persuasive words, *logia*]. (Col 2:4)

To recap, Scripture, from Genesis to Revelation, offers a unified message on the pervasive presence, impact, and seductive nature of the spirit of antichrist. This dark spirit is spread by evil kingdoms and kings, seductive magicians, false prophets, antichrists, the man of lawlessness, false apostles, false messengers of God, false teachers, false teachings, false children of God, false Jews, angels of light, synagogues of Satan, the beast, the false prophet, the antichrist, false cities, symbolic Babylon, and Satan. Jesus and the New Testament expressly affirm the continued need for the faithful to be alert and always prepared for antichristism:

- "You offspring of vipers, how can you, being evil, express any good things? For the mouth speaks from that which fills the heart" (Matt 12:34).

- "Beloved, do not believe every spirit, but test the spirits to see whether they are from God, for many false prophets have gone out into the world. By this you know the Spirit of God: every spirit that confesses that Jesus Christ has come in the flesh is from God, and every spirit that does not confess Jesus is not from God. This is the spirit of the antichrist, which you heard was coming and now is in the world already" (1 John 4:1–3 ESV).

- "For false christs and false prophets will arise, and will provide signs and wonders, in order to mislead, if possible, [even] the elect" (Mark 13:22).

- "For the time will come when they will not tolerate sound doctrine; but wanting to have their ears tickled, they will accumulate for themselves teachers in accordance with their own desires" (2 Tim 4:3).

VERBAL SEDUCTION, ANTICHRISTISM, AND LOGOCENTRISM

As has been demonstrated, a root cause of an undiscerning and feeble faith community or church is the anti-Christian and deceptive use of words, redefining reality by redefining words. It follows, then, that a key cure for the root disease is the proper definition of terms and reality based on the Logos who created reality and words. Logocentrism ultimately triumphs over antichristism or false-Logocentrism.

"Hold on to the example of sound words [true logōn] which you have heard from me, in the faith and love which are in Christ Jesus" (2 Tim 1:13).

In the Old Testament, Israel is the primary locus of God's redemptive work in the world. In the New Testament, the church is the primary locus of God's redemptive work in the world. Accordingly, the strongest ire is stirred up in Jesus, Paul, and John when those claiming to be children of the promise actually seek to deceive, distort, or redefine every biblical belief, practice, or term.

The root of the solution for synagogue, church, and state is a return of God's faithful to biblical words, definitions, beliefs, practices, spirit, and loves. Believers are to be Messiah-centered or Messiah-centric. Logocentrism counters the deception of the City of Antichrist and lays the foundation for the City of Kingdom Approximation. Logocentrism also lays the foundation for the coming City of God and the New Creation.

Faith communities that remain faithful to the spirit, doctrine, and practice of the Messiah and Scripture can mediate God's restoration to the world because the biblical gospel (good news and words) deals with the root problem, which is the human heart, and the "mouth speaks from that which fills" the heart (Luke 6:45). World-influencing Logocentrism, centered in the personal and written Word, embraces the heart, head, reality-creating words, and hands—actions, practice, or praxis.

Political, intellectual, and cultural engagement is a manifestation of loving the King and kingdom expressed by renewed Logocentric faith communities and human hearts, but such engagement is the fruit, not the root, of the solution. Cultural engagement is critical, but apart from a spiritual renewal of God's people any social change is flawed and/or unsustainable. Political and cultural engagement without the Logocentric spirit of Christ simply breeds unnecessary rebellion and resentment and enables antichristism.

The biblical and effective prescription for the present, cancerous, antichristism moment is neither cultural, political, and intellectual engagement nor a simplistic and spiritualized call for revival. The answer is both, with the thoroughgoing biblical reformation of God's people, beliefs, practices, words, language, loves, minds, thoughts, and creative imaginations being the root of the root of the underlying problem and solution. Civilizational engagement is urgent and necessary, yet for God's people, such kingdom influence must begin and end with the Spirit of Messiah, Christ, Logos, and God.

ALWAYS PREPARED TO RESPOND TO ANTICHRISTISM AS KINGDOM CITIZENS WITH THE "FACE OF AN ANGEL" (ACTS 6:15)

Biblical narrative or stories may be the perfect means for teaching how to respond to AJCism in the present age before Christ's return. Authentic kingdom citizens of the future should counter antichristism in alignment with how the faithful responded in key New Testament stories. An essential and biblical primer or introductory textbook on always being prepared citizens of time and eternity would especially include the Gospels, Acts, Heb 11, and Revelation. Story after story recounts how those truly blessed by God responded to antichristism and modeled, like Christ (Hebrews), biblical faith and New Creation citizenship. From the opposition to and crucifixion of Jesus in the Gospels, to "Father forgive them," to the warnings, beatings, and persecutions of those advancing the kingdom in Acts, to those running the race led by the Messiah in the hall of true faith, fame, and an imperishable citizenship and city (Heb 11 and 12), to the faithful martyrs and citizens of the coming City of God in Revelation, these narratives norm the biblical response to antichristism. All Scripture is inspired and profitable, but these books and chapters are particularly relevant in our accelerating antichristism world.

Perhaps the story of Stephen (Acts chapters 6–8), however, is most instructive today. First, the book of Acts may well be a narrative textbook for how to respond to AJCism. Acts and the question of how to respond to AJCism would be a worthy subject for an entire dissertation or book, if such does not already exist. Second, Stephen models always being prepared. He was "full of grace and power" (6:8), courageously spoke the truth in love to power, mastered Scripture and rightly discerned the hearts of his audience, was more than ready with his verbal defense, forgave his murderers (7:60), and likely contributed to the divine conversion of the man who turned civilization upside down (8:1, Saul/Paul).

Stephen spoke the truth in love even when offering a rebuke, was always prepared as a true citizen for antichristism and approximation, ran the race to perfection, and did so with the compassionate but divinely illumined and authorized "face of an angel" (6:15). Stephen laid an inspiring foundation and became a post-resurrection pace-setter for the faithful citizens who overcome and are always prepared for the spirit of antichristism, like Peter, Paul, Apollos, Hebrews' faith heroes, and the martyrs of Revelation. Today's complex context still requires the compassionate face of an angel—especially in global regions where believers still retain some measure of freedom of faith and speech, competing future-visions still can be influenced and history can bend for the better, just as with the apostle Paul's influence and impact.

FLESH-AND-BLOOD REPRESENTATIVE AND TOXIC FUTURE-VISIONS

As noted, this work can only introduce the very real, influential, and numerous future-visions writing the present and future of history and culture. And as referenced earlier, a subsequent, more academic, and lengthier work is forthcoming that will more fully and directly assess these visions. Appendix D includes abbreviated assessments and additional examples. The toxic dimensions of these eschatologies often include strong elements of AJCism. A few examples will suffice for this chapter.

The *Enlightenment* vision (roughly 1650–1850) led to real civilizational wins but worshiped reason and science and often viewed Christianity or traditional Christianity as the key obstacle to progress. The related vision of post-Christianity (eighteenth century to the present) included discarding or replacing Christianity (Voltaire). Likewise, post-Christendom eschatology (also eighteenth century to the present) rejected church-state unions and/or went so far as to reject most or all Christian influence on civilization. Faith was welcome if privatized in the closet.

The future-vision of *Romanticism* (nineteenth century but ongoing) understandably reacted to the life-denying overemphasis on reason/science by emphasizing better ways to experience and connect to reality (e.g., refined feelings or ethics), which contributed to why many Judeo-Christian leaders and educational institutions discarded basic beliefs while trying to preserve religious feelings. Basic beliefs were typically redefined. The divinity of Jesus simply meant that the totally human Jesus fully sensed God's presence such that we see God in Jesus' experience and/or ethics. This redefinition of all beliefs, God, Jesus, sin, and salvation, redefined Christianity, and this redefined Christianity redefined the surrounding culture and the future.

The *Liberationist* vision (especially recent centuries) takes many forms (e.g., Marxism), and identifies some form of oppression (economic, social, racial, religious, gender) as central, and typically views biblical faith as complicit in oppression—as an oppressor and/or a happy drug or opiate. Liberationism is certainly alive and well in the present decade.

Appendix D briefly introduces and evaluates numerous *other future-visions* that may on occasion contain some legitimate concerns yet often contribute to the City of Antichrist and the spirit of AJCism. They are all contemporary forms of liberalism, properly defined—often expressly wanting to be liberated from biblical and Judeo-Christian influence. These legion movements include: Some varieties of Postmodernism or Ultramodernism, Syncretism, Nazism, Neo-Marxism (new forms of Marxism), Critical Race Theory, "Wokism," Dystopian Anarchism, Personal and/or Cultural Relativism, Anti-Westernism, Anti-Capitalism Anti-Colonialism, the Great Reset, Radical Environmentalism, and Nihilism. Many have pronounced liberationist and/or Marxist assumptions, and most overtly or covertly seek to eradicate biblical assumptions.

These various and many forms of modernism, or the late, or last, or ultra/extreme forms of modernism, often referred to as postmodernism, all seek to be liberated from the orbit and influence of the Logos. There are powerful though often shifting alliances between future-visions in the City of Antichrist.

As noted, all of these future-visions, properly classified, are also forms of contemporary liberalism—including the quest for the City of Antichrist and opposition to the City of Kingdom Approximation. Many are seduced by these future-vision sirens, and many sirens are intentional angels of light.

Contemporary liberalism, properly defined previously, is arguably the primary face of evil and much human, cultural, and civilizational carnage in recent centuries. The considerable evidence for this thesis will have to be explored in another publication, yet Marx, Stalin, Nietzsche, Pol Pot, and Hitler are illustrative for now. By the way, unintentional plagues and carnage by colonial powers are certainly evil and tragic but in a different ethical category than calculated and premeditated reeducation, torture, and death camps. The slavery issue is also repeatedly raised to cancel Judeo-Christian–influenced civilizational experiments, yet non-colonial powers not only have practiced slavery across the centuries and across the globe but fueled colonial slavery. The influence of the Logos abolished slavery. And the intentional carnage of kingdoms claiming to be Judeo-Christian does not hold a candle to the sins of contemporary liberalism. Besides, false claims to be Judeo-Christian–influenced kingdoms are simply counterfeit kingdoms, cities, and counterfeit approximation.

FLESH-AND-BLOOD REPRESENTATIVE AND ENABLING FUTURE-VISIONS

This work also has contended that the true problem and solution, the real reason for the success of the City of Antichrist, is enabling conservative future-visions that birth anemic faith communities and organizations (colleges, seminaries, etc.). This means that the true problems and solutions today and in every age largely include church, synagogue, and supporting organizations.

Those claiming to conserve, promote, or protect Judeo-Christian influence have often poisoned the Judeo-Christian cultural and civilizational living waters with enabling or toxic future-visions. Some visions have no real desire or reason to advance Judeo-Christian influence (escapists). Some may redefine Judeo-Christian beliefs (liberal Christians). Others want to protect the free exercise of Judeo-Christian faith and practice even while enabling those who want to bury faith (separatists). This approach also would include most forms of political Libertarianism, as well as separatist and escapist Christianity discussed and critiqued previously.

Some enabling future-visions may view Judeo-Christian faith and practice as positive for culture as long as there is a strict wall of legal separation between the supposedly neutral state and Judeo-Christian influence. Indeed, in some respects, classical liberal political theory—in contrast to the contemporary liberal and the often AJC eschatologies already mentioned—both protects and restricts Judeo-Christian influence. Classical liberals typically want to restrict any sector of civilization, especially government, from encroaching on individual liberty, but some viewed religion as assisting with this liberty and others viewed at least some types of religious activity or influence as a threat.

These enabling future-visions are many, varied, and as with many countless toxic eschatologies will be briefly enumerated and assessed in appendix D. Some of these visions claim to conserve Judeo-Christian assumptions, values, beliefs, practices, and cultural influence even if they ultimately do the opposite. Others simply believe it is wrongheaded and counterproductive to pursue civilizational influence.

Relative to the introductory purpose of this chapter, the more conservative enabling future-visions include two representative categories that seek to conserve Judeo-Christian beliefs in one fashion or another. (1) The *separationist, isolationist, and apolitical visions* conserve biblical beliefs for biblical believers and largely abandon cultural impact. Perhaps these are what Reinhold Niebuhr once referred to as the doves, who seek to remain pure yet who actually dirty their hands by enabling evil. Some naively believe that if they stay out of the public square, the public square will leave them alone and perhaps they can even serve as an indirect positive influence—just like nations that have tried to appease international bullies, terrorists, and genocidal maniacs. (2) On the other end of the spectrum are future-visions that think they honor the Logos by largely or entirely *conquering culture and civilization*. Appendix D explores tragic approaches such as destructive forms of imperialism and colonialism, and this text already has introduced postmillennial and theocratic dangers, even while acknowledging the social concern/biblical justice contributions of views such as postmillennialism (e.g., education, poverty relief, abolitionism, feminism).

The enabling aspects of conservative visions are numberless. Why are so many Judeo-Christian conservatives unbiblical and inappropriately otherworldly, or escapist, or separatist, or monastic or neo-monastic? Why are some proudly apolitical, naively Libertarian, anti-intellectual, simplistically spiritualizing (we just need to pray for revival and preach the gospel), reactionary, politically engaged without refinement or preparation, angry, or simplistically nationalistic? Why have so many tried to take over countries (Cromwellianism, Constantinianism or dominionism or reconstructionism), or save a country, or usher in the kingdom (postmillennialism). Or why do millions still hold tenaciously to a voyeuristic addiction to last-generation darkness (eschatomania)?

The answer seems to point back toward a largely distorted church, misled by a wrong spirit and seduced by redefined words and an enabling future-vision. The conservative visions are often unawares, rushing themselves, the church, the synagogue, and civilization into the orbit of the City of Antichrist. These future-visions enable AJCism. These eschatologies fall well short of always being prepared as true citizens of time and eternity to respond to antichristism and advance the City of Kingdom Approximation.

CONCLUSION

ALWAYS BE PREPARED FOR THE THREE CITIES AND NEW CREATION

The philosophers [and theologians] have only interpreted the world, in various ways; the point is to change it.

—Karl Marx, Theses on Feuerbach, 1845[1]

Like a dog that returns to its own vomit is a fool that repeats his folly.

—Proverbs 26:11-12 (ESV)

FLOUNDERING FAITH COMMUNITIES AND DRIFTING CIVILIZATIONS

Faith communities and churches are often floundering and most civilizations are drifting out of orbit from the influence of the Logos toward a routinely outraged world. Logocentrism is waning. Words, phrases, values, beliefs, meaning, loves, passions, ethics, and practices have moved far beyond merely not being Logocentric. Unbiblical antichristism is on the march and even gaining a foothold inside faith communities, churches, and synagogues. Many are seduced. Individuals, families, communities, states, regions, nations, and civilizations—all kingdoms of sorts—are loving and serving the City of Antichrist and advancing the Age of Antichrist and antichristism. Yet there is far more to this epic story, for we are navigating three cities, not just one or two. There is real hope for the present and ultimate future.

1. Marx, "Theses on Feuerbach," thesis 11.

AGE OF ANTICHRIST OR APPROXIMATION?

As noted previously, the answer to whether we are currently living in the Age and City of Approximation and kingdom influence or the Age and City of Antichrist and antichristism is yes. There are three major, foundational, and overlapping cities (antichrist, approximation, New Creation) that frame our trek from creation to the final consummation of history and all things. And this three-cities "yes" applies to all generations prior to the return of Messiah. However, to recap, this three-cities framework can be subdivided in to five kingdoms or cities: the Kingdom/City of Eden; the Kingdom/City of Antichrist; the Kingdom/City of Approximation; the Kingdom/City of Millennial or New Creation Transition and Restoration; and the Kingdom/City of Cosmic Resurrection.

The City or Kingdom of Eden was corrupted and overthrown by the City of Antichrist. The City of Antichrist received a fatal death blow, a D-Day magnitude in-breaking already of the future and ultimately victorious kingdom, through the "it is finished" birth, life, teaching, death, bodily resurrection, and sending of the Triune Spirit of the Christ. Today, believers are called to faithfully navigate the City of Antichrist and the City of Kingdom Approximation on the journey toward the City of New Creation Transition and Restoration that sets the final redemptive table for the City of Cosmic Resurrection. We are primarily navigating three cities today, fully rooted in the first city while already illuminated and drawn forward by the dawning of the fifth city. This multi-city framework both gratefully builds upon and takes a quantum leap beyond prior two cities frameworks that have helpfully and unhelpfully guided so much of our Judeo-Christian mission, history, understanding, and practice of discipleship, formation, spirituality, holiness, worship, and piety.

Augustine's ever influential and often dualistic future-vision of the City of Man, dominated by lust, pride, self-glory, false glory, and false human wisdom and knowledge, is brilliant and well-grounded in the biblical narrative, including the temptation narrative in the garden of Eden. Yet Augustine's approach can be enhanced by retaining his emphasis on self-glory while also placing the serpent at the core of the city's narrative, concept and loves. Don't forget the serpent—serpent theology is everywhere in the Pentateuch and throughout Scripture and Revelation. Don't overlook the serpentine darkness influencing and inspiring civilizations such as Egypt and Babylon. Don't simplistically claim that "the devil made me or us or them do it" but recognize the powers, forces, and unseen realities that shape a City of Antichrist that silences and crucifies usurpers. The City of Antichrist is both humanity at its worst and the usurping darkness at its best.

Biblical theology enhances Augustine's magisterial view of the two cities by emphasizing real, flesh and blood, earthly and heavenly cities in all their complexity and both real or false glory. Biblical theology emphasizes that there are real cities of antichrist and antichristism already in the present age. Biblical theology and eschatology repeatedly emphasize that current cities can also, at times and to some degree, approximate, *contribute to*, and participate in the real, earthly, flesh and blood, true future of the New Creation.

Biblical theology guides the church with a potent, world-influencing future-vision and calling in the present age: an approximated but not yet resurrected New Creation. Yet this vision, influence, and dawning reality play out on a cosmic stage with the key actors of antichrists, enablers, and the faithful remnant of approximators who truly mediate the ultimately victorious global Abrahamic blessing to every generation prior to Messiah's return.

Yet this glorious approximation already is regularly short-circuited not only by improper responses to antichrists and enablers inside and outside of the key change agents of faith communities. Approximation, as we have seen, is also thwarted or diminished by the well-intentioned faithful seeking approximation who confuse the roots and fruit of antichristism in church, synagogue, state, and culture.

Biblically, the Triune work of God in the church, through the Spirit, is the only true cure. The Spirit can influence the civilizational root and fruit. The Spirit can influence the world and "all" flesh (Joel 2:28 ESV; John 16:8), all human beings, directly and especially through the faithful who have already stepped into God's true future and mediate that future today. Countless future-visions have been documented that undermine the biblical vision and birth, empower, embolden, and fortify the City of Antichrist. Many of these false future-visions, as we have seen, rule church, synagogue, cities, and state.

Unfortunately, those of good will inside and outside faith communities often do not join hands and reflect and partially realize the coming restoration. If those of good will who are influenced by the Spirit of the future do not partner together, the City of Kingdom influence is overcome by the City of Antichrist. The arrow of redemptive time runs backward—the dog returns to its own vomit. And as quoted earlier, either we all hang together in the City of Kingdom Approximation, or we all hang separately in the City of Antichrist.[2]

---

2. As noted, most credit Benjamin Franklin with this "hang together" quotation.

ENABLERS, AUGUSTINE, AND FLESH-AND-BLOOD CITIES

Tragically, church, synagogue, and the faithful are often the major obstruction of God's true future via anemic future-visions and living as if the City of Antichrist has not received a fatal death blow already. The faithful often live as if D-Day has not taken place, as if the watershed invasion has not transpired. They often live as the fearful faithful or as spectators, thus enabling antichristism. Or they sometimes naively rush forward with utopian dreams of kingdom influence, and to their credit sometimes make incredible civilizational gains, only to have such unrealistic dreams crushed by the City of Antichrist. They harness the rocket fuel of eschatology but spend the fuel too quickly and recklessly in a single and sometimes self-congratulatory historical moment.

The faithful desperately need specific and clear marching orders. They need a future-vision with some teeth and muscle that includes clarity on the future, on precisely what cultural gains can possibly be made before Messiah's return (see appendix A and prior discussion), and guidance on collaborative, strategic, tactical, and practical planning and implementation.

N. T. Wright's *The Day the Revolution Began* and Augustine's Two Cities are brilliant but incomplete, overly general, and, with Augustine, sometimes interpreted as largely spiritual or ethereal—not clearly connected to this flesh-and-blood earthy/earthly world. Wright's contribution can be enhanced with more future-vision or eschatological specificity.[3] Augustine's Two Cities contribution can be enhanced by removing some of the otherworldly, dualistic, and amillennial elements that diminished the positive interpretation, influence, and impact of his eschatology.[4]

Augustine's future-vision perceptively and most creatively views the desire for biblical salvation as central to the city of God, and the serpent's elixir and desire for false glory, pride, along with the lust for earthly power as central to the City of Man. Two loves lie at the root of culture and civilization in the present age (or *saeculum*). The first is the love of self (self-glory), which creates vain thinking, false wisdom, and imaginations that can even despise God. The second is the love of God, which glorifies God; generates humility, godly wisdom, and true cultural and civilizational creativity; and dethrones self.

We love and make or shape cities or kingdoms. Those loving either or both cities, for Augustine, can and will impact culture and civilization

---

3. See Matthews, *Theology*, ch. 11, and previous comments in this work concerning N. T. Wright's limitations, such as the latter part of ch. 1.

4. See previous comments in this work concerning Augustine's limitations, such as chs. 3 and 4.

because both loves tarry together in the present age, just like the tares (weeds and thorns) and the wheat—often in the same individual or city or kingdom. Cities, families, kingdoms, institutions, cultures, communities, and influential public entities, for Augustine, participate in either the City of God or the City of Man, or both. Loves or misdirected loves determine the alignment or misalignment with the City of God.

Augustine's diagnosis is truly magisterial. Yet this present work has argued that Augustine's vision can be enhanced. He rejects an earthly reign of the Messiah (amillennialism), perhaps due to his disillusionment with carnal premillennial excesses and the fall of Christian Rome in the early fifth century. As N. T. Wright and others have argued, medieval theology, influenced by Augustine, leans toward an otherworldly, individualistic, escapist, and somewhat Platonic narrowing of salvation and the goal of salvation to avoiding God's wrath and a somewhat otherworldly heaven and the beautiful (beatific) vision of God.

Perhaps, again, because of Augustine's disillusionment with the fall of Rome, he emphasizes that the wheat and tares grow together until the final judgment, which will be addressed shortly. More critically, even though his system provides a means for the City of God to influence current kingdoms, communities, actual cities, culture, and civilization, his lack of clarity and precision has tended to reduce this influence to the realm of internal spirituality and individual loves, desires, affections, attitudes, experiences of God, and salvation. These foci's of influence are important but often limited to the individual or the church.

The Two Cities teaching of Augustine is too easily spiritualized or over-spiritualized. The Two Cities of Augustine are too dualistic, too theoretical, too over-spiritualized, and too internalized—either by Augustine or his interpreters over the centuries.

His "City of Man" concept, whether intentional or not, casts a dark shadow over all legitimate human attempts in the present age to approximate the heavenly city and the New Creation—already on earth as it is in heaven. The City of God for Augustine clearly is not attainable already. The present City of Man is evil. The third City of Kingdom of Approximation is largely missing from his future-vision, which explains much otherworldly dualism among the faithful caught in Augustine's orbit.

The Two Cities are also too exclusive to spark and build broad partnerships with people of many faiths, or even with many within Judeo-Christian faith communities, because God's grace is only applied to the elect—all others are not elect and passed over according to Augustine. And Augustine's passed over "mass of perdition"[5] may not be the best candidates for lovers of God who can mediate or approximate the true future of the City of God in the present age.

This work and the remainder of this concluding chapter only lay possible foundations for more incarnational, strategic, and tactical future-visioning. However, understanding that actual flesh-and-blood cities and civilizations can tilt toward real earthly futures of either the City of Antichrist or the City of Kingdom Approximation revolutionizes our loves, future-vision, education, parenting, preaching, teaching, training, faith communities, strategy, and tactics.

The wheat and tares will remain until the future Day of the Lord, but the flesh-and-blood civilizational landscape today can be overrun with tares (the City of Antichrist) or can be leavened, salted, and illuminated with the City of Kingdom Approximation—the wheat can flourish already. The biblically faithful, via the Triune Spirit and overflowing cruciform love, can serve as authentic and powerful light, and salt, and leaven—already.

Real cities, culture, and civilizations can change in the present age, even given all their beauty, disfigurement, complexity, brilliance, stupidity, false wisdom, arrogant wisdom, real glories, false glories, entertainment, politics, law, education, inspiring architecture, humor, music, values, semantics, human creation, technological opportunities, technological tyranny, and human and demonic oppression and destruction. And such great tribulation or approximation is providentially but largely conditional and based on the state of church and synagogue.

Current history and culture creation are headed somewhere, and not to an otherworldly spiritual realm or cosmic annihilation. The future, it has been argued based on Scripture, theology, human nature, and reason, must include a transitional reign of Messiah that completes and fulfills the entirety of past history. This transition sets the stage for the true future—cosmic restoration and, even better, cosmic resurrection. This transitional era will likely be much longer than one thousand years, but he reigns already in one sense, and he shall reign then and he shall reign forever and ever in the ultimate destination—the New Heaven and the New Earth.

Faith communities, including churches and synagogues, are lovingly and sacrificially involved in an epic and cosmic conflict and advance. The church should be overflowing with love for God, God's creation, and others, plus engaged (the gracious, winsome, prophetic Church Militant in this age), unified, influential, cruciform, and most collaborative with those of

---

5. Including unbaptized babies.

other faiths as much as is possible, as we journey to the New Creation of the Church Triumphant.

THE EXTREME URGENCY OF THE STRATEGIC, TACTICAL, AND PRACTICAL

As we have seen, Karl Marx's hopelessly flawed and naive future-vision did indeed change the world, reshape education, send the masses to reeducation camps or genocide, spark revolutions, raise kingdoms, move military battalions, launch state-of-the art weapons of exploration and death, destroy or remake empires, try to abolish religion and free speech, redefine social justice and economic theory, and liberate millions upon millions to a new and more toxic form of dependent slavery to the state and tyrant liberators. Future-visions rule. Future-visions or eschatologies are the rocket fuel or nuclear power source for cosmic change.

Marx was not advocating for "fire, ready, aim," for he affirmed careful reflection, but he was insistent that such reflection could not be divorced from real-world and historical consequences and action. For Marx, the point of his future-vision was not to understand the world but to change it. In Scripture, both understanding and transformation are essential and one.

Judeo-Christian future-visions (e.g., revival and Spirit-influenced abolitionist anti-slavery movements) also have influenced and reshaped the world. Unfortunately, these corrupted Judeo-Christian visions have too often been obsessed with almost frantically interpreting the present generation as the dark and predetermined, fatalistic last days. Eschatomania rules. Such visions are more pagan than biblical or Judeo-Christian.

Many "Christian" future-visions only misinterpret the world in various pathological ways and not only fail to advance the biblical kingdom but often obstruct it. For many today, their biblical future-vision is largely unbiblical and has become an escapist, narcissistic spectator sport.

Eschatomania has shaped the very life, preaching, teaching, worship, and mission of faith communities and families. Eschatomania has included escapism and short-circuited and reduced or redirected the social concern of the faithful for culture and civilization from large-scale, sometime utopian, programs for change to lifeboat evangelism and small-scale and symptomatic social concern (e.g., soup kitchens and addiction recovery ministries). These symptomatic concerns have great kingdom value and can have some civilizational influence, but such limited future-visions hand over the primary role of writing the pages of future-history to non– or increasingly anti–Judeo-Christian movements.

Judeo-Christian critics of eschatomania have often responded to eschatomania with eschatophobia and have successfully and surgically removed much of the biblical and future-vision nuclear power and jet fuel from the core of the Judeo-Christian movement. And the excesses of eschatology have led some eschatophobes to exorcize eschatology from the faith once delivered. And to paraphrase and modify a number of authors (e.g., Lewis, Kierkegaard, Machen), a Judeo-Christian faith without kingdom eschatology at the core is a watered-down faith. And a watered-down faith is no longer a biblical faith at all. And a non-biblical faith will fail to mediate the true future to the present age.

Other social justice warriors, rightly concerned about the state of the world, have unequally yoked and sometimes "woked" the faith into unbiblical or anti-biblical, naive, flawed, and undiscerning future-visions. Their hearts are often ablaze with future-vision and social justice rocket fuel and they daily cry out "thy kingdom come," yet their minds are seduced by counterfeit kingdoms and verbal deceptions (e.g., "compassion"). They partner with movements that undermine their own Judeo-Christian faith, assumptions, and kingdoms.

Marx, Adam Smith (invisible hand economics), Herbert Spencer, Marcuse, Kant, Hume, Foucault, Nietzsche, Voltaire, Sartre, de Beauvoir, Freud, Dawkins, Teresa Delgado, Kafka, and countless other luminaries, who should be discerningly heard, are not only spiritually baptized, circumcised, and taken to church. They—via various reformulations of their views—are now regularly given access to the pulpit and very life of faith communities and movements (e.g., as we have seen, the Southern Poverty Law Center [SPLC], Social Darwinism, or the Sojourners movement).

Sojourners mixes evangelical theology with predictable and almost guaranteed alignment with one political party—with rare but courageous exceptions. The once noble but now fallen SPLC, for example, defines virtually any groups or individuals that affirm traditional and biblical marriage, the positive value of Judeo-Christian and biblical influence on culture, or those having concerns about reckless illegal immigration as "hate groups" that need to be canceled. As would be expected, SPLC completely redefines numerous terms such as "democracy," which they claim to be saving, and "voter suppression," which in many cases is exactly what they are doing. Their actual bumper sticker (2023) is "Fight Hate," a classification which includes Roman Catholics who believe in the traditional sacrament of heterosexual marriage—see their very "inclusive" "hate" map on their web site. Their current bumper sticker would at least have some integrity if it were changed to

"Fight Hate Hatefully," or, better yet, "Hate and Silence Scripture and Biblical Christians."[6]

Many of these messianic and liberationist kingdom manifestos often redefine or rival the very biblical kingdom itself, often promising liberation and heaven and delivering various new forms of oppression and hell on earth. We should not understate or overlook the civilizational and human carnage that has followed—and is following—in their wake. The City of Antichrist is populated by much more than simply bad ideas—there are very real consequences. And ironically, the corrupt City of Antichrist that claims to liberate disproportionately crushes the marginalized, the powerless, and especially its urban children.

THE WAY FORWARD: THE CITY OF THE FUTURE ALREADY

The daily headlines and cultural realities in the dark shadows of the City of Antichrist in the globally influential North American context, documented earlier in this work, continue to proliferate.[7] A sampling of this ominous evidence and quagmire is included in appendix D.

This work has documented that such is the quagmire of postmodernism, or mod-rot, where the civilizational center no longer holds and every word, value, belief, and practice is up for grabs, shameless spin, and endless, seductive redefinitions. We have moved from Logocentrism to Logo-insanity and pomo-insanity (word usage that is now nearly insane in our postmodern age).

We should not be surprised at this madness, given that many think that all beliefs and words are just manipulative tools for individuals and tribes to gain power. We should not be astonished at our post-truth and post-Logos quagmire. Postmodernists have been telling us for decades, if not longer if Nietzsche is included, that there is no such thing as a reality that is not created through the interpretive spectacles/glasses of language. The result

---

6. Sojourners, "Who We Are." Also see https://www.splcenter.org/. Some will endlessly argue that conservative believers and American evangelicals also align with one political party or presidential candidate. That is often true, but some conservatives are more Libertarian; some are very concerned about certain presidential candidates; and, most importantly, lesser-evil calculations are and have to be made regarding political parties. No political party or candidate represents or incarnates the kingdom of God, but some political parties and organizations, quite regularly, either redefine the biblical kingdom or fuel AJCism.

7. These recent headlines and contemporary issues listed in appendix D are typically paraphrased in order to illuminate clearly the contemporary context for kingdom influence today.

of this semantic or verbal revolution? We've moved from civilizations with at least some sense of community and a moral compass to the loss of community, alienation, isolation, and tribalism. Technology, tech-tyranny, and social media have often only fanned the flames of such fragmentation and vitriol.

Scholars that argue that postmodernism/ultra-modernism or late modernism and syncretism were fads and we have moved on either are very confused and misinformed or they are covering up for their own acceptance of radical postmodern beliefs, practices, redefined and corrupted words and a redefined Christianity. And, for some, they are now in bed with intentional post-Logos-ism or even AJCism. The daily events, issues, and headlines of shameless spin and deceit; the redefining everything, everywhere, and always; the reckless spending of nations into oblivion in the name of compassionate justice; the technological tyranny; the fading of religious, political and economic freedom; and the pervasive and manipulative tribal truth and morality relativism are exactly what a postmodern quagmire and cultural rot looks like. Nietzsche is surely dancing joyfully in his grave at what is emerging from cultures who view churches as the sepulchers of the Judeo-Christian God.

This reality quagmire should jar at least some faithful out of the false visions of both eschatomania and eschatophobia—at least those who care for God's future, their own posterity, and the world and those that God so loves. Eschatology rules and should not be feared but redeemed and harnessed. Eschatomania makes endless false and escapist predictions about the timing of the Great Tribulation and almost ensures a self-fulfilling prophecy of great tribulation.

Our cultural unravelling obsesses over human sexuality issues because sexual and romantic relationships have replaced God and become ultimate concerns, and because human sexuality has become a wedge issue. Such sexuality issues are often a distracting lightning rod, focusing on the fruit and not the root of decay. And such sexuality issues are often a "boil the frog" incremental issue, using the argument for compassion or social justice to mainstream practices that undermine or directly seek the elimination of Judeo-Christian influence on the city.

Judeo-Christian–influenced civilization is being dismantled one issue and one word at a time.

Human sexual relationships and designer sexuality have, for many, replaced the foundational relationship with God that should lie at the center of our loves, purpose, and meaning. The eternal King of kings alone can bear the weight of that role and truly fulfill our deepest desires and calling.

The way forward, however, is not to fixate on the shadows but, instead, to step into the dawning light of the City of Kingdom Influence and Approximation. The answer to the perennial question prior to Messiah's return—are we in the Age and City of Antichrist or the City of Kingdom Approximation and Advance—is, as noted, yes and yes. Indeed, some have also stepped into the Third City already. History, civilizations, cities, communities, and individuals are fluid and not determined. Neither kingdom approximation nor antichristism is inevitable.

History is God's history, moving toward God's true future yet always fluid or plastic. And Judeo-Christian faith communities can enable and empower the City of Antichrist in countless ways, or they can bring the influence of the future already into the very warp and woof of the present civilizational moment.

OUR CALLING TO SERVE THE CITY

The game plan of authentic evangelism and kingdom influence has many pillars, but a few are worth reemphasizing in this conclusion. Living and ministering in the light of the New Creation means that the faithful are not just called to believe something intellectually or secure a ticket to heaven. They are truly called to be God's people and advance the Abrahamic blessing to all nations/kingdoms and peoples—already. They are ultimately called to reign over the fruit of Abraham's blessing, the redeemed cosmos, with the Messiah—but not just yet. That great day of creation restoration and fulfillment, which includes global reconciliation with God and others, is certain and already dawning because of the Messiah's bodily resurrection, sending of the Spirit, and victory over the City of Antichrist.

> They will not hurt or destroy in all My holy mountain,
> For the earth will be full of the knowledge of the Lord
> As the waters cover the sea.
> Then on that day
> The nations will resort to the root of Jesse [the Christ],
> Who will stand as a signal flag for the peoples;
> And His resting place will be glorious. (Isa 11: 9–10)

The way forward involves returning to the powerful and biblical future-vision and then passionately stepping into the future already. We live already as if our true citizenship, which transforms our current citizenship, is in the resurrected New Creation. We seek to eradicate dual allegiances as much as is possible, by grace, in this life.

We are not only expectant of advancing and participating in and representing the Future City today. We are adequately prepared and ever preparing to serve as effective citizens, princes, and princesses for time and eternity. Imagine the implications for education and spiritual formation! Our core and ultimate identity is as vice-regents or co-regents in a redeemed and resurrected creation. Consonant with this high and holy calling is biblically transformed and influential faith communities.

FAITH COMMUNITY CORRUPTION

As Martin Luther pointed out, even biblically reformed faith communities are ever being reformed by the Triune God's Spirit in the light of authoritative Scripture: *Ecclesia Reformata, Semper Reformanda*. The church is reformed but ever being reformed.

False future-visions have birthed or aided and abetted darkness on an unprecedented level inside and outside faith communities. As noted, in prior centuries some harnessed the rocket fuel of eschatology or future-visions to influence the world radically, but when utopia did not materialize, they exchanged that powerful fuel for a new escapist formula, sedative/happy drug, and future-vision. Eschatologies rule.

Indeed, the magical, otherworldly (and partially Platonic and Augustinian) happy drug, which includes some forms of otherworldly praise and worship and otherworldly views of heaven, is unbiblical, un-Hebraic, and absolutely catastrophic for the ministry, teaching, theology, and the mission of the church. We will in one sense be changed in an instant by bodily resurrection or being caught up to meet the Messiah, but in the more important sense the Messianic reign of Christ on earth is a transition that continues our growth in love, holiness, Christlikeness, mental and spiritual maturity, and that likely includes multiple millennia prior to the fullness of the resurrected New Creation.

Many believers are relying on the magical moment of death or rapture to make them instantly and fully like Christ in every necessary respect. In contrast, while all are saved by grace, Scripture clearly teaches eschatological rewards, eschatological accountability, and boldly affirms that everything will be revealed and proclaimed from the rooftops.

Our faithfulness will be assessed, including our fitness to co-reign with Christ the Creator. Where we are on our journey of restoring the image of God and serving as capable stewards of the cosmos will be assessed and revealed. Paul's challenge to believers is clear:

Now if anyone builds on the foundation with gold, silver, precious stones, wood, hay, or straw, each one's work will become evident; for the day will show it because it is to be revealed with fire, and the fire itself will test the quality of each one's work. If anyone's work which he has built on it remains, he will receive a reward. If anyone's work is burned up, he will suffer loss; but he himself will be saved, yet only so as through fire. (1 Cor 3:12–15)

CO-REGENCY: LEARN IT NOW OR LEARN IT LATER

When it comes to growth in and preparation for co-regency with Christ during the reign of Messiah and the New Heaven and New Earth, it is an understatement to say to *every* believer: Learn it now or learn it later; be transparent, honest, and open about the state of our hearts today, even if embarrassing, or be uncomfortable later when standing before others and Christ; work through the difficulties and complexities of forgiveness and reconciliation now or be judged by your own standard later; joyfully learn music, and art, and psychology, and history, and science, and general relativity, and quantum physics, and organizational management and politics now or regret such anti-Logos anti-intellectualism and learn it later; pursue radical transformation now and impact the world now and be rewarded in the next age or plan on taking a heavenly journey from the back of the school bus line later; and become overflowing with the Spirit and love for God and others now or risk waiting until the *eschaton* to fulfill the essence of the holy commandments.

We are called to childlike faith but not to being childish forever. We need to put on our big girl and big boy pants in our churches and synagogues. We are the church, the called-out ones. Preparation for heaven is not achieved by a magical machine or moment, and heaven is not a happy drug and far more than a feeling. Heaven requires heavenly citizens with New Covenant heavenly hearts that have been through cleansed and spiritual open heart surgery (Ezek 36). Heavenly citizens are kingdom citizens.

God does not overrule our character and free will and does not magically give us Logocentric wisdom and profound knowledge in a "heavenly" nanosecond. We are kings and queens and princesses and princes of the most-high God, the Logos, the King of kings and Lord of lords, and the great Alpha and Omega. We are eschatological to the core. Future-visions rule. We are co-regents, and "He shall reign forever and ever" (Rev 11:15).

BIBLICAL FAITH, CO-REGENCY, AND THE FUTURE CITY

Authentic biblical faith is central. To modify the reformer Melanchthon slightly, authentic faith involves personal, radical (goes to the root and heart and core of who we are), eschatological, transformative trust (*fiducia*). Biblical faith is grounded in essential understanding (*notitia*), unwavering assent (*assensus*), repentance, and allegiance. Biblical faith has at least three dimensions: understanding, assent, and radical trust. These three dimensions mature over time and are the key to becoming and advancing God's future (Heb 11).

Today, faith communities lacking a truthful vision practice faith without truth, faith without New Creation kingdom passion/love, faith without kingdom action, faith without cultural engagement, or all of the above. Faith communities without a truthful vision often emphasize religious experience without truth, kingdom passion, and kingdom influence. Faith communities without a fully biblical vision seek blessings without truth, kingdom passion, and cruciform kingdom influence. Faith communities without an utter commitment to the "whole Bible for the whole world"[8] and Abraham's cosmic blessing want to go to heaven without being heavenly. Faith communities who have redefined the faith and key beliefs and terms mislead and promote, without resurrection power or biblical norms, very distorted and unbiblical kingdoms. To summarize how faith intersects with the present and future:

- Faith without Logocentric truth is dead. Faith without truth, passion, and action is dead.
- Faith without Logocentric ethical norms is dead.
- Faith without cultural engagement is dead.
- Escapist faith is dead faith.
- Moving, ecstatic, and powerful worship experiences without truth are dead. Experience without truth is dead. Real praise and worship is God-encountering, world-influencing, and eschatological rocket fuel.
- Faith without truth draws seekers to church services that are more interested in a Starbucks, movie theater, or rock concert experience rather than to "repent for the kingdom of heaven is at hand" (Matt 3:2; 4:17; Acts 2:38).

---

8. This quote is traceable to Asbury Theological Seminary and its founder as well as to various well-known statements from John Wesley (e.g., "The world is my parish").

- Prayers and quests for blessings without truth and kingdom influence are dead.
- Redefined faith, biblical terms, and beliefs without truth are dead.
- Dead faith is not biblical faith or kingdom faith.
- Dead faith is not saving eschatological faith.
- Dead faith is missionally dead and does little to advance the City of Kingdom Approximation or prepare the way for the glorious fourth and fifth cities (Transition/Restoration and Resurrection).

VERBAL CORRUPTION AND SEDUCTION IN THE CITY

It has been argued repeatedly in this work that a key and necessary pillar for authentic, positive, and biblical faith and kingdom influence is bringing all words, terms, phrases, and beliefs back in alignment with Scripture and the Logos (the essential core and Creator of communication). Those who are scholars must therefore contribute to the common good of all (public theology), via semantic (verbal) apologetics.

Semantic apologetics is a gentle and reasoned verbal defense of the faith that reclaims the true meaning of words and the meaning of meaning. Our culture is increasingly moving out of orbit of the Logos relative to our words, terms, definitions, redefinitions, beliefs, spirit, loves, character, culture, and values. Change the definition of words (e.g., marriage, gender, compassion, social justice) and change the world. Words are the building blocks of future-visions. Words guide loves and loves shape words.

The idea that the church can improve or significantly influence the future of culture and civilization simply by being loving, winsome, feeding the poor, or saving individual souls is patently absurd. The current, global, and verbal *coup d'état* of redefining every word and term and value is anti-Logos.[9] Language is unquestionably and increasingly anti-Judeo-Christian (AJC) at the core in many regions of the globe, including formerly Christian-influenced cultures. Faith communities are often verbally asleep.

The Logos is the Creator and sustainer of all things, including the meaning of meaning, the true future, and truthful communication about ourselves and past, present, and future reality. The City of Antichrist wants to dethrone every remaining or vestigial influence of the Logos on words so

---

9. The phraseology of a "global and semantic *coup d'état*" was first used, as far as I know, by Hank Hanegraaff in his introduction to a feature article I was requested to write for the *Christian Research Journal*. Matthews, "Seduced?"

that the dark city can reign supreme over every word, thought, deed, and future-vision.

Words and phrases are polysemous (i.e., many possible meanings based on usage and context, such as tree bark or a dog's bark). Logos or Christ-centered biblical marriage, however, is not designer marriage; it has a normative definition. Redefine marriage and family and redefine the future of individuals, communities, and nations. The redefinition of marriage is a verbal (or semantic) pillar of the current cultural revolution and future-vision. And as many predicted, polyamory or legalized polygamy is the next step and "just" and "compassionate" cause after the redefinition of marriage advanced to chip away at the Judeo-Christian or Logos foundation.

Words are also polypotent or pluripotent—defined here as the ability to influence or change many things. Words and phrases are powerful and influential in countless ways. "I have a dream" or "tear down this wall" would be but two examples of the power of language and words, which Martin Luther King, Malcolm X, Karl Marx, Nietzsche, and many others understood.

All words and phrases align either, to one degree or another, with the City of Antichrist and/or the City of Pure Light. A relevant and influential Judeo-Christian future-vision includes the gentle and persuasive case for the Logocentric word pillars of a Logocentric-influenced civilization that can be already. For scholars, this means that public theology, or public eschatology, must include semantic apologetics outside of the church and semantic polemics, preserving correct beliefs and definitions inside the church. All words must be at least partially defined, shaped and redeemed by the Logos inside and outside faith communities for any lasting kingdom influence, beginning with the church and synagogue.

Words in orbit around the Logos create and influence culture and civilization. AJC words are in orbit around the City of Antichrist. Kingdom influence falters apart from Logocentric semantics.

SEEK FIRST TO APPROXIMATE THE TRANSITIONAL REIGN OF MESSIAH ON EARTH

To recap, our end game must be clear and properly defined. In the present age we seek to approximate the next redemptive age—the transitional reign of the Messiah on earth that prepares humanity and the cosmos for the fully resurrected New Creation. While our present approximation also participates in the ultimate or final state of the New Creation, a needed yet optimistic realism is achieved by recognizing that we do well simply to approximate the next age or City which is also an approximation of the concluding age of the resurrected New Creation City. This theological boundary counters distortions.

Optimistic Postmillennialism

Since the purpose of biblical future-visions is both to understand and influence the world that God so loved, this easily can take on the form of tentative and illustrative manifesto-like calls to action. As we have seen, some postmillennial believers recklessly and absurdly thought they could usher in the golden or utopian era—the millennium—*before* the actual return of the Messiah. Yet they changed the civilizational landscape by drinking this eschatological rocket fuel. For example, the postmillennial manifesto that the kingdom could be ushered in even before the Messiah returned resulted in countless schools founded to abolish slavery and hospitals raised to heal the broken.

Pessimistic Premillennialism

Others became disillusioned with such grand cultural crusades and gravitated toward charting the last days (i.e., eschatomania) while waiting for the Messiah to establish a literal millennium. The manifesto or action plan of these eschatomaniacs increasingly focused on things such as charts, the fulfillment of prophecy in the details of current events, the weeks of Daniel, the coming Antichrist, the rapture escape, lifeboat and/or symptomatic social concern and evangelism, predicting the last generation or decade, and heralding the predetermined slide toward Armageddon.

Eschatophobia and/or Otherworldly Amillennialism

Still others, cringing at eschatomania, put eschatology on the back burner or in the closet (or literally in the appendices of some theology books) due to eschatophobia. Some joked about being pan-millennial and certainly did not consume eschatological jet fuel for breakfast, lunch, and dinner—which is a clear biblical mandate. Some amillennialists did imbibe greatly of the escapist eschatological happy drug, just like their eschatomaniac premillennial sisters and brothers. Their game plans for cultural engagement varied widely.

For some eschatophobes and amillennialists, the millennium became a speculative and largely irrelevant conversation or curiosity, hardly a call to action. Others, throughout much of church history, viewed the millennium as very important but spiritual or heavenly (i.e., Christ reigns spiritually in heaven and/or through the church) and thus less of a call to action and more of a call either to individual or familial salvation in an otherworldly heaven or an enclaved and isolated faith community, or to a church that should be supreme amid the wheat and tares until the great harvest.

As documented previously, many church leaders had very otherworldly or Platonic-influenced views of the millennium and heaven. The wheat and tares would grow together in this dark world before the light of the coming deliverance when all was replaced with a very spiritual new heaven and earth. For these amillennialists, there would be no earthly reign of the Messiah on earth. The present cosmos, according to many in this camp, will most likely be annihilated.

Liberal and Liberationist Transformers

Yet many who rejected both eschatomania and eschatophobia discovered a new and very progressive eschatological nuclear fuel, largely formulated by movements not centered in orthodox theology, Scripture, or the Logos, though they quickly baptized their political agendas with Judeo-Christian and biblical terms. For example, the exodus is not so much about holiness, miraculous plagues, redemption from sin, and being right with God. The exodus is primarily, if not entirely, a story about political and economic liberation, and to be saved and right with God is to either resist oppression or to quit oppressing others and to liberate others from oppression.

To borrow a category from Millard Erickson, theological transformers didn't just translate and apply Scripture and basic Judeo-Christian beliefs. They didn't just emphasize that those who are truly redeemed and right with God care for the oppressed. They marginalized the actual and intended meaning of the exodus text and redefined and transformed some, many, or most basic Christian teachings. This redefined biblical future-vision, or even this gospel redefined and transformed, is primarily about liberation from some form of political, social, economic, gender, or racial oppression—to name just a few. To be clear, the actual biblical future-vision has enormous cosmic, social, and political implications, but it is grounded in orthodox biblical theology and beliefs/practices/words with normed meanings.

APPROXIMATION INTEGRATES THE BEST OF BIBLICALLY INSPIRED FUTURE-VISIONS

Relative to all of these future-vision options, this work has argued that faith communities today desperately need to drink and be nourished by the dynamic, biblical future-vision and harness the eschatological nuclear power or jet fuel of postmillennialism; learn from the premillennial sensitivity to and awareness of darkness and antichristism in every generation; be informed by the "wheat and tares will grow together until Christ returns" realism of amillennialism; embrace the social justice passion of the orthodox postmillennialists; and fully affirm the pro-creation theology of those who believe that Christ will actually reign on earth and restore and fulfill the creation and the entirety of human and cosmic history.

Some amillennialists now affirm New Creation restoration but would rather die than be associated with a literal understanding of the millennium. The reality is that believing in the necessity and reality of Christ's transitional reign on earth does not require getting in bed with eschatomania. Hence, this work prefers pre-restorationism rather than premillennialism when trying to find common eschatological ground for kingdom influence.

The core, essential biblical, and eminently logical belief that the Messiah must return *before* the Messianic reign on earth simply affirms that the actual return of Christ, and a glorious but not fully perfected reign of Christ on earth, is a very biblical and Hebraic understanding of the future. This view affirms that a transitional period on earth is the commonsense next phase in the unfolding of God's future (see Isa 11).

The actual length of this transitional period, loosely referred to as a millennium, is open for debate. This may be a literal thousand years or, much more likely, a longer period represented by the fullness or completion of a thousand years. The point is that the return and reign of the Messiah is the next, rational, and theologically necessary transition step in the elevation, restoration, redemption, and consummation of history on the journey to the fullness of God's kingdom.

In Revelation (Rev 20), not always easy to interpret, the affirmation that a bound Satan will be loosed one final time after the transitional and actual reign on earth of Messiah, amid much symbolism, primarily underscores that even the transitional reign of Messiah is not the fullness of God's consummation of history and the New Heaven and Earth. The theology of Revelation is clearly less about precise chronology and more about a theology that affirms that human history needs a transitional period that fulfills the past and opens the door to the even greater future. The best part of the journey is yet to come.

The transitional binding of Satan fits well with the thesis that cosmic annihilation overemphasizes discontinuity with the present creation, and mere cosmic restoration overstates the continuity of the present with the ultimate future. Taken together, countless passages like 2 Pet 3, Isa 11, Revelation, and especially sound theology all point toward a transitional Messianic reign that prepares the way for cosmic and glorious resurrection. The meticulous biblical interpretation or exegesis of key passages like 2 Pet 3:10 is helpful, and has pointed out that cosmic annihilation is not a necessary or required interpretation, but this issue is best resolved via a sound theology that emphasizes both the radical continuity and radical discontinuity of the present fallen creation with the final redemptive future—just like the bodily resurrection of Christ and the crown of creation, humanity. All things are interconnected. All things must die. All things must be resurrected.

Cross and Kingdom and Glory

It has been argued in this work and elsewhere that the journey toward what some have referred to as the Omega Point or Logos Point New Creation includes the cruciform way of the cross, the *Via Dolorosa*, in an often upside-down world.[10] The cross of sacrifice precedes and is often required for genuine kingdom influence amid the culture of the City of Antichrist. Virtue is rewarded in the City of Approximation and scorned and crucified in the City of Antichrist.

The Dark City views genuine believers as potential or actual usurpers, just like the baby Jesus in Herod's kingdom. The faithful must be marginalized, silenced, and, if need be, silenced permanently and eliminated. The City of Antichrist loathes and despises true freedom of speech because it also allows for true freedom of religion—it allows the voice of the usurpers from the future. The cultural death of Logos leads to the death of truth, words, free speech, biblically flourishing civilizations and, ultimately, the death of the martyrs. On the hill overlooking the City of Antichrist is Golgotha or Calvary. Yet the blood of the martyrs is never silenced forever and births a new already and not-yet future. Every drop of blood sows the seeds of the New Creation.

And, just as with the suffering, cross, and death of Messiah that glorifies God (John 1:29; John 3:14–15; John 8:28; John 12:23; John 12:27–28; John 12:32; John 13; John 17; Rom 3:25), in a fallen or upside-down world all such cruciform mission mediates the glory of the true future. "Now He

---

10. Matthews, *Theology*.

said this, indicating by what kind of death he [Peter] would glorify God. And when He had said this, He said to him, 'Follow Me!'" (John 21:19)

In an often upside-down world, the way of the cross and true glory (the Via Dolorosa) is often the window to the true future. Hence, even within faith communities theology must be aligned with Scripture and purged of beliefs that enable the City of Antichrist by obstructing the *Via Dolorosa*.

Relative to words, terms, concepts, and language creating biblical culture in faith communities and beyond, this work has argued for these critical and representative verbal shifts that reflect a more biblical movement toward the Logos and the City of Kingdom Approximation and influence (also see the chart in appendix A):

- From Last-Generationism to Any-Generationism;
- From Great Tribulationism to Conditional Tribulationism;
- From Historical and Theological Determinism to Conditional Tribulationism and Historical Fluidity;
- From Fatalism, Pessimism, and Utopianism to Cruciform Approximationism;
- From Contemporary Last-Daysism to Biblical Last-Daysism—Christ's first coming inaugurated the last days' era nearly two thousand years ago (Heb 1);
- From an often Escapist Addiction to Darkness (Darkism) to a love of Cruciform Kingdom Approximation;
- From Eschatomania and Eschatophobia to rocket fuel Eschatopraxis;
- From Rapture-Escapism and Fatalism to Cultural Engagement and Approximation;
- From shallow and Simplistic Evangelism, Discipleship, and Experientialism to Approximation and presenting a blameless bride of Messiah that is fit for heaven: "My children, with whom I am again in labor until Christ is [fully] formed in you" (Gal 4:19);
- From fatalistic, pessimistic, escapist, last-generation Great Tribulationism to being prepared for great tribulation and antichristism and the complex realities of the dark city in every generation;
- From the Great Tribulation in this generation to Conditional Tribulationism in every generation;
- From naive Utopianism to Biblical Approximationism; from misdirected, ill-defined, and catastrophic social justice and compassion to

biblical justice, biblical compassion, and appropriate approximation prior to Messiah's return;
- From otherworldly, Platonic, and escapist Millennialism to creation-affirming Approximationism, Millennialism, and New Creation resurrection and Consummationism.

A CHECKLIST: KEY CONCEPTS, STRATEGY, AND TACTICS

In our extraordinary historical moment and the globally influential North American context, the next few decades will determine whether we and many other global regions increasingly move into militant AJCism, properly defined, or an age of dynamic Judeo-Christian kingdom influence and approximation, or some combination thereof. The global balance of the cultural, civilizational, and historical scales will either tip toward the City of Kingdom Approximation or the City of Antichrist. Framed more as tentative elements of a manifesto or public, strategic, big-picture, and tactical game plan, some of the representative elements discussed already in this work are listed in appendix D (e.g., Judeo-Christian believers must learn to partner with all persons of good faith) and should be reaffirmed and implemented.

I'LL FLY AWAY OR STAND UP FOR JESUS?

For many faithful in the globally influential evangelical movement today, passion for and actions emerging from the cruciform City of Kingdom Approximation first require a shift from a posture, perspective, theology, future-vision, and love of the non-cruciform "I'll Fly Away" to "Stand Up, Stand Up for Jesus":

> Some glad morning when this life is o'er, I'll fly away;
>
> To a home on God's celestial shore, I'll fly away (I'll fly away).
>
> I'll fly away, Oh Glory
>
> I'll fly away; (in the morning) When I die, Hallelujah, by and by, I'll fly away (I'll fly away).
>
> When the [less than real Platonic?] shadows of this life have gone, I'll fly away;

> Like a bird from [bodily Platonic?] prison bars has flown, I'll fly away (I'll fly away)
>
> I'll fly away, Oh Glory
>
> I'll fly away; (in the morning) When I die, Hallelujah, by and by, I'll fly away (I'll fly away).
>
> Just a few more weary days and then, I'll fly away;
>
> To a land where joy shall never end, I'll fly away (I'll fly away)
>
> I'll fly away, Oh Glory
>
> I'll fly away; (in the morning) When I die, Hallelujah, by and by, I'll fly away (I'll fly away).[11]

The partial truth of a better world in this hymn is acknowledged, yet in stark contrast to this sometimes escapist worship experience, and an otherworldliness that can be traced back through church history and to some degree even found in Augustine, is the jet fuel future-vision and eschatology that was harnessed in the abolitionist movement and reflected in "Stand Up, Stand Up for Jesus":

> *Stand Up, Stand Up for Jesus* was a hymn inspired by the dying message of Dudley Tyng, a young preacher in Philadelphia who was forced to resign from his Episcopal church pastorate for speaking out against slavery in the mid-1800s.
>
> In addition to starting a new church, Tyng and other ministers preached revival meetings at the local YMCA during lunch and soon began to attract thousands (this revival period is known as "The Work of God in Philadelphia"). In March of 1858 [on the eve of war] Tyng preached a rousing sermon to 5,000 young men at the YMCA and over 1,000 made a profession of faith. During his sermon he supposedly said, "I would rather that this right arm were amputated at the trunk than that I should come short of my duty to you in delivering God's message."
>
> Only a few days later, Tyng left the study of his country home to visit his barn where a mule was harnessed to a machine that was shelling corn. When he patted the mule, his sleeve was caught in the cogs of the wheel and his arm was badly maimed. He passed away the following week from the injury.
>
> Before he died, he was asked if he had a message for the ministers at the revival and he replied, "Tell them, 'Let us all

---

11. Brumley, "I'll Fly Away." Used by permission.

stand up for Jesus.'" His friend and fellow preacher, Dr. George Duffield, was touched by the words and wrote the hymn Stand Up, Stand Up for Jesus. Duffield concluded his sermon the following Sunday by reading the lyrics as a tribute to his friend.

Duffield's Sunday School superintendant [sic] printed copies of the poem, the lyrics soon found their way into a Baptist newspaper and the hymn spread from there.[12]

The Age of Antichrist and the City of Antichrist are not predetermined and fatalistic realities that entertain or from which one should seek, above all, to escape or fly away from the world that God created, so loved, and united with in the cosmic healing Christ event. Instead, the Age and City of Kingdom Approximation and Influence is a glorious and ever-present possibility, but such small steps into the ultimate future in the present age partially depend on the preparation, character, and passion of God's people. Emancipation Day was a real and glorious advance of kingdom influence in the present age. Such days are still possible in Approximation theology and will be for many generations to come, if believers lovingly take a stand.

While, as noted, "Stand Up, Stand Up for Jesus" clearly reflected the utopianism and postmillennialism of the mid-nineteenth century, it also captured and harnessed the indomitable spirit and eschatological jet fuel that, if properly reframed, did and can issue forth in genuine kingdom approximation already. This vision guided every major social reform movement in revival-influenced nineteenth-century America on the eve of the Civil War and most thereafter. Military analogies, pervasive in Scripture, are biblical if carefully utilized, and Scripture defines the core of such taking a stand for kingdom influence in the present age as overflowing love for God and others, including the oppressed:

> Stand up, stand up for Jesus,
> Ye soldiers of the cross;
> Lift high his royal banner,
> It must not suffer loss.
> From victory unto victory
> His army shall he lead,
> Till every foe is vanquished,
> And Christ is Lord indeed.
> Stand up, stand up for Jesus,
> Stand in his strength alone;
> The arm of flesh will fail you,
> Ye dare not trust your own.

12. Chapman, "Unusual Story."

> Put on the gospel armor,
> Each piece put on with prayer;
> Where duty calls or danger,
> Be never wanting there.
> Stand up, stand up for Jesus,
> The strife will not be long;
> This day the noise of battle,
> The next the victor's song.
> To those who vanquish evil
> A crown of life shall be;
> They with the King of Glory
> Shall reign eternally.[13]

APPROXIMATION COLLABORATION AND SERENITY

It has repeatedly been argued that because of God's Triune grace and Spirit, poured out on and influencing all humans (Joel 2; Acts 2), the Judeo-Christian faithful can partner with all women and men of good faith (e.g., the Roman centurion), not for a perfect union but for *more perfect civilizational unions or cities*. Some of the key elements of such a partnership would include

- God's Triune Spirit is at work, influencing and making all humans capable of responding in some measure to God's grace from positively impacting culture and civilization to experiencing salvation. All are the objects of God's love, sacrifice, healing, salvation, and biblical flourishing.

- People of various faiths and perspectives can and must find common ground for halting civilizational decay, enhancing civilization, or even creating new culture and civilizations that properly steward God's good and very good creation until Messiah returns. Cities set on a hill that radiate true light and the true future to the world should be pursued biblically and appropriately.

- Individualistic, rock star, and Lone Ranger attempts to save any country or civilization are doomed. Media and religious stars and cultural leaders have to move beyond self-interest, revenue generation for their own organizations, ministries, or careers, and self-promotion. No leader or even two or three leaders can save a nation and should never imply such. God's grace is primary, and God's grace typically works

---

13. Duffield, "Stand Up."

through relationships and strategic teams, such as the church or body of Christ God founded to stand up against the gates of hell or religious societies and parachurch organizations that have raised so many from brokenness and despair.

- No nations are perfect, but some are more perfect unions than others. The inability to discern and discriminate between cultures and nations is a bankrupt moral and cultural relativism that reeks of immoral moral equivalency. Nations worthy of emulation at least set out to form more perfect unions; subject kingdoms and law at least to some degree, on bended knee, to the only true King and Kingdom; promote and protect religious, political, and economic freedom, which are all interrelated; and enshrine and properly define free speech and ground human rights in something and someone infinitely greater than passing kings and kingdoms—the true future. Such nations, on bended knee, view themselves only as temporary but faithful stewards of God's good creation and creatures.

- Truly influencing the world long-term means avoiding utopianism, escapism, fatalism, pessimism, and otherworldly disengagement.

- Global impact or influence is rooted in a biblical and eschatological wisdom, confidence, humility, transformation, empowerment, and serenity.

The modified Serenity Prayer referenced earlier can capture the spirit of global collaboration and become a present reality only when enabled and guided by God's Spirit:

> God, give me your Spirit and grace to accept with *discerning* serenity the things that cannot be changed,
> Courage to change the things which *should and can* be changed already in the Kairos kingdom moments of history,
> *Confidence, shrewd optimism, passion, and realism* concerning what can and cannot be changed prior to Messiah's return,
> and the Wisdom to distinguish the one from the other.[14]

Scripture calls us to speak the truth in love, to be gentle, reverent, wise, engaged, and content, and always to be profoundly and increasingly prepared while standing up for the City of Kingdom Approximation. The dawning of the New Creation is an ever-present possibility already. The best truly is yet to come now and forevermore.

---

14. Shapiro, "Who Wrote." As noted, this prayer has been eschatologically modified.

APPENDIX A
Future-Vision Distortions and Corrections

Question or Issue	Future-Vision Distortions	Future-Vision Corrections
Will Christ return in our generation?	Yes: *Last-Generationism* The last generation (typically 40–70 years) has arrived. The last generation countdown likely began in 1948 with Israel's founding.	Maybe: *Any-Generationism* Christ may return in this generation or in one thousand years; prepare for both scenarios. The significance of 1948 for date-setting is uncertain or questionable.
Are we about to enter the Great Tribulation?	Yes: *Great Tribulationism* The great tribulation (typically seven literal years) will occur in this generation. The Great Tribulation time table is predetermined and likely within years or a few decades.	Unlikely: *Conditional Tribulationism* An ineffective church may be significantly responsible for civilizational decay and horrific and lengthy periods of tribulation and persecution. The reality, nature, and timing of the Great Tribulation should be open to honest debate.

Are end-time events predetermined?	Yes: **Historical and Theological Determinism** The *Divine Clock* is ticking and, based on Old Testament prophecies, the founding of Israel, and Revelation (e.g., the weeks of Daniel), the end times have arrived.[1]	Yes and No: **Conditional Tribulationism & Historical Fluidity**, *plus* **Providential Kingdom Approximationism** Some future events are determined to occur (Messiah's return, the New Heaven and Earth), but such events could occur now or in ten thousand or more years. The present age may, in a limited fashion, approximate God's future already.
Are we in the last days?	Almost Certainly: **Contemporary Last-Daysism** The last days have arrived, even possibly the last days of the last days. No one can know the exact day or hour, but we can know that the last generation or perhaps even the last few years have arrived. Or we can't know anything for sure, but it appears highly likely that the rapture and Armageddon are just around the corner.	Yes: **Biblical Last-Daysism** We have been in the last days or age (and "last hour") since Christ's first coming (Heb 1; 1 John 2:18). The "last days," and even "Children, it is the last hour" (1 John 2:18), clearly do not refer to literal days or hours and are not failed prophecies but refer to the last age of an undetermined (indeterminate) length between the first and second comings of the Messiah.

Is the world getting darker and darker?	• Yes: **Darkism (Addicted to Darkness)** • The world is rushing toward Armageddon. • We are inundated on all fronts with *This Present Darkness*.	• Maybe: Realistic and Hopeful **Approximationism** (Focused on Kingdom Influence and the Ultimate Future) is possible. • Kingdom light has advanced during many prior generations that were very dark, and such can happen again.

1. Vogt, *Divine Clock*.

What is the psychological mind-set of our future-vision?	- *Eschatomania* - An unhealthy, almost spectator-like obsession and harnessing of the emotional life and the use of the mind relative to some or all of the following: end-time charts, darkness, the last generation, identifying the false prophet, identifying the antichrist, correlating contemporary realities and events with Scripture fulfillment (e.g., Cobra helicopters, the pope, world leaders, the European Union, Middle Eastern events), and certainty with the notion that the rapture will occur within a few decades or years.	- *Eschatopraxis* - Harnessing the emotional life and the rocket fuel of eschatology, including head, heart, and hand, toward kingdom practice, influence, and approximation. - Truly discipling the peoples from all nations in authentic and holistic/wholistic Christlikeness, holiness, and effective kingdom teaching and influence. - Historical faith-based examples: founding educational institutions; abolishing slavery; taking a stand against Nazism; protecting Jews; founding hospitals; contributing to science and medicinal healing; creating beautiful music and art that illuminates and is included in the true future; disaster and poverty relief.
What is the value of eschatology?	- *Eschatomania, Evangelism, Apologetics, Entertainment, or Therapy* - Getting people saved. - Comfort, encouragement, entertainment, proof that the Bible is true.	- *Eschatopraxis and Approximationism* - Harnessing the unavoidable and pervasive human drive toward future-visions in support of a realistic and optimistic future-vision of Approximationism. - Eschatology rules persons and nations.

What is the primary focus and hope for the present age before Messiah returns?	• ***Rapture-Escapism*** • Understand that we are in the last days or even the last days of the last days. • Get people saved (on the lifeboat). • Look forward to escape via the rapture from the coming carnage. • Warn those who are not saved and who won't be raptured of the current and coming deception.	• ***Kingdom Approximationism*** • Kingdom influence, including salvation; the great salvation (radical and robust Christlikeness in this life); discipleship; neighbor-love; service as light, salt, and healing leaven; positive civilizational influence; fulfilling the image via discovery and invention; kingdom-influenced culture preservation and creation.
What is the typical focus of the church's mission in the present age before Messiah returns?	• ***Shallow and Simplistic Evangelism, Discipleship, and Experientialism*** • Get people genuinely saved, discipled in basic morality and sincerely repentant when they fail, and deeply experiencing God in worship and in how God meets daily emotional and physical needs. • ***Ecclesiotherapy***: the church (*ekklesia; ek-klay-see'-ah*) proclaims that the last days have arrived; the unfolding story is riveting and entertaining; escape/salvation is possible; and church should entertain, make one feel good, and know how to access God's blessings to get through the week.	• ***Kingdom Approximationism*** • The radical transformation and preparation of believers in this life, such that their sincere and overflowing love for others and God influences and/or serves as a witness to the nations and prepares them for heavenly living in community. • The development of well-trained citizens of time and eternity who are capable of leading approximation in the present and reigning with Christ over culture and civilization in the future.

What is the City of Antichrist?	• *Great Tribulationism, Last-Generationism, and Last-Daysism* • The literal reign of the antichrist will take place within the present generation, if not within a decade or a few years. This reign and city will likely only last for a literal seven years or less.	• *Historic Pre-Restorationism* • There are and have been many antichrists (1 and 2 John) and a spirit of antichristism that vies for the beliefs and very souls and deepest desires of individuals and nations and which seeks to influence culture and civilization. • The City of Antichrist lures individuals and nations toward the abyss through tyrannical rule *and/or* through the seduction of countless angels of light. • If a literal and singular antichrist rules on earth in the present or any future generation, this seductive reign of terror would be the culmination and consummation of opposition to individuals and nations aligned with God's kingdom rule. • "Children, it is the last hour; and just as you heard that antichrist is coming, even now many antichrists have appeared; from this we know that it is the last hour" (1 John 2:18). • Cosmic transitional restoration is and glorious cosmic resurrection are coming.

Does eschatology matter?	- **Premillennialism:** Yes, as we need to prepare for the end and save souls.
	- **Traditional Amillennialism:** Yes, as it explains the conflict of good and evil, the present role of the church, and points to our true home beyond this broken world.
	- **Pan-Millennialism**
	  - It doesn't really matter what you believe about the millennium, as it will all pan out in the end.
	  - Eschatology should be downplayed and should not divide us.
		- **Eschatopraxis and Approximationism**
		- Not only does it matter, but it frames the very life and mission of families, individuals, and faith communities, their positive influence or lack thereof, their cultural engagement, and the vision (or lack thereof) for developing the entire person, including the mind, and becoming effective citizens of time and eternity; eschatology has guided the church over the centuries, for good or ill; eschatology is very potent; eschatology lies at the very center of the biblical redemptive story, and the life and teaching of Jesus; eschatology rules everywhere and always, and the question is not whether it matters but which eschatology will shape church and state.

What is the City of the Kingdom?	- **Premillennialism and/or Otherworldly Escapism** - The faithful can escape tribulation by the rapture and then reign with Christ in a temporary millennium (one thousand years on earth) prior to the cosmos being annihilated as true believers are taken to a somewhat and often rather otherworldly heaven.	- **Approximationism, Pre-Restorationism, and Consummationism** - The City of Kingdom Approximation is a present reality that anticipates, participates in, contributes to and points toward the final victory and the only true and eternal City and Kingdom of God realized on earth and throughout all of created reality.

APPENDIX A

What is the focus of eschatology?	• ***Individual Eschatology*** • The key is for the believer to escape God's judgment, the Great Tribulation, and to assist as many others as possible with gaining eternal salvation. • The final defeat of evil is often framed more in terms of the individual as opposed to a glorified cosmos, at least in many contemporary understandings of eschatology.	• ***The Theology of the Three Cities*** • The starting point for eschatology is the New Creation of all things, not merely the new creation of individual believers. • Individual eschatology that is biblical must be framed within the broader redemptive story of the three cities: Antichrist, Approximation, and the Heavenly City and/or the New Creation City; one could also argue for fourth and fifth cities or kingdoms, Eden plus the City of the Transitional Restoration prior to the Eternal City.
What is a proper view of the millennium?	• ***Premillennialism*** • Christ returns before a literal one-thousand-year reign on earth.	• ***Pre-Restorationism*** • Christ returns before an actual, historical, transitional reign on earth that largely restores the original intent of the creation and lays the foundation for cosmic resurrection and the eternal state of all things.

What is the final or ultimate destiny of God's creation and cosmos?	• ***Cosmic Annihilationism or Restorationism*** • The Petrine passage (2 Pet 3:10) affirming that "the heavens will pass away with a roar and the elements will be destroyed with intense heat, and the earth and its work will be discovered" is interpreted very literally, and is based on late manuscripts that replace "discovered" (NASB 2020) or "exposed" (ESV) with "burned up" (KJV); the KJV, "burned up," which is often interpreted as cosmic annihilation, is still used or mandated in many otherworldly premillennial churches. • "Burned up" also appears in these versions: NKJV, NASB 1977, NASB 1995, ASV, AB, ERV, and Douay-Rheims, to name a few. The Good News Translation uses the term "vanish." • Both traditional amillennial and premillennial faith communities have often interpreted this passage in an otherworldly, Platonic, and cosmic annihilationist fashion; the present cosmos is annihilated and replaced with a new cosmos, and, for some, a rather spiritualized or largely non-physical cosmos.	• ***Cosmic Resurrectionism*** • As argued throughout this work, the final destiny of reality is better framed as resurrection than mere restoration or purification; cosmos annihilationists lose the essential, biblical, pro-creation, and Hebraic continuity between the present and the future; continuity is lost; cosmic restorationists or cosmic purificationists retain too much continuity between the present fallen creation and the eternal state, and fail to see that the creation, and even the restoration of the creation, is only the beginning of God's eternal plan and glory—eye has not seen and ear has not heard and no one has imagined what God has prepared (1 Cor 2:9).

• Cosmic Annihilationists increasingly understand the need to be pro-creation in view of decades and decades of biblical scholarship; yet they can't ignore their profound sense of the total and systemic depravity not simply of individuals but of all things; they also believe that they can't ignore the strong biblical language throughout the Bible, and especially in biblical texts like this passage and Revelation, that imply if not affirm the replacement of the present creation with an entirely New Creation. Cosmic Restorationists are to be commended for reaffirming the value of the creation, yet this work, including this Appendix A, has enumerated many and substantial reasons for preferring resurrection over mere restoration. Restoration is better applied to the transitional, sometimes referred to as the millennial, reign of the Messiah prior to cosmic resurrection.	• More fundamentally, the bodily resurrection of Christ, which has both continuity and discontinuity with the crucified body of the Savior, is at the center of the gospel, redemptive history, and God's cosmic game plan; resurrection includes but more biblically and robustly defines the cosmic future than restoration or purification; Jesus really died but his body was resurrected not annihilated and yet he was the same Jesus; the cosmos will die, which includes but is not limited to purification and restoration, but will also be resurrected with continuity such that the present universe will fully retain its identity, just like Jesus the Logos. • In addition, the Petrine passage in question (2 Pet 3) strongly emphasizes both discontinuity and continuity in the entirety of this passage, which concurs with the rest of Scripture; proper interpretation does not only hinge on the translation of one Greek term ("burned up" or "discovered"); the entire Petrine passage proclaims a righteous and glorious New Heaven and Earth, but there are other references in 2 Pet 3:8–18 (the "heavens will pass away," "all these things are to be destroyed," "the heavens will be destroyed by burning") that are relevant.

			- The whole of Scripture and key eschatological passages frame the final and ultimate state of all things as preceded by transitional restoration, followed by New Creation cosmic resurrection.

APPENDIX B

Nietzsche and Truth

"There are many kinds of eyes. Even the Sphinx has eyes—and consequently there are many kinds of 'truths,' and consequently there is no truth."[1] Nietzsche's argument about language contains some Truth (capitalized to refer to normative or even cross-cultural or global truth rather than mere personal or tribal truth), at least it contains valid deductive reasoning. If the nonexistence of God obtains, and if the modernistic project has failed, especially regarding normative Truth and reason, then truth may be described (though not True) merely as embodied, evolutionary correspondent will-to-power. Infinite interpretations obtain and the only facts are interprefacts.

> What, then, is truth? A mobile army of metaphors, metonyms, anthropomorphisms, in short a totality of human relations which have been poetically and rhetorically intensified, transferred, and decorated, and which after long use people think are fixed, canonical, and binding. Truths are illusions which people have forgotten are illusions, metaphors which have become worn-out and impossible to perceive, coins whose imprints have worn off and which now are useful only as metal, no longer as coins.[2]

This is not to contrast Nietzsche with the naive belief that any finite and sinful human being in the present age can always rise above seeing through a mirror darkly (1 Cor 13:12) and fully possess something akin to absolute or True Truth. This is to say that Nietzsche entirely rejects the notion that God is revealing Truth to Spirit-influenced humans created in his image. Hence, he also rejects the biblical teaching that, for believers, "you will [personally

---

1. Nietzsche, *Principles*, 291.
2. Nietzsche, "On Truth," 6–7.

and intimately] know the truth and the truth will set you free" (John 8:32). For Nietzsche, God's nature and moral will can never be clearly known from his creation, human conscience (Romans chapters 1–2), or the teaching and leading of the Holy Spirit. This especially follows if the biblical God does not exist.

An analysis of truth, absolute truth, perspectivalism, or Nietzsche's nuanced view of truth far exceeds the purpose, thesis, and necessary limitations of this book. Suffice it to say that while Nietzsche properly identified the volitional and emotional influences on the truth quest and philosophical quest, as well as arrogant modernist claims to objectivity (see the quote at the end of this appendix), his utter theological failure relative to the epistemological implications of the existence of a Triune, personal, transcendent, revelatory and immanent Creator who created humanity *imago Dei* undermined all of his affirmations concerning the nature and attainability of Truth. It is critical for evangelicals to affirm that the rejection of modernism does not require the rejection of all normative Truth. Normative Truth can be maintained and even integrated with passion and life or desire or longing without accommodating either to modernism or postmodernism, and the future of church and civilization may well depend on this important semantic distinction. Nietzsche creatively observes, "To eliminate the will, to suspend the emotions altogether, provided it could be done—surely this would be to castrate the intellect, would it not?"[3]

No suggestion is being made that Nietzsche directly or simplistically influenced everyone involved with AJCism or singularly created our contemporary culture and quagmire. While certainly and massively influential, Nietzsche both reflected emerging ideas and contributed to writing the future. He simply serves as an enormously significant source and post-truth patron saint, and a very creative and articulate spokesperson for AJCism and the cultural and civilizational death of the Judeo-Christian worldview.

---

3. Nietzsche, *On the Genealogy of Morals*, 256.

APPENDIX C

The Incremental Advance of Nietzsche's City of Antichrist?

Historical Snapshots from 1995 and 2016

Nietzsche died as a madman, with various theories explaining why, in 1900. His creatively insane ideas greatly reflected, encapsulated, and influenced the twentieth-century academy and various cultural leaders and forms. Nietzsche's future-vision continues to rule. Foolish faith communities ignore Nietzsche to their own peril and to the hazard of any possibility of spiritually and culturally flourishing expressions of religion and state.

The lists below are worthy of reflection. Whether accurate or not, they document both the future predictions and contemporary descriptions of what Mary Eberstadt and Lynne Cheney perceived as an escalating anti-Western and anti-Christian sentiment toward Judeo-Christian influence on culture.

Taken together, these lists from Cheney and Eberstadt serve as their perceptions or prophetic snapshots from 1995 and 2016 that illustrate Nietzsche's spirit of antichristism. More contemporary illustrations have been peppered and are pervasive throughout this text.

A good theory or argument should have some predictive ability. These assessments and predictions below from 1995 and 2016 have been rather spot on in charting at least some aspects of the future journey of civilizations and the slow, steady, incremental, and intense ideological advances that, by historical terms, have wrought a very swift victory over much of the City of Kingdom Approximation. The prophetic accuracy in formerly Logos-influenced civilizations on some issues is conspicuous.

Cheney's predictions from over a quarter century prior, previously introduced, summarized, and abbreviated in chapter 6, will be expanded and commented upon below in brackets. To make this simple for the reader: (1) Material directly from Cheney will never appear in brackets. Some material from Cheney will summarize her assessments and predictions, and some material will be direct quotations. Direct quotes from Cheney will, of course, always appear within quotations marks. (2) I will make some editorial comments on Cheney's material either in italicized font within brackets in the main text or in the footnotes. Cheney's focus was on how the future-visions emanating from colleges and universities were redefining the present and future. This work has repeatedly made the case that, for some, these single issues ultimately have been used as an often indirect, subversive, wedge or incremental strategy to weaken the influence of the Logos on culture and civilization.

CHENEY'S 1995 SNAPSHOT EVIDENCE OF A DECAYING CIVILIZATION AND HER IMPLIED OR STATED FUTURE PREDICTIONS

Cheney argues that, increasingly, as of 1995:

- It does not matter if a crime such as sexual harassment or a hate crime actually occurred because even false accusations are true, for even the false accusation is symptomatic of systemic oppression and a means for liberation. Lying is therefore good; all words and statements are about power anyhow rather than truth.[1] [*If Cheney is correct, then this means that the only lie possible in a post-truth world, which really isn't ultimately a lie per se and must be battled with lies, is oppression.*[2]]

- Fairness, quality, and merit are code words for the marginalization of nonwhites and non-Westerners.[3]

- The facts that native Africans participated in slavery and the slave trade and that the West contributed to political and economic gains

---

1. Cheney, *Telling the Truth*, 17–18.

2. This redefinition of truth and falsity is likely grounded in the framework of oppression, which could be informed by key and traditional Marxist assumptions: "The history of all hitherto existing society is the history of class struggles. Freeman and slave, patrician and plebeian, lord and serf, guild-master and journeyman [male and female, binary and non-binary, transgender and non-transgender, white and other, Christian and other, Jewish and other, Western and other], in a word, oppressor and oppressed." Marx and Engels, *Manifesto*, 28.

3. Cheney, *Telling the Truth*, 19.

for women and minorities were being intentionally omitted from classroom instruction.[4]

- Proponents of multiculturalism were very open about the hope that multiculturalism ideology could serve as an incremental tool or weapon to divide the nation and destroy the myth that Judeo-Christian and Enlightenment influences created an exceptional American experiment.[5]

- Grade inflation in kindergarten through collegiate instruction was a growing and widespread means for dumbing down and weakening the cultural literacy needed to preserve the Judeo-Christian–influenced experiment of a more perfect union.[6]

- College students were being taught that ancient female deities created peaceful, utopian civilizations in contrast to the male deities of most world religions and especially as contrasted with the misogynistic Judeo-Christian faith.[7]

- All knowledge is situated and perspectival—knowledge and truth are not absolutely true but a matter of one's situation or context, perspective, and tribe (e.g., one's geographical, religious, or cultural situation).[8] [*In the present decade one's gender preference is also contextual and perspectival, and not normed by the Logos. Logos-normed values, ethics, and culture are typically viewed as some form of an oppressive "ism" such as white Christian supremacism. Post-truth culture has much more to do with political and cultural power and the marginalizing of the Logos than with the philosophical question concerning the existence of truth.*]

- History is not about what actually happened, which is virtually impossible to know, but is socially constructed spin used to exercise power over others.[9]

- Agreeing with Nietzsche, in both popular and academic culture, there is no truth.[10]

---

4. Cheney, *Telling the Truth*, 26, 28.
5. Cheney, *Telling the Truth*, 29.
6. Cheney, *Telling the Truth*, 37–39.
7. Cheney, *Telling the Truth*, 40.
8. Cheney, *Telling the Truth*, 44.
9. Cheney, *Telling the Truth*, 44.
10. Cheney, *Telling the Truth*, 44–45.

- Religion is an artificial illusion, and the major religions are "male chauvinist murder cults."[11]
- Cleopatra was a completely dark, black person.[12] [*This mid-1990s observation and prediction of where things were headed came to the big screen in 2023 with the highly controversial Netflix docudrama* Queen Cleopatra.]
- The "holy trinity of race/gender/class" is impacting the entirety of culture, including hiring practices.[13]
- The "ethnic cleansing" of the majority Judeo-Christian–influenced Western views and persons in formerly Judeo-Christian–founded or influenced universities is well underway.[14]
- Rationality is a dream and has become a nightmare. Truth is nonexistent and "rationality is a white, male, practice."[15]
- Ideology, meaning whether a student agrees with the ideology of the professor, is impacting grading [*and graduation, promotions, tenure, and job placement and preservation*].[16]
- Personal [*or tribal*] experience is the only real truth.[17]
- There is no normative or absolute truth, only tribalistic stories, and the Jewish Holocaust is nothing more than a tribal story used to advance Jewish tribal power.[18]

---

11. Cheney, *Telling the Truth*, 50.
12. Cheney, *Telling the Truth*, 45–47.
13. Cheney, *Telling the Truth*, 67.
14. Cheney, *Telling the Truth*, 72.
15. Cheney, *Telling the Truth*, 73–74.
16. Cheney, *Telling the Truth*, 77.

17. Cheney, *Telling the Truth*, 79. Hence, to illustrate what Cheney is observing and predicting, if you are pro-life, you have no right to reflect on the ethics of millions of abortions each year worldwide, unless you have been poor, female, and/or a minority. Of course, by that irrationality, almost no one has the right to affirm anything about anything to anyone else. For example, how can you condemn the Holocaust unless you have been an angry German after the injustice of the Versailles Treaty and the alleged oppression by rich Jews, for who is to judge you when you are just explaining "My Struggle" (*Mein Kampf,* 1925)? Indeed, many on the political left today actually align with anti-Semitism. Note: This observation concerning anti-Semitism was made in the early manuscripts of this work well before the stunning anti-Semitism that emerged in relationship to the Gaza situation in late 2023.

18. Cheney, *Telling the Truth*, 80.

APPENDIX C 265

- The reality is that "different groups construct different realities" and "different regimes of truth."[19]
- According to the late radical and influential postmodernist Foucault, in one of his stories the torturing murderer is portrayed as the hero, which reflects the "truth" that all is a matter of perspective and that (as with Nietzsche) the torturing hero represents going "beyond good and evil."[20]
- In the area of science, Thomas Kuhn (*The Structure of Scientific Revolutions*, 1962) introduced the still-influential term "paradigm" to affirm that in all areas of life, including science, the idea that we know or increasingly know the truth about external reality is now dead.[21] [*"Paradigm" became a buzzword of the 1970s, 1980s, and 1990s that created the current culture of everyone obsessing over their personal or tribal perspective and "stories," as if such stories were the only "truth" anyone could dare have or affirm, and that there simply was no way to judge some stories as wrong, silly, destructive, illogical, and evil.*]
- The late postmodern scholar Foucault, as with Nietzsche and many others, had an incredible impact in the twentieth century on relativizing all truth claims, yet as with all relativists, he enthusiastically supported the totalitarianism of the French Maoists. Other Marxists in education continued to believe that they could "scientifically" understand history, politics, and economics, and that they had the normative truth about what was right and where history was headed.[22]
- Professors boasted that they were "paid by the state to subvert the [Judeo-Christian and Enlightenment-influenced democratic] state."[23]
- Intellectual and cultural leaders [*including self-labeled feminists*] persisted in supporting all forms of abortion, including the use of amniocentesis and other tests to determine if an abortion might be justifiable. Unfortunately, one study of abortion and pre-natal testing demonstrated that only one out of eight thousand unborn children aborted were male.[24]

19. Cheney, *Telling the Truth*, 89.
20. Cheney, *Telling the Truth*, 88–89.
21. Cheney, *Telling the Truth*, 92.
22. Cheney, *Telling the Truth*, 95–96.
23. Cheney, *Telling the Truth*, 103.
24. Cheney, *Telling the Truth*, 110.

- Professors paid by the state affirmed that "the law . . . is no more definitive than a poem or play."²⁵ [*Justice is therefore in the eye of the beholder—this became a mantra at the O. J. Simpson trial by those defending Simpson. Once again, the worthy quest for at least some normative, timeless, cross-cultural norms for truth and justice has been reduced to "just us" truth and morality.*]

- Equal outcomes [*gender/race/class/anti-Western/antichristism*] is the goal, not fair legal processes, legal opportunities, or just legislation.²⁶ [*This ultimately could or should justify the rejection of fair elections.*]

- Critical Race Theory and feminist legal theory were standard instruction, came from the same intellectual sources, and were different applications of the same approach.²⁷

- There has been no real progress made relative to racism in the United States, no truly substantial changes, and racism is not an isolated choice amidst some progress. Racism is "systemic, structural, and cultural."²⁸ [*This means—and it was said even in the 1960s and since—that Martin Luther King Jr. fundamentally got things wrong. King's approach failed to see the need for a radical, perhaps violent, overhaul of the Judeo-Christian- and Western-influenced system, was too indebted to Scripture and Ghandi, and had little understanding of systemic oppression and intersectionality.*]

- The postmodern educational leaders today have moved legal theory, practice, and legislation from being grounded in eternal principles to nothing more than the exercise of [*"just us" conceptions of*] "group power."²⁹

- George Orwell captured the antichristism spirit of education, cultural elitism, and the general spirit of the times in the 1990s with this classic quote: "Just pronounce the magic word 'art,' and everything is OK. Rotting corpses with snails crawling over them [*or urinals*] are OK; kicking little girls on the head is OK."³⁰ [*Unfortunately, Orwell missed the mark by just a bit. Not only is this okay but it is often viewed as commendable, and truly beautiful art is often denigrated as passé, bankrupt, and simply is no longer good art. Bad artistic expression and values are*

25. Cheney, *Telling the Truth*, 129.
26. Cheney, *Telling the Truth*, 130.
27. Cheney, *Telling the Truth*, 130.
28. Cheney, *Telling the Truth*, 131–32.
29. Cheney, *Telling the Truth*, 142.
30. Cheney, *Telling the Truth*, 143.

APPENDIX C

now good and vice versa. In the morality of much popular culture—and this has persisted now for decades—it is good to be bad and bad to be good.]

- All truths are "contingent, contextual, and relative." This "truth" [or post-truth "truth"] includes the so-called truths of science and history.[31]

- History is a "dysfunctional idea." "Truth" is whatever is believed. The rejection of this relativistic conception of truth and its attendant historical relativism is also why the awareness of the truthful and factual history of the Soviet Union actually helped to bring down the totalitarianism of the former Soviet Union.[32]

- Higher education became fixated with narratives of victimization, which then permeated public education and the general culture, including legislation and the practice of law.[33]

- Some went so far as to suggest that all males should be defined as "potential rapists."[34]

- This emerging truth relativism and entertainment culture led to presidential election soundbites being reduced from "42.3 seconds to 9.8 seconds" from 1968–1988, and then to 8.4 seconds just prior to the publication of Cheney's book (1995).[35]

- The idea that "objectivity is an illusion that only the foolish value" moved from the academy to the very nature of journalism by 1992.[36]

- Future journalists were indoctrinated in the idea that journalistic balance, integrity, and objectivity were impossible, so there is nothing wrong with "aggressive interpretation" in journalism in order to shift the balance of power in society.[37] [*White House and other press secretaries have now often moved far beyond the expected and opportunistic framing or spin to what can only be viewed as intentional and*

---

31. Cheney, *Telling the Truth*, 146. Again, this is Cheney's assessment as of the mid-1990s. Incremental totalitarianism may be returning to at least some of the major regions of the former Soviet Union, perhaps, in part, because of the inadequate foundation for political and economic freedom after generations of anti-Christian Marxist rule.

32. Cheney, *Telling the Truth*, 148, 195.

33. Cheney, *Telling the Truth*, 155.

34. Cheney, *Telling the Truth*, 173.

35. Cheney, *Telling the Truth*, 173.

36. Cheney, *Telling the Truth*, 179.

37. Cheney, *Telling the Truth*, 180.

- manipulative deception. Press briefings are mere power games with not even an attempted norm whatsoever for truth and objectivity, all the while appealing to truth and objectivity in order to seduce those unaware of this contradiction.]

- This academic and journalistic shift means that "New News is evolving."[38] [*News often is not a sincere attempt at delivering a balanced reporting of the news but shameless political advocacy. Lying is moral, if anything can be moral, for it liberates the oppressed. The average citizen is too intellectually illiterate to understand all this and is therefore easier to manipulate with such deceptive news, which is justifiable since everything is viewed as merely a matter of perspective and power.*]

- Paul Begala, who often represented the White House in the 1990s, was explicit about his postmodernism, where the role of or only rule for political speech was simply to "define and create the reality that you want."[39] [*I well remember listening to Begala in the 1990s and, even with my background in relativistic postmodernism and post-truth higher education, being stunned at the magnitude of his shameless deception. Classical liberalism, defined in this work multiple times, viewed truth as central to political, economic, and religious freedom, human flourishing, and liberation from tyranny. Today, in the age of a radically transformed liberalism, the abuse of truth and the free exercise of tyranny, including tech tyranny, is applauded by many, from activists and elitists to corporations and entire political parties and organizations.*]

- Politics in the 1990s then moved from occasional or frequent political spin and schemes to a new postmodern or post-truth reality where politicians were truly at home with being chameleons, forever reinventing themselves as needed, operating in multiple value universes, not having any fixed core of integrity, and thus becoming *homo rhetoricus*, where politics rests almost entirely on "artful fictions."[40] [*I remember as a very young professor in the 1990s submitting an article to a popular magazine suggesting that a current US president was our first thoroughly postmodern president. The magazine declined due to the length of the article, but then within a year, I believe, made the same argument in an editorial.*]

- The well-defended and articulated idea affirmed by Professor Frank M. Snowden Jr. that in much of Western history "racism is an unnecessary

---

38. Cheney, *Telling the Truth*, 181.
39. Cheney, *Telling the Truth*, 182.
40. Cheney, *Telling the Truth*, 186–91.

part of the human condition" ran counter to the new orthodoxy that race, ethnicity, and skin color had to be the first and foremost preoccupation of proponents of justice.[41]

- This new orthodoxy is why the well-known truth maxim that Martin Luther King Jr. persuasively proclaimed, that the content of one's character, not the color of one's skin, should be the norm, is naive and should be buried. But Cheney asked a deeper question: "What can it mean to say we should treat one another fairly when there is no external reality in which we can seek a standard that would allow us to know whether we are doing so?"[42] [*Hence, by the 2020s the only fleeting and transitory norm for racial relations becomes skin color and tribal power.*]

Cheney's ending illustration, the murder of Mr. Jaberipour, referenced in chapter 6, is a rather haunting historical event and prediction of the hardening of human hearts and the civilizational heart that enables the advance of the City of Antichrist to utilize heartless brutality. For Cheney, this atrocity was a foretaste of things to come and life as expected in the City of Antichrist, and a window into why the defenders of victims are now viewed as oppressors.

EBERSTADT'S 2016 SNAPSHOT, EVIDENCE, AND IMPLIED PREDICTIONS

Eberstadt essentially extends the argument and prolific documentation of Cheney some twenty years later and names and frames it as anti-religious bigotry, or especially what this book has referred to as AJCism. A limited number of illustrations should suffice to demonstrate that, at least for Eberstadt, the Age and City of Antichrist is ascending or ascendant. As with the Cheney material, bracketed material in the bulleted items below is editorial clarifications or comments by the author of this present work, *A Tale of Three Cities*.

Hence, for Eberstadt, as of 2016:

- "These [antichristism] activists share an understanding that if the problem in America today has a name, 'Christian' is somewhere in it. It

---

41. Cheney, *Telling the Truth*, 198–200.
42. Cheney, *Telling the Truth*, 204.

- is this new coalition—not the real or imagined traditionalist minority of years past—that is now ascendant" in all areas of culture.[43]

- "Doctrinally faithful Christians, Protestant and Catholic alike, are not only culturally disenfranchised. They are the only remaining minority that can be mocked and denigrated—broadly, unilaterally, and with impunity. Not to mention fired, fined, or otherwise punished for their beliefs."[44]

- "Even so, one doesn't need to posit the end of Western Civilization to grasp this much: 2016 looks very different from 1980, let alone 1950."[45]

- The evidence of AJC censorship, discrimination, canceling others, and slander is widespread and tragic:

  > There is no moral high ground in putting butchers and bakers and candlestick makers in the legal dock for refusing to renounce their religion; or in stalking and threatening Christian pastors for being Christian pastors; or in denigrating social science that doesn't fit preconceived ideology about the family; or in telling a flight attendant she can't wear a crucifix; or in firing a teacher for giving a student a Bible; or in other attempts to drive believers into cultural exile these days. Above all, there is no mercy in slandering millions of men and women—citizens, colleagues, acquaintances, schoolmates, neighbors, and fellow members of the human family—by saying that people of religious faith "hate" certain people where [or when] they do not; or that they are "phobes" of one stripe or another, when they are not. Neither should religious believers be slurred as "theocrats" and charged with secretly trying to bring about "theocracy"—that is, of being traitors and fifth columnists in their own country, another accusation with odious historical echoes. All these kinds of slander, to speak figuratively rather than legally, have insinuated themselves into accepted conversation of our time, with objection from practically no one.[46]

- "More recent history confirms that neither modernity nor postmodernity offers insurance against literal or metaphorical witch hunting."[47]

---

43. Eberstadt, *Dangerous*, 9.
44. Eberstadt, *Dangerous*, 11.
45. Eberstadt, *Dangerous*, 13.
46. Eberstadt, *Dangerous*, 14.
47. Eberstadt, *Dangerous*, 21.

- "It is only if we understand the quasi-religious impulse behind the tenacity with which *each and every abortion* [no matter when] is defended that the otherwise puzzling, resolutely uncompromising character of the 'pro-choice' position makes sense."⁴⁸

- "The witch trials in Salem depended for their very existence on 'spectral evidence,' that is, evidence that did not meet ordinary standards of empiricism."⁴⁹ [*Today mere allegations of "isms" are treated as compelling evidence; hence, our age is a spectral age of guilt by accusation.*]

- "'I am not a hater' is the contemporary equivalent of 'I am not a witch'—or for that matter, 'I am not a poisoner,' 'I am not plotting espionage,' 'I am not committing ritual murder/blood libel,' or 'I am not controlling the media/Pentagon/banks/world.'"⁵⁰ [*Judeo-Christian believers in America and the West are gradually but increasingly and more frequently being put in a similar place as Jews in Hitler's Germany or freedom thinkers in Stalin's Russia or China's slave and serf state.*]

- The conviction rate of witches in colonial America, according to historians, was roughly 25 percent. Today, Eberstadt, right or wrong, argues and laments that the conviction rate of the accused Judeo-Christian faithful who have not redefined or corrupted their basic biblical beliefs in order to accommodate to culture is pressing toward 100 percent.⁵¹

- By 2014 the evangelical campus ministry group known as InterVarsity, accepted for decades, found that over forty campuses were trying to challenge its presence as a legitimate student group.⁵²

- Today many believers truly are facing the choice of "my faith vs. my job"—while so many other believers act as if nothing has changed. And today many Jews and Christians likewise face the dilemma of "my faith vs. my social standing," or "my faith vs. my future."⁵³ [*Separatist and escapist believers who fail to use remaining political, economic, and religious freedoms and power to bend the arrow of history away from the City of Antichrist most certainly are tragically falling short of proper stewardship of resources and loving their neighbors and the world that God so loved.*]

48. Eberstadt, *Dangerous*, 25. Emphasis added.
49. Eberstadt, *Dangerous*, 36.
50. Eberstadt, *Dangerous*, 38.
51. Eberstadt, *Dangerous*, 42.
52. Eberstadt, *Dangerous*, 45.
53. Eberstadt, *Dangerous*, 102.

Hence, if Cheney and Eberstadt are to any significant degree properly interpreting the present age, we have moved from incrementally undermining the pillars of Judeo-Christian–influenced civilization, or the City of Kingdom Approximation, to a more direct, aggressive, and somewhat successful siege. Regardless of how exact these two cultural analysts and prophetesses are, sufficient evidence has been presented in this work and the appendices to acknowledge that the City of Antichrist is ascendant.

APPENDIX D

How to Always Be Prepared for Antichristism

There are many antichristisms with one underlying and intangible spirit of opposition to the future and already initiated biblical kingdom. Given the limitations of this present work, we will need to focus on the globally influential Western context. Being prepared requires properly defining and understanding the spirit of many recent expressions of contemporary liberalism.

DEFINING CONTEMPORARY LIBERALISM FOR THE PURPOSE OF THIS PRESENT WORK

Especially in recent centuries and decades, the spirit of antichristism, cloaked by the seductive name of a more progressive, tolerant, just, compassionate, and inclusive future, seeks to marginalize or eradicate authentic and biblical Judeo-Christian influence on church, synagogue, and state. This future-vision seeks not only to be *liberated* from Judeo-Christian church-state political unions (theocracies) but also from Judeo-Christian civilizational influence almost entirely or altogether. Advocates for the elimination of Judeo-Christian influence frequently, and perhaps sometimes intentionally, confuse and conflate influence with calls for church-state unions. If someone suggests that, even in a small measure, Judeo-Christian virtues, values, and beliefs could contribute constructively to the common good, they are accused of trying to take over civilization, politicize religion, or set up a theocracy. There simply are more options than either eradicating Judeo-Christian influence or establishing a church-state union; these two options are a false dichotomy.

Some antichristisms push for Judeo-Christian believers, beliefs, and practices to go back into the closet or the catacombs. Other antichristisms believe that the faithful and their catacombs need to be interred forever. In the West, such AJC future-visions or eschatologies typically align with or are certainly enabled and empowered by what is referred to as more liberal or progressive and contemporary political ideologies.

However, this AJC flavor of liberalism is, technically or more accurately, referred to as one of the many varieties of *contemporary* political liberalism—illustrated by Marx (largely modern) and Nietzsche (largely postmodern). Both Marx and Nietzsche wanted to be liberated from traditional Judeo-Christian influence—as did Hitler's socialistic fascism, even while the Nazis were glad to use the organized "church" in their seduction and conquest of Germany.

Contemporary liberals are "generally willing to experiment with large-scale social change to further their project"[1] and are increasingly willing to sacrifice individual freedoms (e.g., religious freedom or even freedom of speech) to advance their tribe and establish their very idealistic, progressive, or "woke" kingdoms.

Some refer to such contemporary political liberalism as progressivism, but this is a misnomer.[2] There is nothing particularly progressive about undermining freedom in the name of justice, returning to tyranny, and nostalgically returning with Nietzsche to the so-called glories and virtues of ancient Rome or Greece. Eradicating the Judeo-Christian influence in the West, which inspired Michelangelo, Handel, Mendel, Lister and Pasteur, Wilberforce, Lincoln, Carver, Stowe, Wheaton College, Mother Teresa, Frances Townsley,[3] Oberlin College, Lemaître, Martin Luther King Jr., and which liberated countless millions, is regressive not progressive.

Classical political liberalism is illustrated by John Locke and many of the founders of the American political experiment in the United States. To one degree or another, classical liberals "regard the state as the primary threat to individual freedom and advocate limiting its powers to those necessary to protect basic [and, typically, divinely sanctioned, given, and guaranteed] rights against interference by others."[4]

---

1. *Encyclopaedia Britannica* editors, "How Does Classical Liberalism?" This article is valuable but somewhat confused on the distinctions between contemporary and classical liberalism, a confusion that is dispelled in this work.

2. For a quick, nonspecialist overview of types of progressivism, see Milkis, "Progressivism."

3. Sohn-Kronthaler and Albrecht, *Faith and Feminism*; Hardesty, *Women*.

4. *Encyclopaedia Britannica* Editors, "How Does Classical Liberalism?"

Classical liberals are a diverse group and include both Libertarians, who often are leery of any religious influence on the state, as well as numerous founders of the American experiment (US), who concurred with George Washington concerning the need for some measure of Logocentrism:

> Of all the dispositions and habits which lead to political prosperity, *Religion and morality are indispensable supports.* In vain would that man claim the tribute of Patriotism, who should labour to subvert these great Pillars of human happiness, these firmest props of the duties of Men and citizens. . . . The mere Politician, equally with the pious man ought to respect and cherish them.[5]

Liberal future-visions—liberated from Judeo-Christian influence—are only briefly introduced in this work. This work focuses on the common or shared spirit of these many attempts to be liberated from the influence of the Logos. It is important to remember that many conservative future-visions enable this spirit of antichristism, so there is plenty of shame and plus opportunities for redemption to go around. A more academically robust analysis of such views exceeds the scope of this current work and will be included in the previously referenced, already drafted, and forthcoming publication. Examples of such views and their pathologies that are addressed in this and my future work include the toxic:

- Aspects of the Enlightenment and Modernist Liberal Visions
- Dimensions of the Vision of Romanticism
- Points of Legion Utopian Visions
- Elements of the Vision of Liberationism and Traditional or Stalinist Marxism
- Goals of the Postmodern or Ultramodern Vision
- Vision of Syncretism
- Nazi (National Socialist) Vision
- Characteristics of the Neo-Marxist (New Marxist) Visions
- Elements of the Vision of Critical Race Theory
- Extremes of the Twenty-First Century "Woke" Visions
- Vision of Dystopian Anarchism

5. Federer, *America's God*, 661. Emphasis added. For additional documentation and information, see Washington, "George Washington's Farewell Address"; Ross and Smith, *Under God*, xx.

- Vision of Personal Relativism
- Vision of Cultural Relativism
- Belief That Western Civilization Is the Core and Highest Expression of Evil
- Aspects of Anti-Colonial and Anti-Western Vision
- Dimensions of the Vision of Radical Environmentalism
- Nihilist Vision
- Elements of the Consensus Vision of Ultramodern Liberalism

Those claiming to conserve, promote, or protect Judeo-Christian influence have, however, often poisoned the Judeo-Christian cultural living waters with other enabling or toxic future-visions:

- The Enabling Separationist, Isolationist, Escapist, and Apolitical Visions
- The Toxic Elements of Imperialist, Colonialist, Theocratic, and Post-millennial Visions
- The Enabling Aspects of Various Conservative Visions

The proper and biblical response to these toxic and/or enabling future-visions is the Theology of Approximation introduced in this work (see also Matthews, *A Theology of Cross and Kingdom*). The improper responses within Judeo-Christian faith communities to such future-visions are many and addressed throughout this work and the appendices.

Hence, these bulleted lists illustrate the many, varied, shifting, and shape-shifting forms of toxic antichristism and enabling antichristism. The point of including this list in this appendix is to make the connection between the spirit of antichristism and the very tangible, flesh and blood contemporary liberal future-visions that move entire cities and civilizations toward the City of Antichrist or the City of Kingdom Approximation. It is impossible to be properly prepared as true and effective kingdom citizens in the City of Antichrist without at least some ability to understand and respond to such eschatologies. The spirit and the beliefs of these eschatologies must be lovingly but shrewdly countered. It is also impossible to advance the City of Kingdom Approximation if unequipped.

To be clear, some conservative future-visions are less naturally or precisely labeled as antichristisms—though they have just such an effect on church and state. They are more precisely viewed as flawed distortions of Judeo-Christian teaching that often masquerade as being Judeo-Christian, intentionally or not, when in fact they ultimately and indirectly enable opposition to God's will and coming kingdom. Enablers of alcoholics, or decaying cities, are morally liable. For example, in the name of being holy or pure, or in view of being convinced that only ten or so years remain before Christ returns, many believers have trended toward intellectual and cultural disengagement, or inconsistent and confused engagement, and thus also have drifted from being salt, light, and healing leaven, thereby contributing to civilizational decline.

In a secondary or soft sense, unbiblical otherworldliness, escapism, and fatalism could be classified as opposed to authentic biblical teaching (hence anti-Messiah or anti-Christ). Direct and indirect, intentional and unintentional opposition to Messiah certainly exists inside faith communities.

It is at least arguable that the unbiblical otherworldliness and escapism of the faithful contributed to the progress of contemporary liberal views such as Marxism and Nietzschean antichristism (and their many children). Jews and especially Christians were viewed as so medicated by the happy drug (opium or opiate) of religion/heaven that they looked the other way when confronted with horrible economic and social injustice or health disasters (e.g., apocalyptic and devastating plagues) and exchanged the happiness of the religion drug for the real and alleged happiness of medical and scientific advance or political and economic liberation. Or, agreeing with Nietzsche, some Christians and Jews appeared rather life-denying.

In the case of Karl Marx, who continues to undergird countless contemporary liberal future-visions, not only is religion the opiate of the masses, the common people (German *volk*), but "the abolition of religion as the illusory happiness of the people is the demand for their real happiness. To call on them to give up their illusions about their condition is to call on them to give up a condition that requires illusions. The criticism of religion is, therefore, in embryo, the criticism of that vale of tears of which religion is the halo."[6] To be clear, traditional and Stalinist "communism abolishes eternal truths, it abolishes all religion, and all morality, instead of constituting them on a new basis; it therefore acts in contradiction to all past historical experience."[7] Contemporary liberalism is increasingly moving in that more radical direction, after decades of faith communities being softened up for manipulation by indoctrinating education and/or the redefinition of core Judeo-Christian beliefs and practices inside of said faith communities.

Similarly, aggressive attempts to concentrate political and economic power in the name and pursuit of social justice (e.g., socialism) often find

---

6. Marx, "Contribution."
7. Marx and Engels, *Manifesto*, 26.

Judeo-Christian beliefs, practices, and assumptions inconsistent with and an obstacle to such socialist future-visions. For Marx, the right to private property must go away early on in the revolutionary process, and Christianity and Scripture supported such a right. Socialism typically concentrates political and economic power and control and requires or leads to *Rex Lex* (the ruling class or king is the law) rather than *Lex Rex* (God-given eternal law or rights are self-evident and rulers must submit to God; rulers are temporary stewards of God's world).

Likewise, other antichristisms known as forms of secular humanism, the belief that humanity is the measure of all things (truth, value, right, and wrong), and the related Freudian future-vision, tend to agree with Nietzsche and view Judeo-Christian religion as self-suffocating, oppressive, socially regressive, and unhealthy. Again, these representative descriptions of antichristism are not comprehensive and fully balanced but are not without some substance. While some criticisms of Judeo-Christian faith and practice should be addressed, these were not constructive criticisms, for with Marx and Freud (*The Future of an Illusion*) and the secular *Humanist Manifesto* (Dewey), or Dawkins (*The God Delusion*), the solution was to replace entirely the illusion and opiate (religion) with something far better.

In the true, biblical or hard, sense, antichristism is an intentional distortion of, rejection of, or opposition to Judeo-Christian faith, beliefs, believers, values, practices, and cultural influence. God's redemptive work in the world, and God's revelation of truth, meaning, values, and the correct definition of words and reality, is opposed. Contemporary liberalism often agrees, to one degree or another, with such anti-Logos opposition. This antichristism may exist inside (legalism or redefined beliefs) or outside (e.g., the man of lawlessness, Marxism, Freud, or the false prophets or deceivers already referenced) of Judeo-Christian faith communities. Paul minces no words when passionately warning believers to "beware of the dogs, beware of the evil workers" (Phil 3:2) who are distorting the faith *inside* of the church and synagogue.

In contrast, toxic conservative future-visions, while not downplaying the all-too-frequent cultural consequences and carnage of such views, are better classified as biblical or Judeo-Christian distortions, deviations, and enablers of liberal antichristisms—enabling contemporary liberalism in the sense of empowering those seeking to be liberated from Judeo-Christian influence. Conservative enablers often think they are conserving biblical truth when in fact on essential issues they often are doing just the opposite.

Influential faith communities understand the times and the magnitude and complexity of the challenge. They are always prepared to engage the City of Antichrist effectively, engage those seduced by the City of Antichrist, and counter the conservative and liberal future-visions that enable or fuel the dark city.

BEING PREPARED FOR CONTEMPORARY LIBERAL AJCISM

The Judeo-Christian faithful in evangelical communities I have interfaced with for decades have often been reactive rather than proactive in the face of contemporary events and news stories. As noted, some are oblivious to the magnitude of the AJC liberal challenge and therefore their salt has lost its saltiness. Some drift from Scripture and become escapist and otherworldly or Platonic. Others truly do respond as if they are angry and want to neutralize unbelievers and set up something like a church-state union, even if such a radical agenda is not their actual game plan. Our goal should be to influence rather than naively believe that we can transform most everything prior to Messiah's return. Both inside and outside of faith communities we should always be prepared to be "speaking the truth in love" (Eph 4:15). As noted, the book of Acts is a textbook on how to engage when led by the Spirit.

Contemporary news events like those listed below should not provoke the faithful to fight or flight but further motivate us to pursue the City of Kingdom Approximation. Regardless of the accuracy of the description of these events, this is the world that God has called us to love and influence as we move toward the third decade of the twenty-first century:

- Madonna's self-described "Jesus"-based, pro-faith advocacy for abortion;[8]
- Religious Coalition for Reproductive Choice's clergy assisted and embraced redefinitions of "pro-family," "pro-faith," "compassion," and "This Little [pro-abortion] Light of Mine," and their March 12, 2020, webpage photo highlighting interfaith religious leaders and "justice" advocates holding hands, bowing in prayer and asking for God's blessings on abortion clinics;[9]
- A historic "Christian" seminary's redefinition of God, prayer, repentance, and chapel inclusive of neo-pantheistic worship, prayer, and repentance directed toward plants;[10]

---

8. Ernst, "Madonna."
9. Religious Coalition for Reproductive Choice, "Clinic Blessings."
10. Union Theological Seminary, "Worship at Union."

APPENDIX D

- Cultural leaders and certain demographics becoming progressively supportive of the significant redefinition and curtailment of "freedom of speech";[11]
- Merchandise from the anti-Christian band Marduk that includes images of a woman using a cross as a sex toy, a demon performing a sex act on the crucified Christ, toilet covers and bathmats with the face of Jesus on them, and a throw pillow that simply declares, "I hate Jesus";[12]
- Countless other frequent and telling events and headlines:
  - "Nonprofit Finds at Least 45 Canadian Churches Have Been Burned or Vandalized in Recent Weeks";[13]
  - "Trans Weightlifter Laurel Hubbard Wins Coveted Sportswoman of the Year Award";[14]
  - "'You've Got to Be Really Hurting to Do This Kind of Destruction': Pro-Abortion Vandals Spray-Paint Church, Topple and Trample Crosses";[15]
  - "Christian Group Targeted by IRS for Teaching Biblical Values";[16]
  - "Catholic Cathedral in Colorado Vandalized with 'Satan Lives Here'";[17]
  - Lady Gaga argues that anyone supporting the norm of traditional marriage for Christian organizations is not an authentic Christian—like she is;[18]
  - Former Soviet Bloc and current Canadian pastor arrested on tarmac over COVID rules and illegal church gatherings says police confiscated luggage, snooped laptop,[19] and warns Americans: "You're next";[20]

---

11. Rizzo, "Do 40 Percent?"
12. Coalition of Americans for Action and Principles Staff, "Anti-Christian Bigotry."
13. Pandolfo, "Nonprofit."
14. *Stationgossip*, "Trans Weightlifter."
15. Urbanski, "You've Got to Be."
16. Pinedo, "Christian Group."
17. MacDonald, "Catholic Cathedral."
18. Henderson, "Lady Gaga."
19. Brown, "Canadian Pastor."
20. Kumar, "Canadian Pastor."

- "ACLJ Delivers CRITICAL Oral Intervention Asking U.N. to Defend Endangered Christians in Afghanistan";[21]
- ACLJ documents multiple incidents of anti-Christian legal bigotry;[22]
- "Observatory Releases Report on Christian Persecution in Europe";[23]
- "Europe's War on Christianity";[24]
- "Christian Persecution in Europe 'Much Closer' Than Many Think, Warns Hungarian Premier";[25]
- "If Christians in the Middle East need to fear the machete, Christians in the Western world need to fear the media, higher education, activist organizations, and government";[26]
- "The 5 Signs of Persecution and Why Canadian Christians Should Be Concerned";[27]
- "In Canada, Persecution of Christians Escalates";[28]
- "Church Buildings Burned in Canada and the United States";[29]
- "The Coming of Persecution for Christian Americans";[30]
- "Is There Christian Persecution in America? While Christian persecution is widely recognized in other countries, most do not realize the persecution happening right at home";[31]
- "Antisemitism: Jews Target of 58% of All Religiously Motivated Hate Crimes in US";[32]
- "Europe's Worrying Surge of Antisemitism";[33]

21. Sekulow, "In the Absence."
22. American Center for Law and Justice, *Relentless*.
23. Williams, "Observatory."
24. Kilpatrick, "Europe's War."
25. Pentin, "Christian Persecution."
26. Bos, "Report."
27. Korkidakis, "5 Signs."
28. Newman, "In Canada."
29. International Christian Concern, "Church Buildings Burned."
30. Creech, "Coming of Persecution."
31. Bailey, "Is There?"
32. Sharon, "Jews Target."
33. Ward, "Europe's Worrying."

¤ "ADL's . . . [2021] Audit of Antisemitic Incidents in the United States recorded more than [2700] acts of assault, vandalism and harassment, an increase of 12 percent over the previous year. This . . . [was] the highest level of antisemitic incidents since ADL's tracking began in 1979. The year included five fatalities directly linked to antisemitic violence and another 91 individuals targeted in physical assaults." However, in 2022, the "ADL tabulated 3,697 antisemitic incidents throughout the United States. This is a 36% increase from the 2,717 incidents tabulated in 2021 and the highest number on record since ADL began tracking antisemitic incidents in 1979. This is the third time in the past five years that the year-end total has been the highest number ever recorded."[34] [*And this spike in antisemitism was prior to when the October 2023 conflict in Gaza further inflamed the situation.*]

BEING PREPARED FOR FUTURE-VISIONS WITH SIGNIFICANT AJC ELEMENTS

In our current postmodern or ultramodern context various perspectives and future-visions from the past and present are often still influential and often illogically mixed together—which we have defined previously as ultramodern syncretism. Those advocating for and modeling the biblical future-vision need to understand and lovingly engage the many alternatives, for these alternatives not only continue to shape the present and future, but they represent real people, organizations, and institutions that God so loves. Each vision will be all too briefly introduced and assessed so that the faithful can be equipped and prepared. Illustrative questions will attempt to clarify the movements and what is at stake:

- The Toxic Aspects of the *Enlightenment Vision* (dominant roughly 1650–1850). Reason, science, Western progress, and toleration of so-called rational differences were emphasized if not worshiped on the road to utopia. Traditional Judeo-Christian beliefs were often not tolerated or at least ridiculed and viewed as outmoded. The naive utopian dream birthed by the Enlightenment never really collapsed until World Wars 1 and 2, depending on the region of the globe. Why did so many put their faith in the saviors of reason and science that nearly destroyed us? Why has turning on the light of reason, with all of its

---

34. Anti-Defamation League, "Audit of Antisemitic."

benefits, also birthed so much darkness? The Enlightenment was sure it could light the way to a better if not golden city. It misunderstood human nature, worshiped human reason and science, was often very intolerant (especially of religious freedom), and utterly failed at ushering in an age of light. While some have tried to move on from this often arrogant vision, its influence continues, especially among the many today who engage in the ultimate postmodern form of syncretism by illogically mixing together modernism and postmodernism. Modernism is also still alive today, especially in some areas of university life, or in some versions of what has been referred to as the New Atheism.

- The Toxic Aspects of the Consensus Vision of *Post-Christianity* (rejecting, discarding, ignoring, or privatizing Christianity) and/or Post-Christendom (rejecting church-state influence or close associations). This multi-century elitist consensus was one aspect of but was much broader than the Enlightenment. It included movements such as deism, agnosticism, atheism, Marxism, secular humanism, and Nietzschean-influenced postmodernism. These ABC and AJC comrades sought liberation from traditional Judeo-Christian influence, especially church-state political unions. Many traditional Judeo-Christian groups also were leery of church-state unions (e.g., the Virginia Baptists), thus the real threat was using church-state separation as a springboard for a post-Christian world largely or entirely devoid of Judeo-Christian influence. Why did so many diverse movements led by individuals from Judeo-Christian families and often parasitizing off of the benefits of Judeo-Christian–influenced culture so frequently turn on their own heritage? Judeo-Christian–influenced culture was demonized as the cause of social regress (e.g., Nietzsche, Darwin, Freud, Russell [*Why I Am Not a Christian*], and Dawkins).

- The Toxic Dimensions of the Vision of *Romanticism* (nineteenth century yet with ongoing forms and influence). In reacting to cold, dry, stale, arrogant Enlightenment and modernist reason and science, many turned to feeling, beauty, art, and music. Romanticism still drank deeply from the consensus vision of a post-Christian world and also naively misunderstood human nature and the pathway to utopia. In theology, basic Judeo-Christian beliefs built on Romanticism (e.g., via the theologian Schleiermacher, 1799) and utterly redefined (classical liberal theology) and reduced central beliefs to profound and deep experiences of God and ethics, which also redefined the church and synagogue. Especially outside of faith communities, it should be no surprise that so many in the arts and entertainment fields have led the way in turning our passions against Judeo-Christian beliefs and values. Feelings and self-expression without norms rule. Judeo-Christian thought used to be viewed as the reservoir of progress, creativity, and freedom, but some Romantics reclassified or recategorized Judeo-Christian faith and culture as regressive poison. Why is it commonplace to worship personal experience and feelings today even in many faith communities—even so-called biblical churches? Why do so many churches today, even within evangelicalism, shy away from doctrinal essentials and present the core of the faith as an ecstatic experience of God in praise and worship—typically contemporary worship—but sometimes also in liturgical worship? Why or on what basis do so many claim to be Jewish or Christian even after abandoning core Judeo-Christian beliefs? Romanticism played a role in this trajectory.

- The Toxic Points of the Future-Vision of *Generic Liberationism*. Why have so many promised liberation from oppression and promised heaven on earth (utopia) while delivering hell on earth, totalitarian dictators, and antichrists? And why do we never seem to learn from the past? Virtually everyone is looking for a better city, but only one Messiah can truly deliver and the job is filled. All others are counterfeiters, unless they humbly serve the true future on bended knee. The proper role of the king today is to serve the true King of kings as a temporary steward (see Smith and O'Donovan). Steward kings know well their own wicked hearts, the depravity of all humans, and the need for grace and prayer and rule accordingly.

- The Toxic Elements of the Vision of *Marxist Liberationism*. Why have millions, perhaps more than half of the planet, followed the seductive sirens toward "for the people and for the working class" ideologies that have repeatedly resulted in mass genocide, oppression, and poverty? Why is the West that restrained Marxism now seemingly enamored if not obsessed with some version of Marxism? We seem to be uneducable—incapable of learning basic lessons of human nature and history.

- The Toxic Goals of the Postmodern or *Ultramodern* Vision. Why does it seem like there is no longer any norm or plumb line for truth and morality? Why does everyone say, "That may be true for you or your tribe but it's not true for me or my tribe, and who are you to judge anyhow?" "You have no right to speak, for your gender or skin color tells me you are by definition an unjust oppressor." Why are we sinking deeper and deeper into a quagmire of shameless spin and deception, lies, fragmentation, conflict, polarization, tribalism, mistrust, and hate? Why does our entertainment, public discourse, and the entire culture seem so dark, unhappy, coarse, and decadent, and how have we almost entirely lost our sense of being a national family or community? How did we once embrace some differences—unity in diversity—but stand united on core values and causes? Why are so many quite happy with canceling others and canceling freedom of religion, freedom of speech, private property, free enterprise, and the freedom to associate with others who disagree with the ruling class? Why does everything seem to be nothing but seductive or manipulative lies and spin? Why do so many seem to affirm that there are no norms for truth and morality and do so with the spirit and judgmental attitude of the extreme fundamentalists that they claim to despise? Why are we surprised that tech-tyrants have emerged from our indoctrination educational centers and increasingly rule the present and future?

- The Toxic Vision of *Syncretism*. Why does it seem like today that many believe in a little bit of anything and everything as long as they feel it, choose it, and like it, or in some fashion it works for them or their tribe no matter how contradictory or absurd or destructive? Why do we have friends that hate reason, science, the West, and America, truth, and morality while also utilizing computers, flying on planes, seeking care from top flight surgeons, condemning others as immoral or unjust, demanding free speech while canceling others' free speech, accumulating wealth while demonizing economic freedom, suppressing toleration in the name of toleration and inclusion, and enjoying the benefits of the West or America while parasitizing and despising both? Syncretism destroys the City of Kingdom Approximation and feeds or fuels the City of Antichrist.

- The Toxic Nazi (*National Socialist*) Vision. How did one of the most advanced civilizations in history lead the way on dictatorial rule; the eradication of religious, political, and economic freedom; political oppression and torture; the pursuit of world conquest; and genocide; and then plunge the world into two devastating world wars? To be clear, Nazism was inherently anti-Judeo-Christian, entirely redefined and manipulated whatever "Christianity" and Christian beliefs/terms/values remained, exterminated Jews and Jewish influence, and advocated for dictatorial and fascist socialistic control. This socialistic vision—National Socialism (Nazism)—was occultist, demonic, tyrannical, genocidal, influenced by the worst of Nietzsche and Darwin, racist, and militantly anti-Judeo-Christian. Hitler's Third Kingdom (Reich) or city certainly and graphically rose up to illustrate human depravity and the City of Antichrist.

- The Toxic Characteristics of the Neo-Marxist (New Marxist) Vision. After so many Marxist failures in practice, why are myriad new forms of Marxism, such as radical sexual-preference based, race-based, or geographically based liberationist movements, popping up everywhere? The simple answer is that when you pour the fuel of ultramodern syncretism on the fire of revolutionary new forms of Marxism the result is an endless list of those believing, rightly or wrongly, that they are being victimized, especially by Western and Judeo-Christian (Jewish and Christian) oppressors. Why have so many contemporary liberals moved far beyond social justice movements and democratic socialism to a full-fledged tyrannical version of Marxism? Why do many politicians now view free speech, Christianity, Judaism, capitalism, and even polite and non-violent liberal Western socialism as obstacles to true liberation? Why have seemingly traditional or classical liberal politicians and political parties moved so far to the political left and so aggressively attacked once-honored Judeo-Christian values and practices? Why have some neo-Marxists, such as Herbert Marcuse, acknowledged that capitalism has been seductively successful, that it has raised the living standards of millions, that it is not the cause of all the problems in the majority or non-Western world, and yet they still affirm that Judeo-Christian–influenced political and economic freedom must be replaced?

- The Toxic Elements of the Vision of *Critical Race Theory*. Does this theory actually exist, is it simply about honestly telling the story of past oppression, or is this yet another rather unhinged neo-Marxist and racist movement? Whatever the correct answers might be, many critical race advocates view traditional Judeo-Christian beliefs and practice as inherently racist and oppressive—biblical beliefs are either radically redefined or rejected.

- The Toxic Extremes of the Twenty-First Century *"Woke"* Vision. Regardless of the status, nature, and reality of Critical Race Theory, why is there such an emphasis on being "woke" today? Where did this vision come from, and why does it seem like being woke requires the canceling not only of genuine bigots and oppressors, but also the rejection of traditional biblical values, practices, entire races and genders, and Judeo-Christian believers? This vision is far more than simply purifying Judeo-Christian beliefs of Western influence. Judeo-Christian core beliefs were birthed in a multicultural context that was often non-Western or pre-Western,[35] so many of the destructive and

---

35. Oden, *Classic Christianity*.

antichristism versions of the woke project emanate from the City of Antichrist. To be candid, the distant or ultimate prize for many woke movements is to cancel the Bible, which clearly misaligns with being woke at critical points, and Judeo-Christian influence. Some are simply shrewd or patient enough in some cultural contexts not to attack Scripture or Christianity overtly. At least for now.

- The Toxic Vision of *Dystopian Anarchism*. Why do so many seem accepting, or quite content, or perhaps even happy, with destroying everything (anarchy) and advancing utter chaos, confusion, and conflict (dystopia)? How does tearing everything down supposedly lead to a better world? Is it because, like the French Revolution, we must begin again, and the twin evils today for many are Judeo-Christian influence and relatively free or non-centralized economic and political power? In addition, many movements seem obsessed with the idea that we are headed to a dystopia. This pessimism for the present age sometimes rivals the pessimism of the archenemies of anarchism—fundamentalist escapist Christians.

- The Toxic Vision of *Personal Relativism*. Why do so many of our friends act as if truth and morality are morally equivalent to choosing a flavor of ice cream or the color of their new car or flooring? And if they are right—that there are no moral absolutes—then why are they so insistent that Judeo-Christian and biblical values are wrong? They typically do want their values to impact civilization. To be clear, the radical redefinition and militant assault on basic Judeo-Christian and biblical conceptions of marriage, gender, and ordination amount to, for some, far more than compassion for the marginalized. This form of antichristism is a subversive get-the-foot-in-the-door or wedge strategy to marginalize or even criminalize Judeo-Christian beliefs and believers. Relativism is a gateway drug to the City of Antichrist.

- The Toxic Vision of *Cultural Relativism*. Personal relativism opened the door to and empowered cultural relativism and tribal relativism. Why do so many insist that truth, right, and wrong are entirely determined by one's country, community, or tribe while also insisting that the Judeo-Christian tribe is wrong, anti-progressive, or even evil? How can it be absolutely true or moral to affirm that truth and morality are relative, or a matter of perception, or merely a personal or tribal opinion? The rejection of any God-given norms for truth and morality is a hallmark of the contemporary City of Antichrist. And the City of Antichrist, as noted, quickly provides and has provided not just ten but ten thousand rigidly enforced new commandments from the new odious lord of the antichristism city. In the City of Antichrist, the contradictions of ultramodern syncretism are often celebrated and a key to cultural victory.

- The Toxic Belief That *Western Civilization Is the Core of Evil*. What happened? How did we move so rapidly from a very Judeo-Christian–influenced civilization, with all its imperfections, to an increasingly repressive AJC culture in less than forty years? As with Cheney, referenced many times in this work as a sort of 1990s prophet, education was critical in this metamorphosis.

- The Toxic *Anti-Colonial and Anti-Western* Vision. Why does it now seem as though Christianity, Judaism, America, and Western culture are viewed by so many today, especially our elites, as lying at the heart of the evil empire or empires? While freely acknowledging all of its past and present flaws, especially in practice, why are the global benefits of Western civilization unmentionables? Why are the virtues of other cultures romanticized and the flaws ignored? Is it true that the authentically Judeo-Christian–influenced kingdoms and cities are the worst forms of government in the world—except for all the rest? Why is it that this question, popularized in one form or another by Reinhold Niebuhr and Churchill in the twentieth century, can no longer be persuasively asked today? The abuse of weak people groups, nations, and individuals by the powerful is historical reality and is often referred to as colonialism. Powerful countries colonize, or more accurately conquer, and exploit the powerless regardless of race, gender, or religion. Why not simply acknowledge the evil of all human hearts, the abuse of religion, as well as the evil acts of non-colonial powers or peoples on each other and on other people groups? Why not also recognize the benefits of some elements of the age of exploration and non-violent missionary work? Utopians often replace the arrogance and utopianism of colonialism with the arrogance and utopianism of anti-colonialism, anti–Judeo-Christian influence, and anti-Western culture. Paul Hiebert's wise words concerning globalism, pluralism, and colonialism continue to be muted or ignored in many circles, including faith communities claiming to be biblical and compassionate, not to mention missions or intercultural Christian academic centers obsessed with contextualism, castigating colonialism, and largely redefining the gospel and biblical evangelism:

> Missions has always had to deal with cultural and religious pluralism. In the past its response has often been colonial. In

recent years there has been a strong reaction that has sought to eradicate the ethnocentrism and arrogance of the previous era. This reaction is an important corrective, but in itself leads us into pragmatism, relativism, and a superficial acceptance of the other. We need to go beyond anti-colonialism to find a solid base for affirming the truth of the gospel.[36]

Hiebert, rooted in biblical assumptions and discerning historical analysis, senses the danger both in the unprincipled future-vision of colonialism and the relativism, now morphing into an intolerant absolutism, of the current and ongoing anti-colonial and anti-Western reaction. He was prophetic.

Relative to colonialism and to the often-despised belief in American exceptionalism, there are many views with three basic options or points on the continuum:

1. Either America (or any country or civilization) truly is exceptional and desirable (e.g., American exceptionalism);

2. Or all countries and civilizations are morally equal (moral and cultural relativism or multicultural relativism), and/or morality is merely a matter of cultural or personal perspective (moral perspectivalism)—and thus there is really nothing to criticize or affirm;

3. Or America (or any country or civilization) is morally inferior, and some other country or civilization is morally superior, which ironically, for relativists, means that exceptionalism and universal morality of some sort are "true," which then also logically entails belief in American mediocrity, American inferiority, or, more common today, passionate anti-Americanism.

If exceptionalism is a possibility, however, then a possible defense of American exceptionalism (or any cultural exceptionalism) is at least theoretically possible; therefore let the debate begin. Let us approach and assess all cultures with great discernment. In any event, we must make, and cannot avoid making, moral distinctions between nations and cultures. To not make such difficult moral distinctions is the essence of immorality for it has real world and devastating consequences for millions.

Churchill and Niebuhr noted long ago, in various ways, that the inability to discriminate ethically between cultures dominated by the demonic (e.g., Hitler's Reich) and very fallible experiments in civilization and freedom laced with or influenced by Judeo-Christian assumptions is

---

36. Hiebert, "Beyond Anti-Colonialism," 263.

devastating to civilization. It is also destructive of the church, missions, and human flourishing. This lack of discrimination and discernment reflects option two from the previous list.

Thus, the only real choice for lovers of normative truth is to identify aspirational countries and civilizations in a less than perfect world prior to Messiah's return and seek to learn from, form, and sustain more perfect civilizations. Loving our neighbor and our progeny requires such difficult discernment.

- The Toxic *Nihilist* (nothing is true, valuable, or meaningful) Vision. How did we get to the point where so many feel like "all we are is dust in the wind," and why does it sometimes seem like our entire culture is awash in a sense of utter meaninglessness? Clearly some segments of the academy and popular culture have replaced the affirmation that humanity is the crown of creation with the deflating affirmation that all we are is dust in the wind. The City of Antichrist welcomes the debasing of human value because antichrist hates humanity and the image of God in humanity.

BEING PREPARED FOR SEDUCTIVE FUTURE-VISIONS THAT ENABLE THE AGE OF ANTICHRIST

Some future-visions are rather seductive, even or especially for the Judeo-Christian faithful. Hence, we need to always be prepared for views that seem compatible with biblical faith. To simplify, these conservative enablers will be grouped in two basic categories. As with the contemporary liberal views previously discussed, these enabling visions will be briefly introduced and assessed, especially via probing questions:

- The Enabling *Separationist, Isolationist, and Apolitical* Visions. How can so many believers today, in the face of the growing manipulation and oppression of antichristism, still cling to the naive belief that if faith communities and others just "stay in their lanes, bro" and are nice to each other then we can all just get along together? Can these well-intentioned individuals not see that these allegedly noble antichristisms never have and never will, over the long haul, "stay in their lane"? Such visions increasingly have the power of the state to assist with keeping the faithful out of the public marketplace of ideas and off of the public highways of the economy, political power, culture, and civilization. Every kingdom has a social glue that binds the community together.

Every civilization, as noted, either has the Ten Commandments or its own thousand commandments. Cultures without glue and stable pillars fragment and collapse. Hence, seductive Libertarianism is very illustrative and hopelessly naive and flawed:

> Libertarianism is the political philosophy that takes individual liberty to be the primary political value. It may be understood as a form of liberalism, the political philosophy associated with the English philosophers John Locke and John Stuart Mill, the Scottish economist Adam Smith, and the American statesman Thomas Jefferson. Liberalism seeks to define and justify the legitimate powers of government in terms of certain natural or God-given individual rights. These rights include the rights to life, liberty, private property, freedom of speech and association, freedom of worship, government by consent, equality under the law, and moral autonomy (the ability to pursue one's own conception of happiness or the "good life"). The purpose of government, according to liberals, is to protect these and other individual rights, and in general liberals have contended that government power should be limited to that which is necessary to accomplish this task. Libertarians are classical liberals who strongly emphasize the individual right to liberty. They contend that the scope and powers of government should be constrained so as to allow each individual as much freedom of action as is consistent with a like freedom for everyone else. Thus, they believe that individuals should be free to behave and to dispose of their property as they see fit, provided that their actions do not infringe on the equal freedom of others.[37]

Apolitical Libertarianism is a seductive experiment that collapses in the face of human nature. Judeo-Christian influence on civilization is a necessary foundation or prerequisite for any sustainable possibility of political and religious toleration and liberty. Consider how even classic political liberalism has now morphed into increasingly authoritarian contemporary political liberalism. Over time, experiments in freedom inevitably "infringe" on the "equal freedom of others" apart from the norm of the Logos.

American Libertarianism not only presupposes countless values and assumptions that are ultimately religious in nature, if not Judeo-Christian at the core, but the final blow is attempting to define precisely when the "equal freedom of others" is infringed upon apart from a divinely sanctioned value system. In a nutshell, Libertarianism is naive.

37. Boaz, "Libertarianism."

Libertarianism requires Judeo-Christian influence and assumptions about reality for its very existence. Smith and O'Donovan's "craters of the gospel" argument referenced earlier makes this clear. The Libertarian assumption that the law is or should be king (*Rex Lex*) rather than the assumption that the king is law (*rex lex*) owes a great debt to Judeo-Christian political influence and theory. Libertarianism that tries to affirm the supremacy of liberty or the kingship of the law apart from divine sanction or revelation is especially naive.

All attempts to be neutral apart from overt, direct, intentional, and indirect Judeo-Christian influence on kings and kingdoms are absolutely futile. Such futility is gullible concerning human nature, the nature of human beliefs and actions, the relationship between beliefs and culture, and the Judeo-Christian basis for placing all kings and kingdoms in a subordinate and temporary stewardship role.

Hence, all attempts at neutrality and "live and let live" are either naive or mere smokescreens for yet another ideology to rule. Recent political theories such as Common Good, Uncommon Ground, Uncommon or Common Virtues, or Confident Pluralism, far from helping the current age of tribalism and outrage, actually enable civilizational fragmentation and the emergence of tyranny. Freedom requires the influential spirit and reality of the pure and brisk breath or wind radiating from Judeo-Christian living waters.

The myth of neutrality is hence truly seductive and deadly. Polite social discourse is a value in Logos-influenced civilizations, but "can't we all just get along" is simplistic and fatal. This is increasingly evident today. So-called neutral public education has proven to be a farce. Postmodernists have correctly been trying to tell us for decades, if not longer, that such neutrality is a pipe dream. Indeed, Judeo-Christian assumptions about reality and human nature—that we are radically fallen and dependent on grace—are the only hope for anything resembling true tolerance, relative neutrality, and humble objectivity.

- The Toxic Elements of *Imperialist, Colonialist, Theocratic, and Postmillennial* Visions. Why did so many believers and Westerners feel comfortable with using political power, economic power, cultural power, and even military power to try and usher in and impose a religious or political vision on others? Was this biblical? Was it because of the very optimistic spirit of the Enlightenment and modernism influencing and infecting faith communities? Certainly human nature played a role, but so did distorted eschatologies. And while some good came out of this eschatological optimism (reform movements, ministry to the poor, educational institutions), the unbelievably naive attempt to usher in the kingdom before Messiah returns, or the attempt to Christianize the world fully, or the attempt completely to unify church and state in a fallen world with fallen religious and political leaders led to extreme disillusionment and escapism. Utopianism is partially noble but also reflects arrogance and elitism and departs from core Judeo-Christian values, beliefs, and biblical eschatology. It especially departs from the biblical teaching that all need spiritual open-heart surgery prior to the New Creation because the heart is desperately wicked, the human imagination is evil continually, and there is no one righteous, no, not even one (Gen 6:5; Jer 17:9–10; Ezek 36:26; Rom 10–12).Everything must die and be resurrected to eventually arrive at the New Creation.

ALWAYS BE PREPARED FOR ANYTHING

Meeting the present and endless challenges and opportunities clearly requires a team effort, with the faithful serving as salt, light, and healing together and in countless capacities. We must not lose heart or fall into fight or flight responses, including single-issue fight responses. Our love, passion, and mission is to be part of the epic story of the inbreaking kingdom—together.

A critical part of being prepared, however, is to be prepared for most anything, from marginalization to persecution. Being tuned in to contemporary events is deflating for some, but for kingdom Christians is it our mission field to the people and world system that God so loved.

Hence, our cultural and civilizational engagement should be open-eyed and optimistic in the face of daily events and news headlines. We should not shrink back if we read in the news, in late 2023, that a drag queen admits that their movement's real agenda goes beyond social justice and includes an intentional assault on Judeo-Christian values. There should be no real surprise if a public school teacher confesses that they are intentionally attempting to indoctrinate children to reject Judeo-Christian beliefs or believers.

The illustrations are endless concerning the contours of our future journey through the dark city toward the City of Kingdom Approximation. Man and woman have been redefined in prestigious dictionaries. Very progressive or liberal comedians have complained about everyone redefining everything because we can't deal with reality. National radio programs have compared the beauty of childbirth to the beauty of abortion. Teachers and professors have lost their jobs for not using specified transgender pronouns. Major evangelical and biblical universities are toying with or have moved forward with hiring LGBTQ+ employees. News and polling have become advocacy rather than fact-based. Legislation has been proposed to prosecute parents who refuse to support so-called gender-affirming surgery for children. Public claims are made that polyamory and Christianity are compatible. Politicians and entertainers increasingly invoke God, Jesus, and the self-labelling of being Christian to support unbiblical and anti-biblical practices. Consensual sex between children and adults is increasingly getting a hearing, as some seek to revive the so-called glories of ancient Greece. A broadcaster is fired for using the phrase, also found in legal governmental documents, of illegal alien. Christian and Jewish marginalization and persecution seem to be in a phase of significant increase.

Pages could be added that would recount such realities. One only has to follow the news periodically for such a reality check. The faithful need to be aware, informed, shrewd, compassionate, collaborative, and creative when responding, while especially focusing confidently on the reality and power of the inbreaking future kingdom and the ultimate victory of the New Creation. God is in the business of resurrecting the entire cosmos, the work is well underway, and we are the responsible and engaged citizens of the only true and hopeful future.

Appendix E

A Kingdom Approximation Manifesto: Tentative and Foundational Elements of a Kingdom Approximation Manifesto and Strategy

In many formerly Logos-influenced cultures and nations, the siege by the City of Antichrist has often advanced slowly and incrementally, typically through educational institutions, by *not* engaging in a direct, frontal, and wholesale assault on the Judeo-Christian faith and the tolerant pursuit of normative truth and justice for all. Instead, all words, concepts, and values—like the boiled frog urban legend allegory—have been slowly and gradually redefined over the course of decades. Single issues like the redefinition of marriage, family, gender, and freedom/democracy have been attached to non-Logos definitions or redefinitions of compassion, inclusion, and especially social justice. Rather than overtly, clearly, and publicly announcing that biblical and Judeo-Christian influence and influencers must be silenced or removed from culture and civilization, the more shrewd leaders and soldiers of the City of Antichrist have shattered the pillars and cornerstones of the City of Approximation, drawn the faithful into endless and single Whac-A-Mole issues while missing the deeper tectonic shifts, and redefined and relabeled believers, Scripture, and Judeo-Christian values as not only unhelpful or irrelevant (ABC[1]) to the common good but hateful, non-inclusive, and unjust. Such AJC cultures are on the precipice of banning Judeo-Christian Scripture, beliefs, and practices altogether as hateful, unjust, and violent. Hence, AJCism and post-truth, post-toleration culture is thriving and the marginalization, oppression, silencing, canceling, and criminalization of the faithful is accelerating, and increasingly militant if not violent. AJCism

---

1. ABC, anything but Christian, was a concept previously introduced in this work on p. 17 and borrowed from Os Guinness.

is now applauded on soil once dedicated to and tilled by Logos-influenced and Enlightenment-influenced leaders pursuing more perfect civilizational unions who sought to subject all things to divinely revealed and self-evident justice, equality, rights, freedom, morality, and Truth. It is within the context of this extraordinary post-truth and post–Judeo-Christian historical moment that, perhaps, the pillars of a Third City Approximation Manifesto that have been emerging throughout this work will assist the reader with additional understanding and applications. Consistent with the argument of this work, an actual manifesto would need to be created collaboratively with key partnerships that might use the following as a primer or conversation piece:

- Faith communities will play a significant, if not the critical role, in shaping the present and the future.
- Based on biblical theology and history, history and civilizations are somewhat plastic or moldable by Spirit-led biblical churches and synagogues. Churches should train future leaders to fully engage all of reality.
- Fatalistic and escapist "last days" approaches to the future are unbiblical, irrational, and inattentive to a mountain of historical evidence, and such future-visions actually enable the spirit of antichrist.
- Believers who contort and distort their faith into a last-days, otherworldly, end-times spectator sport, a means to escape trials and sacrifice, or into merely a ticket to an otherworldly heaven actually clear the path for the flourishing of the kingdom of antichrist. Such believers are enablers of the City of Antichrist.
- While comfort and praise are essential to mission and the purpose of churches and synagogues, those who contort their faith, almost entirely, into an escapist means of ecstatic worship or emotional support enable those who are advancing the cause of antichrist.
- The Messiah is not an emotional support animal but the one who tells authentic believers that while he will send the Comforter, all are called to repent and "deny themselves and take up their cross" and "Come, follow me, . . . and I will send you out to fish for people" (Matt 16:24; 4:19).[2]
- As Bonhoeffer put it, when God calls someone, he bids them to "come and die"—to choose the way of the cross, or what N. T. Wright refers

---

2. The origin of this utilization of emotional support animal is unknown. My wife and I have been referencing this for some time.

to as a cruciform service and a cruciform world impacting revolution that began the day Christ died; taking on the form of the cross is key to loving kingdom advance.

- Humble, loving, pure but shrewd and well-prepared faith communities and believers shaped by the cross, on bended knees, referred to in this work as "cruciform" believers, are best positioned to advance the Judeo-Christian kingdom in such heated, fragmented, tribalistic, AJC, polarized, and Balkanized times.
- While it is certainly true that Messiah comforts and counsels, he primarily calls us to kingdom service, to being transformed influencers overflowing with love for God and others.
  - ¤ The kingdom rule of God, which has already decisively broken into human history, means that individuals, marriages, families, churches, communities, cultures, and nations can already, to one degree or another, approximate God's true future. This already-but-not-yet kingdom rule and reality means that individual believers, via Scripturally normed means, can be radically transformed in this life from one degree of glory to another (2 Cor 3) and approximate the day when "we shall be like Him" (1 John 3:2). Such transformed believers and believing communities can bend the arc of history and influence the nature, desires, and destinies of humanity and nations. Such critical influence is possible because of the grace that has been poured out on all humanity, including fallen humanity created in God's image (Acts 2:17), plus the gifts of God-given reason, commonsense, lessons about God and morality "clearly perceived" or revealed (Rom 1:20) to all, conscience (Rom 2:15), and humanity's Triune and inescapable spiritual hardwiring. Believers can serve as radically changed civilizational influential change agents already.
  - ¤ Prayers and calls for revival, when revival is properly defined, are essential and appropriate if framed within the biblical teaching of the Third City, where the glorious future that is centered in God's faithful is approximated already and radiates throughout God's good creation. Prayers and calls for revival which are escapist or uninformed pleas for magical silver bullets, and which ignore the "in the trenches" realities and cruciform dimension of the truly great and influential historical revivals, actually can enable the City of Antichrist. True revival and a truly revived church may be

opposed, mocked, and persecuted, but it can never be quarantined "and the gates of hell shall not prevail against it" (Matt 16:18).

- ¤ Needless to say, wisdom is needed concerning the fine and sometimes messy line between appropriate moral and political engagement by churches versus individuals or faith based organizations and action committees. That fine line conversation likely requires an additional book to adequately address the history and complexity of the issue.

- Legion other future-visions assessed in this work, such as Platonic or otherworldly conceptions of heaven and salvation, Libertarianism, strict political separationism, Jeffersonian or Madisonian separationism, baptistic church-state separationism, or the myth of secular neutrality, especially enable the spirit of antichrist and the City of Antichrist. Cultures and civilizations that are not Logocentric inevitably become AJC over time. It's that simple. Every community and nation has a spirit and cultural glue or soul, even if it is a deified emperor, *or* they drift toward toxic fragmentation and tribalism which typically births more tyranny.

- Logocentrism dethrones every attempt to allow a temporary steward of a civilization to masquerade as king and God. Bonhoeffer properly called out Hitler, the *führer* or leader, as the misleader, days after Hitler came to power in 1933.[3]

- History, culture, and civilization are "cruciplastic": They can be reformed and they can emerge from a Spirit-led passionate love and desire (pathos) to impact positively individuals, communities, and the world that God so loved. Great caution, service, sacrifice, and humility are required. Cruciform service and suffering draw the present into the future and undermine the City of Antichrist.

- This self-giving love (agape) and cruciform passion or pathos is known as "crucipathy," and such kingdom advance is known as "crucipraxy" (theologically driven cruciform practice).

- Crucipathy and crucipraxy lie at the heart of authentic spiritual formation, holiness, and the character, integrity, and kind of ministry and cultural engagement that advances the City of Kingdom Approximation and awakens the dawn of the New Creation.

---

3. Bonhoeffer, "Younger Generation's Altered View." This radio address was broadcast on "Berliner Funkstunde" at 5:30 p.m., on February 1, 1933.

APPENDIX E

- This historic watershed moment and the character and actions of faith communities will determine whether America and other influential regions of the globe will empower a lengthy age of antichrist and tribulation or an age of kingdom advance and approximation.
- Spirit-led faith communities and other partners informed and energized by a realistic but hopeful theology of approximation can partially write the future in the present era prior to when divine providence brings the Messianic transitional future kingdom more fully to planet Earth.
- The fullness of the glorious new kingdom on earth can only be realized by the Messianic, supernatural, miraculous work of God that judges and redeems the world. This assumption is essential for biblical theology and practice and constructive civilizational engagement.
- The next, summative, mighty, and consummative act of God emerges from but is even greater than the Old Testament exodus and the New Testament bodily resurrection of Messiah. This next transitional period in history on the journey to the New Creation is the earthly reign of the Messiah—the great Restoration of the intent of the Creator and the great Transition to the New Heaven and Earth.
- Those who are trying already to establish the Messiah's kingdom on earth prior to the Messiah's return often contribute, honorably and with good intentions and some good but mixed results, to kingdom advance via various causes but ultimately have a confused, utopian, disillusioning, and dangerous future-vision.
- Such utopianism often leads to movements and leaders with dangerous Messiah complexes, not to mention eventual and great disappointment and disillusionment with leaders and movements and institutions. Such revolutionaries are often very sensitive to the sins, personal and systemic, of others but not self-aware concerning their own depravity and carnage.
- Those trying prematurely to establish Messiah's rule on earth without the actual return of the Messiah especially fail to understand the necessity and implications of God's next redemptive act—the transitional phase of history of the Messiah's earthly rule. Such utopianism may have short-lived and even some long-term victories, but the net effect often if not ultimately aids large scale antichristism.
- The necessity of this transitional phase of Christ's actual and earthly rule guards against utopianism and properly understands the human

and cultural condition in our age. We can improve but not perfect the world; we can influence or impact but not change the world in the strong or idealistic sense. We don't need overconfident world changers; we need cruciform and confident world influencers.

- The present age can, in a limited and typically localized fashion, approximate the redemptive work of the coming and earthly reign of the Messiah but is utterly incapable of approximating the New Heaven and Earth on a scale significantly resembling the world after Messiah's return.

- Future-visions and attempts to establish the kingdom now misunderstand the present realities of human nature and the nature and timing of God's redemptive program (e.g., theocracy, dominion theology, and some forms of liberation theology).

- Approximation, in this current age, does not refer to approximating the entirety of the New Heaven and Earth but instead refers to approximating some aspects of the next intermediate and transitional phase of human history—phase one of the Messiah's return and reign on earth.

- The immediate goal of approximation is the partial though sometimes fleeting realization of the Messianic reign on earth already, just as the Messianic reign on earth approximates the ultimate perfection of the New Heaven and Earth.

- This dual and progressive approximation guards against both naive pessimism and naive optimism, both of which are dangerous to the mission of Judeo-Christian faith communities.

- The springboard, core, or primary locus of global approximation is in and through the biblically transformed church, believing families, and the new hearts and lives of the faithful. The primary failure leading to the emboldened City of Antichrist lies with faith families and communities, the interconnected loci of God's work in the world.

- The secondary sense of approximation is the cultural and civilizational presence, mirroring, artifacts, or craters of the future already resulting from the appropriate influence of the faithful on culture and civilization (e.g., medical healing, beautiful music, transformed lives, transformed families, transformed communities, life-giving culture, or the partial abolition of slavery).

- This future, Messianic, glorious transitional period on earth can be approximated provisionally, partially, and proleptically in the present.

- Proleptic theology refers to how God is granting a beautiful and impactful glimpse, down payment, foretaste, and real-world approximation of the future such that we live and act in many respects as if the future is already present even though much is to be fulfilled after the Messiah's return.

- This potent and practical theology is an already-but-not-yet kingdom approximation that is hopeful, realistic, shrewd, cruciform, relevant, prophetic, purpose-filled, strategic, tactical, biblical, cruciplastic, fluid, Spirit driven, and grace based.

- Approximation in the present is based in the favor, power, and gracious presence of the Triune God, God's Messiah, and God's Spirit, which various theological traditions refer to as some form of grace (unmerited/undeserved favor and/or influence).

- God's primary means of impacting civilization is to approximate the future in the church directly as the primary locus of God's redemptive work in the present age. Such churches inevitably mediate or radiate the true future and overflow with love for each other, profound magnetic unity (John 17), and agape love for those outside the circle of faith.

- In a secondary sense, Judeo-Christian faith communities are also Spirit-led means of bearing witness to the future and sometimes rebuking, influencing, creating, or bending culture and civilization, while influencing presidents, prime ministers, emperors, princes, princesses, kings, queens, cities, and kingdoms that participate in God's true and certain future.

- God also lovingly bestows grace (favor and influence) upon the whole world and all of humanity to offer an alternative to human hard-heartedness, brokenness, other-destruction, and self-destruction.

- God's grace creates the possibility of all peoples and groups partnering together, not for utopia prior to Messiah's return, but for more perfect futures already. Not only do believers all hang separately in the City of Antichrist if they fail to hang together, but Judeo-Christian influence or impact is undermined by largely siloed individuals and organizations that seek to save nations and advance the kingdom.

- Contributing to the common good through public theology or public eschatology is mostly futile apart from team partnerships with a variety of Logos-centered Judeo-Christian leaders, organizations, faith communities, and all those of good will seeking more perfect unions.

Perhaps the spirit of the Roman centurion (Matt 8:5–13) is instructive—for "many will come from east and west, and recline at the table with Abraham, Isaac, and Jacob in the kingdom of heaven" (8:11).[4] Team partnerships are especially essential when attempting to persuasively influence powerful governmental, educational, and corporate realities.

- While church and synagogue are in many respects both the problem and the solution to the present crisis, there is no question that the slow, incremental corruption of the educational establishment has fueled antichristism and fragmented spiritually, politically, and economically flourishing civilizational experiments in more perfect unions. Hence, education runs a close second relative to being both the problem and the solution of the present crisis. The educational solution will require creativity, tact, strategic initiatives, boldness, and numerous partnerships.

- The fullness of the City of God and the New Creation requires the actual return of the Messiah, yet the Spirit-led work of the faithful can advance the oft forgotten Third City of Kingdom Approximation which counters and provides an alternative to the City of Antichrist and its spiritual, physical, and relational carnage in the present age.

- The true future that providentially guides, animates, redeems, norms, frames, influences, and lures the present and the loving faithful is the return of the Messiah, followed by the lengthy transitional period that largely restores the Creator's original intent for humanity and the cosmos and which prepares and effectively launches all things toward the fullness of the final New Creation cosmic resurrection.

- It has often been said that all thought is to some extent a footnote on either Plato, who pointed to the true, ultimate, non-shadowy reality of otherworldly perfection, or Aristotle, who pointed to the physical world before us as the only true reality that exists. The epic biblical journey and tale of five cities traverses from the first City or Kingdom of Eden through the three key cities and kingdoms framing our

---

4. This suggestion is not affirming universalism, that all will ultimately be saved whether they receive grace or not, or that sincere belief in anything is salvific. The point here is that the centurion was not a Jew but was viewed as an oppressor, and certainly as a Roman, yet he had a faith the Messiah had not found "with anyone in Israel" (Matt 8:10). Surely there are individuals and groups outside of Judeo-Christian faith communities with whom believers should partner in neighbor love of present and future generations, loving the world that God so loves, and moving civilization toward its true future.

present age, and then culminates in the glorious fifth City of Cosmic Resurrection. In this final city that fulfills the true desires of humanity and nations Plato marries Aristotle, and the real flesh and blood physical world finally becomes the ideal world of illuminating and radiant perfection. Yet the final chapter of this mighty tale absolutely requires the death and resurrection of all things. The incredibly good news is that "Christ is risen" and has "become the firstfruits" (1 Cor 15:20) of the singular, cosmic, true future.

Appendix F

Seven Representative Objections and Misunderstandings Briefly Considered

One can only anticipate possible objections to or misunderstandings of this work, though interaction with students and colleagues have assisted with grasping seven likely and representative perceptions below.

This work aligns with conservative evangelical American (US) political positions. If there is a primary concern of this work, it is with the future-vision of conservative American evangelicalism and how it may be adversely impacting American evangelical political and cultural engagement. Evangelical eschatology is confused at best and detrimental at worst to church, culture, and state. However, it also has been argued that the solution is not to redefine basic Christian beliefs and ethics, which almost everyone is doing these days, inside and outside of communities of faith. The solution is to redeem the future-vision of those solidly committed to biblical authority, biblical morality (e.g., the Ten Commandments), and historic, orthodox Judeo-Christian beliefs and practices such as are reflected in the great creeds (Nicaea, Constantinople, Chalcedon) and declarations (Barmen, 1934). If this book is properly interpreted, few existing Judeo-Christian–influenced political groups will not at least be required to engage in a self-inventory or internal theological audit. The author has found the more conservative group Acton Institute actually to be more self-reflective and open to debate concerning which political postures are reasoned and biblically influenced than groups like Sojourners or the SPLC. This is of course anecdotal, but I clearly remember one Acton conference presentation that basically undermined much of what Acton stood for, but it was allowed and welcomed, in contrast to what I had experienced at other more progressive or politically liberal conferences. Acton is greatly influenced by the late political philosopher (and former socialist) Michael Novak—indeed Acton provides an annual Novak Award. Perhaps Novak's dialogical approach and journey from a more politically liberal ideology to a rebooted vision of free enterprise has contributed to Acton culture, though every organization changes over time. Similarly, there are exceptions, but the mainstream media also seems more averse to honest debate and dialogue than many of their more conservative competitors, and more shameless relative to spin, redefinitions, and deception. This work makes the argument for and documents the thesis that many media groups have largely or fully embraced shameless spin, redefinitions, and deception as a morally justifiable means of political and social justice advocacy. "By any means necessary" is not a Judeo-Christian position. Some political parties have become fertile soil for AJCism. None of these groups, left or right on the political spectrum, are the fullness of the kingdom of God and are subject to biblical and prophetic challenges. The careful reader will find an approach or template that recommends significant reforms for most politically engaged American evangelicals.

This work fails to appreciate the contributions of political liberalism to faith communities seeking to live out their faith. Actually, the argument has been more than clear that there is a significant difference between classical or traditional political liberalism and contemporary political liberalism. Some forms of classical liberalism found great value in how Judeo-Christian beliefs could contribute to human freedom and flourishing. Some classical liberals viewed any form of traditional Judeo-Christian religion as a threat to progress—or Enlightenment progress. Classical political liberals in the United States tended to be more favorable to traditional Christianity, for example, than such liberal counterparts in Europe (especially the liberals on the European continent like Voltaire or architects of the French Revolution). Contemporary political liberalism often identifies real or imagined injustice but redefines the solution to injustice, including the key values of justice and compassion, in a fashion that is fertile soil for antichristism. Faith communities in bed with contemporary political liberalism typically redefine biblical and Judeo-Christian beliefs and terms to align with an ideology that looks to a powerful, centralized government for salvation. The individual political, economic, and religious freedoms purchased with centuries of political reflection and much shed blood are easily dispensed with as needed in the quest for some measure of utopian "social justice." However, even this distinction between contemporary and classical political liberalism misses the real point of the argument in this book. Liberalism, and its vast and well-documented human and civilizational carnage, is specifically defined in this work as the attempt to be liberated from authentic biblical and Judeo-Christian civilizational influence. Some forms of liberalism are overt in their AJCism (Nietzsche), but most have been, up until recent years, covert and incremental. The focus of this work is not political liberalism but AJC liberalism, which is present to one degree or another in numerous future-visions writing the pages of history.

This work does not acknowledge that evangelical future-visions are changing. Actually, it has been clearly argued both that a very powerful and influential American evangelical pessimistic eschatology is still prevalent, and that some attempts at reform have been made and younger generations may be more open to just such a reform as postulated in this work. N. T. Wright's popularity among some evangelicals may reflect this trending, though this work argues that his eschatology has needed areas of improvement and more precision.

The key question of this text, concerning what age we are living in, was never fully answered. To be fair, this work intentionally gave hints of the answer early to keep the reader interested, but the entire text must be thoroughly read in order to comprehend the answer. The answer related directly to the theology of the multiple cosmic cities in the book.

The concept of the city is never clearly defined. I would argue that the theology of the city, as with Augustine, is never comprehensively or exhaustively defined, and for good reason—to not get too far beyond Scripture and too far down the road toward additional speculation. However, I would argue that the city is repeatedly and at least adequately defined throughout the work—it simply has many layers and meanings (e.g., actual flesh and blood cities, kingdoms, cultures, and civilizations that reflect core beliefs and loves and a spirit of the times). This approach to defining the key theological cities of this work is needful, powerful, and participatory in nature. The faithful can shape the cities, even via persecution, and certainly through political freedoms. Indeed, the term city is directly and historically related to the term *citizen*. The call to be well-prepared citizens for all cities, for time and eternity, is central and almost redundant in this work. Theological drama or imagery is essential to sharing a future-vision that can energize the faithful by harnessing and properly directing civilizational-influencing and already ignited eschatological jet fuel. And such harnessing has been done before.

This book is responding to a dispensational evangelical eschatology that is largely passé or dead. First, this book and a forthcoming publication irrefutably document that much of the fatalism, escapism, cultural disengagement, confused political engagement, otherworldliness, anti-intellectualism, and last-generationism of dispensationalism is very much alive and well across the globe, based on countless surveys, book sales, and the general culture, assumptions, and the preaching and teaching of the media luminaries of American evangelicalism. The common refrain of "No one knows the hour or day, but I'm just sayin' it certainly looks like the time is near" almost always moves the masses. The story of the The Rise and Fall of Dispensationalism is in some respects a true story of decline if properly qualified,[1] but this death has been greatly exaggerated. Dispensationalism is still leaving its fingerprint on church (including worship), state, and the future. Major political figures are still in orbit and sometimes advised by last-generation evangelical leaders. In addition to the data, recent global events and rapid cultural change and chaos in the United States have spawned much additional anecdotal evidence such that many are interpreting current crises, once again, as proof that the Bible is true and that the last generation has arrived. Rarely does a month go by that someone in my wide circle of contacts does not raise the last-generationism white flag. Many of the evangelical and academic power centers, as well as younger evangelical scholars, may have moved on from Darbyism or dispensationalism, but millions if not more globally frame their faith with some or many of these dispensational assumptions just referenced. It is possible someday that younger evangelicals will marginalize key dispensational assumptions to the point that a funeral service is appropriate, but that seems unlikely in the near future given the staying power of the last-generationist vision and how the vision serves as fuel for apologetics (civilizational decline is proof of biblical prophecy), evangelism, missions, fundraising to save Judeo-Christian civilization, conservative politics, and eschatological entertainment. Millions may no longer be sitting on pins and needles wondering if they will miss the rapture, but the last-generation future-vision is energizing, provides hope and assurance, and makes sense out of some current events that seem apocalyptic, dystopian, and the vision seems to be spot on relative to predictions that evangelicals have heard since childhood. And, as this work argues, there are hidden truths in the vision. Any generation can experience apocalyptic tribulation, a powerful antichrist or multiple antichrists, runaway governmental control if not tyranny, and militant antichristism. However, biblically speaking, any generation can also witness amazing kingdom advance and step into God's true future, and most of the fatalistic and escapist echoes of dispensationalism only enable the City of Antichrist rather than persuasively exposing the dark city and empowering the City of Kingdom Approximation.

It is never clearly stated as to whether there will be a literal, future, singular antichrist at the end of history as we know it before Messiah returns. That statement is true, and the issue may be the subject of a future work. There has been too much distracting speculation on the who and when of the singular Great Tribulation antichrist. There certainly are many antichrists

---

1. See Hummel, *Rise*.

and many antichrist figures to be expected throughout history who wield tremendous power and influence over the faithful and much of the globe, and there certainly could be a singular such figure in the future given our globally connected world. Hitler was certainly AJC and an antichrist, and for that generation he arguably was the functional, singular, epic antichrist. What is plainly stated in this work is far more important and productive than any speculations. It has been clearly and repeatedly argued that we should be prepared for antichristism and approximation in every generation of human history until Messiah comes. The focus in Revelation is not on whether details like the thousand years are literal—the time period is likely much longer. The daily north star for God's people is the fulfillment of history and creation via the actual coming transitional restoration of all things by the literal Messiah, and the ultimate and final resurrection of all things in the New Creation. And we are already stepping into that future victory today.

BIBLIOGRAPHY

Adams, James Luther. "Arminius and the Structure of Society." In *Man's Faith and Freedom: The Theological Influence of Jacobus Arminius*, edited by Gerald O. McCullough, 88–112. New York: Abingdon, 1963.

"The Age of the Enlightenment." In *History of Western Civilization II*. Lumen Learning. https://courses.lumenlearning.com/suny-hccc-worldhistory2/chapter/the-age-of-enlightenment/.

Alinsky, Saul D. *Rules for Radicals: A Practical Primer for Realistic Radicals*. New York: Vintage, 1971.

Allen, Scott D., et al. *A Toxic New Religion: Understanding the Postmodern, Neo-Marxist Faith That Seeks to Destroy the Judeo-Christian Culture of the West*. Phoenix: Disciple Nations Alliance, 2020.

Allman, William F. "Fatal Attraction." *US News and World Report*, April 30, 1990, 12–13.

Alper, Becka A., and Aleksandra Sandstrom. "The U.S. as 100 People: Two Jews, One Muslim and 71 Christians." Chart 1 in "If the U.S. Had 100 People: Charting Americans' Religious Affiliations." Pew Research Center, November 7, 2016. https://www.pewresearch.org/fact-tank/2016/11/14/if-the-u-s-had-100-people-charting-americans-religious-affiliations/.

Althaus, Paul. *The Theology of Martin Luther*. Translated by Robert C. Shultz. Philadelphia: Fortress, 1966.

Amazon.com. "Best Sellers in Christian Prophecy." Accessed March 1, 2022. https://www.amazon.com/Best-Sellers-Christian-Prophecy/zgbs/digital-text/158404011.

American Center for Law and Justice. "ACLJ Victory Report: Churches Have Equal Right to Police Protection." January 26, 2012. https://aclj.org/us-constitution/aclj-victory-report-churches-have-equal-right-police-protection.

———. *Relentless: 2019 Freedom Report*. https://static.aclj.org/2019-ACLJ-AR.pdf.

Amico, Sam. "JK Rowling Not Invited to Harry Potter Reunion because She Said Men and Women Are Different." *OutKick*, November 17, 2022. https://www.outkick.com/jk-rowling-not-invited-to-harry-potter-reunion-because-she-said-men-and-women-are-different/.

Anderson, R. Lanier. "Friedrich Nietzsche." In *Stanford Encyclopedia of Philosophy*, edited by Edward N. Zalta. Last updated May 19, 2022. https://plato.stanford.edu/entries/nietzsche/.

Anthony, Abigail. "'Queer and Trans Nuns': Dodgers Disinvite, Then Re-invite, Anti-Catholic Group to Pride Night." *National Review*, May 23, 2023. https://www.

nationalreview.com/news/queer-and-trans-nuns-dodgers-disinvite-then-re-invite-anti-catholic-group-to-pride-night/.

Anti-Defamation League. "Audit of Antisemitic Incidents 2022." March 22, 2023. https://www.adl.org/resources/report/audit-antisemitic-incidents-2022.

———. "What We Do: Fight Antisemitism." https://www.adl.org/what-we-do/fight-antisemitism.

"Approximator." *The Free Dictionary*. https://www.thefreedictionary.com/Approximator.

Arminius, James. *The Writings of James Arminius*. Translated by James Nichols and W. R. Bagnall. 3 vols. Grand Rapids: Baker, 1956.

"Artifact." *Merriam-Webster*. https://www.merriam-webster.com/dictionary/artifact.

Athanasius. *On the Incarnation*. 2nd ed. Translated by Archibald Robertson. London: David Nutt, 1891.

Augustine. *The City of God*. Translated by Marcus Dods. Peabody, MA: Hendrickson, 2018.

Aylesworth, Gary. "Postmodernism." In *Stanford Encyclopedia of Philosophy*, edited by Edward N. Zalta. Last updated February 5, 2015. https://plato.stanford.edu/entries/postmodernism.

Bahnsen, Greg L. "In What Ways Is Christ's Kingdom to Be Evident Today?" Paper presented at the Evangelical Theological Society, 43rd Annual Meeting, Kansas City, MO, November 22, 1991. Audiocassette EV91005.

———. *No Other Standard: Theonomy and Its Critics*. Tyler, TX: Institute for Christian Economics, 1991.

Bailey, Megan. "Is There Christian Persecution in America?" *Beliefnet*, July 27, 2017. https://www.beliefnet.com/news/is-there-christian-persecution-in-america.aspx.

Bakke, Raymond J. *A Theology as Big as the City*. Downers Grove, IL: IVP Academic, 1997.

Barna Group. "Christians React to the Legalization of Same-Sex Marriage: 9 Key Findings." July 1, 2015. https://www.barna.com/research/christians-react-to-the-legalization-of-same-sex-marriage-9-key-findings/.

———. "The End of Absolutes: America's New Moral Code." May 25, 2016. https://www.barna.com/research/the-end-of-absolutes-americas-new-moral-code/.

Barth, Karl. *The Epistle to the Romans*. Translated by Edwyn C. Hoskyns. New York: Oxford University Press, 1968.

Baucham, Voddie T., Jr. *Fault Lines: The Social Justice Movement and Evangelicalism's Looming Catastrophe*. Washington, DC: Salem, 2021.

Bauckham, Richard J. *Moltmann: Messianic Theology in the Making*. Bastingstoke, UK: Marshall Pickering, 1987.

Bayer, Oswald. *Martin Luther's Theology: A Contemporary Interpretation*. Grand Rapids: Eerdmans, 2008.

Beasley-Murray, George R. *Highlights of the Book of Revelation*. Nashville: Broadman, 1972.

———. "Premillennialism." In *Revelation: Three Viewpoints*, edited by David C. George, 11–70. Nashville: Broadman, 1977.

Beck, Glenn. *The Glenn Beck Show*. October 20, 2021. WLAP. Lexington, KY. iHeartradio.

Beck, Glenn, and Justin Trask Haskins. *The Great Reset: Joe Biden and the Rise of Twenty-First-Century Fascism*. N.p.: Forefront, 2022.

BIBLIOGRAPHY

Beckwith, Francis J., and Gregory Koukl. *Relativism: Feet Firmly Planted in Mid-Air.* Grand Rapids: Baker, 1998.

Bell, Rob. *Love Wins: A Book about Heaven, Hell, and the Fate of Every Person Who Ever Lived.* New York: HarperOne, 2012.

Biggar, Nigel. "Theology in the City: A Theological Response to Faith in the City." *Themelios* 17.2 (January 1992) 26–27.

Black, Conrad. "America's Not Back, It's Gone Mad." RealClear Politics, October 27, 2021. https://www.realclearpolitics.com/2021/10/27/americas_not_back_its_gone_mad_555078.html.

Black, James M. "When the Roll Is Called Up Yonder (541)." In *Trinity Hymnal.* Rev. ed. Suwanee, GA: Great Commission, 1990. https://hymnary.org/hymn/TH1990/541.

Blackburn, Simon. *Truth: A Guide.* Oxford: Oxford University Press, 2005.

Bloesch, Donald G. *Life, Ministry, and Hope.* Vol. 2 of *Essentials of Evangelical Theology.* San Francisco: Harper and Row, 1979.

Blumenthal, Stephen. "In a World Gone Mad Rationality Is More Important Than Ever." *Telegraph,* July 3, 2020. https://www.telegraph.co.uk/global-health/science-and-disease/world-gone-mad-rationality-important-ever/.

Boaz, David. "Libertarianism." *Encyclopaedia Britannica Online.* Last updated August 28, 2023. https://www.britannica.com/topic/libertarianism-politics.

Bonhoeffer, Dietrich. "Cheap Grace and Discipleship." In *Readings in Christian Thought,* edited by Hugh T. Kerr, 348–52. Nashville: Abingdon, 1966.

———. *The Cost of Discipleship.* Rev. ed. New York: Macmillan, 1966.

———. *Ethics.* Edited by Eberhard Bethge. Translated by Neville Horton Smith. New York: Macmillan, 1955.

———. *Letters and Papers from Prison.* Edited by Eberhard Bethge. New York: Touchstone, 1971.

———. "The Younger Generation's Altered View of the Concept of Führer." Radio address, February 1, 1933. *Dietrich Bonhoeffer Works.* Vol. 12, *In Berlin: 1932–1933,* edited by Larry L. Rasmussen, translated by Isabel Best and David Higgins. Minneapolis: Fortress, 2009.

Bonino, Jose Miguez. *Toward a Christian Political Ethics.* Philadelphia: Fortress, 1983.

Bos, Stefan J. "Report: 'Growing Persecution of Christians in North America, Europe.'" *Eschatology Today* (blog). https://www.eschatologytoday.org/worthy-news/?story=report-growing-persecution-of-christians-in-north-america-europe.

Boteach, Shmuley. "Americans Have Gone Insane Hating Each Other—Opinion." *Jerusalem Post,* December 16, 2020. https://www.jpost.com/opinion/americans-have-gone-insane-hating-each-other-opinion-652355.

Braaten, Carl E. *Eschatology and Ethics: Essays on the Theology and Ethics of the Kingdom of God.* Minneapolis: Augsburg, 1974.

Brian, Rustin E. *Covering Up Luther: How Barth's Christology Challenged the Deus Absconditus That Haunts Modernity.* Eugene, OR: Cascade, 2013.

Brown, Jon. "Canadian Pastor Arrested on Tarmac over COVID Rules Says Police Confiscated Luggage, Snooped Laptop." Fox News, October 2, 2021. https://www.foxnews.com/politics/polish-canadian-pastor.

Brown, Robert McAfee. "'Eschatological Hope' and Social Responsibility." *Christianity and Crisis* 13 (1953) 146–49.

Brumley, Albert E. "I'll Fly Away." 1929. https://popularhymns.com/ill-fly-away.

Bunyan, John. *The Pilgrim's Progress: From This World to That Which Is to Come*. Edited by C. J. Lovik. Wheaton, IL: Crossway, 2009.

Cahn, Jonathan. *The Harbinger: The Ancient Mystery That Holds the Secret of America's Future*. Lake Mary, FL: FrontLine, 2012.

———. *The Oracle: The Jubilean Mysteries Unveiled*. Lake Mary, FL: FrontLine, 2019.

———. "The Oracle: The Jubilean Mysteries Unveiled Part 3." Interview by James Dobson. Dr. James Dobson Family Institute, December 4, 2019. https://www.drjamesdobson.org/broadcasts/the-oracle-the-jubilean-mysteries-unveiled-part-3.

———. *The Return of the Gods*. Lake Mary, FL: FrontLine, 2022.

Carlisle, Belinda. "Heaven Is a Place on Earth." Track 1, *Heaven on Earth*, 1987.

Carter, A. P. "This World Is Not My Home, I'm Just Passing Through." In *Hymns of Faith*, 311. Carol Stream, IL: Tabernacle, 1980.

Carter, Joe. "Founding Believers." *First Things*, September 22, 2010. https://www.firstthings.com/web-exclusives/2010/09/founding-believers.

CBS News Staff. "Obama Calls Out Call-Out Culture: 'That's Not Bringing about Change.'" CBS News, October 30, 2019. https://www.cbsnews.com/news/president-obama-calls-out-woke-culture-says-not-bringing-about-change-2019 10-30/.

Center for the Study of Global Christianity at Gordon-Conwell Theological Seminary. "Frequently Asked Questions [Quick Facts]." https://www.gordonconwell.edu/center-for-global-christianity/research/quick-facts/.

Chapman, Don. "The Unusual Story behind 'Stand Up, Stand Up for Jesus.'" HymnCharts, July 27, 2015. https://www.hymncharts.com/2015/07/27/the-unusual-story-behind-stand-up-stand-up-for-jesus/.

Cheney, Lynne. *Telling The Truth: Why Our Culture and Our Country Have Stopped Making Sense—and What We Can Do About It*. New York: Touchstone, 1995.

The Christian Century. "About Us." https://www.christiancentury.org/about.

Christianity Today Editors. "Is It Time for Evangelicals to Strategically Withdraw from the Culture? Four Evangelical Thinkers Consider What Rod Dreher's Benedict Option Means for the Church." *Christianity Today*, February 27, 2017. https://www.christianitytoday.com/ct/2017/february-web-only/benedict-option-evangelicals-strategically-withdraw-culture.html.

Cleary, Finn. "Understanding the Trivium and Quadrivium." Hillsdale College (blog), February 15, 2017. https://www.hillsdale.edu/hillsdale-blog/academics/understanding-trivium-quadrivium/.

Coalition of Americans for Action and Principles Staff. "Anti-Christian Bigotry Is the Last Acceptable Prejudice." Coalition of Americans for Action and Principles, March 12, 2019. https://caapusa.org/2019/03/anti-christian-bigotry-is-the-last-acceptable-prejudice/.

Coates, Ta-Nehisi. "The Myth of Western Civilization." *Atlantic*, December 2013. https://www.theatlantic.com/international/archive/2013/12/the-myth-of-western-civilization/282704/.

Cole, Devan. "Virginia Governor Faces Backlash over Comments Supporting Late-Term Abortion Bill." CNN, January 31, 2019. https://www.cnn.com/2019/01/31/politics/ralph-northam-third-trimester-abortion/index.html.

Copan, Paul. *True for You, but Not for Me: Overcoming Objections to Christian Faith*. Rev. ed. Minneapolis: Bethany House, 2009.

Cox, Harvey. *Religion in the Secular City: Toward a Postmodern Theology*. New York: Simon & Schuster, 1984.

Crawley, William. "A Disgustingly Evil Man . . ." *Will & Testament* (blog). BBC, September 23, 2007. https://www.bbc.co.uk/blogs/ni/2007/09/a_disgustingly_evil_man.html.

Creech, Mark H. "The Coming of Persecution for Christian Americans." *Christian Post*, July 24, 2019. https://www.christianpost.com/voices/the-coming-of-persecution-for-christian-americans.html.

Crosswalk Editorial Staff. "The Sinner's Prayer—4 Examples for Salvation." Crosswalk.com, August 6, 2020. https://www.crosswalk.com/faith/prayer/the-sinners-prayer-4-examples.html.

Cruz, Ted. *Unwoke: How to Defeat Cultural Marxism in America*. Washington, DC: 2023.

Cullmann, Oscar. *Christ and Time: The Primitive Christian Conception of Time and History*. Translated by Floyd V. Filson. Rev. ed. Philadelphia: Westminster, 1964.

———. *Salvation in History*. Translated by Sidney G. Sowers. New York: Harper and Row, 1967.

"David Leong: What Is the Theological Meaning of the City?" *Faith and Leadership*, September 4, 2018. https://faithandleadership.com/david-leong-what-the-theological-meaning-the-city.

Dayton, Donald W. *Discovering an Evangelical Heritage*. Grand Rapids: Baker Academic, 1976.

Decision Staff. "Hostility on the College Campus: A Conversation with Os Guinness." *Decision: The Evangelical Voice for Today*, May 27, 2016. https://decisionmagazine.com/hostility-on-the-college-campus-a-conversation-with-os-guiness/.

Dillard, Raymond B. "Glory." In *Baker Encyclopedia of the Bible*, edited by Walter A. Elwell, 1:870–73. Grand Rapids: Baker, 1988.

Dillenberger, John, ed. *Martin Luther: Selections from His Writings*. New York: Anchor, 1961.

Dochuk, Darren, et al., eds. *American Evangelicalism: George Marsden and the State of American Religious History*. Notre Dame: University of Notre Dame Press, 2014.

Dreher, Rod. *The Benedict Option: A Strategy for Christians in a Post-Christian Nation*. New York: Penguin Random House, 2017.

———. "Social Justice: Our New Civil Religion." The American Conservative, July 10, 2019. https://www.theamericanconservative.com/lgbt-pride-social-justice-our-new-civil-religion/.

Dreisbach, Daniel L., et al., eds. *The Founders on God and Government*. Lanham, MD: Rowman and Littlefield, 2004.

Duffield, George. "Stand Up, Stand Up for Jesus." 1858. https://hymnary.org/text/stand_up_stand_up_for_jesus_duffield.

Duignan, Brian. "Postmodernism." In *Encyclopaedia Britannica*. Accessed October 25, 2018. https://www.britannica.com/topic/postmodernism-philosophy.

Eberstadt, Mary. *It's Dangerous to Believe: Religious Freedom and Its Enemies*. New York: Harper, 2016.

———. "Regular Christians Are No Longer Welcome in American Culture." *Time*, June 29, 2016. https://time.com/4385755/faith-in-america/.

Echols, Hannah. "UAB Hospital Delivers Record-Breaking Premature Baby." *UAB News*, November 10, 2021. https://www.uab.edu/news/health/item/12427-uab-hospital-delivers-record-breaking-premature-baby.

Elkins, Chelsea. "The Antichrist by Friedrich Nietzsche: Summary & Analysis." Study.com. Last updated March 6, 2022. https://study.com/learn/lesson/antichrist-friedrich-nietzsche-summary-analysis.html.

Ellul, Jacques. *The Meaning of the City*. Translated by Dennis Pardee. The Jacques Ellul Legacy Series. Eugene, OR: Wipf & Stock, 2011.

Encyclopaedia Britannica Editors. "How Does Classical Liberalism Differ from Modern Liberalism?" Accessed October 17, 2023. https://www.britannica.com/question/How-does-classical-liberalism-differ-from-modern-liberalism.

———. "Uncle Tom's Cabin." *Encyclopaedia Britannica Online*. Accessed May 25, 2020. https://www.britannica.com/topic/Uncle-Toms-Cabin/Major-themes-and-influences.

Erickson, Millard J. *Christian Theology*. Grand Rapids: Baker, 1985.

Ernst, Douglas. "Madonna Wants Meeting with Pope Francis to Convince Him of Pro-Choice Jesus." *Washington Times*, June 19, 2019. https://www.washingtontimes.com/news/2019/jun/19/madonna-wants-meeting-with-pope-francis-to-convinc/.

Evans, Jimmy. *Tipping Point: The End Is Here*. Texas: XO, 2020.

Federer, William J. *America's God and Country: Encyclopedia of Quotations*. St. Louis: Amerisearch, 2000.

———. "Colonial Clergy John Wise, Thomas Hooker & John Witherspoon, Who Signed Declaration of Independence: 'A Republic Must Either Preserve Its Virtue or Lose Its Liberty.'" American Minute, November 15, 2019. https://americanminute.com/blogs/todays-american-minute/a-republic-must-either-reserve-its-virtue-or-lose-its-liberty-rev-john-witherspoon-signer-of-declaration-of-independence-american-minute-with-bill-federer.

Franks, Gabriel. "Marxism as a Christian Heresy." *Forum for Social Economics* 1.3 (1971) 13–18. https://doi.org/10.1007/BF02757756.

Freeze, Trevor. "Franklin Graham: 'Every Demon in Hell Has Been Turned Loose.'" *Charisma*, May 23, 2023. https://charismamag.com/spiritled-living/franklin-graham-every-demon-in-hell-has-been-turned-loose/.

Gander, Kashmira. "Why We Should Reconsider Assigning Babies as 'Boys' or 'Girls' at Birth." *Independent*, September 7, 2017. https://www.independent.co.uk/life-style/health-and-families/baby-gender-why-not-boys-girls-trans-assign-birth-non-binary-reveal-party-gendered-intelligence-doctor-queer-nhs-a7933871.html.

Gaustad, Edwin S. *Faith of the Founders: Religion and the New Nation, 1776–1826*. Waco, TX: Baylor University Press, 2004.

Gaustad, Edwin S., et al. *A Documentary History of Religion in America to 1877*. 3rd ed. Grand Rapids: Eerdmans, 2003.

Gibbs, Nancy, and Michael Duffy. "Why Christopher Hitchens Is Wrong about Billy Graham." *Time*, September 18, 2007. https://content.time.com/time/nation/article/0,8599,1662757,00.html.

Gorman, Michael J. *Inhabiting the Cruciform God: Kenosis, Justification, and Theosis in Paul's Narrative Soteriology*. Grand Rapids: Eerdmans, 2009.

Grenz, Stanley J. *The Millennial Maze: Sorting Out Evangelical Options*. Downers Grove, IL: InterVarsity, 1992.

Grider, J. Kenneth. "Arminianism." In *Evangelical Dictionary of Theology*, edited by Walter A. Elwell, 79–81. Grand Rapids: Baker, 1984.

———. *A Wesleyan Holiness Theology*. Kansas City: Beacon Hill, 1994.

Groothuis, Douglas. *Truth Decay: Defending Christianity against the Challenges of Postmodernism*. Downers Grove, IL: InterVarsity, 2000.

Gushee, David P., and Glen H. Stassen. *Kingdom Ethics: Following Jesus in Contemporary Context*. Grand Rapids: Eerdmans, 2003.

Guttmacher Institute. "United States Abortion." https://www.guttmacher.org/united-states/abortion.

Habermas, Gary. *Beyond Death: Exploring the Evidence for Immorality*. Eugene, OR: Wipf & Stock, 2004.

Hall, Mark David. "Did America Have a Christian Founding?" *Heritage Lectures*. Heritage Foundation, June 7, 2011. https://www.heritage.org/political-process/report/did-america-have-christian-founding.

Hamilton, Alexander, et al. *The Federalist*. Edited by Benjamin Fletcher Wright. New York: Barnes and Noble, 2004.

Hanegraaff, Hank. "The Word Crisis That Threatens to Undo Western Civilization with D. K. Matthews." Interview with D. K. Matthews. *Hank Unplugged Podcast*, August 5, 2020. https://www.equip.org/hank-unplugged-podcast-and-shorts/the-word-crisis-that-threatens-to-undo-western-civilization-with-d-k-matthews/.

Hannam, James. *The Genesis of Science: How the Christian Middle Ages Launched the Scientific Revolution*. Washington, DC: Regnery, 2011.

———. "Medieval Christianity and the Rise of Modern Science." BioLogos, October 31, 2012. https://biologos.org/articles/medieval-christianity-and-the-rise-of-modern-science/.

Hanson, Victor Davis. "America Does Not Have to Be Perfect to Be Good (Despite What Radical Progressives Tell Us)." Fox News, July 18, 2019. https://www.foxnews.com/opinion/victor-davis-hanson-america-does-not-have-be-perfect-to-be-good-despite-what-radical-progressives-tell-us.

Hardesty, Nancy A. *Women Called to Witness: Evangelical Feminism*. Knoxville: University of Tennessee Press, 1999.

Harrison, E. F. "Glory." In The *Evangelical Dictionary of Theology*, edited by Walter Elwell, 443–44. Grand Rapids: Baker, 1984.

Harvey, Anthony, ed. *Theology in the City: A Theological Response to "Faith in the City."* London: Society for Promoting Christian Knowledge, 1989.

Hauerwas, Stanley, and William H. Willimon. *Resident Aliens: A Provocative Assessment of Culture and Ministry for People Who Know That Something Is Wrong*. Nashville: Abingdon, 1989.

Henderson, Cydney. "Lady Gaga Slams Mike Pence as the 'Worst Representation of What It Means to Be a Christian.'" *USA Today*, January 21, 2019. https://www.usatoday.com/story/life/people/2019/01/21/lady-gaga-slams-vice-president-mike-pence-christianity/2636241002/.

Henry, Carl F. H. *God, Revelation and Authority*. 6 vols. Wheaton, IL: Crossway, 1976–1999.

———. *Twilight of a Great Civilization: The Drift toward New Paganism*. Westchester, IL: Crossway, 1988.

———. *The Uneasy Conscience of Modern Fundamentalism*. Grand Rapids: Eerdmans, 1947.

Hick, John. *Evil and the God of Love*. London: Macmillan, 1966.
Hiebert, Paul G. "Beyond Anti-Colonialism to Globalism." *Missiology: An International Review* 19.3 (1991) 263–81.
Hillard, Graham. "The Social-Justice Movement's Unjust Crusade." *National Review*, March 7, 2019. https://www.nationalreview.com/magazine/2019/03/25/the-social-justice-movements-unjust-crusade/.
Hitchens, Christopher. "Mommie Dearest." *Slate*, October 20, 2003. https://slate.com/news-and-politics/2003/10/the-fanatic-fraudulent-mother-teresa.html.
Hodgkinson, Tom. "How *Utopia* Shaped the World." BBC, October 6, 2016. https://www.bbc.com/culture/article/20160920-how-utopia-shaped-the-world.
Hoehner, Harold. "Is Christ or Satan Ruler of This World?" *Christianity Today* 34 (1990) 42–44.
Holocaust Encyclopedia. "Martin Niemöller: 'First They Came For . . .'" United States Holocaust Memorial Museum. https://encyclopedia.ushmm.org/content/en/article/martin-niemoeller-first-they-came-for-the-socialists.
Hoonderdaal, G. J. "A Dutch Theology of Toleration." *Religion in Life* 41.1 (973) 449–55.
Hoyt, Herman. "Dispensational Premillennialism." In *The Meaning of the Millennium*, edited by Robert G. Clouse, 63–116. Downers Grove, IL: InterVarsity, 1977.
Hubbard, D. A. "Antichrist." In *The Evangelical Dictionary of Theology*, edited by Walter Elwell, 55–56. Grand Rapids: Baker, 1984.
Hummel, Daniel G. *The Rise and Fall of Dispensationalism: How the Evangelical Battle over the End Times Shaped a Nation*. Grand Rapids: Eerdmans, 2023.
Huttar, David K. "Glory." In *Baker's Evangelical Dictionary of Biblical Theology*, edited by Walter Elwell. Grand Rapids: Baker, 1996. https://www.biblestudytools.com/dictionaries/bakers-evangelical-dictionary/glory.html.
Inazu, John D. *Confident Pluralism: Surviving and Thriving through Deep Difference*. Chicago: University of Chicago Press, 2016.
International Christian Concern. "Church Buildings Burned in Canada and the United States." Persecution.org, July 27, 2021. https://www.persecution.org/2021/07/27/church-buildings-burned-canada-united-states/.
Irenaeus. "Incarnation, Recapitulation, Redemption." In *Readings in Christian Thought*, edited by Hugh T. Kerr, 34–35. Nashville: Abingdon, 1966.
Isaacson, Walter. "Benjamin Franklin Joins the Revolution." *Smithsonian Magazine*, July 31, 2003. https://www.smithsonianmag.com/history/benjamin-franklin-joins-the-revolution-87199988/.
Jackson, Griffin Paul. "No Matter Where You Are, Religious Freedom Is Getting Worse." *Christianity Today*, July 15, 2019. https://www.christianitytoday.com/news/2019/july/religious-freedom-getting-worse-pew-ministerial.html.
James, Christopher B. "John Wesley's Doctrine of Salvation (and Perfection)." *Jesus Dust* (blog), February 2013. http://www.jesusdust.com/2013/02/john-wesleys-doctrine-of-salvation-and.html.
Jaschik, Scott. "Professors and Politics: What the Research Says." *Inside Higher Ed*, February 27, 2017. https://www.insidehighered.com/news/2017/02/27/research-confirms-professors-lean-left-questions-assumptions-about-what-means.
Jeremiah, David. *The Book of Signs: 31 Undeniable Prophecies of the Apocalypse*. Nashville: Thomas Nelson, 2019.
———. *Escape the Coming Night: A Message of Hope in a Time of Crisis*. With C. C. Carlson. Nashville: Thomas Nelson, 2018.

BIBLIOGRAPHY

Johnson, Jesse. *City of Man, Kingdom of God: Why Christians Respect, Obey, and Resist Government*. Edited by Michael T. Hamilton. Self-published: BookBaby, 2022.

Juza, Ryan P. *The New Testament and the Future of the Cosmos*. Eugene, OR: Pickwick, 2020.

———. "The New Testament and the Future of the Cosmos." PhD diss., Asbury Theological Seminary, 2017.

Kadai, Heino O. "Luther's Theology of the Cross." *Concordia Theological Quarterly* 63.3 (1999) 169–204.

Kairos Theologians. *Kairos Document: Challenge to the Churches*. Grand Rapids: Eerdmans, 1986.

Kandiah, Krish. "God Turns Up in All the Wrong Places at Christmas." *Christianity Today*, December 20, 2017. https://www.christianitytoday.com/ct/2017/december-web-only/god-turns-up-in-all-wrong-places.html.

Keener, Craig S. *The IVP Bible Background Commentary*. 2nd ed. Downers Grove, IL: IVP Academic, 2014.

Keller, Tim. "A Theology of Cities." *Cru* (blog). https://www.cru.org/us/en/train-and-grow/leadership-training/sending-your-team/a-theology-of-cities.html.

Kelley, Stewart E., and James K. Dew Jr. *Understanding Postmodernism: A Christian Perspective*. Downers Grove, IL: IVP Academic, 2017.

Kelly, Walt. "We Have Met the Enemy and He Is Us." Billy Ireland Cartoon Library & Museum, The Ohio State University Libraries. January 5, 2020. https://library.osu.edu/site/40stories/2020/01/05/we-have-met-the-enemy/.

Kennedy, D. James, and Jerry Newcombe. *What If Jesus Had Never Been Born?* Rev. ed. Nashville: Thomas Nelson, 1994.

Kesler, Charles L. "America's Cold Civil War." *Imprimis*, 47.10 (October 2018). https://imprimis.hillsdale.edu/americas-cold-civil-war/.

Kestenbaum, Sam, and Andrew White. "#MAGA Church: The Doomsday Prophet Who Says the Bible Predicted Trump." *New York Times*, Mar 15, 2019. https://www.nytimes.com/2019/03/15/nyregion/trump-preacher-magachurch.html.

Kilpatrick, William. "Europe's War on Christianity." *Crisis Magazine*, April 1, 2019. https://www.crisismagazine.com/opinion/europes-war-on-christianity.

King, Martin Luther, Jr. "I Have a Dream." Speech. Washington, DC, August 28, 1963. https://www.npr.org/2010/01/18/122701268/i-have-a-dream-speech-in-its-entirety.

Kinnaman, David, et al. *Faith for Exiles: 5 Ways for a New Generation to Follow Jesus in Digital Babylon*. Grand Rapids: Baker, 2019.

Kirkpatrick, David D. "Evangelical Sales Are Converting Publishers." *New York Times*, June 8, 2002. https://www.nytimes.com/2002/06/08/books/evangelical-sales-are-converting-publishers.html.

Korkidakis, Jon. "The 5 Signs of Persecution and Why Canadian Christians Should Be Concerned." *Jon Korkidakis* (blog), October 29, 2019. https://jkorkidakis.com/blogs/jon-korkidakis/the-5-signs-of-persecution-and-why-canadian-christians-should-be-concerned.

Kumar, Anugrah. "Canadian Pastor Arrested at Airport Warns Americans: 'You're Next.'" *Christian Post*, October 3, 2021. https://www.christianpost.com/news/canadian-pastor-arrested-at-airport-warns-americans-youre-next.html.

Labberton, Mark. Introduction to *Still Evangelical? Insiders Reconsider Political, Social, and Theological Meaning*, edited by Mark Labberton and Shane Clairborne, 1–18. Downers Grove, IL: InterVarsity, 2018.

———. "Political Dealing: The Crisis of Evangelicalism." Fuller Theological Seminary, April 20, 2018. https://www.fuller.edu/posts/political-dealing-the-crisis-of-evangelicalism/.

Labberton Mark, and Shane Clairborne, eds. *Still Evangelical? Insiders Reconsider Political, Social, and Theological Meaning*. Downers Grove, IL: InterVarsity, 2018.

Ladd, George Eldon. "Can the Kingdom Be Both Future and Present?" In *Crucial Questions about the Kingdom of God*, 63–74. Grand Rapids: Eerdmans, 1952.

———. *The Presence of the Future: The Eschatology of Biblical Realism*. Grand Rapids: Eerdmans, 1996.

———. *A Theology of the New Testament*. Grand Rapids: Eerdmans, 1974.

LaHaye, Tim, and Jerry B. Jenkins. *The Left Behind Collection*. 12 vols. Carol Stream, IL: Tyndale, 1995–2007.

Landes, Richard. "The Views of Augustine." *Encyclopaedia Britannica Online*. Accessed October 17, 2023. https://www.britannica.com/topic/eschatology/The-views-of-Augustine.

Lebrecht, Norman. *Genius and Anxiety: How the Jews Changed the World, 1847–1947*. New York: Scribner, 2019.

Lencke, J. Scott. "The Average Church Size in America." *The Prodigal Thought* (blog), January 26, 2011. https://prodigalthought.net/2011/01/26/the-average-church-size-in-america/.

Lepore, Jill. "A Golden Age for Dystopian Fiction." *New Yorker*, June 5, 2017. https://www.newyorker.com/magazine/2017/06/05/a-golden-age-for-dystopian-fiction.

Lerner, Maura. "He, She, or Ze? Pronouns Could Pose Trouble under University of Minnesota Campus Policy." *Star Tribune*, July 14, 2018. https://www.startribune.com/he-she-or-ze-pronouns-could-pose-trouble-under-u-campus-policy/488197021.

Levin, Mark R. *American Marxism*. New York: Threshold Editions, 2021.

Lewis, C. S. "Our English Syllabus." In *Rehabilitations and Other Essays*, 79–94. Oxford: Oxford University Press, 1939.

LifeWay Research. *Pastor Views on the Return of Jesus Christ, Biblical Prophecy, and End Times*. https://lifewayresearch.com/wp-content/uploads/2020/04/2020-Eschatology-Pastor-Study-Final-Report.pdf.

Lincoln, Abraham. "The Gettysburg Address." Speech. Gettysburg, PA, November 19, 1863. Cornell University Library. https://rmc.library.cornell.edu/gettysburg/good_cause/transcript.htm.

Lindsey, Hal. *The 1980s: Countdown to Armageddon*. New York: Bantam, 1980.

———. *The Terminal Generation*. Old Tappan, NJ: Revell, 1976.

Lindsey, Hal, and Carole C. Carlson. *The Late Great Planet Earth*. Grand Rapids: Zondervan, 1970.

Livesay, Bruce. "Have Americans Gone Crazy?" *Canada's National Observer*, May 5, 2020. https://www.nationalobserver.com/2020/05/05/opinion/have-americans-gone-crazy.

Livingston, James C. *Modern Christian Thought: From the Enlightenment to Vatican II*. New York: Macmillan, 1971.

Lowry, Rich. "Australia Exemplifies Western Society Gone Mad." *Boston Herald*, September 9, 2021. https://www.bostonherald.com/2021/09/09/lowry-australia-exemplifies-western-society-gone-mad/.
Lull, Timothy. *Martin Luther's Basic Theological Writings*. 2nd ed. Minneapolis: Fortress, 2005.
Luther, Martin. *A Compend of Luther's Theology*. Edited by Hugh T. Kerr. Philadelphia: Westminster, 1966.
———. *D. Martin Luthers Werke: Kritische Gesamtausgabe (Weimarer Ausgabe)*. Weimar: Böhlau, 1883–1929.
———, trans. *Das Neue Testament, nach der deutsche* Übersetzung *D. Martin Luthers*. Philadelphia: National, 1956.
———. *Luther's Works*. Edited by Jaroslav Pelikan. 55 vols. American ed. St. Louis: Concordia, 1955–86.
———. *Martin Luther's Basic Theological Writings*. 3rd ed. Edited by William R. Russell. Minneapolis: Fortress, 2012.
———. *The Sermon on the Mount and the Magnificat*. Vol. 21 of *Luther's Works*. Edited by Jaroslav Pelikan. St. Louis: Concordia, 1956.
Lutzer, Erwin W. *Hitler's Cross*. Chicago: Moody, 1995.
Lyotard, Jean-Francois. *The Postmodern Condition: A Report on Knowledge*. Translated by Geoff Bennington and Brian Massumi. Theory and History of Literature 10. Minneapolis: University of Minnesota Press, 1993.
MacDonald, Cassandra. "Catholic Cathedral in Colorado Vandalized with 'Satan Lives Here.'" *Gateway Pundit*, video (0:07) and text, October 10, 2010. https://www.thegatewaypundit.com/2021/10/catholic-cathedral-colorado-vandalized-satan-lives-video/.
Machen, J. Gresham. *What Is Christianity? And Other Addresses*. Grand Rapids: Eerdmans, 1951.
Maclaine, Shirley. *Going Within: A Guide for Inner Transformation*. New York: Bantam, 1990.
Maddox, Randy L. *Responsible Grace: John Wesley's Practical Theology*. Nashville: Kingswood, 1994.
Madsen, Anna M. *The Theology of the Cross in Historical Perspective*. Eugene, OR: Pickwick, 2007.
"Maher Torches People Who Change Words because They Can't Deal with Reality: 'Repeat Kindergarten.'" *Daily Wire*, October 30, 2021. https://www.dailywire.com/news/maher-torches-people-who-change-words-because-they-cant-deal-with-reality-repeat-kindergarten.
Mains, David R. *The Rise of the Religion of Antichristism*. Grand Rapids: Zondervan, 1985.
Marx, Karl. "A Contribution to the Critique of Hegel's Philosophy of Right." In *Marx: Early Political Writings*, edited by Joseph J. O'Malley with Richard A. Davis. Cambridge University Press Online, June 5, 2012. https://www.cambridge.org/core/books/abs/marx-early-political-writings/contribution-to-the-critique-of-hegels-philosophy-of-right-introduction/0B51DEBE7A0D7379187EDE1369F8C8B8.
———. "Theses on Feuerbach." In *Karl Marx: Selected Writings*, edited by David McLellan, 171–74. New York: Oxford University Press, 1977.

Marx, Karl, and Frederick Engels. *Manifesto of the Communist Party*. In *Marx/Engels Selected Works*, translated by Samuel Moore, 1:14–21. Moscow: Progress, 1969. https://www.marxists.org/archive/marx/works/download/pdf/Manifesto.pdf.

Massing, Michael. "Making Sense of Evangelicals' Support of Trump." *Guardian*, June 7, 2019. https://www.theguardian.com/commentisfree/2019/jun/07/evangelical-americans-trump-supporters-progressives.

Matthewes, Charles. *A Theology of Public Life*. Edited by Daniel W. Hardy. Cambridge Studies in Christian Doctrine. Cambridge: Cambridge University Press, 2007.

Matthews, D. K. "Approximating the Millennium: Toward a Coherent Premillennial Theology of Social Transformation." PhD diss., Baylor University, 1992.

———. "Seduced? The Crisis of Word and the Fragmentation of Civilization." *Christian Research Journal* 43.1 (2020). https://www.equip.org/articles/seduced-the-crisis-of-word-and-the-fragmentation-of-civilization/.

———. *A Theology of Cross and Kingdom: Theologia Crucis after the Reformation, Modernity, and Ultramodern Tribalistic Syncretism*. Eugene, OR: Pickwick, 2019.

Maxouris, Christina. "You Can Now be Fined up to $250,000 If You Call Someone an 'Illegal Alien' in New York City." CNN, October 1, 2019. https://www.cnn.com/2019/10/01/us/nyc-illegal-alien-discrimination-guidance/index.html.

McCallum, Dennis, ed. *The Death of Truth: What's Wrong with Multiculturalism, the Rejection of Reason and the New Postmodern Diversity?* Minneapolis: Bethany House, 1996.

McClain, Alva J. "A Premillennial Philosophy of History." *Bibliotheca Sacra* 113 (1956) 111–16.

McDowell, Josh, and Bob Hostetler. *Right from Wrong: What You Need to Know to Help Youth Make Right Choices*. Nashville: Thomas Nelson, 1994.

McGrath, Alister E. *Luther's Theology of the Cross*. Malden, MA: Blackwell, 1985.

Middleton, J. Richard. "Does Tom Wright Believe in the Second Coming?" *Creation to Eschaton: Explorations in Biblical Eschatology* (blog), June 2, 2014. https://jrichardmiddleton.wordpress.com/2014/06/02/does-tom-wright-believe-in-the-second-coming/.

———. *A New Heaven and a New Earth: Reclaiming Biblical Eschatology*. Grand Rapids: Baker Academic, 2014.

———. "Singing Lies in Church." *Creation to Eschaton: Explorations in Biblical Eschatology* (blog), November 2, 2014. https://jrichardmiddleton.com/2014/11/02/singing-lies-in-church/.

Migdon, Brooke. "Harry Potter Cast Reuniting for 20th Anniversary Special, without J. K. Rowling." *Changing America*, November 18, 2021. https://thehill.com/changing-america/enrichment/arts-culture/582247-harry-potter-cast-reuniting-for-20th-anniversary/.

Milkis, Sidney M. "Progressivism." *Encyclopaedia Britannica Online*. Last updated August 21, 2023. https://www.britannica.com/topic/progressivism.

Mojtabai, A. G. *Blessed Assurance: At Home with the Bomb in Amarillo, Texas*. Boston: Houghton Mifflin, 1986.

Moltmann, Jürgen. *The Experiment Hope*. Translated and edited by M. Douglas Meeks. Philadelphia: Fortress, 1975.

———. "Hope and History." *Theology Today* 25 (1968) 369–86.

———. "Politics and the Practice of Hope." *Christian Century* 87 (1970) 288–91.

———. *Theology of Hope: On the Ground and the Implications of a Christian Eschatology*. Translated by James W. Leitch. New York: Harper and Row, 1967.

Moody, D. L. "The Return of the Lord." In *The American Evangelicals 1800–1900: An Anthology*, edited by William G. McLoughlin, 180–85. New York: Harper and Row, 1968.

Morris, L. L. "Antichrist." In *The Illustrated Bible Dictionary*, edited by J. D. Douglas, 1:69–70. Leicester, England: InterVarsity, 1994.

Morrow, Lance. "Evil." *Time* 137 (1991) 48–54.

Muehlhoff, Tim, and Richard Langer. *Winsome Persuasion: Christian Influence in a Post-Christian World*. Downers Grove, IL: IVP Academic, 2017.

Murawski, John. "Our Idea of Heaven Wrong, Says N. T. Wright." *Christian Century*, May 24, 2012. https://www.christiancentury.org/article/2012-05/our-idea-heaven-wrong-says-n-t-wright.

Nash, Ronald H. *Evangelicals in America: Who They Are, What They Believe*. Nashville: Abingdon, 1987.

———, ed. *Liberation Theology*. Milford, MI: Mott Media, 1984.

———, ed. *Process Theology*. Grand Rapids: Mott Media, 1987.

National Institutes of Health. "Alcohol-Related Deaths Increasing in the United States." January 10, 2020. https://www.nih.gov/news-events/news-releases/alcohol-related-deaths-increasing-united-states.

Nelson, Marcia Z. "Frank Peretti: The Father of Christian Fiction Doesn't Want to Look Back." *Publisher's Weekly*, September 25, 2013. https://www.publishersweekly.com/pw/by-topic/authors/profiles/article/59186-frank-peretti-the-father-of-christian-fiction-doesn-t-want-to-look-back.html.

Newman, Alex. "In Canada, Persecution of Christians Escalates." *New American*, April 16, 2021. https://thenewamerican.com/in-canada-persecution-of-christians-escalates/.

Niebuhr, H. Richard. *Christ and Culture*. New York: Harper and Row, 1975.

———. *The Kingdom of God in America*. New York: Willett Clark, 1937.

Niebuhr, Reinhold. *Christian Realism and Political Problems*. New York: Scribner, 1953.

———. *Man's Nature and His Communities*. New York: Scribner, 1965.

———. *Moral Man and Immoral Society: A Study in Ethics and Politics*. New York: Scribner, 1932.

Nietzsche, Friedrich. *The Antichrist*. Translated by H. L. Mencken. Whithorn, Scotland: Anodos, 2017.

———. *Beyond Good and Evil: Prelude to a Philosophy of the Future*. Cambridge Texts in the History of Philosophy. Cambridge: Cambridge University Press, 2001.

———. *Book Three: Principles of a New Evaluation*. In *The Will to Power*, edited by Walter Kaufmann, translated by Walter Kaufmann and R. J. Hollingdale, 261–453. New York: Random House, 1967.

———. *The Gay Science*. Edited by Janet Kopito. Translated by Thomas Common. Mineola, NY: Dover, 2020.

———. "The Madman." In *The Gay Science; or, The Joyful Wisdom*, translated by Thomas Common, 47 (par. 125). Newton Stewart, UK: Anodos, 2019.

———. *On the Genealogy of Morals*. Translated by Francis Golffing. New York: Doubleday, 1956.

———. "On Truth and Lie in an Extra-Moral Sense." Translated by A. K. M. Adam. Oxford: Quadriga, 2019. https://www.academia.edu/39824687/On_Truth_and_Lie_in_an_Extra_Moral_Sense_Friedrich_Nietszsche.

———. *Twilight of the Idols; or, How to Philosophize with a Hammer*. Translated by Richard Polt. Indianapolis: Hackett, 1997.

———. *The Twilight of the Idols and the Anti-Christ; or, How to Philosophize with a Hammer*. Edited by Michael Tanner. Translated by R. J. Hollingdale. Rev. ed. London: Penguin Classics, 1990.

Nitzberg, Alex. "Baby Delivered at 21 weeks and 1 Day Breaks Record for Most Premature Infant to Survive." *TheBlaze*, November 10, 2021. https://www.theblaze.com/news/baby-delivered-at-21-weeks-and-1-day-breaks-record-for-most-premature-infant-to-survive.

Novak, Michael. Foreword to *The Founders on God and Government*, edited by Daniel L. Dreisbach et al., ix–xv. Lanham, MD: Rowman and Littlefield, 2004.

———. "Social Justice: Not What You Think It Is." In *Poverty and Inequality*. The Heritage Foundation. December 29, 2009. https://www.heritage.org/poverty-and-inequality/report/social-justice-not-what-you-think-it.

———. *The Spirit of Democratic Capitalism*. Rev. ed. Lanham, MD: Madison, 1990.

———. *The Spirit of Democratic Capitalism: Thirty Years Later*. McLean, VA: Institute for Faith, Work & Economics, 2015.

———. *Writing from Left to Right: My Journey from Liberal to Conservative*. New York: Image, 2013.

Obama, Barack. "'Call to Renewal' Keynote Address." *New York Times*, June 28, 2006. https://www.nytimes.com/2006/06/28/us/politics/2006obamaspeech.html.

Oden, Thomas C. *After Modernity—What? Agenda for Theology*. Grand Rapids: Zondervan, 1990.

———. *Classic Christianity: A Systematic Theology*. New York: HarperOne, 2009.

———. "The Long Journey Home." *Journal of the Evangelical Theological Society* 34.1 (1991) 77–92.

———. *Requiem: A Lament in Three Movements*. Nashville: Abingdon, 1995.

O'Donovan, Oliver. *The Desire of the Nations: Rediscovering the Roots of Political Theology*. Cambridge: Cambridge University Press, 1999.

Olaskey, Marvin. *The Tragedy of American Compassion*. Washington, DC: Regnery, 1992.

Pacienza, Rob. "God-Given Rights and 'Christian Nationalism.'" *The Washington Stand*, March 4, 2024. https://washingtonstand.com/commentary/godgiven-rights-and-christian-nationalism.

Pallardy, Richard. "Christopher Hitchens." *Encyclopaedia Britannica*. Last updated April 9, 2022. https://www.britannica.com/biography/Christopher-Hitchens.

Pandolfo, Chris. "Nonprofit Finds at Least 45 Canadian Churches Have Been Burned or Vandalized in Recent Weeks." *TheBlaze*, July 14, 2021. https://www.theblaze.com/news/nonprofit-finds-at-least-45-canadian-churches-have-been-burned-or-vandalized-in-recent-weeks.

Pannenberg, Wolfhart. *Theology and the Kingdom*. Edited by Richard John Neuhaus. Philadelphia: Westminster, 1969.

Pearcey, Nancy. *Total Truth: Liberating Christianity from Its Cultural Captivity*. Wheaton, IL: Crossway, 2004.

Pentin, Edward. "Christian Persecution in Europe 'Much Closer' Than Many Think, Warns Hungarian Premier." *National Catholic Register*, November 27, 2019. https://www.ncregister.com/blog/christian-persecution-in-europe-much-closer-than-many-think-warns-hungarian-premier.

Peretti, Frank E. *This Present Darkness*. Rev. ed. Wheaton, IL: Crossway, 2003.

Perrotta, Al. "CHOP . . . as in Madam Guillotine: We're Watching the Reboot of the French Revolution." *The Stream* (blog), June 24, 2020. https://stream.org/chop-as-in-madam-guillotine-were-watching-the-reboot-of-the-french-revolution/.

Pettit, Emma. "'My Merit and My Blackness Are Fused to Each Other.'" *Chronicle of Higher Education*, January 11, 2019. https://www.chronicle.com/article/my-merit-and-my-blackness-are-fused-to-each-other/.

Pew Research Center. "Americans Express Increasingly Warm Feelings toward Religious Groups." February 15, 2017. https://www.pewforum.org/2017/02/15/americans-express-increasingly-warm-feelings-toward-religious-groups/.

———. *Life in 2050: Amazing Science, Familiar Threats, Public Sees a Future of Promise and Peril*. June 22, 2010. https://www.pewresearch.org/wp-content/uploads/sites/4/legacy-pdf/625.pdf.

———. "Public Sees a Future Full of Promise and Peril." June 22, 2010. https://www.pewresearch.org/politics/2010/06/22/public-sees-a-future-full-of-promise-and-peril/.

Pinedo, Peter. "Christian Group Targeted by IRS for Teaching Biblical Values." Texas Right to Life, June 23, 2021. https://texasrighttolife.com/christian-group-targeted-by-irs-for-teaching-biblical-values/.

Quebedeaux, Richard. *The Worldly Evangelicals*. San Francisco: Harper and Row, 1978.

———. *The Young Evangelicals: Revolution in Orthodoxy*. New York: Harper and Row, 1974.

Radcliff, Kaylena. "A War Story: 'There Is No Pit So Deep God's Love Is Not Deeper Still.'" *Christian History Magazine* 121 (2017) 40–43. https://christianhistoryinstitute.org/magazine/article/there-is-no-pit-so-deep.

Rassmussen Reports. "31% Think U.S. Civil War Likely Soon." June 27, 2018. https://www.rasmussenreports.com/public_content/politics/general_politics/june_2018/31_think_u_s_civil_war_likely_soon.

Rauschenbusch, Walter. *A Theology for the Social Gospel*. New York: Macmillan, 1917.

Reader's Digest Illustrated Story of World War II. New York: The Reader's Digest Association, 1969.

Religious Coalition for Reproductive Choice. "Clinic Blessings." Accessed March 12, 2020. https://rcrc.org/clinic-blessings/.

Renn, Aaron M. "The Three Worlds of Evangelicalism." *First Things*, February 2022. https://www.firstthings.com/article/2022/02/the-three-worlds-of-evangelicalism.

Richard, Ramesh P. "Elements of a Biblical Philosophy of History: Parts 1–3 of Premillennialism as a Philosophy of History." *Bibliotheca Sacra* 138 (1981) 108–18.

Richardson, Bradford. "Liberal Professors Outnumber Conservatives Nearly 12 to 1, Study Finds." *Washington Times*, October 6, 2016. https://www.washingtontimes.com/news/2016/oct/6/liberal-professors-outnumber-conservatives-12-1/.

Richardson, Joel. "N. T. Wright and Eschatology." *Joel Richardson* (blog), June 24, 2014. https://joelstrumpet.com/?p=6773.

———. "N. T. Wright's Perversion of Biblical Hope." *Joel Richardson* (blog). July 1, 2018. https://joelstrumpet.com/?p=6799.

Rizzo, Salvador. "Do 40 Percent of Young Americans Think Free Speech Is Dangerous?" *Washington Post*, April 12, 2018. https://www.washingtonpost.com/news/fact-checker/wp/2018/04/12/do-40-percent-of-young-americans-think-free-speech-is-dangerous/.

Rogers, James R. "N. T. Wright's Epicurean Enlightenment." *Law & Liberty* (blog), November 15, 2009. https://lawliberty.org/n-t-wrights-epicurean-enlightenment/.

Rosenberg, Joel C. *The Kremlin Conspiracy*. Carol Stream, IL: Tyndale, 2018.

Ross, Tara, and Joseph C. Smith Jr. *Under God: George Washington and the Question of Church and State*. Dallas: First Colonial, 2009.

Rottenberg, Isaac C. *The Promise and the Presence: Toward a Theology of the Kingdom of God*. Grand Rapids: Eerdmans, 1980.

RT Staff. "Get Woke, Go Broke: Oberlin College Hit with $44 MILLION Penalty for Accusing Local Bakery of Racism." *RT*, June 14, 2019. https://www.rt.com/usa/461913-oberlin-bakery-racism-fine/.

Russell, Bertrand. *Why I Am Not a Christian and Other Essays on Religion and Related Subjects*. New York: Touchstone, 1957.

Rutherford, Samuel. *Lex, Rex, or the Law and the Prince: A Dispute for the Just Prerogative of King and People*. Seattle: CreateSpace, 2012.

Saler, Robert Cady. *Theologia Crucis: A Companion to the Theology of the Cross*. Eugene, OR: Cascade, 2016.

Salo, Jackie. "Why You'll No Longer Find 'Convicted Felons' in San Francisco." *New York Post*, August 22, 2019. https://nypost.com/2019/08/22/why-youll-no-longer-find-convicted-felons-in-san-francisco/.

Sartre, John Paul. *Being and Nothingness*. New York: Washington Square, 1966.

Schaeffer, Francis A. *How Should We Then Live? The Rise and Decline of Western Thought and Culture*. L'Abri 50th Anniversary ed. Wheaton, IL: Crossway, 2005.

Schillebeeckx, Edward. *The Schillebeeckx Reader*. Edited by Robert J. Schreiter. Translated by Crossroad Publishing. New York: Crossroad, 1987.

Schleiermacher, Friedrich. *On Religion: Speeches to Its Cultured Despisers*. Translated by John Oman. New York: Harper and Row, 1968.

Seattle Times Staff. "Seattle-Area Protests: Live Updates on Sunday, June 14." *Seattle Times*, June 15, 2020, 4:44 am. https://www.seattletimes.com/seattle-news/seattle-area-protests-live-updates-on-sunday-june-14/.

Sekulow, Jordan. "In the Absence of Leadership from President Biden, ACLJ Delivers CRITICAL Oral Intervention Asking U.N. to Defend Endangered Christians in Afghanistan." American Center for Law and Justice, October 1, 2021. https://aclj.org/persecuted-church/in-the-absence-of-leadership-from-president-biden-aclj-delivers-critical-oral-intervention-asking-un-to-defend-endangered-christians-in-afghanistan.

Shapiro, Fred R. "Who Wrote the Serenity Prayer?" *Chronicle Review*, April 28, 2014. https://www.chronicle.com/article/who-wrote-the-serenity-prayer/.

Sharon, Jeremy. "Jews Target of 58% of All Religiously Motivated Hate Crimes in US." *Jerusalem Post*, August 31, 2021. https://www.jpost.com/diaspora/antisemitism/antisemitism-jews-target-of-58-percent-of-all-religiously-motivated-hate-crimes-in-us-678228.

Shellnut, Kate. "Americans Warm Up to Every Religious Group except Evangelicals." *Christianity Today*, February 15, 2017. https://www.christianitytoday.com/

gleanings/2017/february/americans-warm-feelings-religious-groups-evangelicals-pew.html.

Sine, Tom. *The Mustard Seed Conspiracy*. Waco, TX: Word, 1981.

Sire, James W. *The Universe Next Door: A Basic Worldview Catalog*. 6th ed. Downers Grove, IL: IVP Academic, 2020.

Smith, Cam. "Connecticut Parents Petition to Ban Transgender Track Athletes." *USA Today High School Sports*, June 6, 2018. https://usatodayhss.com/2018/connecticut-parents-ban-transgender-track-athletes.

Smith, James K. A. *Awaiting the King: Reforming Public Theology*. Grand Rapids: Baker Academic, 2017.

———. *Who's Afraid of Postmodernism? Taking Derrida, Lyotard, and Foucault to Church*. Grand Rapids: Baker Academic, 2006.

———. *You Are What You Love: The Spiritual Power of Habit*. Grand Rapids: Brazos, 2016.

Smith, Mandy. "How a Theology of the City Helps the Whole Church: A Review of Urban Spirituality by Karina Kreminski." *Missio Alliance* (blog), July 6, 2018. https://www.missioalliance.org/how-a-theology-of-the-city-helps-the-whole-church-a-review-of-urban-spirituality-by-karina-kreminski/.

Smith, Timothy L. *Revivalism and Social Reform: American Protestantism on the Eve of the Civil War*. Baltimore: Johns Hopkins University Press, 1980.

Snyder, Howard A. "The Holy Reign of God." *Wesleyan Theological Journal* 24 (1989) 83–84.

Sohn-Kronthaler, Michaela, and Ruth Albrecht. *Faith and Feminism in Nineteenth-Century Religious Communities*. Atlanta: SBL, 2019.

Sojourners. "Who We Are." https://sojo.net/about-us/who-we-are.

Stafford, Tim. "The Abortion Wars." *Christianity Today*, October 6, 1989. https://www.christianitytoday.com/ct/1989/october-6/abortion-wars-what-most-christians-dont-know.html.

Stanton, Glenn T. *The Myth of the Dying Church: How Christianity Is Actually Thriving in America and in the World*. New York: Hachette, 2019.

Stationgossip. "Trans Weightlifter Laurel Hubbard Wins Coveted Sportswoman of the Year Award." October 2021. http://www.stationgossip.com/2021/10/trans-weightlifter-laurel-hubbard-wins.html.

Stetzer, Ed. *Christians in the Age of Outrage: How to Bring Our Best When the World Is at Its Worst*. Carol Stream, IL: Tyndale, 2018.

Stockwell, Clinton E. "The Enchanting City: Theological Perspectives on the City in Post-Modern Dress." *Transformation* 9.2 (April 1, 1992) 10–14.

Stowe, Harriet Beecher. *Uncle Tom's Cabin: Life among the Lowly*. Coppel, TX: Independent Publisher Reprint, 2020.

Strand, Daniel. "Religious Left Misdiagnoses Crisis of Evangelicalism." *Providence: A Journal of Christianity and American Foreign Policy*, May 1, 2018. https://providencemag.com/2018/05/religious-left-misdiagnoses-crisis-evangelicalism-power-donald-trump/.

Swaim, Barton. "The Left Won the Culture War. Will They Be Merciful?" *Washington Post*, May 27, 2016. https://www.washingtonpost.com/opinions/the-left-won-the-culture-war-will-they-be-merciful/2016/05/27/5c5014c2-2024-11e6-8690-f14ca9de2972_story.html.

Taylor, Sarah. "JK Rowling Pillories Trans Activists Who Shared Her Address on Social Media, Says She Will Never Stop Defending Biological Women's Sex-Based Rights." *TheBlaze*, November 22, 2021. https://www.theblaze.com/news/jk-rowling-trans-activists-shared-her-address.

Teilhard de Chardin, Pierre. *The Divine Milieu*. Translated by William Collins. New York: Harper Colophon, 1960.

———. *The Phenomenon of Man*. Translated by Bernard Wall. New York: Harper, 1959.

Union Theological Seminary. "Worship at Union." *Union News*, September 18, 2019. https://utsnyc.edu/worship-at-union/.

Urban, Linwood. "Was Luther a Thoroughgoing Determinist?" *Journal of Theological Studies* 22.1 (1971) 113–39. https://www.jstor.org/stable/23962345.

Urbanski, Dave. "Menacing Speaker Asks Far-Left Seattle Protesters What Happened to Those Who Didn't Support French Revolution. 'Chopped!' They Reply." *TheBlaze*, June 15, 2020. https://www.theblaze.com/news/seattle-protester-french-revolution-chopped.

———. "'This Little Light of Mine, I'm Gonna Let It Shine': Clergy Members Sing, Pray, Speak Out in Support of Yet Another Abortion Clinic." *TheBlaze*, October 4, 2019. https://www.theblaze.com/news/clergy-members-sing-pray-in-support-of-yet-another-abortion-clinic.

———. "'You've Got to Be Really Hurting to Do This Kind of Destruction': Pro-Abortion Vandals Spray-Paint Church, Topple and Trample Crosses." *TheBlaze*, October 1, 2021. https://www.theblaze.com/news/pro-abortion-vandals-spray-paint-church.

Urrutia, Adam. "John Wesley's Theological Framework of Authority and the Enlightenment." *The Pulse* 2.3 (Spring 2005). https://www.baylor.edu/pulse/index.php?id=27756.

Van Engen, Charles, and Jude Tiersma, eds. *God So Loves the City: Seeking a Theology for Urban Mission*. Eugene, OR: Wipf & Stock, 2009.

VanHoose, Benjamin. "J. K. Rowling Not Returning for HBO Max 'Harry Potter' Reunion but Will Appear in Archival Footage." *People*, November 17, 2021. https://people.com/movies/jk-rowling-not-returning-for-hbo-max-harry-potter-reunion-special/.

Veith, Gene Edward, Jr. "'The World Has Gone Mad.'" *Cranach* (blog), October 25, 2021. https://www.patheos.com/blogs/geneveith/2021/10/the-world-has-gone-mad/.

Vogt, Frederick. *The Divine Clock, with Visions of the Future*. London: Marshall, Morgan & Scott, 1929.

Wallis, Jim. *America's Original Sin: Racism, White Privilege, and the Bridge to a New America*. Grand Rapids: Brazos, 2016.

Walvoord, John. "Why Must Christ Return?" In *Prophecy and the Seventies*, edited by Charles Lee Feinberg, 31–44. Chicago: Moody, 1971.

Ward, Benjamin. "Europe's Worrying Surge of Antisemitism." *Human Rights Watch*, May 17, 2021. https://www.hrw.org/news/2021/05/17/europes-worrying-surge-antisemitism.

Washington, George. "George Washington's Farewell Address." George Washington's Mount Vernon. https://www.mountvernon.org/library/digitalhistory/digital-encyclopedia/article/george-washington-s-farewell-address/.

———. "Washington's Farewell Address, 1796." Mount Vernon. https://www.mountvernon.org/education/primary-source-collections/primary-source-collections/article/washington-s-farewell-address-1796/.

Webber, Robert E. *The Secular Saint: A Case for Evangelical Social Responsibility*. Grand Rapids: Zondervan, 1979.

———. *Younger Evangelicals: Facing the Challenges of the New World*. Grand Rapids: Baker, 2002.

Weber, Timothy P. "Premillennialism and the Branches of Evangelicalism." In *The Variety of Evangelicalism*, edited by Donald Dayton and Robert K. Johnston, 5–21. Downers Grove, IL: InterVarsity, 1991.

Wesley Center Online. "A Word of Explanation." *The Sermons of John Wesley (1872 Edition)—Chronologically Ordered*. http://wesley.nnu.edu/john-wesley/the-sermons-of-john-wesley-1872-edition/the-sermons-of-john-wesley-chronologically-ordered/.

Wesley, John. *A Farther Appeal to Men of Reason and Religion, Part I*. In *The Works of Reverend John Wesley*, 34–96. New York: Emory and Waugh, 1831.

———. "From the Journal: Wednesday, May 24, 1738." *Christian History* 2 (1983). https://christianhistoryinstitute.org/magazine/article/john-wesley-journal.

———. "The General Spread of the Gospel." In *Sermons II*, edited by Albert Outler, 485–99. Vol. 2 of *The Works of John Wesley*. Nashville: Abingdon, 1985.

———. *John Wesley*. Edited by Albert C. Outler. New York: Oxford University Press, 1980.

———. *Journal and Diaries I*. Vol. 18 of *The Bicentennial Edition of the Works of John Wesley*. Edited by W. R. Ward and Richard Heitzenrater. Nashville: Abingdon, 1984.

———. *Journal and Diaries II*. Vol. 19 of *The Bicentennial Edition of the Works of John Wesley*. Edited by W. R. Ward and Richard Heitzenrater. Nashville: Abingdon, 1984.

———. *Letters I (1721–1739)*. 32 vols. Edited by Frank Baker. Oxford: Clarendon, 1982.

———. *The Letters of the Rev. John Wesley*. Edited by John Telford. 8 vols. London: Epworth, 1831.

———. "The New Creation." The Sermons of John Wesley 64. *Wesley Center Online*. http://wesley.nnu.edu/john-wesley/the-sermons-of-john-wesley-1872-edition/sermon-64-the-new-creation/.

———. "Original Sin." The Sermons of John Wesley 44. *Wesley Center Online*. http://wesley.nnu.edu/john-wesley/the-sermons-of-john-wesley-1872-edition/sermon-44-original-sin/.

———. "Salvation by Faith." In *The Sermons of John Wesley: A Collection for the Christian Journey*, edited by Kenneth J. Collins and Jason A. Vickers, 125–33. Nashville: Abingdon, 2013.

———. "A Short History of the People Called Methodists." In *The Bicentennial Edition of the Works of John Wesley*, edited by Rupert E. Davies, 425–503. Vol. 9 of *The Methodist Societies, History, Nature, and Design*. Nashville: Abingdon, 1989.

———. "What Is an Arminian?" In *Readings in Christian Thought*, edited by Hugh T. Kerr, 193–95. 2nd ed. Nashville: Abingdon, 1966.

———. *The Works of John Wesley*. 1st American ed. New York: J. and J. Harper, 1827.

"Whack-a-mole." *The Free Dictionary*. Accessed May 24, 2023. https://idioms.thefreedictionary.com/whack-a-mole.

Wikipedia. "Criticism of Mother Teresa." Updated June 12, 2024. https://en.wikipedia.org/wiki/Criticism_of_Mother_Teresa.

Williams, Donald T. "Discerning the Times: Why We Lost the Culture War and How to Make a Comeback." *Journal of International Society of Christian Apologetics* 9.1 (2016) 4–11. https://www.isca-apologetics.org/sites/default/files/JISCA-2016-v9.pdf.

Williams, Thomas D. "Observatory Releases Report on Christian Persecution in Europe." *Breitbart*, November 19, 2019. https://www.breitbart.com/faith/2019/11/19/observatory-releases-report-on-christian-persecution-in-europe/.

Wright, N. T. *The Challenge of Jesus: Rediscovering Who Jesus Was and Is.* Downers Grove, IL: IVP Academic, 1999.

———. *The Day the Revolution Began: Reconsidering the Meaning of Jesus's Crucifixion.* San Francisco: HarperOne, 2016.

———. "Heaven Is Not Our Home." *Christianity Today*, March 24, 2008. https://www.christianitytoday.com/ct/2008/april/heaven-is-not-our-home.html.

———. "NTWrightPage." 2019. https://ntwrightpage.com.

———. *On Earth as in Heaven: Daily Wisdom for Twenty-First Century Christians.* San Francisco: HarperOne, 2022.

———. *Surprised by Hope: Rethinking Heaven, the Resurrection, and the Mission of the Church.* 2008. New York: HarperCollins, 2008.

Young, Stephen. "Robert Jeffress: Christians Who Don't Back Trump Are Morons, Like Christians in Nazi Germany." *Dallas Observer*, February 13, 2019. https://www.dallasobserver.com/news/dallas-pastor-robet-jeffress-says-anti-trump-christians-are-morons-11561290.